Plow Women Rather Than Reapers:

An Intellectual History
of Feminism
in the United States

by

Sarah Slavin Schramm

The Scarecrow Press, Inc.
Metuchen, N.J. & London
1979

SARAH SLAVIN SCHRAMM

B. A. , University of Iowa, 1962; M. A. T. , Webster
College, 1973; Ph. D. , the George Washington Uni-
versity, 1978.   Author of articles; editor, Female
Studies Series, vol. VIII Women in the Political
System; editor, The Study of Women and Politics:
A Symposium Exploring Methodological Issues;
feminist; activist.

The author and publisher wish to thank the individuals and institutions listed on page iv for
granting permission to reproduce the items cited.

Library of Congress Cataloging in Publication Data

Schramm, Sarah Slavin, 1942-
    Plow women rather than reapers.

    Bibliography: p.
    Includes index.
    1.   Feminism--United States--History.   II.   Feminists
--United States.   I.   Title.
HQ1426. S34   301. 41'2'0973   78-10907
ISBN 0-8108-1183-9

For my mother,
Ruth Martin Slavin,
who made everything possible

ACKNOWLEDGMENTS

Jane Wells Schooley, "Alice Paul," copyright 1978.

Excerpt from Lillian Hellman, Pentimento: A Book of Portraits, (Boston: Little, Brown), p. 3; copyright © 1973 by Lillian Hellman. By permission.

Stephan Sinding, "The Captive Mother" (Den Fangre Mor), Nasjonalgalleriet Oslo, Norway.

"Old Vic," courtesy of Gotfred O. Hoffmann, Miniature Mansions of Cheshire, Connecticut.

John Rae, drawing of Vassar College Calisthenic Hall, engraving dated 1865; hurdle race at Vassar College Field Day, 1913--Vassar College Library.

Woman's brassiere, about 1917, Smithsonian Institution, Photo No. 74-8640.

Blanche Ames Ames cartoon, Sophia Smith Collection, Smith College.

The Statue of Liberty, Tyrone Dukes/New York Times.

Andrew Wyeth, "Christina's World," Collection, the Museum of Modern Art, New York.

Suzanne Benton, "Susan B. Anthony," cast on loan to the Hon. Ella Grasso, Governor of Connecticut, original in the collection of Mr. and Mrs. David Mishkin.

Eleanor Roosevelt and Helen Keller, United Press International.

Gertrude Kasebier, "Blessed Art Thou Among Women," Collection, the Museum of Modern Art, New York, Gift of Mrs. Hermine M. Turner.

Suzanne Benton, "Hagar's Mask."

Benjamin Franklin Reinhart, "The Emigrant Train Bedding Down for the Night," in the collection of the Corcoran Gallery of Art, Gift of Mr. and Mrs. Lansdell K. Christie.

Photograph of overhead conveyor belt at North American Aviation plant, Franklin Delano Roosevelt Library.

Sarah Slavin Schramm, "Women's Studies: Its Focus, Idea Power and Promise," reprinted from Readings in Women's Studies: Interdisciplinary Collection, edited by Kathleen Blumhagen and Walter Johnson, with permission of the publisher, Greenwood Press.

Grandma Moses (1860-1961): "A Quilting Bee," painted in 1950. Copyright Grandma Moses Properties, Inc., N.Y.

PREFACE

In writing this book--a research project begun in
Linda Grant De Pauw's 1975 doctoral seminar on women's
history at George Washington University, I attempt to eschew a great woman (or man) theme. In that spirit, I
have tried to avoid biography and autobiography but am not
always successful in the attempt. In compiling an intellectual history, overlooking great women/men is not all that
easy, for many feminist and prefeminist thinkers are great
women/men. It must be said that even though the feminist
movement over time becomes more and more a mass movement, feminist thinkers are in many ways a product of the
colonial gentry class. There is a very interesting tension
at work here as a result, something highlighted by the not
always successful attempts to eschew a great woman theme.
I am aiming for balance with historical intellectual
trends, women's social history and feminist and prefeminist thought.

This book in part stipulates a special definition for
feminism by examining what feminist thinkers say it is.
The process is not as tautological as it sounds. Beginning
with feminist thinkers who identify themselves as feminists,
we work outward in concentric circles, drawing in the work
of others on whom our subjects rely. Thus, we avoid defining feminism through the works of those whom we alone
identify as feminists. Fortunately, although time consuming,
this is not a difficult task. Feminist thinkers are quite generous in their dedications and references to contemporaries
and forebears alike.

The works themselves for the most part were easy to
come by--once identified. The Library of Congress, where
the original research was done, lists about seven entries under feminism in its card catalog. (Several of these are
written by severe critics.) The Library nonetheless is a
veritable goldmine on this topic--if you have a triptik and
the ability to either outwait or cajole the runners. Univer-

v

sity of Pittsburgh's Hillman Library has an excellent collection, much of which undoubtedly is due to Mary Louise Bris-
coe's early direction of the women's studies program. Robert Darcy at George Washington University kindly forwarded
a few volumes which were eternally checked out at Pitt and
hence unavailable. Wherever possible, the numerous reprints and collections now available are cited to aid the access of future scholars in this area to the materials.

I have tried to the best of my ability to transcribe
the ideas and ideals discussed herein as feminist and prefeminist thinkers present them, and hope that I am not judgmental. I am far more interested in knowing what feminist
and prefeminist thinkers have to say. I do take a critical
overview at times, asking hard questions of this body of
thought, but I feel the seriousness of this literature warrants
such an overview. Sometimes the answers to the questions
are less than satisfactory: I hope in that event I have been
sympathetic to the problems which limit the answers. Since
I name myself feminist, in some ways I am writing this book
subjectively. Since I also name myself scholar, I at least
have tried to attain a measure of objectivity and distance
from the subject. It is for you, the reader, to decide how
successful this endeavor as participant observer is.

There would be no book were it not for the assistance,
input and support of numerous others whom I would like to
acknowledge. There are those who participated in my training. First and foremost of these is my mother, Ruth Martin Slavin, to whom this book is dedicated. There are my
teachers and mentors. Linda Grant De Pauw and her careful scholarly manner always are the source of great inspiration to me. Both Stow Persons and Christopher Lasch in
different ways contributed to my world view during my under-
graduate training at the University of Iowa (completed in
1962). I benefitted from the independent doctoral reading on
women and Western political theory that I undertook with
Carl Linden. I am sure neither he nor I will forget the discussions which ensued. To Lane Davis at the University of
Iowa I owe my intrigue with normative thought. Florence
Lee Cahlan--a lifelong resident of Las Vegas, Nevada, my
home town--long has encouraged and shared my interest in
frontier history.

More particularly, I wish to acknowledge a number of
individuals who helped me with this book in a number of ways.
Heidi and Beth Schramm, who call me mother (or less decor-

ously, "Ma"), shared their own research: Heidi, on Gertrude Stein's relation to Cubism; Beth, on the correspondence between Elizabeth Cady Stanton and Susan B. Anthony. Ruth Slavin and Mort and Alice Silverblatt assisted in obtaining a picture of the Statue of Liberty. Molly Shanley located the Vassar illustrations. Anne Pride facilitated the inclusion of Alice Paul's portrait, which first appeared in Do It Now. Margo Barnett helped locate Phillis Wheatley's "Liberty and Peace" after an absurdly frustrating search which included correspondence with the Schlesinger Library and Harvard University's Houghton Library. (It was in Hillman Library all along but not cross-referenced.) Herdes Bull Teilman at Pittsburgh's Museum of Art set the author in the right direction to find Stephan Sinding's magnificent sculpture, "The Captive Mother." Raphael Paganelli at the New York Times corresponded with me above and beyond the call of duty, as did Joyce E. Mathes and Roberta A. Diemer at the Smithsonian Institution. Shelby Cave at the Corcoran Gallery of Art helped to locate a suitable frontier illustration.

Gerry Gallucci, Elaine Heffernan, Alice Silverblatt, Ruth Slavin and Corey Venning read parts of the manuscript and offered suggestions, which were taken very seriously. I give thanks to my fellow graduate students in Professor De Pauw's doctoral seminar for their penetrating comments about the findings. Stow Persons seconded the choice of a beginning, feminism and the family, and William L. O'Neill offered useful comments on the introduction's format. Elaine Heffernan and Linda Grant De Pauw helped chase down a number of small details. The librarians at Hillman Library's Afro-American collection were consulted on whether to publish Sojourner Truth's speeches in dialect; the author has abided by their decision. The librarian at the University of Pittsburgh's Darlington Room was of assistance even though the Room was undergoing extensive repairs. Janet Altenbaugh, who typed the manuscript, did impeccable work and demonstrated great patience with the author. Kendall Stanley sorted and typed the annotated bibliography. Victor L. Schramm, Jr., who calls the author spouse, expressed interest in the project and extended numerous acts of kindness through the manuscript's preparation. Correspondence with Melissa Butler, who knows a great deal about women and Western political thought, and about this book as well, has been very rewarding. Theo Tamborlane gave kind words of encouragement. Finally, to Kirstie Morna McClure, who helped me find my way back to feminism and this book after a short but unconscionable absence, I owe lasting gratitude.

Without these good people, there truly would be no book. Yet in spite of them, I may err. If I do, I err on my own in the face of all the advice tendered me.

Sarah Slavin Schramm
Pittsburgh, Pennsylvania
January 1978

TABLE OF CONTENTS

Plow Women Rather Than Reapers:
An Intellectual History of Feminism
in the United States

FEMINISM:
ITS HISTORICAL INTELLECTUAL FRAMEWORK*

Old paint on canvas, as it ages, sometimes becomes transparent. When this happens, it is possible, in some pictures, to see the original lines:
a tree will show through a woman's dress, a child
makes way for a dog, a large boat is no longer on
an open sea.... Perhaps it would be well to say
that the old conception, replaced by a later choice,
is a way of seeing and then seeing again....
    That is all I mean about the people in this book.
The paint has aged now and I wanted to see what
was there for me once, what is there for me
now. --Lillian Hellman.[1]

    If feminism has not become a household word since
1960,[2] it is no fault of those involved in its resurgence or
of the media. Juliet Mitchell suggests it surely must be
"the most public revolutionary movement ever to have existed."[3] Certainly never before has it been so exposed to
public scrutiny. Probably never before has it been more
evident that there is virtually no agreement as to what feminism means, what it encompasses, what it entails for those
who advocate it (or detract it). In fact, it is clear that even
those who call themselves feminists do not agree on the meaning of the word. The conflict in movement ranks over the
different activities women--and occasionally men--set about
under the label of feminism underscores this lack of agreement.[4]

    If we want to be able to communicate with each other

---

*An earlier version of this introduction was prepared for the
Chesapeake Area Group of Women Historians Conference, Na-
tional Anthropology Archives, Museum of Natural History,
Washington, D.C., April 1976.

about this very visible cause, then we need to be able to identify and relate it. To define feminism simply by identifying its salient historical intellectual characteristics--by looking at "the original lines"--would be useful for analytic purposes. To define feminism also would have a practical aspect to it. Those of us who consider ourselves feminists at least could see what there was in it for bygone feminists, what there is in it for us still. Those who are critical of feminism generally--for example, Roman Catholic bishops or, particularly, the Redstockings--could utilize such a definition as a taking-off point for their critiques. Those who read the critiques at least would have a frame of reference within which to evaluate them.[5]

For a beginning in the direction of definition, and this book must be seen in that context, we are going to focus on what writers since the late seventeenth century up to about 1960 and mostly in the United States think feminism is. Matilda Gage writes in 1893 about the historical struggle of women for liberation of their thought and for the right to share their thought with the world.[6] This is an exercise in sharing that thought through an intellectual history. After we engage in it, we will be able to identify feminism's intellectual framework, at least in the United States. As we examine what writers say about feminism, we will look for those characteristics on which they agree.

In order to maximize clarity, we will try to distinguish between writers who make value judgments and those who claim they are relating only what they observe in the "real world." There is quite a lot of variation among writers here, and some of the writings we will consider legitimately could be described as both normative and empirical. This is not so much a failing of the categories, which facilitate our grasp of the writer's approach to the topic, as it is an indication of gradations in the types of writing. For example, in The Subjection of Women, John Stuart Mill establishes his approach by stating at the beginning "that the principle which regulates the existing social relations between the two sexes ... is wrong in itself ... and ... ought to be replaced by a principle of perfect equality...."[7] This is a clear and simple statement of intellectual preference and hence a value judgment. Later on Mill maintains "that the course of history, and the tendencies of progressive human society, afford ... a strong [presumption] against [this system of inequality of rights],"[8] an appeal to real-world observations for validation of his preference. Still, on the whole, Mill fairly may be typed as a normative theorist.

To give this study as much depth as possible, we will look at writers who advocate feminism as well as those who detract from it. For those who suggest it is possible that detractors partially misinterpret feminism, perhaps intentionally in order to be especially convincing in their arguments, remember it is equally possible that advocates partially misinterpret feminism as they understand it in order to disguise some of its further-reaching implications. Whatever the validity of the interpretations involved, it still is useful for us to compare these divergent writings. For example, Virginia Woolf writes in A Room of One's Own,

> Lies will flow from my lips, but there may perhaps be some truth mixed up with them; it is for you to seek out this truth and to decide whether any part is worth keeping. If not, you will of course throw the whole of it into the wastepaper basket and forget all about it. [9]

She is writing in 1929.

In 1962, at the very moment feminism is reasserting itself, Edward Albee writes in Who's Afraid of Virginia Woolf? that Martha is afraid of her. [10] We see that Woolf's thinking is still important 33 years later and that Albee perceives it as a direct threat to Martha. Furthermore, he tells us Martha is going to lead the band, which we must attribute to Woolf's world view as Albee understands it when he writes the play. Nancy Topping Bazin, who gives us a very provocative study of Woolf, notes that she saw every mind including her own as potentially bisexual; that is, characterized by an equilibrium between the feminine and masculine aspects of human nature. [11] If as Albee suggests, Martha is going to lead the band, but is afraid of doing so, then we have a glimpse of what one critic thinks about the potential for bisexual equilibrium. Albee suggests Martha will be more aggressive (or masculine), but she is afraid of such aggression (and hence feminine). Woolf tells us about Shakespeare's gifted sister who ran away to London, only to have men laugh in her face and finally to kill herself. [12] Woolf concludes by telling us that his sister still lives in each of us, even though she never wrote her poetry and was buried in an anonymous fashion. [13] She seems to live in Martha too, however unsympathetic her portrayal. We know, though, that Shakespeare's sister does not get a sympathetic hearing in her day either. In fact, Woolf warns us that it is even harder now for such a mind to attain a hearing. [14]

From a comparison of Woolf, feminism's advocate, and Albee, its detractor, we see that both writers are concerned with merging the characteristics of males and females, a kind of role congruency. We see that both believe assertions in this direction by women will be painful experiences. On this much, they are consistent. Other writers we will examine show this same consistency. We are, however, getting ahead of ourselves in this justification for including feminism's advocates and detractors in an attempt to identify its intellectual framework. Even if we are able to identify areas of agreement about the characteristics of feminism in writings such as these, why do we have to go to all of this trouble? Why is it that we cannot just look feminism up in the dictionary and be done with it, if we want to know what it means?

Webster's New Collegiate Dictionary tells us feminism is "the theory of the political, economic and social equality of the sexes." The Oxford English Dictionary defines it as "the opinions and principles of the advocates of the extended recognition of the achievements and claims of women," a more open-ended stipulation. Sociologist Alice Rossi prefers the latter[15]; historian Linda Grant De Pauw prefers the former.[16] These are not the only definitions of feminism which are available, but they are two major ones. If we must preface any discussion we are going to have about feminism with a reference to one or the other definition, we are bound to an awkward procedure.[17] The stipulation of a special definition for feminism after an examination of its intellectual history is so much the better for our future analyses of it. It is so much the better too for our insight into women's history and social change. (As we already know, feminism always is concerned with women's condition even if all women do not espouse it.) We also can bring American history into sharper perspective by looking at social reality as it is perceived or prescribed by a select progressive group and its critics, all of whom play active roles in that history.

This book is going to define feminism in terms of an ongoing series of generalizations. These generalizations cover, first of all, intermingling concerns with women's family relations and education; secondly, inapposite ideologies of liberty and equality; and finally, inconsistent images of women and men's roles. Each of these generalizations and the writings which compose them are going to be examined.

It must be said that defining feminism in terms of what thinkers say it is, however, is no measure of what feminists actually do. That is a study yet to be written. Furthermore, writing down a definition in this fashion is no guarantee it is going to be adopted by historians and/or analysts of feminism in the future. That much remains to be seen.

We shall proceed developmentally, in order to account for the many streams of thought which feed into one another, culminating in feminism per se around the end of the nineteenth century. Rossi tells us the word feminism comes into accepted usage during the 1890s. She believes it first is used in this fashion in a book review published in The Athenaeum, a British journal, on April 27, 1895. She also tells us the word commonly is set off in quotation marks until the early 1900s.[18] The confluence of the streams of thought which she pinpoints in The Athenaeum but which can be traced back earlier still--for example to Avrom Barnett's Foundations of Feminism: A Critique, published by the American Tract Society in 1870--marks an identity of feminism's own.

Running throughout the writings of those who agitate for change designed to benefit women in either or both the family and education are deep and powerful ideological undercurrents of liberty and equality. The libertarians speak of woman's individuality and inner-self development along with her fulfillment of duty. The egalitarians call for recognition of women's and men's comparable value. The two ideological currents do not necessarily run compatibly side-by-side. Emma Goldman recognized the problem as seeking "to be one's self and yet in oneness with others; to feel deeply with all human beings and still retain one's characteristic qualities."[19] The impelling force of this paradox could engulf feminism once and for all, a likelihood intellectually circumvented by the accommodation of the egalitarian creed to the libertarian one.

The stream begins, for our purposes, in the eighteenth century with the genius of Mary Wollstonecraft. She has her forerunners, rationalistic and mystic both, just as she has compatriots, i.e. Lady Mary Wortley Montague. She writes about both the family and education, and we shall consider her thoughts on both topics. A careful reading indicates she reacts strongly and particularly to Jean Rousseau's Emile. Whereas Emile, prototypical young man, is taught to be self-reliant, Sophy, prototypical young woman, is viewed essentially as a child. This has strong implications both for woman's role in the family as well as for the content of her education. According to Wollstonecraft, however, women and men, both of whom have souls, attain virtue and happiness the same way. The power of virtue is that of discerning truth through reason. In this respect, every human is a world in itself. Women and men have access to the same degree of reason. They must be educated, therefore, by rules deduced from pure reason and applied to the whole species.

Women and men alike have human duties to fulfill as rational creatures; they are ennobled only by that which is obtained through their own exertions. Women may have been rendered gentle domestic brutes, but they should not depend on men for happiness because both are subject to similar limitations when it comes to attainment of that transient state. The ideal wife/husband relationship is friendship which, unlike love, is founded on principle and cemented by time. A woman's first duty is to herself as a rational creature, and next, to herself as a citizen at the station of wifeliness and motherhood, with some allowance made for expanded usefulness and independence for "women of superior cast."[20]

In 1829, Frances Wright cautions men that the level in life they will achieve is related to that which women achieve. The equality which has "its seat in the mind" is ill served by attempts to increase woman's utility through her subordination.[21] By 1929, 100 years later, Virginia Woolf takes a more confrontational stance: "Lock up your libraries if you like; but there is no gate, no lock, no bolt that you can set upon the freedom of my mind."[22] In addition to moving from persuasion to confrontation, the economic implications of an education are full upon us. Where Wright speaks of utility, Woolf is conscious of a whole dimension of poverty and obscurity which--worthwhile though it may be-- can be overcome only by the attainment of some means of subsistence. We are left with the facts that educated women have truncated outlets for their abilities and, as we know after the fact, working-class women who must attain the means of subsistence have limited access to formal education.

Discourse about the family stemming from Wollstonecraft focuses on both the marriage relationship--human and legal--and motherhood. It is pregnant with its implications for women's work. In 1870, Lizzie Bates emphasizes motherhood, obedience and religious fervor mixed with work in social and domestic circles and the church as woman's proper

role.[23] Amelia Moore Nation, in her autobiography, represents herself as the "distracted, suffering, loving motherhood of the world, Who, becoming aroused with a righteous
fury rebelled at this torture."[24] Charlotte Perkins Gilman,
in 1903, suggests that if motherhood is to be honored, mothers must foreswear instinct in favor of developing their intelligence through study and experience. She stresses scientific advances and argues for love based in reason.[25] She
argues that "the true home" is retarded in her time but can
become whole and good.[26] If it does not, the ideal society
is going to be a long time in coming.[27]

    We are back to education, the essential means--or as
Beth Bradford Gilchrist puts it in 1910, "the Golden Fleece"--
by which women are to realize their potential in the home
and in the world. We see an increasing emphasis placed on
women's work outside the home in a reform context which
brings better-educated women more into contact with the
reality of life as lived by other less well-educated women
and their children. We see the marital relationship undergoing an increasingly penetrating examination. Elizabeth
Cady Stanton in her autobiography published in 1898 notes the
number of women writing articles about divorce in the North
American Review and takes it as a sign that women are
speaking out about relations which are vital to them.[28] These
selections from eighteenth-, nineteenth- and twentieth-century
writings demonstrate a continuing concern with the problems
of family and education for women. They indicate an intellectual shift from persuasion to confrontation. They move
from a focus on women's work in the home to women's work
in society. A consideration of other writings in this vein
will show increasing interest in the economic, political and
cultural implications of the family and an education.

    These selections also give us a glimpse of the extent
to which some writings tend to support egalitarian ideals and
others, libertarian ones. For example, Wright and Gilman
think in terms of collectivity and society; Wollstonecraft and
Woolf are more in the classical liberal line and hence individualistic. Elizabeth F. Ellett, in her The Women of the
American Revolution, quotes a lady of Philadelphia during
the period: "I know this--that as free I can die but once;
but as a slave I shall not be worthy of life. I have the
pleasure to assure you these are the sentiments of my sister Americans."[29] Constantia, on the other hand, is asserting woman's soul is equal to man's in 1770.[30] Both of these
lines of thought are echoed in the Declaration of Sentiments

and Resolutions issued at the Woman's Rights Convention in
Seneca Falls in 1848; women and men's equality as well as
their inalienable right to life, liberty and the pursuit of happiness are asserted. [31]

By 1925, Elizabeth Breuer is writing that feminism
has taken on new life and direction in the choosing and dividing of self and that the problems which feminists face are
nearer those of the artist than of the average man in the material realm. [32]   By the 1950s, Doris Lessing, in her Children of Violence series, is tracing the inner and outer life of
a modern woman from her parents' home in Central Africa
through two marriages and the abandonment of her child, past
conventional boundaries and the path of duty into freedom to
self actualize. [33]   Compare the above thoughts to the more
egalitarian ones of Correa Moylan Walsh writing in 1917:
"full feminism demands that practically all differences between the male and the female of the human species shall
be obliterated except the one big difference: begetting and
bearing children. "[34]   In 1948, Ruth Herschberger is looking
at inequality, whatever its source, with more than just a
jaundiced eye when she writes about roughriding male cells
and flowering female eggs which overnight--depending on
whether we are reading a patriarchal or matriarchal account--
change places. [35]

We are past the late nineteenth-century confluence
marking the emergence of feminism per se and seem either
on the brink of a vortex or a fork in the torrent.   James L.
and Sheila M. Cooper suggest the roots of American feminist
thought lie in Enlightenment rationalism but are nourished by
nonrationalist dimensions which extoll feminine virtues.   They
see feminist theory growing within what they describe as masculine intellectual models, resulting in a conflict of loyalties
for those who espouse them. [36]   We do see both rationalistic
and mystic elements in Mary Wollstonecraft's thought; we can
trace the influence of John Locke and Rousseau's thought on
her work.   The Declaration of Sentiments, a meta-Declaration
of Independence, seems to be part of a similar sequence.

The question whether inapposition in the undercurrents
of libertarian and egalitarian ideologies is attributable to prevailing intellectual tempers nevertheless may be the wrong
question.   Granted, the inherent contradition of that thought
is apparent.   Feminist thought, however, has a further intellectual dimension which is intrinsic and potentially troublesome.   This dimension cuts across both intermingling con-

cerns about family and education and inapposite ideologies of liberty and equality. Some writings about feminism see women's and men's roles as complements; each is necessary to complete the other which is less than whole, as in the reproduction function. Then again, some writings about feminism see those roles as congruents; women and men essentially coincide with each other, not excepting the reproduction function. Let us examine briefly several examples of these approaches, both of which are part of feminism. [37]

In the late eighteenth century, Abigail Adams admits she is content for "the lords of creation" to continue governing the world's states and kingdoms, however badly they may do so. Government in the domestic area, however, she contends is best left to women. [38] Margaret Fuller, almost midway through the nineteenth century, wants

> every path laid open to woman as freely as man. Were this done, and a slight temporary fermentation allowed to subside, we believe that the Divine would ascend into nature to a height unknown in the history of past ages, and nature, thus instructed, would regulate the spheres not only so as to avoid collision, but to bring forth ravishing harmony. [39]

Simone de Beauvoir, writing over 100 years later, argues that men and women best can achieve the goal of brotherhood by stressing their natural differentiation. [40] Each of these writers accepts complementary, specialized roles for women and men which spring from natural and potentially harmonious differences between them.

In contrast to this approach, Mary Wollstonecraft in 1792 is writing, among other things, that it is important for females to base their conduct on the same principles and to have the same end as males. The abuse of power which has characterized humankind suggests that the more equality is established, the more virtue and happiness will reign in society. We know she stresses domestic duties for females, but we also know she suggests that females do today what they did yesterday merely because they did it yesterday. She suggests that the actual place of the female sex on any intellectual scale cannot be determined until females develop their rationality fully. Sojourner Truth's "Ar'n't I a Woman" speech, given at a woman's convention in Akron, Ohio, in 1851, dramatically belittles those who advocate male protection for females. As a woman she can plough, plant and gather into barns; she can work and eat as much as a man and endure the lash as well as he can too. She scarcely can be expected to support those who argue women by their nature need men to provide what they as women cannot.[41] Sixty-five years later, Robert H. Lowi and Leta S. Hollingsworth point out that restriction of woman's sphere is not natural and that there are no scientific grounds on which to base any artificial limitation of woman's activities.[42] Each of these writers sees women's and men's roles as basically (or potentially) congruent. They downplay so called natural differences and appeal to real-world observations to vindicate them.

Margaret Mead observes these differing approaches to women's and men's roles in a broader anthropological con-text. She concludes that societies which realize "the extent to which male and female personalities are socially produced" either can standardize those personalities as complementary or cease to make such distinctions. She also suggests there is a third alternative to be found in the recognition of diverse potentials which transcends sex.[43] From Mead's suggestions we can extrapolate further development of feminist thought. We do not need to conclude that a division among these think-ers is logically necessary because of their differences with regard to women's and men's roles. In fact, the intellectual history of feminism itself suggests continuing development is quite likely.

Many of the thinkers we are examining share imagery such as Lucy Stone projects:

> I used to think we girls (in my time) were like the
> cows we saw which were in barren pastures, but
> which could look over where grass and waving,
> growing grain grew beyond their reach, and now
> the bars are down and open.[44]

Elizabeth Cady Stanton, in her 72nd year, tells the Interna-tional Council of Women about the feelings of tenderness she has for young women about to receive the burdens of pre-judice and ridicule which have marked her efforts for 40 years.[45] Earl Conrad reports on an interview Harriet Tub-man once had with a New York World reporter in which she mentions a special fondness she had for apples as a child. "I said to myself: 'Someday I'll plant apples myself for other young folks to eat,' and I guess I did."[46]

All this brings to mind Frederick Jackson Turner's

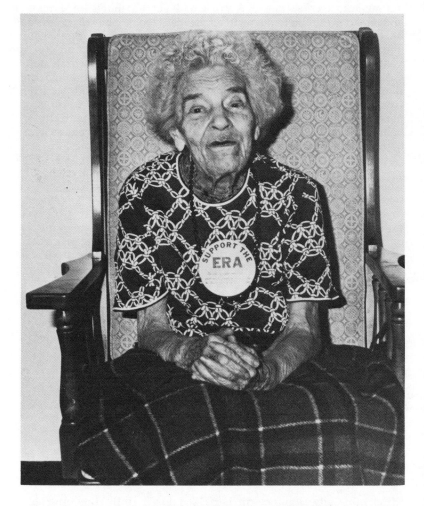

Alice Paul (© Jane Wells-Schooley, 1978).

"frontier hypothesis" which states that as settlers move into free lands, customs give way to new practices better suited to life as it is being lived. [47] Wollstonecraft tells us society as it is necessarily must be reconstituted. Time sanctions innovation. There is an impetus toward the end, even though it may be temporarily impeded. As customs give way to the realities of life, feminism--truly "a way of seeing and then seeing again"--looks ahead for passage past rough places in the torrent. Inez Haynes Irwin, in her Angels and Amazons: A Hundred Years of American Women, says: "this book has concerned itself with plow-women rather than reapers; with important beginnings, no matter how humble they seemed in their time, rather than with fulfillment. "[48] Alice Paul, at 85 years of age, echoes her when asked by a reporter about present day women's liberation: "When you put your hand to the plow, you can't put it down until you get to the end of the row. "[49] That there may be no end to the row is no cause for discouragement. After all, the frontier now is light years into space. So it may be for the cause that is feminism.

References

1   Pentimento: A Book of Portraits (Boston: Little, Brown, 1973), p. 3.
2   Jo Freeman in her book about social movements, public policy and feminism sees the origin of the contemporary movement about this time in establishment of federal and state Commissions on the Status of Women, issuance of Betty Friedan's The Feminine Mystique and insertion of the class "sex" into Title VII of the 1964 Civil Rights Act. The Politics of Women's Liberation (New York: McKay, 1975), pp. 52-54.
3   Woman's Estate (New York: Pantheon Books, 1971), p. 13.
4   For example see Redstockings, Feminist Revolution, 1975. In "The Retreat to Cultural Feminism, " p. 65, Brooke asserts that the current impasse in the women's movement "is due to a deradicalizing and distortion of feminism. " This deradicalizing includes, among other things, "changing the definition of radical feminism. "
5   We need to keep in mind here that definitions are neither true nor false. They are rather symbolic representations which allow us to communicate something usefully. For a helpful discussion of language and definitions, see George J. Graham, Methodological Foundations for Political Analysis (Waltham, Mass.: Xerox College Publishing, 1971), pp. 36-53.
6   Woman, Church and State: An Historical Account of the Status of Women through the Christian Ages: With Reminiscences of the Matriarchate (1893) (New York: Arno, 1972), p. 525.

7   In Essays on Sex Equality. John Stuart Mill and Harriet
    Taylor Mill, ed. Alice S. Rossi (Chicago: University
    of Chicago Press, 1970), p. 125.
8   Ibid., p. 142.
9   (1929) New York: Harbinger Book, 1957, p. 4.
10 Who's Afraid of Virginia Woolf: A Play (New York:
    Atheneum, 1962).
11 Virginia Woolf and the Androgynous Vision (New Bruns-
    wick, N.J.: Rutgers University Press, 1973).
12 Room of One's Own, pp. 49-50.
13 Ibid., p. 117.
14 Ibid., p. 103.
15 The Feminist Papers: From Adams to de Beauvoir (New
    York: Bantam Books, 1973), p. xiii.
16 "The American Revolution and the Rights of Women: The
    Feminist Theory of Abigail Adams," paper prepared for
    the annual convention of the Organization of American
    Historians, Boston, 1975, pp. 15-16.
17 Lexical or dictionary definitions such as we are discus-
    sing are not to be confused with technical definitions
    (even if both are equations of the stipulative variety).
    A lexical definition is a conventional meaning which is
    likely to be characterized by ambiguity and vagueness.
    A technical definition has a special meaning. The two
    kinds of definitions are not interchangeable.
18 Feminist Papers, p. xiii.
19 Anarchism and Other Essays (Port Washington, N.Y.:
    Kennikat Press, 1969).
20 The Rights of Women (1790) (New York: E. P. Dutton,
    1929), p. 160.
21 "Of Free Inquiry," Course of Popular Lectures (New
    York: Free Enquirer, 1829), p. 41.
22 Room of One's Own, p. 79.
23 Woman: Her Dignity and Spheres, By a Lady (New York:
    American Tract Society, 1870).
24 The Use and Need of the Life of Carry A. Nation (Tope-
    ka, Kan.: F. M. Steves and Sons, 1908), Preface. For
    those who might not believe that the words of Carry Na-
    tion belong in a book about the intellectual history of
    feminism, let us quote a section from Adela Rogers St.
    John's Some Are Born Great (New York: Doubleday,
    1974), p. 36, based on research done for a screenplay
    by Robert Thom: "'You are a madwoman,' a judge said
    to her when she was handed before him on the usual
    charges of destruction of property and disturbing the
    peaceful drinking of American citizens. 'Of course I
    am,' Carry cried. 'One, because I am a woman. Two,

because I am sober. <u>Three</u>, because I believe it is possible for a sober woman to change the face of the world. ''

25 <u>The Home: Its Work and Influence</u> (1903) (Urbana: University of Illinois Press, 1972), p. 61.
26 Ibid., pp. 302, 315.
27 <u>Ibid.</u>, p. 317.
28 <u>Eighty Years and More: Reminiscences 1815-1897</u> (1898) (New York: Schocken, 1973), p. 219.
29 Philadelphia: George W. Jacobs, 1900.
30 Judith Sargent Murray, ''On the Equality of the Sexes, '' <u>The Massachusetts Magazine</u> (March/April 1790), 132-35, <u>223-26.</u>
31 Elizabeth Cady Stanton, Susan B. Anthony and Matilda Joslyn Gage, eds., <u>The History of Woman Suffrage</u>, 2d ed. (Rochester, N.Y.: Charles Mann, 1899), vol. 1, p. 70ff.
32 Feminism Is Awkward Age, '' <u>Harper's Magazine</u> (April 1925), 545-52.
33 New York: Simon & Schuster, 1952-1958.
34 Feminism (New York: Sturgis and Walton, 1917).
35 <u>Adam's Rib</u> (1948) (New York: Harper & Row, 1970), p. 78.
36 <u>The Roots of American Feminist Thought</u> (Boston: Allyn & Bacon, 1973), Introduction, passim.
37 As we shall see later, among feminist thinkers, there are fewer advocates of congruent than of complementary roles; the latter seemingly is the broader protest in terms of its appeal. Even fewer are those who advocate congruent roles and believe that they are widespread in the advocate's own time. This apparently is a case of looking to the future.
38 Quoted in Janet Whitney, <u>Abigail Adams</u> (Boston: Little, Brown, 1947), p. 290.
39 ''The Great Lawsuit. Man versus Men. Woman versus Women, '' <u>The Dial</u>, 4 (July 1843), 16.
40 <u>The Second Sex</u> (New York: Bantam Books, 1970), p. 689.
41 See Olive Gilbert, <u>Narrative of Sojourner Truth, a Bondswoman of Olden Time ... Drawn from Her Book of Life</u> (Battle Creek, Mich.: Rev. and Harold Office, 1884), for Frances Gage's report of that speech and the crowd's reaction to it.
42 ''Science and Feminism, '' <u>Scientific Monthly</u> (September 1916), pp. 277-84.
43 <u>Sex and Temperament in Three Primitive Societies</u> (1935) (New York: Dell, 1971), pp. 285-86, 292.
44 Elinor Rice Hays, <u>Morning Star: A Biography of Lucy</u>

Stone, 1818-1893 (New York: Harcourt, Brace & World, 1961).

45 Quoted at the beginning of Feminism: The Essential Historical Writings, ed. Miriam Schneir (New York: Vintage, 1972).

46 Harriet Tubman: Negro Soldier and Abolitionist (New York: International, 1973), p. 46.

47 "The Significance of the Frontier in American History," paper prepared for the annual convention of the American Historical Association, Chicago, 1893. For a discussion of this hypothesis see Ray Allen Billington, Westward Expansion: A History of the American Frontier, 2d ed. (New York: Macmillan, 1960), pp. 1-11. David M. Potter points out the hypothesis neglects the fact women shared in the opportunities of the West only on an affiliated basis in "The American Woman and the American Character," Stetson University Bulletin, 62 (January 1962).

48 Garden City, N.Y.: Doubleday, Doran, 1933, p. 429.

49 "Where Are They (National Woman's Party) Now?" Newsweek (March 23, 1970), 18.

Part I

Monumental Issues

1

THE TRUE HOME: FEMINISM AND FAMILY

Feminist thought about the family is basic to its every
aspect. It is extraordinarily cohesive for an intellectual
trend coming into being over 200 years. This is not to say
that one feminist thinker always agrees with his/her sister or
brother, or that each intellectual period is like every other.
There is much continuity to this body of thought nonetheless;
it cleaves together. Imagine, if you will, that these thinkers
gain the opportunity to visit in a home apart from time and
space, a true home. They ponder the nature of the personal
relationship of woman and man. They recall that Jean
Jacques Rousseau characterizes it as harmonious in woman's
and man's mutual dependence. I think their discourse would
go something like this:

Mary Wollstonecraft says that woman's and man's relationship is the very cement of society. Margaret Fuller
thinks Rousseau describes only the first plane of the relationship, a sort of household partnership. Yes, says Harriet
Martineau, woman's all or nothing. An association in which
woman has no choice of servitude, adds John Stuart Mill.
The second plane, continues Fuller, is that of either mutual
trust or idolatry. It will be transcended by a state of religious harmony. Marked by profound love and sympathy, adds
Elizabeth Cady Stanton. She goes on. All progress depends
on changing the marital state as it is now. Yes, Mill agrees,
it must become a voluntary association. One in which women
and men can experience oneness in their love for each other,
says Emma Goldman.

So much of our time was devoted to explaining how this change would take place, sighs one visitor.   Mary understood from the beginning, though.   Mary Wollstonecraft smiles.   I still believe it is an inevitable end state of virtue. Virtue is the perfection from which all happiness flows.   As perfect as nature permits, reminds Fuller.   But in the United States, virtue is constrained by man's law, protests Martineau.   In the United States, virtue came to be recognized as a law of woman's own, states Alexis de Tocqueville.   Angelina and Sarah Grimke speak simultaneously: woman's law nurtures the public spirit that Mary believes will be forthcoming from perfection.   This time Fuller and Mill speak together: women are their own best helpers in that regard. Woman will achieve liberation through her own efforts, contributes Emma Goldman.   That's why her law unto herself is based on personal responsibility and self-reliance, adds Mary Wollstonecraft.   The Grimke sisters agree.

Wollstonecraft keeps speaking.   If man only would snap woman's chains that she might begin.   Fuller shakes her head.   He never will until woman shows him how.   Antoinette Brown Blackwell reminds her friends, just as Stanton did earlier and lest they stray from the topic, that monogamic marriage is at the base of all progress.   She goes on.   Spouses need only cooperate to develop woman's naturally evolving tendencies.   Woman's law is subject to an even higher one, the law of natural evolution.   Justice is natural, Ellen Glasgow recalls.   Everyone remembers that nature is symbolically female. That's why women are the interpreters of natural or physical religion--Blackwell and Frances Willard speak as one person.

Willard returns to the topic at hand.   In the correct scheme of things, spouses are peers.   Yet there can be no correct scheme of things so long as woman is unequal to

man economically, Charlotte Perkins Gilman reminds Willard.
Only woman's economic independence from man can improve
home life. And that isn't going to come about through the
courts or at the polls, insists Goldman--although women need
the vote to continue their interpretive work, Willard injects.
Keep in mind, Frances, that the interests of state and society
are diametrically opposed: Suzanne LaFollette speaks up.
Emancipating woman will destroy the state but greatly enhance
society. Women are individualizing, says Gilman. In a context of social diversity, adds Jane Addams. Feminist programs are for all women, not just the few, says Beatrice
Forbes-Robertson Hale. Gilman and Addams pass over her
remark to point out that the home has real social connotations and responsibilities which must be filled to preserve it.

     Olive Schreiner continues, woman has the right to
honored and socially useful toil. What we're talking about is
first of all a universal social duty and secondly a great necessity. Love is at the base of it all, recalls Goldman.
Motherhood must not be lost sight of, cries Ellen Key looking
directly at Gilman and Schreiner, who understand. Key goes
on. If we lose sight of motherhood, we are in danger of accepting the public and private nonmorality of men. Hale
sums it up: women and men's lives are linked, but men
must live up to whatever standards are demanded for women
in the changes still to come. Yes, says Margaret Mead, the
marriage standard in America is so difficult, juxtaposing
choice and self-sufficiency with innocence and complete commitment. Doris Lessing speaks of Martha Quest, who
dreams of the destruction of her childhood home. In its
place she sees herself keeping house in a bungalow in which
each of her selves--daughter, mother and activist devoted to
social change--are kept separate and apart that she might
preserve them through a time of disintegration.

* * * * *

Feminist thought about the family, its search for the
true home, begins for our purposes in what may seem an
inhospitable cradle. Rousseau writes that a happy or unhappy
marriage is determined by the personal relationship on which
it rests. In mutual harmony, woman and man contribute to
a common purpose. They are made for each other, and one
depends on the other. Man, the master, is naturally and inexorably dependent on woman, who controls him through his
desire.[1] Woman's charm is her strength; she reigns by nature's decree. Out of coquetry--kept within bounds of mo-
desty and truth--springs the law of right conduct for woman.[2]
Sophy is neither child nor woman, partaking of both. It
would be a mistake for her to complain of legal inequality
springing from the use of reason to hold her responsible for
child care to her child's father. Woman is inferior only
when she tries to usurp man's rights.[3]

Mary Wollstonecraft reads Rousseau's Emile during
her Irish exile in 1787. She loves the paradoxical, fanciful
air of it and attributes sensibility and penetration to the
author.[4] She goes on in her writing later to elaborate on
the wife/husband relationship as the "cement of society."[5]
Her end-directed theory encompasses a whole in which females and males are united as reasonable creatures, earning
their own subsistence--the true definition of independence.
A properly organized society compels females and males to
discharge their respective duties by making esteem contingent
on it. Females must have the protection of civil laws as
they discharge their civil duties. They also ought to have
representatives, as men do, rather than arbitrary authority
over them. Married or single, they must have a civil existence in the state.

So do the first brush strokes touch the intellectual
canvas to be known as feminism. Woman, the weaker sex
who is mutually dependent on the stronger, in some perfect
end state will be independent and self-sufficient. She will
continue to discharge her duties as wife and mother; these
really are not disputed for in discharging them she acquires
the virtue which is perfection. The benevolent legislator will
endeavor to make it in a human's interest to be personally
virtuous; this is the common center of public happiness.
Public spirit is nurtured by private virtue, and women must
have a share in public spirit.

In the public sphere at this time women are subject to substantive and procedural legal disabilities. These stem from the feudal doctrine of coverture, by means of which a married woman's legal existence is suspended or incorporated and consolidated with her spouse's. A husband owns his wife's services, the value of which in one case is equated with the value of his horse. A husband has in his wife a legal property right by virtue of their marital status, and that right is inviolable. A wife, as the inferior party in the marriage relationship and much as a child, has no property in her husband parallel to that he enjoys in her. Equity somewhat mitigates the financial disadvantage here. Overall, women are subject to the embrace of a law in whose composition they have no say.

Marriage for women in the colonies which become the United States entails much more than legal status. Marriage is an economic partnership facing a potentially bleak existence. Just as married men have "homemaking duties," married women have money-making responsibilities.[6] Among the considerations about who will marry whom is economics. Paternal economic authority may follow men into marriage through continuing legal control over the land on which they settle their families.[7] It is a material culture, one in which quantitative valuation is to play a large role.[8] In it, women move toward a self-subsistent existence, but they still are dependent on their spouses. Their spouses' dependency on them does not mitigate the limitations dependency poses for women. Women do earn and are treated to esteem for their discharge of duty. Nevertheless, their civil existence is canceled when they enter the relationship from which esteem stems.

Loss of a civil existence is not the only limitation on married women. Abigail Adams writes to John Adams about women as domestic beings whose geographic mobility is circumscribed, even when they enjoy their spouses' protection. Woman's discharge of duty stands in the way of greater mobility.[9] Abigail Adams experiences her geographic limitations most painfully in her beloved friend and spouse John's absence. She writes him--often signing herself Portia--about her wish to travel to him as easily as her friend Mercy Otis Warren travels to Watertown. "But it is not my lot."[10] She charges him to "remember the ladies" more than is customary and to bypass man's natural tyranny by limiting his power. She mentions a ladies' rebellion against laws to which they do not assent.[11] Abigail tells John that she writes of things about which she cannot speak.[12] Admittedly spoiled by indulgence, she takes the liberty to be saucy.[13] She expresses her fancy "for a closet with a window, which I could more particularly call my own," something indulgence does not provide.[14]

Woman's bittersweet dependence upon her husband is opposed by some. "The [sic] Equal Laws let Custom find,/ And neither sex oppress;/ More freedom to Womankind/ Or give to Mankind less," writes an anonymous poet in 1736.[15] Women take their domestic duties more seriously than their legal status, however. Life in America is democratic enough in practice.[16] Human energy typically is directed toward survival first and then getting ahead in life; people do believe their condition in life can be improved indefinitely. The common law codified in Sir William Blackstone's Commentaries embraces this doctrine. Law demonstrably, automatically and inevitably improves the institutions based on it; to attempt to change law manually is hazardous and certainly in vain.[17] In American eyes, law is necessary to restrain the fallibility of human reason in the face of its perfectibility and excesses or oversights in law are understandable as the imperfect work of still imperfect man. Chances are existing law is the best the political situation, habits and opinions of the population will admit. *

If women think about law at all, they are not likely to undertake a systematic effort to change it. Mary Wollstonecraft's thought is received favorably in this country when it becomes available in 1790. It is not widely distributed, however, and even had it been, there is no reason to believe it would have spurred legal change in married woman's status. Such is not the intellectual tone of the Enlightenment period. Better discover empirically while it happens the process by which change takes place than systematize normative rules, in effect, a priori. Women, with men, are expected to adapt to the existing order, even though the order is subject to investigation.[18]

Mary Wollstonecraft begins the analysis from which feminist thought about the family stems. It is received by the forebears of feminism in the United States in an optimis-

---

*James Madison makes these arguments in Federalist Papers nos. 10 and 85 for the Constitution's ratification. It is fair to relate them to accepting the portions of English common law adopted in the New World. They represent the state of American mind toward law.

tic spirit. Practically speaking, the fulfillment of domestic
duties comes first. As with the common law, prefeminist
thought is adapted in a practical fashion by prefeminist thinkers. Improvement in woman's domestic status is anticipated;
change is not instigated because it will come in its own mysterious and inevitable way. The rationalistic and practical
roots of feminism are entwined with idealism and optimism.
As Wollstonecraft puts it: "Rousseau exerts himself to prove
that all WAS right originally; a crowd of authors that all IS
now rights; and I, that all will BE right."[19] The end state
is something to be taken on faith. Reflection on it is the
changing.

In 1837 Harriet Martineau, an Englishwoman visiting
the States, observes that while "laws and customs may be
creative of vice ... [they] cannot be creative of virtue."[20]
Her statement challenges Wollstonecraft's faith in civil law.
Martineau suggests that one might expect the course of true
love to run smoothly in America and American morals to be
pure. These expectations are unfounded, however, as long
as the male sex dominates the female sex. Despite nearly
universal marriage relationships in the New World's material
prosperity, their mercenary character impairs their moral
sanctity.[21] There is nothing for women to do but marry,
and in so doing, their morals are destroyed. Women are in-
dulged largely and generally, but justice is denied them.

Alexis de Tocqueville, a Frenchman visiting the States,
notes the loss of independence which marriage entails for
American women. He adds that married women submit to
the austere duties required of them in a knowledgeable fashion
and without complaint. Unlike Martineau, he believes their
morals remain pure for having made this choice. Their spirit remains that of a young girl, despite "abnegation ... and
a continual sacrifice of pleasure for the sake of business."[22]
The paternalistic family has gone out of existence for the
father and his sons. Loss of aristocratic lineage is replaced
by kindred ties. Tocqueville seems to intimate that this
change has profound implications for woman's status. Women
now are shaping the mores of American society, and mores
constitute a kind of law unto themselves.

There are those who believe American mores are con-
formist in their Puritanic overview.[23] There also are those
who contest this judgment and the interpretation of Puritanism
which goes along with it.[24] The important point here lies not
so much in the content of social mores as in the development

of a law of woman's own. In the context of such a law, Tocqueville can speak of the purity of woman's morals; Martineau can speak of their destruction in the context of man's law. To Martineau, woman is granted the responsibility for society's ethical customs because she submits to the demands of business and prosperity. Her native ability is channeled into emotions and intuitive streams and away from systematic investigation of her inferior status. Woman's capacity for virtue seems circumscribed.

Martineau and Tocqueville are sociologists, objective observers of the American experience, each having a distinct informative position on the implications of his/her own observations. They come to different but not incompatible conclusions. Their conclusions will be met again; both are part of feminist thought. Angelina Grimke incorporates both in her "Appeal to the Christian Women of the South."[25] She acknowledges that women are subject to law not of their own making and she acknowledges their capacity for moral leadership. She then provides a synthesis. Promising women they can overthrow the licentious slavery system, she urges them to appeal to their legislators. They, after all, are wives, mothers, sisters and daughters of law makers; their counterparts will find such moral suasion irresistible. Women through the bonds of womanhood can use their moral leadership to influence the law-making process.

Angelina Grimke relies on a Rousseauian argument here; men are dependent on women, and women can capitalize on that by following their own law of right conduct. Since the patriarchal institution of slavery is a carnal one contrary to natural order, it must be overthrown through women's devotion to truth and personal regeneration. It is in their power to do so; justice will not be denied them. Shortly after, Angelina's sister Sarah Grimke addresses another slavery-related issue--abolitionist women speaking from the pulpit:

> [Women] will soon discover that danger is impending ... danger from those who, having long held the rains of usurped authority, are very willing to let us fill that sphere which God created us to move in, and who have entered into league to crush the immortal minds of women.[26]

Men have overstepped the bounds of their authority without right. Sarah does not contradict Angelina's assertion that women can use their leadership capabilities, but she delivers a cautionary note. She also introduces the injustice which at last calls for action by women on their own behalf.

In the meantime, Margaret Fuller assures her readers that there is ample justification for abolitionists to seek more freedom for women. The grounds of the search ought to be based on right and not on abolition.[27] Women are their own best helpers, and for that reason she speaks to them rather than men. Men can assist women by removing arbitrary barriers from their path, once women in their natural dignity show men how. With Rousseau, Fuller sees men and women as mutually dependent household partners. Marriage is in a transitional state, however. At the next grade, men and women will participate either in the mutual trust which characterizes a meeting of the minds or in mutual idolatry. The highest grade is a religious one in which men and women engage in a pilgrimage toward a common shrine. By ascertaining women's true dignity, giving her herself and the standard within her, the marriage relationship will be harmonized as much as nature permits. Most women undoubtedly will choose to inhabit the domestic sphere then as now, but they all need not be tied to it. Better they should have this element of choice than continue as overgrown children.[28] This is Wollstonecraft's goal as well.

Fuller's argument, often conducted as a sort of Socratic dialogue,[29] has a dialectical format to it. Her thesis is the household partnership men and women have; men furnish the house, and women manage it. Should woman not acquire a more dignified self-subsistent state, however, she will become an unlovely siren to man, and he will become an effeminate boy to her. The tension inherent in the relationship can generate something quite antithetical: intellectual companionship. From that grade, an ecumenical synthesis of all going before is achievable. The analysis is romantic, despite its economic implications. There is a religious fervor to it. Mysticism rather than rationalism is prevailing. This is especially evident in the utopian movement of Fuller's time and in the wave of social reform which parallels it. The utopians are social planners. Unlike the practical men and women of yesteryear who deal with society as it is, they deal with the reorganization of society.

Mary Griffith is a utopian who looks 300 years into the future from 1836 to a time when the United States is democratic in practice and theory both. Her own day is characterized by theoretical democracy; Abigail Adams' day, by practical democracy. In Griffith's day, ladies are homemakers and consumers; working women would aspire to this state if they could.[30] In Adams' day, women work in the

home and help to keep a business as well. The prosperity
of the future is based largely on woman's work. Women no
longer are contented to keep house and consume material
goods. They are responsible for all mercantile pursuits.
They have made war impossible by training their children
not to kill. * They are protected against drunken husbands by
prohibition and divorce. Government at last is concerned
with people's real problems. [31] Woman in 2136 is upwardly
mobile. The key to her success is the self-mastery of which
Fuller speaks. As an individual, woman ultimately will be
freed of her customary status. Her liberal morals will triumph. It is an idealistic vision in which the nature of woman
as it is commonly understood overcomes the conventional constraints which limit her world sphere.

The vision is reflected by Lydia Maria Child as well.
In a classical Greek setting, the beautiful, pure and reverent
Philothea marries Parolus, only son of Pericles and Aspasia.
Philothea dutifully follows Parolus in death soon after, only
to overcome death by being reunited with him. (Compare
woman's civil death upon marriage to Fuller's belief it will
be transcended by a state of religious harmony). Philothea
stands in remarkable contrast to the beautiful but jaded and
designing Aspasia, a woman of distinction who lives with
Pericles in spite of the laws of religion and morality. [32] All
of these prefeminist thinkers seem convinced woman's status
will improve. They believe she has the means at her disposal. They do not wish to change women's essential character in changing her status, however. Woman's character is
part of nature and must be right. Prefeminist thinkers are
suggesting that woman assert herself on behalf of what is
right. Woman is to act within the mores of which she is
the acknowledged guardian. Woman, in effect, is a law unto
herself and apart from the laws of men. Should men invade
her domain--which is domestic but far more than that--she
must work with other women to re-establish it. The end
state will be harmonious, and the world of women and men
will be better for it.

Nathanial Hawthorne critically ponders this body of
thought in The Blithedale Romance in 1852. Zenobia and
Priscilla are half sisters on a utopian venture, but the
sibling resemblance at first is not a strong one. Priscilla
flutters about leaflike, no free will to her, much as Eve does

---

*Enthusiasm about the War for Independence has been super-
seded by dissension over the War of 1812, a near rout.

before the Fall. Zenobia, having tasted of the fruit of knowledge, rails at woman's destiny. "Did you ever see a happy
woman in your life? ... How can she be happy after discovering that fate has assigned her by one single event, which
she must contrive to make, the substance of her whole life."[33]
At least she is a woman and not a girl, whatever the faults
she may share with other women. Were but small changes to
take place in her earthly destiny, were God to smile upon her
and were a heart true to her to offer encouragement and direction, she would realize her potential.[34] Fate is not kind,
however, and the heart in question is given to Priscilla instead. Zenobia's choice is to drown herself in a dark muddy
river, a latter-day Ophelia, "as so many village maidens
have, wronged in their first love, and seeking peace in the
bosom of the old, familiar stream--so familiar that they
could not dread it--where, in childhood, they used to bathe
their little feet."[35] Her body is recovered, bent in prayer,
but hands clasped eternally in unrelieved defiance.

Hawthorne injects a note of hopelessness to which prefeminist thinkers do not subscribe. His suggestion seems to
be that by defying her customary status, woman dooms herself to a morbid fate even worse than death. Zenobia better
might have been an actress, realizing her energetic impulse
while keeping her heart under control. She really could not
expect to channel her impulse on behalf of women and society,
playing at philanthropy and progress. Zenobia laments near
the end that she has had only a mock life, characterized by
hollow mockery, partaking in an effort to establish the one
true system.[36] What prefeminist thinkers perceive as being
well within woman's domain and true to her nature, Hawthorne
perceives as a futile struggle with nature doomed to defeat.

To backtrack a bit, Maria Weston Chapman notes
comically in 1837 that, properly conceived, these are the
times that try men's souls. She writes poetically in response
to a widespread clerical appeal in New England against women
speaking from the pulpit.

> Confusion has seized us, and all things go wrong,
> The women have leaped from their "spheres,"
> And, instead of fixed stars, shoot as comets along,
> And are setting the world by the ears!
> ...
> They've taken a notion to speak for themselves,
> And are wielding the tongue and the pen;
> They've mounted the rostrum; the termagant elves,
> And--o horrid!--are talking to men.[37]

Women are doing more than talking. They decide in the company of several men to convene to declare their independence from men, quite literally. Their Declaration of Sentiments, promulgated July 19, 1848, is modeled after the Declaration of Independence. "All men" is substituted for "King George." The 18 colonial grievances are matched one by one with 18 female grievances after searching through statutes and recollecting church and social customs. The Declaration is delivered at the Wesleyan Church in Seneca Falls, New York, despite the fact the church door is locked. It cites the laws of nature and God as entitling women to a position on earth different from that which they occupy.

Among the grievances which impel women to assume this new position in relation to men are that: man refuses woman her inalienable right to vote; he denies her representation in forming the laws to which she is subjected; he renders the married woman civilly dead; he deprives her of her property; he has as her husband the legal power to restrain and chastise her; he frames unjust divorce laws which award child guardianship arbitrarily, and he does so without fear of punishment; he limits woman to few occupations, and for those she receives meager remuneration; he establishes different moral codes for women and men, the greater burden of these being assigned to women; and he tries to make women submit to a dependent and abject life, destroying her self-confidence and lessening her self-respect.

It is a controversial document for the times. As Frederick Douglass puts it, discussing rights of animals probably would be more acceptable than discussing rights of women![38] The authors of the Declarations of Sentiments, among them Elizabeth Cady Stanton, firmly resolve that these injuries and usurpations ought not be so. Afterwards Stanton reminds a critic that the purpose of the meeting was not "fashions, customs, or dress, the rights of man or the propriety of the sexes changing positions, but simply our own inalienable rights, our duties, our true sphere." Woman's true sphere should not be assigned her because of her sex. With man, every woman has a different sphere for which she may or may not be adept, and she may occupy different spheres at different times.[39] It is useless to expect woman to rise above her condition while she is degraded by marriage, however. "The right idea of marriage is at the foundation of all reforms,"[40] and only profound love and sympathy can constitute the correct marital state. Woman is degraded by man's idea that she is made for him. All progress now is based on the issue of marriage.[41]

Marriage is the female all or nothing, just as Martineau observes. Whatever she may achieve is conceptualized in marital terms. Harriot K. Hunt celebrates 25 years as a physician in the summer of 1860 amidst friends, flowers and bridal offerings with a silver wedding party. "Her love element has all centered in her profession."[42] Five years before, Lucy Stone and Henry Blackwell marry but protest as they do existing marriage laws. They protest laws "unworthy of the name" out of reverence for law and its essence, which is justice.[43] Lucy Stone keeps her maiden name at a time when women customarily use their spouses' surnames. "There is a great deal in a name. It often signifies much and may involve a great principle," writes Elizabeth Cady Stanton.[44] It is worth recalling Henry Blackwell's eulogy to Mary Wollstonecraft in 1853: Wollstonecraft was true to what she believed to be her duty despite pressure to the contrary. As a result, she gained a noble character. In William Godwin, she found someone worthy of her own nobleness. She spawned a child who married the poet bard Percy Bysshe Shelley and who wrote his biography. It behooves us all to resemble that child of parents whose relationship was one of absolute right.[45] The unjust nature of the relationship between most women and men, especially in the marital state, is recognized. No one questions whether women and men should marry. The laws and their makers are at fault. It is only justice that this wrong should be put to rights. No one questions whether, when it is put to rights, women and men's relationships will change.

Married Women's Property Acts are adopted widely throughout the United States at the time of Blackwell's eulogy. These laws include a woman's right to sue and be sued, to manage and control property of her own, to enter into contracts, to work in the paid labor force without her spouse's permission and to keep her salary. These laws are not nearly as comprehensive as they might be. Judicial interpretation and construction of what there is leaves a great deal to be desired. Legislation nonetheless is the focus of reform at this time. Social change is conceptualized as institutional change.[46] Women involve themselves in missionary (1826), temperance (1826) and abolition (1833) associations to emancipate certain unfortunate beings from institutional repression. The same has been said for women's rights voluntarism. Stow Persons sees an inherent paternalism in these movements and others like them.[47] Alice Rossi describes them as benevolent.[48] Zenobia bemoans their counterfeit nature. Women's involvement in their own cause is more than pater-

nal, benevolent and counterfeit, however.   It goes beyond the
institutional changes for which they call, whatever their reform orientation.   John Stuart Mill puts it this way in 1851:
"It is a movement not merely FOR women, but BY them."[49]
It has to do with their own lives.

Consider what Elizabeth Cady Stanton writes to Susan
B. Anthony in 1855:

> I wish that I were as free as you and I would stump
> the state in a twinkling.   But I am not, and what
> is more, I passed through a terrible scourging
> when last at my father's.   I cannot tell you how
> deep the iron entered my soul.   I never felt more
> keenly the degradation of my sex.   To think that
> all in me of which my father would have felt a
> proper pride had I been a man, is deeply morti-
> fying to him because I am a woman. [50]

She accepts the facts of her existence, much as Abigail
Adams accepts hers.   She does not stop there, however.
She feels the mortification of it deeply and exerts the one
power within her grasp to deal with it: her ideas and her
ideals.   These will work the change ultimately, she believes.
That she bends them toward institutional change is beside the
point.   That she accepts with others the fact most women,
herself included, will enter relationships with men is beside
the point as well. She knows the injustice being done herself.

* * * * *

"The prairie years, the war years, were over." [51]
The middle class is growing, and liberal individualism must
give way.   Industrialism displaces what is left of the rural
Jeffersonian and Jacksonian world view.   The western frontier is expanding and with it notions of equality.   Woman's
subordination remains the exception to institutional demo-
cratization in the United States.   The ratification of the 14th
Amendment to the Constitution (in 1868) provides for reducing
the representative basis in any state denying voting rights to
male inhabitants over 21 who are citizens.   The fifteenth
amendment (1870) forbids qualifying voting rights because of
race, color or previous condition of servitude.   In a century
in which the theoretical equation of citizenship with suffrage
is so important, [52] women are left behind.   Why?   John
Stuart Mill, an Englishman, writes in 1869 that it cannot be
because general experience pronounces the existing system

fit. No one ever has tried anything else. It cannot be because the nature of the two sexes renders them fit only for
their existing relationship. No one ever has seen them in
any other relation. [53] The answer to the question for Mill
lies with women's experiences and the use of their natural
aptitudes. Most importantly, the answer lies with women.
The problem is, however, that women once they marry, and
most do, are slaves in the fullest sense of the word. In becoming one person with their spouses, they have no further
choice of servitude. Furthermore, they are subject to the
animal desires of the spouse who is their master. Mill
points out all of this is based on the syllogistic assumption
that: (1) it is socially necessary for women to marry and
produce children; (2) women will not do so unless they are
compelled; (3) therefore it is necessary to compel them. [54]

Mill asserts there is a need for more voluntary association between married women and men, and there is no
place in such association for a master. Voluntary association
will develop from the legal equality of women and men. The
actual division of power between them requires their mutual
consent, however, and can be set forth in a marriage contract. The rule of property can be subsumed in this mutually
agreed-upon association. In the absence of independent property, the power of earning can be advanced as essential to
dignity. Self-subsistence for women seems more important
than ever. The problem in Mill comes with distinguishing
between, on the one hand, the need for sanction by a state
agency and, on the other hand, the need for individual choice.
How far must the law go? How far may the individual go?
Mill is writing normatively about the fine line between institutional and individual solutions to woman's subjection. He
is doing so at a time of growing suspicion that the problem
is moral and not economic or political.

Woman's law unto herself, a moral code based on personal responsibility, is confronted by a social situation much
too unwieldy for personal solutions alone, however. Woman's
law also is confronted by another law superseding that of
Blackstone and coopting that of her own. The new law is social Darwinism. Evolutionary principles attest to "a universe
governed by Law and the progressive destiny of Man ... by
the irreproachable findings of science." Evolutionary conclusions (but not methods) are similar to those of the Enlightenment and Transcendentalism. Progress still is necessitated
by nature, but it is scientific determinism that is benevolent;
morality now has a scientific foundation. Most importantly,

evolution pledges perfection independent of human contribution.[55] Mores no longer are to be entrusted to women, and the assertion of personal responsibility is irrelevant.

The positive implications of this are not lost on those concerned with woman's position. Questions of custom and convention now are subjects for scientific inquiry. The equivalence of females and males is potentially demonstrable. The "theory of sex selection" currently may be indicative of male superiority, but theory-generated hypotheses along this line are subject to empirical validation. Who could be better suited to approach such testing from a feminine standpoint than woman?[56] Antoinette Brown Blackwell sets out to do just that. She establishes the universally admitted distinction: females nurture offspring; males do not. The theory built on the basis of this distinction is false, however. Responsibilities entailed by the nurturing function, supplemented by demands of human justice, actually require that family duties be shared equitably. "Defrauded womanhood, as unwittingly to herself as to man, has been everywhere naturally avenged for the system of arrogant repression under which she has always stifled hitherto; the human race, forever retarding its own advancement, because it could not recognize the need for a genuine, broad and healthful equilibrium of the sexes...."[57] Nature, in other words, compensates for conventional restraints on feminine force.

Blackwell points out that in the process of evolving, women are acquiring a sphere ever more complex than home life. It is morally assured that women will neither relinquish their domestic relations nor evade their corresponding duties, however. "If Evolution, as applied to sex, teaches any one lesson plainer than another, it is the lesson that the monogamic marriage is the basis of all progress."[58] Spouses only need cooperate in developing woman's prevailing, naturally-selected tendencies. To obstruct these would be to delay human progress and thus hamper a basic evolutionary law. Essentially, though, nature will take care of woman's status. The interested observer, through the use of scientific method, will learn woman's place in the evolutionary scheme. Human beings otherwise play a passive role in the evolutionary process.

Nature, it must be remembered, is symbolically female. To invoke mother nature is to evoke a nurturing image. Woman no longer may be a law unto herself, but the higher law to which she now is subject is female. The traditional theological account of creation presented in Genesis is being forced into a defensive position. In 1855 Henry Ward Beecher publishes Evolution and Religion in which he distinguishes between theology as a potential science and religion as an art form. Theology will have a new authoritative basis from here on out. Methodologically that authority is scientific; substantively it is natural or female. The promulgation of institutional reform will take a similar direction as time passes.

In 1883, Frances Willard, president of the Women's Christian Temperance Union (WCTU), suggests the antidote to the age's skepticism lies in linking the relationship between New Testament religion and philanthropy with the relationship between church and civilization. In this context the economics of cooperative housekeeping take on a whole new air for women. Women now know the value of time and money expended for a Christlike benevolence from their work for the WCTU. Furthermore, to the degree that a home is Christian, it will embrace spouses who are "peers in dignity and power."[59] This Christian sentiment will be realized in law, but law must be supported by public sentiment as well.

For Willard, the WCTU stands as an interpreter of the authority of a physical or natural religion which matches Christ's religion of the soul. This is in addition to its interpretive work to curb drunken lapses by men.[60] To further its interpretive work, WCTU members need the vote. They do not need it so much for their own sake as for the sake of others who are directly affected by man's fall from evolutionary grace through his drinking habits.

> I thought that women ought to have the ballot as I paid the hard earned taxes upon my mother's cottage home--but I never said as much--somehow the motive did not command my heart. ... [F]or love of you, heart-broken wives, whose tremulous lips have blessed men; for love of you, sweet mothers, who in the cradle's shadow, kneel this night beside your infant sons, and you, sorrowful little children, who listen at this hour, with faces strangely old, for him whose footsteps frighten you, for love of you have I thus spoken.[61]

This is not paternalism as it ordinarily is understood. It is maternal. It is not alone for their own benefit that women seek the ballot. It is because their understanding of nature compels them to do so. With the ballot, they may con-

front animalistic aberrations which stand in the way of human
progress. No longer should the relationship between married
women and men be one of dignity and comradeship. It is
thusly characterized in the correct scheme of things. Woman
suffrage would be just one further example of this.

Use of the word feminist for these thinkers and writers
now seems appropriate. They have moved from awareness of
customary restraints upon women, to assertion of the right to
confront infringement of woman's sphere properly defined, to
assertion of authority above and beyond mere human law.
Their understanding of woman's sphere has moved from the
domestic to the mystical to the world. They have survived
the Jacksonian displacement of the colonial gentry class, those
early keepers of this nation's intellectual and cultural heritage. They have kept their heads above the mass tide which
follows the middle class's emergence. They know their gene-
alogical roots spread among the gentry, however, and they
have kept its tradition alive. [62] "It is the ultimate irony that
a tradition that has always prided itself upon its masculinity
should come to find its best represented by its women."[63]
From this time on, there is a literal explosion of creative
talent on behalf of feminism. It has an identity of its own.

Its identity does not go unnoticed. In a poorly received but aptly titled 1886 novel, The Bostonians, Henry
James writes about a blue-stocking get together. Among
those in attendance is Olive Chandler, "a female Jabin--a
nihilist, whatever is, is wrong ... [and a woman] unmarried
by implication of her being ... a woman without laughter."[64]
Also there is Verena Tarrant, the beautiful daughter of a
mesmerizer who succeeds in mesmerizing the group and
Olive before the evening is out. Dr. Prance is present, "impatient of the general question and bored with being reminded,
even for the sake of her rights, that she was a woman--a
detail that she was in the habit of forgetting, having as many
rights as she had time for."[65] The hostess is Miss Birdseye, a frumpy little missionary committed to unpopular
causes in the last line of the gentry tradition and with an
aroma of martyrdom about her. The guest of honor is Mrs.
Farrinder, a suffragist, factual to the core and of an intellectual nature, a woman of the world in search of a protago-
nist. It is Tarrant who draws the group together, bypassing
Farrinder and speaking to women alone about feelings she is
born to feel. "The great sisterhood of women," she tells
them tenderly, might accomplish a great deal with the full-
ness in women's hearts were they to "join hands, and lift up

their voices about the brutal uproar of the world, in which it is so hard for the plea of mercy or of justice, the moan of weakness and suffering, to be heard."[66] Women's day has come, and they have a duty to themselves and to each other.[67]

Olive has a sister, Mrs. Luna, who is not a feminist. In the end she and her sister unite to keep Verena from marrying their cousin Basil Ranson. Ranson is a Southerner with a provincial respect for women; he thinks women are essentially inferior but acknowledges the gracious and grateful woman's claim to man's generosity and tenderness. The widowed Mrs. Luna has matrimony in mind when it comes to Ranson. Olive, however, thinks Verena is born to regenerate the world. There are distinctly sexual implications to her claim on Verena. These implications are not as well defined with regard to Dr. Prance and Miss Birdseye's friendship. In the end, Verena leaves with Basil, betraying her spiritual sister Olive. Apparently the unhappy fate which awaits her with Basil is less unhappy than the fate which awaits her with Olive. Either way she turns, however, she is going to be exploited.

James exhibits a large measure of anxiety about feminist abridgment of time honored traditions and convention. He can understand the factual suffragist and even Dr. Prance, although he may not like them. Miss Birdseye too is given a sympathetic reception. Olive Chandler, however, has an immoral air to her. It is clear that Verena Tarrant never will cause the world's spiritual rebirth. Her questionable origins aside, the association with Olive is fatal. She is stifled permanently. Verena's abstract virtue is no virtue at all, and in fact it introduces a serious ethical problem for the individualist. Whatever one's passion for reform, in the end it must have to do with individuals, or it is worthless.

Intellectual feminism continues to be characterized by a certain abstract quality, but its analyses take on an increasingly sociological and anthropological overview. It is idealistic in an evolutionary context. It is altruistic, and it is gynocentric. Charlotte Perkins Gilman's work stands at its pinnacle. Intellectual feminism in the twentieth century owes her a considerable debt. In 1898 Gilman hypothesizes that unequal economic relations between women and men-- which result in woman's dependence on man and her subsequent unfitness as wife, mother and human being--are beginning to change as the social tendencies of human beings develop. As it is, women are economically dependent on men;

they support themselves by obtaining a husband. Man's primal destructive force now is modified by virtue of the existing sexuo-economic relation between women and men. "Maternal energy is the force through which have come into the world love and industry."[68] With gain tied to love, however, the instincts and processes of self preservation and race preservation are linked for woman. This is how she is modified when man constitutes her economic environment.[69]

According to Gilman, woman increasingly is individualizing, however. The simple family relation of the present will be replaced by a more complex social relation as women and men both become more specialized and differentiated. Woman's distortion will be overcome by personal volition and subjective consciousness. Only woman's economic independence can improve home life for women, men and children. Properly conceived, motherhood's purpose is to produce a child better than its parent.[70] "The child has as much right to the home as any one--more, for it was originated for his own good."[71] Motherhood will become even more pathological than it is if woman continues to be segregated. "The sweet union of the family group" will be possible when the mother can be a human being actively engaged in work for the progress of humanity; only then can she give her child "some true sense of what life is for and how it works."[72]

Gilman makes it appallingly clear that without congenial work, advice and companionship, excitement and change, the thinking and feeling woman will become sick. She has no means to cope with the sensual aspect of her existence. There is little left for her but anger with the impertinence and everlastingness of existence. To follow its pointless pattern to some sort of conclusion is exhausting. The only relief is to say what she feels and thinks in some way. Life becomes more exciting then; there are things to expect, to look forward to, to watch. The end, however, is problematic. The confinement of such an existence is so quiet and empty. The prisoner gets angry enough to do something desperate. She must get out. Gilman presents all this in the intensely subjective context of The Yellow Wallpaper in 1899.[73] The reader might suppose the woman speaking is going mad from her isolation. Perhaps she is mad in her compulsion. Perhaps, however, she is overcoming her distortion.

The heroine of The Yellow Wallpaper tears away the repellent, irritating and provocative reminders of her con-

finement. She creeps about in a primeval gesture, staking
out her territory. She creeps like "every creeping thing that
creepeth over the earth, " created by God. [74] When her husband apprehends what she is doing, that she is out at last,
he faints. "Now why should that man have fainted? But he
did, and right across my path by the wall, so that I had to
creep over him every time. "[75]

For Gilman, home life based on woman's economic
dependence is not the best way to maintain healthy, happy
individuals with high social faculties. Putting aside domestic
mythology, there is socializing the domestic class to anticipate. Working in its favor are more modern methods.
Trained professional service and an appropriate arrangement
of the methods of living are naturally developing social functions. [76] "The home that is coming will not try to be a work-
shop, a nursery or a school. "[77] It will encompass dutiful-
ness, reverence and love and, most importantly, the world. [78]

It is an optimistic statement, founded on scientifically
inspired hope. The reality of it potentially is devastating,
however. In her beautiful and moving novel, Virginia, Ellen
Glasgow expresses its reality for women. Virginia, with the
state bearing her name, must come to grips with the reality
of a new order. "Love, which had seemed to her to solve
all problems and to smooth all difficulties, was helpless to
enlighten her. "[79] Seen through the eyes of her playwright
husband, Virginia is a perfect wife but a nonexistent intellectual companion. Her world is limited to him and their
children. When Virginia loses her husband to an actress after their children have grown, she comes to understand it is
the very structure of life with which she is confronted, not
another woman. Sacrifice, life's fundamental law, governs
her, governs mother love, governs even men's industrial war-
fare. The free woman who commands her husband represents the victory of a type, not an individual. Natural, as
opposed to social, justice sides with this type, because it is
at one "with evolution and with the restless principle of
change. "[80] Virginia's strength in the face of change is endurance, born of her passivity. Coming to grips with life as
it is, duty dogging each step, the fixed quality of her soul
continually returns to the belief that "everything [will] be
right, everything [is] eternally bound to be right from the beginning. "[81] There is no turning back.

Despite the profound meaning of feminist thought for
women's--and men's-- lives, feminist thought as a whole still

is characterized by a buoying sense of optimism. Its goals
are seen in the context of evolutionary progress. Inevitable
they always were, but now there is a driving force behind
inevitability. Rather than dwelling on women who do not keep
up with the pace, feminist thinkers concentrate on those who
do. They begin to notice working women, the new immigrants who have taken the place of early nineteenth-century
mill girls. [82] Glasgow mentions a black woman whose matriarchal heritage shines through her civilized veneer. Some
suffragists are using fear of the immigrant and black vote as
a tactical ploy on behalf of enfranchising women, [83] but feminist thought has a broader social perspective than the suffrage movement does. The suffragist, Mrs. Farrinder, is
bypassed quite realistically for Verena Tarrant in The Bostonians. The "moral heart" of feminism is the idea of self-
reliance, not suffrage. [84]

     There is feminist writing about woman suffrage. It
places suffrage in a slightly different perspective than do
those activists for whom it becomes an obsession. The philosophy of woman suffrage is discussed in terms of its harmony with woman's evolving status and the evolution of the
race. (Men are brought into the discussion in terms of their
fatherhood and need for maternal copartnership.) The New
Woman is not new at all; she always has existed but in advance of her time and place. Women need not be embar-
rassed by their ancestry at all. It is the woman who does
not live up to her hard-earned place today who is cause for
embarrassment. [85] Jane Addams writes in 1910 that many
women are not performing their household duties. Why not?
"... [B]ecause they do not perceive that as society grows
more complicated it is necessary that woman shall extend
her sense of responsibility to many things outside of her own
home if she would continue to preserve the home in its en-
tirety. "[86]

     Feminism is beginning to settle on the fact of woman-
hood as the key issue in its ongoing analysis of family. Women consistently are destroyed in the names of wife and
mother. [87] Those who do the destroying miss the higher significance of being a wife and mother. Science, however, is
coming to grips with this significance, revealing "the feminine principle to inhere in plants, rocks, gems, and even the
minutest atoms.... "[88] Feminine principle has a long history
in civilized and natural worlds both. Mother rule embraces
a divine element above and beyond the original source of life
and its nurturance. Not only can women be self-reliant; they

must be.   They have a responsibility to the world, and only
in fulfilling that responsibility can they preserve the home.

Fulfilling their world responsibility takes women out
of their own class and into contact with another.   Whatever
their prescriptive view of the world, they now are faced with
the world at its worst.   Industrial and urban society is not
pretty.   It is a fertile field for those concerned enough with
social ethics to learn its lessons, however.   "The daintily
clad charitable visitor who steps into the little house made
untidy by the vigorous efforts of her hostess, the washer-
woman, is no longer sure of her superiority to the latter;
she recognizes that her hostess after all represents social
value and industrial use, as over against her own parasitic
cleanliness and a social standing attained only through status. "[89]   Jane Addams minces no words about bourgeois standards.   They are out of place in an urban industrial world.
Truisms about temperance go out the window; notions about
early marriage and child labor are upset.   The experiences
of the working class are larger, admit to more emotion and
even freedom than one would suppose.   Bringing together
such different standards and experiences is a formidable task.
Those who would attempt it must be aware of the diversity
of human experience and sympathetic to it. [90]

According to Addams, this is particularly true for
women who are administering domestic affairs.   In the midst
of industrial transition, households have a social aspect to
them which surpasses individual and family codes of obligation.   Accepting that civilization's foundation is the home,
which must be preserved, does not preclude sharing in community corporate life.   The family should be the unit of that
life. [91]   Isolating live-in household employees makes impossible a well-defined but independent employer/employee relationship.   It also offers no assurance that the duties which
an employer exacts will be curbed by rationality.   Girls in
domestic service often are isolated industrially and socially
and subject to mental and social inequalities inconsistent with
democracy.   When domestic service moves into the field of
social ethics, there still will be a need to supply family
needs by more associated efforts, however. [92]

Concern for the status of the working class and its
women is broadening. [93]   Because this is the case, it is inaccurate to state that feminism dies with ratification of the
nineteenth amendment. [94]   Feminist thought continues to develop.   It is in the process of adapting itself to an industrial

world and a new class structure. The basic problems with which it deals, including the family, still are being analyzed. The context in which it deals with them is changing, however. The writings of Charlotte Perkins Gilman mark the transition from an old to a new world. Everyone was brave, but feminist thinkers are more than courageous; they genuinely are open to the diversity of human experience and sympathetic to it. Jane Addams is ample evidence of this, but there are others. They can be overlooked only if feminism is understood solely in terms of suffrage.

In fact, the tenet of self-reliance implies quite a bit more than the right to vote. Emma Goldman points out in 1911 that "[true emancipation] begins in woman's soul."[95] Woman must obtain liberation by her own efforts. Emancipation alone will not stimulate the self-discovery which comes with giving oneself boundlessly.[96] Woman's present need to buy her right to existence with her sex cannot be overcome at the polls or in the courts. Furthermore, there is little difference between women who make their purchase through marriage and those who do so by prostitution. Both cases stem from woman's economic and social inferiority.[97] Practically speaking, woman's position in the work force is so fleeting that she has no need to organize on her own behalf. Rather she gives herself in marriage to the "first bidder."[98] So much for her fulfillment. Martineau believes woman's morals are crushed as a result and to her detriment. Tocqueville thinks they are enhanced. Goldman sees women crushed by morality and needing to discard it. No one is victimized more by morality than the increasing numbers of middle-class women in the professional work force. At least women of the working class, through economic necessity, often express their physical promptings without regard for convention.[99]

For Goldman, there is something better ahead, though, a time when women and men will meet on a higher plane of companionship and oneness. The possibilities for the force of love in their lives are endless.[100] Woman's law unto herself, which was transformed into a higher law still, takes on a slightly different complexion. Love is permeating everything for which feminists stand.[101] This is not romantic love, which entails sacrifice of woman's selfhood to man. It is love that entails sacrificing convention, morality and property. Once the legal fiction that married women and men are one person, the man, was at the forefront of feminist concerns. Now the hope is that women and men are approach-

ing the time when they can be one in their love for each
other. There is a tenuous consistency to all this, but it
lends itself to reaction against feminism. Feminist thought
does not die, but it comes perilously close to sowing the
seeds of its own destruction.

The problem does not lie so much in claiming that for
the present all labor is within woman's domain, as Olive
Schreiner does. [102] Evolutionary thought can be drawn upon
to support that stance. The problem also is not in claiming
that woman with man is being displaced by industrialization. [103] This strikes a familiar chord in almost everyone's
awareness. No one intelligently can deny that this phenomenon affects most middle-class women in the civilized world
and that it may affect working-class women as well before
long. The logic of feminist analysis is impeccable.

> We do not ask that the wheels of time should re-
> verse themselves, or the stream of life flow back-
> ward.... [W]e demand that in that strange new
> world that is arising alike upon the man and the
> woman, where nothing is as it was, and all things
> are assuming new shapes and relations, that ...
> we also shall have our share of honored and so-
> cially useful human toil.... We demand nothing
> more than this, and we will take nothing less.
> This is our 'WOMAN'S RIGHT!'[104]

Schreiner suggests that an anthropological analysis of
domestic art's evolution makes only too clear the lady's increasing sex parasitism, in short, her prostitution. Woman's
movement advocates are not seeking such personal gain.
They are unique in their consciousness of two impersonal
ends: universal social duty and great necessity. This almost religious consciousness someday will "make more possible a fuller and higher attainment of motherhood and wifehood to the women who will follow...."[105] Such attainment
is crucial for the species' future. Women are "the final standard of the race." As they decay, feeding on wealth which they
themselves have no desire to produce, so must the race. [106]
Feminists must bear whatever loss and renunciation their
stance brings them in order to stem this potentially fatal tide.

Such thinking bespeaks a renaissance for motherhood.
Everything else is subsidiary and justified only as a social
means to that end. Ellen Key, writing coterminously with
Schreiner, Goldman and Addams, attempts to provide the

means: state pensions and supervision for mothers, a year of social service as preparation, study of eugenics. Motherhood must become socially productive labor again. Women do not need to confront morals at all; their relationship to morals, pre- and post-emancipation, is pacific. Women, who apply morals to life, must know that the ideal of the self-supporting wife and mother will mean the death of the family. Woman's demand for the right to remunerative work leads to the realization of her duty to work. This realization contributes to honoring labor, from which it is but a step to social work as an expression of her self assertion. In the meantime other forces in her power go unused. [107]

Key agrees that woman's erotic life has been developed in preference to other aspects of her nature over centuries of sex slavery. This has happened in spite of early worship of divine female principle. An ethical synthesis of self-assertion and self-sacrifice on a higher plane is necessary for women to realize the social value inherent in the duties of motherhood. [108] Key's thought draws heavily on both Charlotte Perkins Gilman and Olive Schreiner here, and she acknowledges her debt to them. She also is initiating a critical overview of their work. It is correct to apply evolutionary law and morals to woman's life. The flaw therein lies with accepting and even encouraging the public and private non-morality of men. [109] Woman's leadership best is exerted with regard to society and the home. Herein lies woman's greatest cultural contribution to civilization. Women should be initiating cooperation as an economic idea with moral bearing, but they are not doing so. [110]

Key is very like Jane Addams in acknowledging that, for many women, motherhood and family life remain their primary concerns. Key sympathizes with their concerns. The industrial labor force must offer them opportunity as well. She seeks to make their endeavor part of that force rather than find them a new occupation within it. This seems practical enough. It does not make for radical institutional change, and it does not confront the industrial system. Key's thought is not even totally at odds with Goldman's. They do disagree about the impact of morality and woman's relation to it. Where Goldman wants to bypass legal/legislative means, Key is eager to bring in state control of motherhood. The fact is, though, that they both want to see a continuance of woman and man's relationship even though its traditional trappings are to be changed. If economic conditions are not favorable to flourishing male/female love relationships, they

"The Captive Mother" (Den Fangne Mor), by Stephan Sinding; bronze, 71. 5 cm.

can be changed one way or another. They must be changed
for the future of humankind.

This turn of thought draws on both a growing pragmatic intellectual atmosphere and the social Darwinist's enthusiasm for nature. Means of adaptation are very important. Weaknesses which inhibit the evolutionary process have
to be overcome. The potential for doing so is virtually unlimited. If industrialization displaces women from their
rightful place in the work force and if female biology dictates
that her place is a nurturing one, then industrialization and
biology must be brought together. There is real social necessity to this, and social cooperation can bring it about.
Whereas the utopians once withdrew from society to engineer
a better world, their predecessors are joining society to reconstruct it. Progress still is accepted as inevitable, but it
can be hastened through social effort to remove obstructions
in its path. The relationships of women and men--once hindered by law, now hindered by economics--can be assisted
in their evolution to a higher plane. It would be inaccurate
to label feminists' acceptance of the fact of industrialization
as merely expedient.[111] They are not sacrificing some
prior principle in doing so. They are trying to find a place
for their principles in a changing world. If, as John Dewey
comes to suggest will be the case,[112] this entails interaction
between selecting adaptive means and determining final principles, it is through no ethical failure of feminism.

Feminist thinkers are a product of their intellectual
environment when it comes to the structure of their thought.
However much feminist thinkers are affected by this structure, they nonetheless are ahead of current-day thinking about
women in a family setting. The problem is that they now are
so far ahead of early twentieth-century thinking that they are
reinforcing the nineteenth-century arguments of their critics.
For those who understand women solely in terms of wifeliness
and motherhood, Ellen Key's call for a renaissance of motherhood can come only as fuel for their fires. No matter that
she bases her call upon Charlotte Perkins Gilman's radical
analysis of woman's economic dependence. No matter that
she would alter radically the shape of motherhood forever after. To her critics' way of thinking, she concedes the basic
point: women are meant to be wives and mothers. Key does
not bring this upon herself by herself. She has ample assistance from all feminist thinkers who pinpoint marriage as the
crux of the matter and then go on to alter it pro forma--main-
taining the fundamental relationship between women and men
all the while.

What else are they to do? Mating still is a biological fact of life. It also is an intellectual fact of life in a period enthralled with evolution and the future of the species. To plead, as Margaret Sanger does in 1928, that motherhood is in bondage[113] is not to eliminate either motherhood or mating. It simply is to call for the means, in this case birth control, by which to loosen its chains. The sexual revolution begins in the late nineteenth century. It focuses on premarital pregnancy, illegitimacy, premarital coitus, attitudes and values about sex and socio-familial change, such as divorce.[114] Early twentieth-century feminist thinkers work within this framework and that of social Darwinism and, increasingly, pragmatism. Their point is to eliminate compulsion--whatever its source--and institute choice for women. They see themselves, and are seen, as symbols of deliverance. They write about "chaos, catastrophe, disaster, the invariable price paid for chance moments of happiness and bliss."[115] Their plan is founded on love; happiness is its end-in-view.[116]

Men are not eliminated from the goal. Woman's cause is perceived as linked inevitably with man's. Whatever standards are demanded for women are to be demanded for men as well.[117] In fact, the earlier tendency to place the blame for woman's dilemma on man's shoulders is disowned entirely by now. Feminists and critics alike see "nothing more depressing than perpetual comparison of the sexes, weighing them against each other ... as rivals for social supremacy."[118] Only a revolt against nature could be behind a revolt against man. Such a revolt would do nothing but add to woman's estrangement from her environment.[119] After all, men are undergoing a trying period as well. If marriage is-- as H. L. Mencken puts it--constant war between an impulse to rebel and social pressure to submit,[120] men are caught in that war too. If marriage incorporates an element of slavery, then men may be slaves.[121] Those who seek human happiness must find the means to deliver men as well as women.

In the midst of discussion about man's situation erupts real concern that feminist thinkers not incorporate man's means. Woman's ways have been discussed for quite some time in an idealized fashion. Now woman's histories are being written, outlining female contributions to civilization.[122] Economics, and law before it, may relegate woman to an inferior position, but she has not behaved in an inferior fashion. Women are beginning to love other women.[123] They recognize that men have lent a helping hand to changes in women's status; now, however, women want to tell their own story

from their own point of view. Telling that story can work
only in feminism's favor. It really is human lapse which
holds women back, not inherent female weakness. In fact,
woman's history shows that females inculcate certain
strengths worthy of emulation.

The trend toward evolutionary anthropological analysis
adds scientific verity to those who look to the principle of
mother rule for guidance. In The Mothers, Robert Briffault
outlines the origins of human sentiments and institutions.
He shows that primitive maternal groups are united by maternal instinct and extra-rational sentiments which stimulate
more extensive ties and diverse loyalties and, ultimately,
human society. The evolution of society itself is rooted in
sexual association and cooperation. Its product is the human
soul, and that product modifies, but does not abolish, the
biological facts on which human life is founded.[124] The masculine intellectual process which once overcame primitive ir-
rationality now is fastening on women's status.[125] The problem is both that women cannot return to the economic dominance they enjoyed in bygone ages and that economic independence for women today is inconsistent with their relationship to men. To fashion a solution, they are going to have
to trust in their "elemental instincts," the spirit of motherhood, while men unlearn patriarchy.[126]

Female instinct is preferable to legislative action.
Here Briffault's line of reasoning is worth quoting at length:

> All legislative regulation of sexual associations de-
> rives from the same principle as the barbaric claims
> which regarded them as subject to the authority of
> the tribe, or rulers, or of parents, and which pro-
> duced infant-betrothal and marriage by purchase.
> ... In our societies a sexual association deriving
> in sanction from the sentiment of the parties to the
> association is immoral. ... [P]eople are either
> united by love and agreement, or they are united
> by an 'institution,' and if the latter is the only bond
> of union, it comes into being synonymous with pros-
> titution. Legislative action cannot institute new
> forms of marriage.... No 'new form of marriage'
> is devisable that shall be of universal applicability
> to all men and women, bestowing perfect harmony
> on their relations, proof against all inadaptations.
> For human nature is not a biological function, but
> [a social product]; ... disharmony between it and

the contrasted primal instincts of men and women
cannot be completely obliterated. Tragedy and
suffering will continue, love will be attended with
pain.[127]

Suzanne LaFollette steps right into this attack on state
domination of women's and men's relationships, implicitly
siding with Goldman but utilizing the most rational of frame-
works in doing so. She makes a careful distinction between
state and society. The state represents the organized,
numerical (with regard to its subjects) interests of a dominant class. Society, if civilized, enlightened and humane,
is an aggregate of individuals of both sexes with its own
qualitative interests at heart. The interests of state and society are diametrically opposed. Given economic conditions
which the state engenders, nothing maintains its subject domination more than marriage. Marriage has been transformed from the natural, instinctive habit it is to an institution, but now as a result of woman's changing industrial and
social position, it is being transformed again into a more
personalized relationship. Marriage and parenthood do concern women biologically, but they also concern men.[128] To
emancipate women would destroy the state but be of inesti-
mable value to society. The key to woman's ultimate emancipation lies in abolishing all restrictions on natural human
rights which subject the mass of humanity to a privileged
class. It does not lie in the sentimental arguments of feminists such as Key and Schreiner. They have abdicated the
scientific spirit of the age by discussing woman's status
solely in superstitious terms as a function.[129]

For LaFollette, genuine change in woman's status,
rather than change for the sake of a dominant class, will
come about in a society not characterized by state interference. Healthy societies grow, and growth is change.[130]
A laissez-faire attitude such as LaFollette's calls for indivi-
dualized solutions to problems. Within a social setting, individuals will work out their problems without the state's
heavy hand upon them. Members of society must cooperate
by maintaining a spirit of tolerance for the diversity of solutions which result. One feminist intellectual trend, ironically
stemming from this temper, is a series of highly personalized
criticisms about the social situation. They do not so much
resemble solutions as they do expressions of distress. There
really is no spur to action in them. They recognize problems
in the love relationships of women and men, and there is irony
in the recognition.

Dorothy Parker, for an example, poetically expresses immeasurable gratitude to the man friend who proves "shallow, false and hateful" and in so doing gives her back herself. Women are silly beings "who meet a slanted gaze, and ever more/ Go build themselves a soul to dwell behind it."[131] One of Parker's favorite themes is the triviality of woman's daily existence, expressed in "Epitaph for a Darling Lady." Lady's hours all are like sand, slipping through her fingers, shaped into yellow castles. Day after day passes, brightly cluttered, as she tosses each one away. "Leave for her a red young rose,/ Go your way, and save your pity;/ She is happy for she knows/ That her dust is very pretty."[132] Shifting sands and dust are often repeated images in Parker's work, as is death. Whatever there is in woman which yearns to nurture, it is wasted, all for nought, similar to giving bread to those who ask only for stones.[133] The pleasures of love, in the end, are realized at best shallowly. In After Such Pleasures, Parker bitingly examines romantic notions about married life and its reality, women who never live and who are empty-headed, sentimental, in frank misery, thinking one thing but doing another for sake of appearances. Woman's talk is small; her capacity for empathy with other women is seriously limited.[134]

Even if it issues no call to action, writing such as this illuminates the dilemma of the wife midway between the Flapper Age and the back-to-the-home movement coming with the thirties. Perhaps no one hits upon the critical point here better than Gertrude Stein. Her very style, independent of traditional form and language, exposes the inner logic of wifehood. Stein shunts artistic posing to the side, and the result is wholly perplexing.

> With a wife. Letting it be as frequently with a wife. She could be an elaboration of having.... With a wife to be with a wife and to be have to be have to be with a wife and to be as income income with a wife and Harry. Let it be uniquely as in fishes. Let it be uniquely as in hyacinths when natural. Let it be uniquely in as if on hats they imitate the blossoms that they have in as uniquely.... With a wife there's to pears. Pear blossoms finish before the late apple blossoms begin and neither make any difference altogether. This is after they come by white and yet.[135]

Having and holding have a mercenary aspect in the flow of things. They also have rhythmic sexual implications: "income income." Having and holding can be as matchless as the hyacinth which once sprang from the blood of Hyacinthus, a youth beloved by Apollo and accidentally killed by him. It can be as matchless as the imitative blossoms on a hat. Real blossoms are indications of things to come, of fruit such as the useful, edible fleshy pear which grows on a tree of the apple family. The pear is an egg-bearing organ. Blossoms may come early; they may come late. It is all alike. Both pear and apple blossoms spring from the same family tree. They make wholly no difference ... after they come. They come white as a bride, pure; they come orgastically. They make no difference ... and yet....

Feminist thinking which stresses personalized perceptions rather than objectified reality is particularly receptive to anthropological findings about women as well as to subjective critiques. Margaret Mead demonstrates why this is the case in discussing how an anthropologist writes: "This book is being written from the standpoint of a woman of middle age, of an American, and of an anthropologist. It is part of the whole argument of the book that women will see the world in different ways than men--and by so doing help the human race see itself more completely."[136] The stress of earlier evolutionary anthropologists on the unity of their findings now is breaking down into greater tolerance of human diversity. Culture is being seen less as the integrated product of evolution and more as the thoughtful consequence of human experience.[137] In order to appreciate such diversity of experience, the anthropologist sets his/her own culture aside to observe and participate in another, without regard for class or racial barriers.[138] Anthropology is drawing on a method incorporated by feminist thought since Jane Addams.

Cultural anthropological findings and methods both are friendly to and with feminist thought. The issue for some scholars and/or feminists such as Margaret Mead becomes not so much innate sex differences as difference in temperament among women and men which exists independently of sex. Exploring the issue necessarily entails a cross-cultural perspective; one cannot test a hypothesis about differences not related to sex without comparing the situation in more than one culture. A single culture will emphasize only certain emotional inclinations at the expense of others less appropriate to its central focus.[139] Mead points out that such inclinations usually are not considered the "imaginative creation of the human mind busy patterning a bare existence with

meaning. "[140] Despite earlier assumptions to the contrary
and after studying social attitudes about temperament in
three isolated cultures, she concludes that it is a mistake to
continue comparing women's and men's personalities. There
is a human temperament capable of variance which is taught
to either women or men or to both of them with differing de-
grees of success. This is what must be studied comparative-
ly. The implications of her findings are of great depth when
extended by inference to her own culture. Here changes in
women's economic status are eliminating part of the support
for man's domination of women, male economic support of
the family unit. Women are becoming confused about their
status because of tension between what they have learned
their household place is and what they suspect it should be,
given their incomes. The matter is complicated by the existence of different expectations in this regard throughout a
complex, stratified culture and by intermarriage among individuals trained to different expectations. While Mead's own
culture is one of those which emphasizes the importance of
such expectations, it also is one which cannot enforce
them. [141]

Mead makes the impossibility of enforcing expectations
as to what constitutes appropriate temperament for men or
women especially clear in a discussion about American cultural complexity. American homes, except for those of isolated subcultures and even for those of the same class, contain many different sets of parents. Similarity among American homes lies in the fact of their differences. Because
there is no single model as to what home life should be,
there is no active preparation for it. This difficulty is met
largely by denying it. [142] The result is a kind of ideal picture about how the things which make up home life are accomplished. If American women and men do not match the
ideal, empathy supplies the missing ingredients. Even at
that, "the American marriage ideal ... is one of the most
difficult marriage forms that the human race has ever attempted," demanding the exercise of choice and self-sufficiency, innocence and complete commitment. [143]

The assertion that a de facto ideal type exists for
marriage in the United States is a long way from belief in
evolutionary progress. To speak about an ideal marriage
type is to speak in platonic terms about its essence. Evolutionary progress, on the other hand, is a teleological concept, Aristotelian in derivation. As feminist thinkers move
away from strict notions of evolutionary progress, they are

confronted with a discrepancy between the norm they espouse
and recognize, diversity in human love relations, and their
ideal type, the self sufficient woman. Clearly most women
are not of this type. Furthermore, accepting diversity means
that, even though they should be self-sufficient to break the
vicious circle of their economic dependence, they need not
be. Feminist thinkers such as Ellen Key in effect circumvent this by advancing a program to render mothers economically independent. Not only does this line of thought provide fuel for critics of feminism, it also advocates social
change through legislation which is still a long way in the
future. Generally speaking, feminist thinkers are no longer
friendly to legislative remedies and state control.[144] The
problem of what women are to do with their lives in an industrial society is much too complex and personal to leave
to impersonal, single-minded authoritative solutions.

The ideal marriage type Mead finds on most people's
minds is not only difficult; it is paradoxical as well. How
can women make choices about marriage in an innocent state?
Innocence is tantamount to ignorance, but choice-making requires awareness if it is to be meaningful. How are women
to be self-sufficient and yet completely committed to their
marriages? Self-sufficiency entails reliance on one's own
person; complete commitment requires sacrifice for another's
sake. For feminists who think women ought to be encouraged
to make intelligent choices about their lives and to rely on
themselves in making them, this bit of reality Mead uncovers
is more than just difficult. It is antithetical to their entire
mind set.

The puzzle is reflected throughout B. F. Skinner's
utopian model, Walden II. A group of people retire from
society at large to engineer their own ideal society in which
technology makes it possible for them to control undesirable
cultural influences. The goal is happiness and a futuristic
orientation. Domestic practices are studied scientifically
and collectivized. Housewifery ("huzzifry") is industrialized.
Because there is no leisure class in the community, women
devote themselves to whatever needs to be done; at least half
of them perform tasks unrelated to domestic technology. The
Housekeeper is a man.[145] Sex differences are not eliminated,
but they are minimized. When women and men are old enough
to attain the capacity for love, there are no economic obstacles in their paths. Child care is institutionalized as group
care, so women may devote their lives to other things. The
Walden community "must solve the problem of the family by

revising certain established practices. That's absolutely inevitable. "[146] Men and women are encouraged to be friends
and to think of all children as their own. Children in turn
are to think of all adults as their parents. "Home is no
place to raise children, " but the community, as revised
family, is. [147] The result is a radically changed place for
women in community life.

Yet women, who have the most to gain by throwing
their lot in with that of the community, are the least certain
about the security of their place in it. 'It's sometimes an
almost hopeless task to take the shackles off their souls but
it can be done. "[148] The important thing, paradoxically, is
that the subjects always are right; they behave as they
should. Any failure in prediction must lie with the experi-
menter. The behavioral control behind Walden II is T. E.
Frazier, a sort of second Thoreau and a Christlike figure.
Walden is an ideal type in itself, predetermined from the
start, although within its bounds every member seems to
make choices and determine outcomes. There is no compulsion involved; the community controls its members by satis-
fying their needs. Through the power of love, community
members can have peace on earth. [149] Somehow the tension
in marriage (and life) between choice and innocence and between self-sufficiency and complete commitment is not erased
in Walden. If anything, it seems more evident. One suspects Skinner is aware of this.

There is an attempt in Walden II to deal with the tension, however. To understand it, a brief consideration of
an earlier work by August Bebel, Woman and Socialism, is
helpful. Bebel suggests that the usually mutually exclusive
ends, satisfaction or personal egotism and service of society,
will be harmonized when human beings serve themselves with
their fully developed abilities and thereby serve society. [150]
This is the sort of harmony Frazier is attempting to engineer.
The parallels between Skinner and Bebel's thoughts are quite
remarkable. For example, Bebel sees the solution to the
woman question in the removal of social extremes and their
attendant evils. [151] Skinner presents a utopian society in
which these influences are controlled carefully and thus eliminated. Both thinkers identify the solution of woman's problem with that of society's. Society discovers the laws which
determine its development and applies them consciously to its
future growth. Skinner's work represents the triumph of what
Bebel refers to as the inevitable "progress of great technical
revolution. "[152] Women are released from their domestic

place through the development of their social lives.   Technology makes it possible.[153]   The details of domestic technology in both books are very much alike.   The only justifiable
difference between women and men for Bebel is that of reproduction,[154] and Skinner agrees with little qualification.

There is no evidence that Skinner read Bebel's book
or that he was influenced by Bebel's thought.   Both thinkers
partake of the naturalistic postulates which are inherent to
Marxism, however.   Where Bebel says communism can be
inferred from the patriarchate,[155] Skinner applies the inference.   It would not be correct to label Skinner a Marxist,
but his provisions for the status of women in Walden II are
similar to those made by certain Marxist thinkers.   The same
may be said for most transitional and early twentieth-century
thinkers, excluding Emma Goldman and Mary Beard.   The
best explanation for this phenomenon may be Stow Persons':
"In the early decades of the twentieth century, although acknowledged American Marxist intellectuals remained few in
number, a pervasive Marxist influence began to permeate
the community, leaving its mark upon the work of many students who were not themselves aware of the affiliations and
sometimes even the derivation of their ideas."[156]   Jane
Addams and B. F. Skinner, for two, undoubtedly are better
informed than all that, but their premises probably are indigenous rather than Marxist.   Goldman and Beard, on the
other hand, often consciously use Marxist premises.

One practical contribution to resolving tension in marriage between choice and innocence and between self-sufficiency and complete commitment is the inclusion of men in its
resolution.   Well-intentioned men are evident throughout the
intellectual history of feminism.   In the beginning, they are
regarded as exceptions, and the blame for existing tension is
laid on men's shoulders.   Now they are taken for genuine
comrades and indicative of things to come.   Accusations
against them are softened, even withdrawn, and they are
seen as victims as well.   Just as there is a New Woman,
there is a New Man.   This is evident in Walden II, but it
also is evident in less utopian and less controlled but nonetheless progressive settings.   Sinclair Lewis tells the story
of Cass Timberlane, a divorced young judge in a small Minnesota community, who persuades his "Cinderella that the
glass slipper [is] pretty," wondering all the while what marriage will do to his intended.[157]   Cinderella is Jinny Marshall, another Virginia, whose real surname is Marshandsky.
She is "different from anyone else, a complete individual,

courageous and joyful and yet so fragile that she must be protected.[158] She admits to having no real ideas and does not aspire to a career, but she is artistically adept. Cass encourages her to realize her ability with to him reasonable qualifications, but not much comes of it.

Jinny's idol is a crystal statuette of Isis, the Egyptian goddess of motherhood and fertility. Not much comes of that either; their baby girl dies, and Isis is first confined to a shelf and then lost altogether. Cass cannot understand what it is that Jinny wants.

> Security, scenery, power, the ability to recognize
> a quotation from Steinbeck, a ruby-and-diamond
> bracelet, a sense of self discipline, the love of a
> tangible God, a red canoe with yellow cushions,
> an unblemished skin, venison with sauce Cumber-
> land, many children, a $75 hat from New York,
> a request to speak on a nation-wide hook-up,
> dawn beside Walden pond, the certainty of her
> husband's affection, or an Irish wolfhound?[159]

Jinny is not sure. At one time each of these things might be what she wants but not all the time. Cass is steadfast in her love for her, through the play-acting after baby's death and Jinny's illness with diabetes, her runaway affair with his best friend and her return under Cass's auspices. Having and holding has real meaning for him. He is not a dupe and is supportive of Jinny's needs, whatever they are.

Cass is not a feminist, by his own admission,[160] but he is the New Man of whom feminists are speaking. Beatrice Forbes-Robertson Hale writes about such a man thirty years earlier, and in her description Cass emerges very clearly. He is, above all, "a human being before he is a male, counting a woman human before female."[161] He faces Jinny's difficulties with sympathy, respect and friendliness. He does not attempt to dominate her or exercise sovereignty over her. He is, as Hale suggests he will be, a member of the enlightened middle class, and he marries a woman in whose qualities he identifies, although she is not a duplicate of himself. He encourages his wife to follow whatever calling she desires after their marriage.[162] One wonders if Lewis read Hale's book; the resemblance between Cass and the New Man is that close. Perhaps the most stunning example of closeness comes as Cass commits "patricide" after Jinny leaves by selling his familial mansion to return to the home Jinny made for him--for good. Hale writes,

"Big Vic" (courtesy of Gotfred O. Hoffmann, Miniature Mansions of Cheshire, Conn.).

---

to paraphrase her, that man must commit "patricide" by tearing down the ancient edifice of his dominance and building on its site a mansion so different from the old that his architectural knowledge may falter.[163]

The message is that the tragi-comedy of married life is not easy for the New Man either.[164] Lewis's novel is an excellent comment on marriage in all its diversity, on divorce and on much feminist writing. It is at all times sympathetic, respectful and friendly, but it makes clear that problems still remain. It is a hopeful book, for all its ins and outs, and it is very much in the stream of feminist thought. Divorce, a state remedy for an intolerable situation, is not necessarily going to be a solution in all or even most cases for tension intrinsic in the marriage relationship. Whatever woman's capacity may be, whatever man's capacity may be, they are into the dilemma together. Love and an occupation are important, but an individual's consciousness of their meaning for him/her makes the difference. Hale comments that the woman's movement might not have developed as it has were it not for the novel.[165] Certainly one can say that about its intellectual superstructure. The novel puts feminist ideas into a very real-feeling environment, a quality sometimes, but not always, lacking in its other manifestations. The author cannot agree with Suzanne LaFollette's judgment of Ellen Key's work and of the whole body of feminist literature, that it lacks seriousness,[166] but she does believe that the novel contributes a great deal to its seriousness.

Not all responses to New Women and their advocates are sympathetic, respectful and friendly by any means. Perhaps the most systematic, comprehensive criticism ever made of feminist thought is that of Ferdinand Lundberg and Marynia F. Farnham. They begin by conceding that being a woman is not easy, especially in the present. The biggest difficulty, however, is that women are a problem individually and collectively to everyone, including themselves and society. They may be enigmatic, and their female power may have been idealized, but more than anything, women are "a bundle of anxieties."[167] Their psyche was shaken disastrously after man "destroyed his material earthly home," "the social extension of the mother's womb," with the coming of progress, industrialization and technology.[168] As a result, women now function as transmitters of the disordered emotions so characteristic in the modern world. They are able to do so by using their influence as mothers. Women, however, are offered a new direction for their troubled lives by feminists, the mother of whom is Mary Wollstonecraft. (Feminists generally are equated with careerists, and non-feminists, with homemakers, although Lundberg and Farnham recognize there is some overlap here.) The program advanced by feminists, insofar as it attempts "to restore earlier rights and privileges," is correct. It is feminist ideology that is "an expression of emotional sickness, of neurosis."[169]

According to Lundberg and Farnham, the chief underlying idea of feminist ideology is that women and men are equal and therefore identical. This means feminists are at-

tempting to gain masculinity for women. In doing so, they--
ironically--are the greatest phallic worshippers ever known.
This is in spite of the fact they hate men, but because they
overvalue and overestimate them. The result is to negate
femaleness and exhibit hostility toward women. Feminists
do this despite known consequential differences between women and men, largely because of the "disturbed [female] li-
bidinal organization" which gives rise to their ideology.[170]
Feminists unconsciously are trying to reform woman's sexual
life or sphere, even though their program bespeaks reform
of woman's ego sphere. Both ideology and program fail.
The program fails because women's egos cannot be strength-
ened by taking on male ways. "Feminists ... attempted to
put women on the essentially male road of exploit, off the
female road of nurture."[171] The ideology fails because it
confuses external sexual gratification for woman with her need
for inner satisfaction through giving birth. Feminists miss
the point; even though environmental influences do play a part
in woman's problems, they are not as crucial as woman's
inner state. "The initial inhibition standing in the way of
woman's gratification was connected directly to the social
inhibition against having children."[172]

One possible response to the Lundberg/Farnham critique is that they are mistaken about feminist ideas. Wollstonecraft, in fact, does not assert that women are identical
to men, that women should have the same work as men, that
women should behave as much like men as possible.[173]
Neither do other feminist thinkers. Furthermore, Lundberg
and Farnham construct what is at best a questionable psycho-
biography for Wollstonecraft[174] and then attribute her traits,
as they interpret them, to all feminists: again, at best a
faulty procedure. Defending feminist ideas against their mis-
apprehensions would be to miss the point that this is the way
feminist thought is perceived by its critics. Part of the
reason for the misconception probably lies in the fact feminist
thinkers constantly are grappling with the premises they are
accused of adopting. This is evident in feminist thought
about the family. The fact that women are not identical to
men with regard to the nature of their reproductive capacity
(and vice versa) is the crux of the problem. The kinds of
work that women and men do and what this means in terms
of self-sufficiency are crucial. The consequence of woman's
behavior for herself, her family and society and what it
would mean were she not able to perform her duties are of
the greatest importance.

If anything, the Lundberg and Farnham critique confirms salient aspects of feminist analysis about the family, for example that women are displaced,[175] and extends them. In discussing the home's destruction, they go beyond the rational aspects of its constitution to delve into its irrational aspects. Ideally "home ... is fixed, permanent, spacious, separate and unique."[176] Beneath its material and physical facade, "it is irrationally felt to be very safe, and therefore extraordinarily valuable" by fearful but intelligent human beings.[177] Hale asserts the New Man is committing patricide by razing the old structure of paternalism.[178] Lewis follows up by saying yes, he is, but it is not easy and in fact, his architectural knowledge is faltering just as Hale suggests it may. Why is it faltering? Mead gives the ostensible reason by uncovering the tension inherent in the ideal conception of marriage. Lundberg and Farnham give the underlying irrational basis for both the ideal conception and the problems faced by those who attempt to resolve it. They also give a good reason why they misapprehend feminist thought. They may be stating their own fears about what they perceive is coming to pass.

Americans have just passed through a Great Depression and a second World War. In this time, woman's political consciousness rises considerably; her social consciousness about herself, however, does not change significantly.[179] Franklin Roosevelt's injunction that there is nothing to fear but fear itself does not strike at irrational fears about the home's destruction; it is aimed at economic and political problems for which political solutions are proposed. Women's efforts are incorporated into the solutions. In giving their assistance, women do not delve automatically into the connection between their own situation, a wildly fluctuating economic environment and political means. As Lundberg and Farnham put it in another context, they are doing what they feel they must under a certain set of circumstances.[180] (So are men.) Recalling Mill, the question still rests with women themselves; it is a matter of trying. Granted, they are not expected to try without the participation of a goodly number of men.[181] Women and men's efforts are directed to controlling their economic environment now. Their fears about the home's destruction are unabated and unaddressed.

Woman's continuing plight is summarized in the fifties by Doris Lessing in her Children of Violence Series. In a South African setting, Martha Quest begins a life marked off by "farm time, that strict measuring rod, where life was kept

properly defined--for there could be no nonsense where the
seasons were used as boundaries."[182] In her first season,
she reads and agrees with Frederick Engel's The Origin of
the Family, acquires "the new skilled vivacity [of] a girl
about town" and is seduced in her innocence by a Jewish
male much as in a magazine story. It is decided that she
will marry someone else on very short notice at the age of
19. She does not want her fiancé's "self-absorbed adoration
of her," but she is passive throughout the rite, "offering
herself to his adoration ... quite excluded."[183] Martha is
alienated from the outside world, caring but impotent. She
is wearily blasé, if analytical. In the confines of her proper
marriage, she often withdraws to her inner self, leaving behind a brittle facade. She and her ulcerous bureaucrat of a
husband have a baby which neither of them wants initially.
In the summer of her life, Martha feels "caught up in an immense impersonal tide which paid no attention to her."[184]
Caroline's birth gives her back herself, but her estrangement in the face of a sickening disgusting mess continues.
She is bored with motherhood, it does not suit her and she
self-righteously admits it.[185]

   Martha is both bored and not bored. She is troubled
by whether there is a woman type who inevitably marries the
civil servant. She does not feel as if she were her civil
servant husband's wife or her daughter's mother. She is uncomfortable because she adjusts to her secure life so well.
Her marriage is fundamentally material (Martha's euphemism
for modern); in it, she can have an affair or involve herself
in Communist activities, even if civil servants' wives usually
do not.[186] She intellectualizes but deserts her spouse and
child in a parting marked by abuse and sentiment. She becomes engrossed in pamphletting ... and in worrying about
her soldier lover's lack of promptness. She anxiously is
dissatisfied with herself; she has an idea of what she wants
to be. "Any real man would be able to see what I could be
and help me to become it...."[187] She marries another man
formally, in the face of social circumstances, in the autumn
of a life only slightly ruffled by the storm about it. All
the while "she was dreaming persistently of that man who
must surely be somewhere close and who would allow her to
be herself."[188] Her second try becomes a marriage after
all, and another two years of her life go by. They are busy,
agitated and happy years, and they are over. Everything is
inevitable; everything is unreal; it is impossible it should be
so. Martha is overwhelmed with futility.[189]

In the winter of her first life, Martha is 24 and attractive but "locked in herself, and ... what a damned waste."[190] She must keep her selves separate at the expense of the best in her; in this way only can she "preserve wholeness through a time of dryness and disintegration."[191] She imagines the home of her childhood destroyed, undercut by some teeming force over her soul's grave. She dreams of a bungalow for which she keeps house, keeping the different furnished rooms and their occupants apart without bridges between them. Martha's husband has a lover; Martha's going to England; Martha has a lover. It is winter, and Martha is still young because her experience has kept her safe. She does not believe in violence, yet she is "the essence of violence.... Conceived, bred, fed, and reared on violence."[192] She cannot use the word love; she does not know what it means.[193] Her father dies; her lover dies. Her re-entry to British citizenship (which she never left) is arranged, just as her divorce is being arranged, and the way is cleared for her passage to England and a new life.

There it is, one woman's history,[194] and in it, every woman's. Martha's three selves--daughter of the land; mother of husband, of child, of lover, of employer; political activist creating a new order--carefully are kept separate from one another to keep them intact. There is a time and season for everything: every season has its seasons and when seasons are over, they will recycle--with Martha's trinity of selves. In the process, though, it all comes out the same. Woman's reproductive function is at the base of it all. The daughter of the land is planted by her father and born of her mother. The mother nurtures and cares for her offspring. In their name she civilizes and reorders society. If woman keeps her selves separately, they never will meet and never will make the fatal connection. The way out? If there is one, it will have to be found. Feminist thinkers undoubtedly will continue their search for that higher plane, the true home, where choice and innocence, self-sufficiency and commitment, are harmonized. They have not found it as the decade of the 1950s comes to a close.

References

1   Jean Jacques Rousseau, L'Emile, trans. Barbara Foxley (1762) (New York: E. P. Dutton, 1911), pp. 362, 345, 322-23.
2   Ibid., pp. 322, 324, 348.

3   Ibid., pp. 359, 322, 327.
4   Margaret George, One Woman's "Situation": A Study of Mary Wollstonecraft (Urbana: University of Illinois Press, 1970), p. 76.
5   Wollstonecraft, The Rights of Women (1790) (New York: E. P. Dutton, 1929), p. 182.
6   I am indebted to Linda Grant De Pauw for her analysis of this phenomenon in Founding Mothers: Women of America in the Revolutionary Era (Boston: Houghton, Mifflin, 1975), pp. 1-44.
7   Philip J. Greven, Jr., "Family Structure in Seventeenth-Century Andover, Massachusetts," in The American Family in Social-Historical Perspective, ed. Michael Gordon (New York: St. Martin's Press, 1973), pp. 86-87.
8   Henry Steele Commager makes this point retrospectively in The American Mind: Thought and Character Since the 1880's (New Haven, Conn.: Yale University Press, 1961), pp. 6-7.
9   April 20, 1771, in Adams Family Correspondence (Adams Papers, Series 2), ed. L. H. Butterfield (Cambridge, Mass.: Harvard University Press, 1963), p. 76.
10 May 7, 1776, in Familiar Letters of John Adams and His Wife Abigail Adams During the Revolution (1875) (Freeport, N.Y.: Books for Libraries Press, 1970), p. 169. Portia is the humorous, intelligent and feminine woman who pleads at the bar for Antonio against Shylock in Shakespeare's Merchant of Venice.
11 March 31, 1776, ibid., p. 148.
12 October 22, 1775, ibid., p. 115.
13 March 16, 1776, ibid., p. 143.
14 August 29, 1776, ibid., p. 221.
15 The Virginia Gazette, October 15, 1736, quoted in Linda De Pauw, Founding Mothers, p. 201.
16 Charles Sellers and Henry May make this point in A Synopsis of American History, 2d ed. (Chicago: Rand-McNally, 1972), p. 35.
17 Daniel J. Boorstin discusses Blackstone's demonstration of this tendency in The Mysterious Science of the Law (Beacon Hill, Mass.: Beacon Press, 1958), pp. 74-81.
18 See Ernest Cassirer, The Philosophy of the Enlightenment, trans. Fritz C. A. Koelln and James P. Pettegrove (Boston: Beacon Press, 1961), pp. 3-36, for further discussion of the Enlightenment mind.
19 Wollstonecraft, Rights of Women, p. 18. Presumably Edmund Burke is among the crowd of authors who assert that all is now rights.

20 Society in America (London: Saunders and Otley, 1837), vol. 3, p. 130.

21 Ibid., pp. 119, 126, 128.

22 Democracy in America, trans. George Lawrence, ed. J. P. Mayer (Garden City, N.Y.: Anchor Books, 1969), p. 592.

23 See for example Commager, American Mind, pp. 22-23.

24 See for example Edmund S. Morgan, "The Puritans and Sex," in American Family, ed. Michael Gordon, pp. 282-95.

25 The Anti-Slavery Examiner, 1 (September 1836), 16-26. See also Elizabeth Margaret Chandler, "An Appeal to the Ladies of the United States" and "Opinions" in her collected works, ed. Benjamin Lundy (1836) (Miami: Mnemosyne, 1969), pp. 17-23.

26 Letters on the Equality of the Sexes and the Condition of Women (1838) (New York: B. Franklin, 1970), p. 15.

27 Fuller, Women in the Nineteenth Century, in The Writings of Margaret Fuller, ed. Mason Wade (New York: Viking, 1941), p. 210.

28 Ibid., pp. 187, 213-16, 122.

29 Vernon Louis Parrington, Jr., quotes Barrett Wendell's Literary History of America as labeling Fuller "an unsexed version of Plato's Socrates," in Main Currents in American Thought: An Interpretation of American Literature from the Beginnings to 1920 (New York: Harcourt, 1930), vol. 2, p. 427.

30 Page Smith offers this thesis in Daughters of the Promised Land: Women in American History (Boston: Little, Brown, 1973). Harriet Martineau would disagree. She suggests in Society in America, vol. 2, p. 355, that mill girls have too much pride for domestic service as it is in America, even if it means doing without a respectable home and class status.

31 Three Hundred Years Hence (1836) (Philadelphia: Prime Press, 1950), is discussed by Vernon Parrington in American Dreams: A Study of American Utopia, Brown University Studies 11, American Studies 2, American Dreams (Providence: Brown University Press, 1942), pp. 17-22. Griffith's book originally is published anonymously.

32 Philothea: A Grecian Romance (1836) (Freeport, N.Y.: Books for Libraries Press, 1969). Cf. Gertrude Atherton's treatment of Aspasia almost 100 years later in The Immortal Marriage (New York: Liveright, 1927).

33 Hawthorne, The Blithedale Romance, in The Works of Nathaniel Hawthorne (New York: Bigelow, Brown, 1923), vol. 3, pp. 56-57.

34 Ibid., p. 218. This passage is strikingly reminiscent
    of Harriet Martineau's recollection of Margaret Fuller.
    See Alice Rossi, ed., The Feminist Papers: From
    Adams to de Beauvoir (New York: Bantam Books, 1974),
    pp. 122-23.
35 Hawthorne, Blithedale Romance, p. 237. Margaret Ful-
    ler too drowns tragically off Fire Island in 1850. She
    apparently chooses death over parting with her spouse
    and child. Ophelia drowns "... incapable of her own
    distress,/ Or like a creature native and indued,/ Unto
    that element ..."--Shakespeare, Hamlet.
36 Hawthorne, Blithedale Romance, p. 227.
37 "The Times That Try Men's Souls," in History of Woman
    Suffrage, 2d ed., ed. Elizabeth Cady Stanton, Susan B.
    Anthony and Matilda Joslyn Gage (Rochester, N.Y.:
    Charles Mann, 1889), vol. 1, pp. 82-83.
38 The North Star (August 28, 1848), reprinted in History
    of Woman Suffrage, ed. Stanton, Anthony and Gage, vol.
    1, p. 74.
39 Letter to George G. Cooper, Editor of the National Re-
    former, September 14, 1848, in Elizabeth Cady Stanton,
    ed. Theodore Stanton and Harriot Stanton Blatch (New
    York: Arno, 1969), vol. 2, pp. 19-20.
40 Letter to Susan B. Anthony, March 1, 1853, ibid., p.
    48.
41 Letter to Anthony, June 14, 1860, ibid., p. 82.
42 History of Woman Suffrage, ed. Stanton, Anthony and
    Gage, vol. 1, p. 260.
43 Ibid., pp. 260-61.
44 Letter to Rebecca R. Eyster, May 1, 1847, in Elizabeth
    Cady Stanton, ed. Stanton and Blatch, vol. 2, p. 16.
45 History of Woman Suffrage, ed. Stanton, Anthony and
    Gage, vol. 1, pp. 126-27. Mary Wollstonecraft Godwin
    Shelley is the author of Frankenstein as well as Shelley's
    biography. She finally marries Shelley, after living
    with him in dire circumstances, when Harriet Westbrook,
    his first wife, drowns. Alice Rossi notes that on Shel-
    ley's death, Mary devotes her life to attaining respecta-
    bility for herself, Shelley and her parents in order not
    to disgrace her son's title and fortune. The Feminist
    Papers, p. 39. It seems that Mary's parents' relation-
    ship of absolute right is of little help in her own troubled
    life.
46 Stow Persons, American Minds: A History of Ideas (New
    York: Henry Holt, 1958), pp. 149-62.
47 Ibid., pp. 160-61.
48 The Feminist Papers, p. 265.

49 "Enfranchisement of Women," in Essays on Sex Equality, ed. Alice Rossi (Chicago: University of Chicago Press, 1970), p. 93.
50 Elizabeth Cady Stanton, ed. Stanton and Blatch, vol. 2, pp. 59-60.
51 Carl Sandburg, Abraham Lincoln: The Prairie Years and the War Years, (New York: Harcourt, Brace, 1954), p. 742.
52 See Persons, American Minds, p. 149. See also Herman Belz, A New Birth of Freedom: The Republican Party and Freedmen's Rights 1861-1866 (Westport, Conn.: Greenwood Press, 1976), for a realistic appraisal of nineteenth-century civil rights and liberties.
53 Mill, "The Subjection of Women," in Essays on Sex Equality, ed. Rossi, pp. 147-48.
54 Ibid., pp. 154, 159.
55 Commager, American Mind, pp. 87-88.
56 Blackwell, The Sexes Throughout Nature (New York: G. P. Putnam's, 1875), p. 53.
57 Ibid., pp. 197, 109.
58 Ibid., p. 136.
59 Willard, Woman and Temperance: or, The Work and Workers of the Women's Christian Temperance Union (1883) (New York: Arno, 1972), pp. 43-44.
60 Ibid., p. 42.
61 Ibid., p. 458.
62 History of Woman Suffrage, ed. Stanton, Anthony and Gage, vol. 1, is dedicated affectionately to its forebears, among them Mary Wollstonecraft, Frances Wright, Harriet Martineau, Lydia Maria Child, Margaret Fuller, Sarah and Angelina Grimke.
63 Stow Persons, The Decline of American Gentility (New York: Columbia University Press, 1973), p. 275.
64 The Bostonians (London: John Lehman, 1886), p. 29. Marius Bewley suggests Bostonians is a conscious effort by James to improve upon Hawthorne's Blithdale Romance--in The Complex Fate: Hawthorne, Henry James and Some Other American Writers (New York: Grove Press, 1954), pp. 11-30.
65 James, Bostonians, p. 53.
66 Ibid., p. 65.
67 Ibid., p. 63.
68 Gilman, Women and Economics: A Study of the Economic Relation Between Men and Women as a Factor in Social Evolution (1898) (New York: Harper Torch Books, 1966), pp. 18, 110, 128, 126.
69 Ibid., pp. 97-98, 38-39.

70 Ibid., pp. 151, 155, 168, 220, 182, 199.
71 Gilman, The Home: Its Work and Influence (1903) (Urbana: University of Illinois Press, 1972), p. 234.
72 Ibid., pp. 250-51.
73 (1899) Old Westbury, N.Y.: Feminist Press, 1973.
74 Genesis, i:26.
75 Gilman, Yellow Wallpaper, p. 36.
76 Gilman, Women and Economics, pp. 210, 241.
77 Gilman, The Home, p. 341.
78 Ibid., p. 347.
79 Virginia (1913) (Garden City, N.Y.: Doubleday, Page, 1923), p. 288.
80 Ibid., p. 486.
81 Ibid., pp. 480, 294-95. Much later, writing autobiographically at 60, Glasgow recalls that she always was a feminist, liking intellectual revolt as she did. "On the whole, I think women have lost something precious, but have gained immeasurably, by the passing of the old order"--The Woman Within (1944) (New York: Harcourt, 1954), pp. 167-68.
82 Edith Wharton, The House of Mirth (New York: Charles Scribner's Sons, 1905), traces the fate of a Gibson girl, the New Woman, who must throw in her lot with women of the industrial working class.
83 Aileen S. Kraditor, Ideas of Woman Suffrage Movement (New York: Columbia University Press, 1965), pp. 163-218.
84 See Christopher Lasch, The Agony of the American Left (New York: Knopf, 1969), pp. 23-24.
85 Clara Bewick Colby, "The Philosophy of Woman Suffrage," in History of Woman Suffrage, ed. Susan B. Anthony and Ida Husted Harper (Indianapolis: Hollenbeck Press, 1902), vol. 4, pp. 254-55.
86 "Why Women Should Vote," in The Social Thought of Jane Addams, ed. Christopher Lasch (Indianapolis: Bobbs-Merrill, 1965), p. 144.
87 History of Woman Suffrage, ed. Stanton, Anthony and Gage, vol. 1, p. 22.
88 Matilda Joslyn Gage, Woman, Church and State (1893), (New York: Arno, 1972), p. 48.
89 Jane Addams, Democracy and Social Ethics (New York: Macmillan, 1911), p. 16.
90 Ibid., pp. 32, 38, 58, 7.
91 Ibid., pp. 103, 106.
92 Ibid., pp. 111-36.
93 In 1912, Beatrice Forbes-Robertson Hale asserts "it must not be forgotten that when feminists speak of women

68 / Monumental Issues

they mean all women, and when they demand a programme
of reform they demand it for women as a whole, not for
any one class"--What Women Want: An Interpretation of
the Feminist Movement (New York: Frederick A. Stokes,
1914), p. 146.

94 For examples of this thesis, see William L. O'Neill,
Everyone Was Brave: A History of Feminism in America
(Chicago: Quandrangle Books, 1969), p. 274; Lasch,
Agony of the American Left, p. 25.

95 "The Tragedy of Woman's Emancipation," from Anarchism
and Other Essays, in Red Emma Speaks: Selected Writings and Speeches, ed. Alix Kates Shulman (New York:
Random House, 1972), p. 142.

96 Ibid., pp. 136-37.

97 "The Traffic in Women," from Anarchism, in Red Emma, ed. Shulman, p. 145.

98 "Marriage and Love," from Anarchism, in Red Emma,
ed. Shulman, p. 165. In 1871 Victoria Woodhull puts it
this way: "where there is no love as a basis of marriage there should be no marriage..."--The Victoria
Woodhull Reader, ed. Madeline B. Stern (Weston,
Mass.: M and S Press, 1974), p. 16.

99 "Victims of Morality," from Mother Earth (March 1913),
in Red Emma, ed. Shulman, p. 132.

100 "Marriage and Love," from Anarchism, in Red Emma,
ed. Shulman, p. 167.

101 One recalls Susan B. Anthony's parting words to the
National American Woman Suffrage Association in 1900
upon her retirement and on the eve of her 80th birth-
day: "I have lived to rise from the most despised and
hated woman in all the world of 50 years ago, until
now it seems as if I am loved by you all"--History of
Woman Suffrage, ed. Susan Anthony and Ida Harper,
vol. 4, p. 394.

102 In her Woman and Labor, 5th ed. (New York: Frederick A. Stokes, 1911), p. 172.

103 Ibid., p. 46.

104 Ibid., pp. 64-65.

105 Ibid., pp. 125, 128, 140.

106 Ibid., pp. 100, 109-10.

107 Ellen Key, The Renaissance of Motherhood, trans.
Anne E. B. Fries (New York: G. P. Putnam's, 1914),
pp. iv, 151, 18-19, 53, 60.

108 Ibid., pp. 34, 23, 91.

109 Beatrice Hale, What Women Want, p. 178, suggests
that where Gilman seeks to minimize the impact of
sex, Key wants to maximize it.

110 Ellen Key, Renaissance of Motherhood, pp. 8, 132, 48.
111 Feminists do not accept its evils. Ida Tarbell writes
in The Business of Being a Woman (New York: Macmillan, 1912), p. 80, about appalling indifference to
the moral quality of commercial and political trans-
actions which comes about under the regime of emancipated women. She is speaking about the suffragists.
112 John Dewey, Theory of Valuation, in John Dewey on
Education: Selected Writings, ed. Reginald D. Archambault (1939) (New York: Modern Library, 1964),
pp. 91-92.
113 Motherhood in Bondage (1928) (Elmsford, N.Y.: Maxwell Reprint, 1956). The book is made up of letters
to Sanger from women in need of assistance; through
their words comes the story.
114 See Daniel Scott Smith, "The Dating of the American
Sexual Revolution: Evidence and Interpretation," in
American Family, ed. Michael Gordon, pp. 321-35.
115 Margaret Sanger, Motherhood, pp. xi, 433.
116 Ibid., p. 434.
117 Beatrice Hale, What Women Want, pp. 242, 55.
118 Ethel Maud Colquhoun, The Vocation of Woman (London:
Macmillan, 1913), p. 27.
119 Ibid., p. 40.
120 Prejudices, first series (New York: Knopf, 1919), p.
205.
121 Mencken, Prejudices, fourth series (New York: Knopf,
1929), p. 115. Mencken does not incorporate any sense
of moral urgency to change the situation.
122 See Alice Ames Winter, The Heritage of Women (New
York: Minton, Balch, 1927); Inez Haynes Irwin, Angels
and Amazons: A Hundred Years of American Women
(Garden City, N.Y.: Doubleday, Doran, 1933); Mary R.
Beard, Woman as Force in History: A Study in Traditions and Realities (New York: Macmillan, 1946).
Cf. earlier biographic woman's histories, the most
well known of which is Elizabeth F. Ellet, The Eminent
and Heroic Women of America (New York: McNenamy,
Hess, 1873). For an example of a man's view of woman's history, see John Langdon-Davis, A Short History
of Women (New York: Literary Guild, 1927).
123 Alice Winter, The Heritage of Women, p. 3.
124 Briffault, The Mothers: A Study of the Origins of Sentiments and Institutions (New York: Macmillan, 1927),
pp. 510-11, p. 513.
125 Ibid., pp. 507, 515. The Briffault volume which I bor-
rowed from the library has such fascinating annotation

by an earlier anonymous (alas) reader that I would like
to share it: "I do not think that the 'superiority of
men' needs to be posited as the causal factor in the
development of higher cultures; as ever, the transforming activities of men--which elaborated the higher cul-
tures--[were] not the effect of 'intellectual superiority'
but of an environing circumstance which directed masculine thought into channels different from those earlier
powerful. The causal factors were probably closely allied to conditions promoted by the formation of an economic surplus, which although the product of woman's
labor affected the status and function of man more than
it did woman." The comment is not dated.

126 Ibid., pp. 515-16, 519, 521.
127 Ibid., pp. 517-18.
128 LaFollette, Concerning Women (1926) (New York: Arno,
     1972), pp. 68-71, 55, 73, 94.
129 Ibid., pp. 5, 117, 55
130 Ibid., p. 5.
131 Parker, "Sonnet for the End of a Sequence," in Death
     and Taxes (New York: Viking, 1931), p. 36.
132 The Collected Poems of Dorothy Parker (New York:
     Modern Library, n.d.), p. 19.
133 Parker, "For a Sad Lady," in Collected Poems, p. 26.
134 Parker, After Such Pleasures (New York: Viking,
     1933), passim.
135 "With a Wife," in Painted Lace and Other Pieces
     (1914-1937) (New Haven, Conn.: Yale University Press,
     1955), pp. 303-04.
136 Male and Female: A Study of the Sexes in a Changing
     World (New York: Morrow, 1949), p. 22.
137 Stow Persons discusses this trend in American Minds,
     pp. 360-62.
138 Mead, Male and Female, pp. 27-38.
139 Mead, Sex and Temperament in Three Primitive Socie-
     ties (1935) (New York: Dell, 1971), p. 11.
140 Ibid., p. 13.
141 Ibid., pp. 18, 282-83.
142 Mead, Male and Female, pp. 248-50, 257. There is
     an implicit but telling criticism of LaFollette's work in
     these findings. Where LaFollette argues to tolerance
     for diversity, Mead shows it already exists. Where
     LaFollette asserts there ought to be no restriction--
     state sanction or social superstition--on women and
     men's personal relationships, Mead shows that what-
     ever the restriction, there is no way to enforce it in
     America.

143 Ibid., pp. 262-63, 342, 348, 353-54.
144 Alice Winter, The Heritage of Women, p. 286, makes the case well: "Alas, it needs more than a law to make a temperate world; more than an amendment to make good citizens. Law, in fact, seems nothing more than a clamp thrust down on a situation to hold it where it is, before we are up and at it again on the long, slow plodding which will bring us up to standard."
145 Skinner, Walden II (1948) (New York: Macmillan, 1972), pp. 209, 59, 63, 72.
146 Ibid., pp. 131-33, 138.
147 Ibid., pp. 140, 142, 147.
148 Ibid., pp. 147-48.
149 Ibid., p. 289 and see especially pp. 217-21, 296, 105-07.
150 Woman and Socialism, trans. Meta L. Stern (Hebe) (New York: Socialist Literature, 1910), p. 377.
151 Ibid., p. 3.
152 Ibid., pp. 369, 237.
153 Ibid., p. 238.
154 Ibid., p. 245.
155 Ibid., p. 33.
156 American Minds, p. 324.
157 Cass Timberlane: A Novel of Husbands and Wives (New York: Random House, 1945), pp. 47, 68.
158 Ibid., p. 46.
159 Ibid., p. 292.
160 Ibid., p. 51.
161 Beatrice Hale, What Women Want, p. 242.
162 Ibid., pp. 263, 256, 258-59, 261.
163 Ibid., p. 255.
164 Sinclair Lewis, Cass Timberlane, p. 331.
165 Beatrice Hale, What Women Want, p. 120.
166 Suzanne LaFollette, Concerning Women, p. 76.
167 Ferdinand Lundberg and Marynia F. Farnham, Modern Woman: The Lost Sex (New York: Harper & Row, 1947), pp. 1-2, 13, 10.
168 Ibid., pp. 118, 114, 91.
169 Ibid., pp. 23, 142-43.
170 Ibid., pp. 147-48, 162, 145, 167, 170, 173.
171 Ibid., p. 174.
172 Ibid.
173 Ferdinand Lundberg and Marynia Farnham attribute these assertions to Wollstonecraft at p. 144.
174 Cf. Ruth Benedict's much more sympathetic, respectful and friendly approach to Wollstonecraft's life in Margaret Mead, An Anthropologist at Work: Writings of

Ruth Benedict (Boston: Houghton, 1959), pp. 491-519.
175 Lundberg and Farnham, Modern Woman, p. 117.
176 Ibid., p. 114.
177 Ibid., p. 115.
178 The New Man thus tries to fulfill Wollstonecraft's plea that he "generously snap [women's] chains and be content with rational fellowship instead of slavish obedience," whereupon he will "find women better citizens"--Rights of Women, p. 164.
179 See Sarah Slavin Schramm, "Eleanor Roosevelt and the Presidency," and Caroline D. Hamsher, "Eleanor Roosevelt: A Study in Irony," in Women in Politics: Six Studies, ed. Marian B. McLeod (Sydney, Australia: Wentworth Press, 1977); Schramm, "Frances Perkins: Too Soon for Equality," paper prepared for the Midwest Regional Conference on Women's Studies, University of Indiana, Bloomington, April 1975; and Schramm, "Section 213 of the Economy Act of 1932: Woman Overboard?," paper prepared for the Berkshire Conference on Women's History, Radcliffe College, Cambridge, Mass., October 1974. The Schramm papers are being revised into chapters for a book, Women in the Political System.
  Also William H. Chafe, The American Woman: Her Changing Social, Economic and Political Roles, 1920-1970 (New York: Oxford University Press, 1972), pp. 135-225, for implicit confirmation of the thesis that woman's political consciousness is rising as her social consciousness about herself is falling, and J. Stanley Lemons, The Woman Citizen: Social Feminism in the 1920's (Urbana: University of Illinois, 1973), passim, for background materials.
180 Modern Woman, p. 143.
181 Subjection of Women, pp. 154, 215.
182 Martha Quest (1952) (New York: New American Library, 1970), p. 197.
183 Ibid., pp. 56-57, 111, 193-94, 224, 220.
184 Lessing, A Proper Marriage (1952) (New York: New American Library, 1970), p. 92.
185 Ibid., pp. 101, 202-04.
186 Ibid., pp. 250, 302, 288.
187 Lessing, Ripple from the Storm (1958) (New York: New American Library, 1970), pp. 1-3, 89.
188 Ibid., pp. 182, 255.
189 Ibid., pp. 256, 261-62.
190 Lessing, Landlocked (1958) (New York: New American Library, 1970), p. 15.

191 Ibid., pp. 15, 14.
192 Ibid., pp. 168, 195.
193 Ibid., p. 218.
194 Or, as Margaret George puts it in her book of the same name, "one woman's situation", pp. v-viii.

2

THE GOLDEN FLEECE:
FEMINISM AND EDUCATION

Woman's education along with the family constitute two monumental concerns for feminist thinkers. These concerns are intermingled in feminist ideas and ideals. Just as there is a true home, there is a true education. Quest for the one true education for women serves the purpose of the Golden Fleece for feminist thinkers. In the beginning, this quest is conceptualized in terms of woman's willing performance of duty and better family management and childhood education. Imagine once again, if you will, that feminist thinkers have the opportunity to commune outside time and space.

Mary Astell is proposing that women begin to reflect seriously on their own minds. Their glass will not do them half so much service, she insists. It is through ignorance and narrow education, along with imitation and custom, that women have come to live in a house of vice. Someone mentions Rousseau, who thinks education must cultivate practical reason in woman, in a habitual context. Ah yes, sighs Mary Wollstonecraft, but reason--perfectly aligned with natural sympathies and feelings--is available to both women and men. We must cultivate the instantaneous association of ideas if we are to prevent habitual slavery to first impressions. The problem is, inserts Constantia, that every educational scheme is calculated to establish the universal error of man's superi-

ority. Well, then, woman needs to cultivate reason and religion rather than her appearance, says Thomas Branagan.
There is no woman now, cries Margaret Fuller, only overgrown children; this impedes the development of man's genius
and use of subjective reason as well as woman's.

Emma Willard thinks the answer is to systematize
woman's education like man's without giving women a masculine education. Frances Wright agrees that progress will obtain through a just educational system. A more republicanized
education, adds Mary Lyon. But there is only one best education for women and men alike, inserts M. Carey Thomas,
looking at Emma Willard. Frances Wright continues: Progress also depends on a fearless spirit of inquiry. Thereby
woman may seek truth for and about herself as a thinking
being. Elizabeth Margaret Chandler muses about the fresh,
beautiful world of feelings, perceptions and the human mind
from which education lifts the veil. Harriet Martineau agrees
that woman's power to act in her own interest depends on the
active use of intellect. Alexis de Tocqueville suggests that
the dangers presented to woman's chastity by democracy far
outweigh any dangers to educating women.

Catharine Beecher adds that, in the future, education
must not allow anything which sacrifices woman's health.
Harriot Hunt points out that much of woman's false position
is premised on her ill health. Intellectual development has
a large role to play here. Don't forget that much of woman's
ill health is the result of her fashionable attire, says Abba
Gold Woolson. Dio Lewis sums it up: true education for
woman must include both her mental and bodily needs. That
way the body becomes an efficient agent of the mind in larger
social service, adds Marion Talbot. Woman's education will
develop her personal, mental and moral qualities, says Sarah

Josepha Hale. What we need is mental reconstruction--it is Charlotte Perkins Gilman speaking. We can obtain mutual help through a collective educational process which serves a social function. Then our developing self-consciousness can evolve into a common consciousness which will yield humanity; that is, being together.

What is important, suggests Anna Garlin Spencer, is the new feminine ideal. Women first must develop as persons. They must avoid excessive discussion of themselves and the mental ferment that goes with it, cautions Ida M. Tarbell. Spencer goes on: Women also must develop as serviceable functionaries in family life. Ellen Key adds that the stress must be on woman's intuition, on educating her feelings, rather than on man's utilitarian God of personal gain. Really what is needed is a marriage of opposites, says Virginia Woolf. This will stimulate an androgynous mind whereby woman may hold her looking glass to life and think of things of themselves. There is need for a fixed income and a room of one's own if we are to live in the presence of reality. Gertrude Stein talks about the configuration which detracts from natural existence. Generic men identify through man's superiority, his need to do things well.

Masculinism as sex monopoly and feminism as sex antagonism are ceasing to exist, though, says Mary Beard. At the center of this tendency is the eternal feminine, the care for life. But for women to quest, we must encourage their divine discontent, insists Margaret Mead. We must educate women to overcome their enculturation if we are to construct a new innocence which is not founded in sacrifice. Unfortunately, adds Marshall McLuhan, coeducation shunts aside acquisition of knowledge in favor of a sterile prepara-

tion for sex production and distribution. Then, says Mary
McLeod Bethune, the quest must be reset by a thirst for
education. Knowledge is the prime need of the hour. She
is speaking to her race, the black, but feminist thinkers
know her legacy is wide and pervasive.

* * * * *

One of feminism's forgotten forebears is Mary Astell. [1]
Writing late in the seventeenth century, Astell proposes to
educate women rightly, ingenuously and liberally, advancing
their wit and wisdom, thereby securing lasting and permanent beauty through their immortal minds. She assures her
readers that her proposition is far more worthy of discussion "than what Colours are most agreeable, or what's the
Dress becomes you best. Your Glass will not do you half
so much service as a serious reflection on your own
minds...."[2] Better women should value themselves than
fashion's latest nuance or how attractive they are to men.
With an education, women will comprehend their duties more
readily and understand Christianity for themselves. Such
practical knowledge will be useful in managing their families and educating their children as well as in all of life's
concerns. It also will enable the unmarried woman, whose
family is the world, to relieve the wants of unfortunate beings and perhaps even to reform the "Prophane and Profligate
Age" in which she lives. [3] Men "may still enjoy their Prerogatives for us, we mean not to intrench on any of their
Lawful Privileges, our only Contention shall be that they may
not out-do us in promoting his Glory who is Lord both of
them and us; ... our only endeavour shall be to be absolute
Monarchs of our own Bosoms. "[4] Astell wants to tear down
the house of vice which woman's ignorance and narrow education in company with imitation and custom construct. Then
only can woman reasonably expect and be capable of enjoying
the life in the hereafter which Eve forfeited. Astell's proposal is not serpentine; rather it seeks to develop woman's
intelligent soul that she may contemplate truth and realize
goodness. [5]

Jean Jacques Rousseau agrees that "nature means
women to think, to will, to love, to cultivate their minds
as well as their persons. "[6] Woman's reason is practical.
The world is her book. She has wit where man has genius;

where man reasons, she observes. Woman and man's faculties are divided fairly. One should consult woman

> in bodily manners, in all that concerns the senses;
> consult the man in matters of morality and all that
> concerns the understanding. When women are what
> they ought to be, they will keep to what they can
> understand and their judgment will be right; but
> since they have begun to criticize books and to
> make them with might and main, they are altogether
> astray. [7]

Because their faculties are divided, woman and man's education must be divided. Little girls do not care to read or
write; they prefer playing with dolls and sewing. Woman
needs only the restraint of early habit to prepare her for her
duties: pleasing man, educating him as a child and caring
for him as a man, counseling and consoling him, making his
life pleasant and happy. To this end, her education is practical, and her science is that of self-possession, penetration
and delicate observation. Despite their different faculties,
woman and man's education partakes of the same method,
"doing rather than talking," drawing upon their senses as the
first means of learning. [8] In this way, they will learn many
things but only those which are suitable for them.

Mary Wollstonecraft does not conceive woman's employment of her mind and her domestic duties as incompatible. [9] She believes that human reason, which is potentially
perfectible through immortality, is available to both woman
and man. Reason, which has an aspect of compulsion to it,
is aligned strongly with natural sympathies and feelings.
Its perfection and human capacity for happiness depend on the
degree of virtue and knowledge which characterize humans
personally. [10] To that end, women ought not marry too
young. First they must attend to their souls, beginning with
a "tolerable education" and adding experience and reflection
on it. Only then can they be responsible for their actions
(although preparation for marriage and maternity needs to
begin early in their lives). Love must have a rational basis
and be supported by esteem to endure. Universal benevolence
rather than passion is the first duty. [11] The harmonious
marriage of two rational and morally disciplined beings
yields parents capable of educating their children. [12]

According to Wollstonecraft, while every rational
creature has a duty to care for its offspring, women do have

special responsibilities here. They should nurse their children, thereby contributing to healthy young constitutions as well as to their own maternal affection. They also must see that children's needs are filled consistently, looking forward to the day when mental discipline begins to develop. [13] Most of all, they need to teach their children to combine ideas. This instantaneous mode of association depends on the original temper of the mind rather than on the will. Such heightened association is the essence of genius and the key to preventing habitual slavery to first impressions. Reason thus replaces prescription, and duty is not placed on arbitrary grounds. [14] "Whatever tends to make a person in such measure independent of the sense, is a prop to virtue."[15] As a result, girls should cultivate simple dress and unaffected manners. Once habits are set and character begins to form, knowledge and taste with it gradually will be acquired. Judicious reading is an act which will enlarge the mind and improve the heart. Woman also needs to study different aspects of domestic concern and family business, including medicine. She must learn to manage servants with benevolence and by setting a good example. [16]

Rousseau and Wollstonecraft both stress experience as the substance of a good education. In that sense, they bypass custom in favor of more natural mental and personal development. With Astell, they advocate practical knowledge for women which has to do with family management and the education of children. Rousseau, however, centers these accomplishments around a woman's spouse, his needs and direction. Astell and Wollstonecraft do not. [17] Astell and Rousseau refer to woman's wit, Astell with reference to wisdom, Rousseau to common sense. Wollstonecraft makes her case for woman's education in terms of critical reason, while concerning herself with woman's soul and happiness as Astell does. Astell and Wollstonecraft have as a goal the growth of woman's power to understand what she perceives. When woman understands her duties, she will fulfill them willingly. Rousseau, on the other hand, refers to placing a yoke on woman that she would fulfill her duties without question, submitting to the authority of her spouse in doing so. Astell does not challenge man's prerogatives in relation to his spouse, but Wollstonecraft seeks to put the relationship on more rational footing. All three thinkers assume such an education will enhance natural tendencies and become part of a child's adulthood. Wollstonecraft's ingenious analysis suggests in and of itself that this influence must precipitate some rather dramatic changes in woman's position, although she couches her predictions in more cautious terms.

In the New World, women largely are illiterate--more so than men. They do not read much beyond the Bible. For the most part, they do not have time for such repast, but they do not have the ability either. What early education they have consists of learning to write and cipher and to read the Bible. Further achievement is limited by the dominant conception of their intelligence and the belief they are destined for marriage and maternity. Woman's preparation for her homemaking duties is attained through an apprenticeship with her mother in the home. [18] This tendency is reflective of Rousseau's overall influence on education; learning comes through observation. Susanna Wesley constitutes a partial exception to this rule so far as her own daughters are concerned. One of the principal rules she observes is

> that no girl be taught to work till she can read
> very well; and that she be kept to her work with
> the same application for the same time that she
> was held to her reading. This rule ... is much
> to be observed, for putting children to learn
> sewing before they can read perfectly is the very
> reason why so few women can read fit to be
> heard, and not to be well understood. [19]

Wesley's rule, while not typical, nevertheless fits comfortably into the Puritan-Evangelical tradition with its stress on education. Everyone must be able to read the Bible, whose authority is paramount. There is a deep-seated humility to Puritanism, but it also admits to a kind of "strenuous asceticism."[20] This undoubtedly stems from its appeal to New England's mercantile or Yankee class, the gentry, and the need for genuine industry to get along in the New World. Pedagogues of this tradition universally agree on the need to control and suppress children's autonomy that they might acquire necessary moral discipline for coping and getting ahead. [21] It seems paradoxical that this body of thought contributes so much normatively to a body of thought concerned with advancing the right of women--who become legally children for life upon marriage--to autonomy or self-governance. A careful reading of John Locke, however, suggests quite a curious situation. The father has only a temporary government in his child, and he shares it with the child's mother. The child tacitly consents to it. Between them, parents must educate the child, for whom they are accountable to God. (Rousseau makes the mother in turn accountable to the child's father). Children's right to act in accordance with their own wills depends upon the state of their reason. Reason is the law by which they will be governed, and once they attain it, they are of age to govern themselves. Political and paternal (parental is more appropriate) powers are perfectly distinct and separate. [22] Mothers clearly have attained enough reason to entitle them to educate their children, although there is reference to the fact naturally equal persons are not always equal in society. It is this ambiguity which works normatively to woman's benefit.

There are schools for women in the New World; for example, the Ursuline Convent in New Orleans is established in 1727; Bethlehem (Pennsylvania) Female Seminary, in 1742. Still, Abigail Adams writes to John in 1778 that "in this country, you need not be told how much female education is neglected, nor how fashionable it has been to ridicule female learning; though I acknowledge it my happiness to be connected with a person of a more generous mind and liberal sentiment. "[23] To one who argues the superiority of the male sex, Constantia replies that every educational scheme is designed to establish such "universal error. " Even so, woman's imagination, reason and memory cannot be doubted, and her judgment merely is depressed by her domestication. The custom of confining woman to needle and kitchen becomes second nature to her, even replaces nature. Despite this, the uncultivated woman is aware of her inferiority here and is mortified by it. Where she instructed to employ her rational mind like her brothers, how different she would be. Rather than abandoning her domestic duties, she would complete them and when her mental attention is no longer required. Woman's immortal soul entitles her to an appropriate education. [24]

There are men other than Rousseau who address themselves to women's educational needs. In 1808, Thomas Branagan asserts that "nothing but poison of false education, the wrong association of juvenile ideas" restricts woman's native genius and inherent endowments. [25] It is envy of woman's mental capacity rather than contempt for it, and failure to be frank rather than want of respectful regard, which mortifies her. Woman in her youth is victimized by her own readiness to believe those who contribute to her degradation and by man's dissemblance of that role. She mimics her fashionable mother, directing her imagination to her appearance and the dictates of her looking glass. She even wears artificial breasts before her own development. The end result is that men consider her an object subject to their passion, all for want of a judicious education. [26]

The blame for her concern with fashion and the subsequent destruction of her intellectual powers rests with her parents and teachers as well as with servants and underlings. Such solicitation of wayward appetites scarcely befits a civilized nation which should be characterized by the cultivation of reason and religion. To give up these characteristics by yielding common sense to "vile and vulgar passion" precedes transformation to more barbarian status. [27]

The frivolity and even moral corruption of female pastimes are abhorrent to those of the Puritan-Evangelical tradition. They are reminiscent of English society in the early Stuart era when the Puritans set out for the virgin New World. They run counter to Puritan moral virtues of moderation and simplicity in all things. Life for the Puritans is a moral process which originates in sin but which hopefully culminates in salvation. [28] Just as Puritanic doctrine with its emphasis on Bible reading supports woman's educational quest, so does Quaker mysticism and its designation of every person as a priest. Where the Puritans dedicate their lives to faith on the authority of the Bible, the Quakers look to God's own word, revealed in the human soul. The Puritans find the mystic aspect of self illumination as abhorrent as female pastimes. Matter and spirit for a Puritan are alien; for a Quaker they are united in a way lending itself to direct intuition of spiritual truth.

Quakerism is largely an eighteenth-century phenomenon. [29] It is followed in the nineteenth century by the Transcendental movement. The Transcendentalists are idealistic, communing with the unreal world of sensations. They want to free the individual from custom and convention. As a result they incorporate both tenets of classical liberalism and a rather conservative view of reality. On behalf of the individual, they protest materialism and advance instinct and intuition. They react to Locke by proclaiming subjective principles of reason rather than an objective reason to which everyone attains and adheres. In positing a relationship between human nature and the world of nature, they acknowledge the existence of an aptitude which transcends the senses and understanding. [30] The abandonment of one standard, objective reason, for a more subjective reasoning process changes the emphasis on woman's education somewhat, although the precept that she should be educated remains. Rather than holding that women share with men the ability to attain and adhere to objective reason which is the same for everyone, the argument now is that women and men have their own unique faculties and neither of them is complete without the other.

Margaret Fuller suggests women and men constitute two halves of one thought, a radical dualism, and the full development of one cannot take place without the development of the other. The two methods of thought are feminine and masculine. The feminine method includes harmony, beauty and love; the masculine method, energy, power and intellect. Woman's essential genius lies in her electrical movement, intuitive function and spiritual tendency.[31] It is important that she develop her genius, however different from man's it may be; in doing so, however, woman and man must develop together in order to be governed by the same fundamental keynote at every stage. The problem is man's mind is so impeded by tradition that he places capricious obstacles in the way of woman's development. She cannot enhance the standard within herself under such conditions. "Now there is no woman, only an overgrown child."[32] Once woman has the opportunity to think and act in accordance with her own needs, she better can show man how to assist her in this.

Woman's education must be an appropriate one; here all prefeminist thinkers are in agreement. They are not totally in agreement about what is appropriate, however. Must education facilitate woman's attainment of objective reason or enhance her own subjective reason? Will she require a solid, disciplinary education or one devoted to domestic science? Constantia discusses astronomy, geography and natural philosophy. Edgar Allan Poe, reviewing Lydia Maria Child's Transcendental novel, Philothea, finds it "might be introduced advantageously into our female academies. Its purity of thought and lofty morality are unexceptionable."[33] The end result, in either case, is expected to turn woman away from frivolity and immoral pleasure, from trifle and fashion. She will devote herself willingly to her pursuit of duty in any case. Astell does refer to unmarried women who ultimately may reform the world. Wollstonecraft makes some allowance for expanded usefulness and independence for "women of superior cast."[34] Constantia allows that the more industrious may commit their ideas to paper or at least refined and rational conversation. The most immediate and practical result of woman's education, however, is expected to be better family management and childhood education.

There are some problems in either educational model. Margaret Fuller in many respects reproduces Rousseau's dichotomy: Emile and Sophy. Rousseau makes a very sharp distinction with regard to intellect. Woman ought not to be criticizing or making books; the world is woman's book. She observes it but does not reason from it. Her use of subjective reason and her experiential education combine to maintain the dichotomy. Fuller does stipulate that woman must think and act in accordance with her own needs apart from encumbering male tradition. It is nonetheless a rather restrictive method which seems more likely to maintain the status quo than to release individuals from custom and convention. Constantia, on the other hand, is closer to Wollstonecraft's emphasis on critical reason available to both sexes. She lacks the sense of compulsion which makes its realization inevitable, however. Granted woman's judgmental power is capable of development. Once it is developed, there is nothing much to do with it but reflect upon her immortal soul. While Wollstonecraft finds mental transition from disappointment in this world to the better land beyond a natural one, she also stresses the love, compassion and happiness which are of this world.[35] Education that results in willingness to perform one's duty either because it is natural to do so or because one understands why duties must be performed is not necessarily the forerunner of happiness or the combatant of custom and convention. *

Elizabeth Cady Stanton's recollections of her childhood bear witness to this fact. She attends Johnstown Academy and is the only girl in the advanced mathematics and language classes; from there she goes on to Emma Willard's Troy Female Seminary. Her first memory is of family friends expressing their pity that her new baby sister is a girl.[36] When her brother--who "filled a larger place in our father's affections and future plans than the five daughters together"--dies, Elizabeth tries to comfort her father. "At length he heaved a deep sigh and said: 'Oh, my daughter, I wish you were a boy.'"[37] She vows to take her brother's place in his heart, hoping to hear her father admit, "'Well, a girl is as good as a boy, after all.' But he never said it."[38] Her father's comment, when she brings home second prize in Greek from school, is, "'Ah, you should have been a boy.'"[39] Her early friend, teacher and pastor, the Rev. Simon Hosack, who tutors her in Greek--and who says he likes girls better than boys--gives her "unbounded praises and visions of future success" when she wins the prize. He

---

*It also might be said that such willingness is not necessarily the forerunner of the civilized nation of which Branagan speaks or Fuller's marital harmony.

leaves her his Greek lexicon, Testament and grammar, plus
four volumes of Scott's commentaries, when he dies. [40] Her
father's attitude, however, does not change.

The content of Stanton's education is not unlike that
Constantia envisions. Whatever her accomplishments in this
regard, however, her sex intervenes in the eyes of the one
person whom she tries hardest to please. She is a girl, and
she will remain a girl; her duty does not lie in bringing home
academic prizes. She is sadly disappointed when she strives
for or expects paternal praise for her academic accomplishments. Had her education been in domestic science, her father probably would have been disinterested. There would
have been no need to wish manhood on her, but the result
still would have been disappointing to young Elizabeth. She
is Wollstonecraft's "woman of superior cast," it is true, and
her life exhibits expanded usefulness and independence in
many ways. The basic problem remains: how to release
woman as a genre from the grasp of custom and convention.
For every accomplishment in Stanton's life, there is a corresponding slap on the hands. What must it be for women
of a less assertive mold. [41] Stanton's experience at Troy
(New York) Female Seminary, opened by Emma Willard in
1821, appears to have been somewhat unhappy. She already
has mastered most of the curriculum in her earlier coeducational experience and is left to concentrate on French, music
and dancing. She notes her instructor has little appreciation
for the stress placed on children by "new and trying experiences." In addition, she leaves Troy convinced that a separate institution of learning for girls and boys is an error,
deleting as it does "a healthy condition of the intellectual and
moral faculties and ... a development they never can acquire
alone." [42]

Willard is remembered best as "the apostle of normal
schools"; her work on behalf of woman's education is tireless.
She asks that it be more systematized even though different
from the education of men. She makes it clear she does not
propose a masculine education for women. [43] As mothers,
women have the responsibility for their children's minds, and
they have to know something about these minds to fulfill their
responsibility. The material improvement of housewifery depends on implementing a uniform educational method. To this
end, Willard advocates that woman's education: cultivate understanding and develop and strengthen reasoning powers to
submit woman's activities to the dictates of reason; teach moral systems and religious sanctions and afford a broader view

of duty and more motivation to perform it; preserve young women from scorning useful labor; develop moral and intellectual taste with due regard for merit rather than "frivolities of dress, furniture, and equipage" and elaborate the nature, extent and obligation of woman's influence over children. [44] This method must have legislative assistance and endowment for the reformation to begin; individual exertion on its behalf is not enough. [45]

Alma Lutz, Willard's biographer and another Troy alumna, reports that the "apostle" supports neither the work of Susan B. Anthony nor Frances Wright.

> Yet she herself was continually stepping out of the
> so-called sphere of woman, and had struggled all
> her life to widen that sphere for other women.
> It is difficult to see where she drew the line, ex-
> cept that she felt that education rather than agita-
> tion would solve woman's problem.... The ballot
> seemed unimportant to her in comparison with the
> value of education to women. [46]

To help women get an education, she provides many who cannot afford one with fellowships. She trains teachers, beginning with her own, even on her vacation. The entrance of women into teaching begins 1835-1860, and Willard is one of those who makes it possible.

Elizabeth Margaret Chandler expresses the high hopes prefeminist thinkers have for women born "from the giddy world afar" to a more cultivated existence. "Such woman is--and shall proud man forbear, / The converse of the mind with her to share? / No! she with him shall knowledge pages scan, / And be the partner, not the toy, of man!"[47] It seems man's prerogatives are to be tampered with, after all. Chandler goes from hope to excitement about access to education and its promise. "It may be compared to lifting the veil of another fresh and beautiful world, or to standing in the midst of a new creation, to be permitted to gaze in among the hidden feelings, the fine and delicate perceptions, and the unveiled mysteries of the human mind."[48] Finally, she lauds Prudence Crandall, an educator who established a girls' school and enrolled first one black and then 17 more in the face of the grossest harassment. "Heaven bless thee, noble lady, in thy purpose good and high! / Give knowledge to the thirsting mind, light to asking eye; / Unseal the intellectual page, for those from whom dark pride, / With tyrant and

unholy hands, would fain its treasures hide. "[49] For Chandler, it is not just white women who must have access to an
education; whatever the cost, their black sisters are included
in the quest.

Frances Wright, an Englishwoman of Scottish descent,
conducts a speaking tour in the United States early in the
nineteenth century, discussing in part knowledge and the spirit of inquiry. [50] The human race can hasten progress with
a just educational system and a fearless spirit of inquiry.
Both attainments are calculated to improve woman's position,
one by entitling her to assume the position good sense and
feeling designate her and the other by enabling her to reason
with those skeptical of her reasoning power. Wright makes
short order of the "vulgar persuasion, that the ignorance of
women, by favoring their subordination, ensures their utility. "[51] More than that, she prophesies that when "women
drink the living waters of knowledge, " they will end the influence of error's mercenaries. [52] Her emphasis is not upon
teaching but upon learning. This change in emphasis has
rather important implications. Rather than being concerned
with the content of knowledge and its impact on the beholder,
she is concerned with its attainment and the method of inquiry. In effect, the power which goes with knowledge is
shifted from one who has it to share to one who would attain
it.

Wright says, "behold in me an inquirer, not a teacher, one who conceives of truth as a jewel to be found, not
to be coined; a treasure to be discovered by observation, and
accumulated by careful, persevering independence.... "[53]
These sentiments epitomize the difference between a Quaker
and a Puritan, between the striving of the human soul and the
authority of the Bible. [54] The independent observer proceeds
apart from common persuasions and error to find truth as it
is, "not invented and manufactured by learned art or aspiring
quackery. "[55] The tenor of Wright's thought is scientific;
reason is objectified and available to all. The education prescribed for woman, even by those who seek her advancement,
heretofore does not afford the means to advance her. With
Wright comes a new conceptualization of the meaning of education generally and for women. Education now is to enhance
woman's reasoning powers that she may seek truth for and
about herself as a thinking being. This is in many ways
Fuller's argument, but where she emphasizes woman's nature,
the standard within her, Wright does not. Wright leaves the
discovery of knowledge to use of objective reason and inquiry.

Harriet Martineau testifies that this method of inquiry could have considerable impact on woman's future intellectual activities. In the New World, she observes more power in this regard among women who have considerably less literary distinction than most American ladies. Generally, "readers are plentiful; thinkers are rare. Minds are of a very passive character...."[56] In short, woman is better educated by Providence than by the literary education man assigns her.[57] Man depends upon the absence of genius in woman to maintain his hold over her as property, but his comeuppance may be in progress. Angelina Grimke is an example of what may be in store when women begin to use their minds for themselves. At any rate, woman's power to act in her own interest cannot be denied until she attempts it.[58] Her success in this regard lies not with literary pursuits but with active use of her intellect. The exploratory and experimental intellectual state Angelina Grimke displays offers the means by which women may advance themselves.

Alexis de Tocqueville speaks of the strength of free determination and confidence in their own powers common both to American women as well as to women in most Protestant, but not Catholic, nations. Female behavioral control is encouraged and exerted to defend woman's chastity. American women, whose morals are notably pure, have minds that are not similarly chaste. Thus the keepers of American mores become judgmental rather than imaginative and stress their chastity to the exclusion of tender, loving companionship with men. The dangers inherent in democratic institutions and mores outweigh the dangers of woman's education in America and, in fact, necessitate it. Before the young American woman "has completely left childhood behind she already thinks for herself, speaks freely and acts on her own."[59] Once again Tocqueville and Martineau seem to be observing wholly different phenomena, worlds apart rather than on the same continent. The answer to the dilemma is forthcoming in Tocqueville. For the most part, he suggests, Americans depend on the individual's mental operations as a means to bypass "imposed systems, the yoke of habit, family maxims, class prejudices and to a certain extent national prejudices as well," seeking "by ... and in themselves for the only reason for things...."[60] It is this trait that Fuller bespeaks and Martineau observes in women of Angelina Grimke's ilk. On the other hand, the only intellectual authority to which Americans submit is that of public opinion. The mind of all pressures the intelligence of each.[61] Herein lies the female mental passivity of which Martineau speaks,

the flawed plan of female education designed to establish the
superiority of the male sex which Constantia confronts.

This tendency makes it possible for Americans to embrace on the one hand woman's statutory inferiority in man's
law and on the other her moral superiority in a law of her
own. The paradox of submission and dominance is encom-
passed in woman's education, tending as it does to confine
her to domestic and religious spheres. The path to a broader education for women generally is justified by her moral
dominance and her need to understand more fully its implications. The limits of her moral and intellectual abilities
are not known yet; they will become more evident as she develops her abilities. This wait-and-see attitude, common to
American philosophy and prefeminist thought both, is a practical adaptation of a scientific temper. As Tocqueville points
out, it does not trouble itself with abstract theory. [62] The
problem with this particular adaptation, noted by Branagan
as well as Tocqueville, is that excessive emphasis on means
may detract from the cultivation of reason. Advocates of
education for women already have encountered this problem.
The tension between "drinking the living waters of knowledge"
and existing "more like ghostly shadows than human flesh and
blood, " between drawing on one's own mental operations and
submitting to the pressure of the mind of all, is a continuing
one. Nowhere is the dualism accommodated in a comprehensive theory or ideology.

The quest after education for women and the intellectual tension following in its wake is evident in the life of
Mary Lyon. She is a doer, a woman committed to "building
her ideas into the tissues of society ... [speaking] most
clearly in her deeds. "[63] Her biographer, Beth Bradford
Gilchrist, sets the theme for a study of feminism and education out of the materials of Lyon's life. As a young woman,
her life ahead of her, Mary Lyon cries only for "living minds
to work upon, " not for "the brick and mortar" with which to
establish an educational institution. [64] Ultimately she founds
Mt. Holyoke, however, receiving its state charter in 1836
and tending its opening in 1837. Her ideas and principles
about woman's education are realized through her school
by means of her own endeavors. She herself does not question social institutions and their meaning for women's lives;
in fact she accepts them. Her quest is after a more republicanized education for women, one which serves "the common
uses of humanity. "[65] She evidences truth in the future, and
in this respect she is an adventurer. "We who live in a

generation widely experienced in the higher education of women have forgotten that it once served the purposes of the
Golden Fleece. "66

The Golden Fleece in Greek mythology is the sacrifi-
cial remains of a winged ram who carried Nephele's two
children, Castor and Pollux, from their stepmother. (Only
Pollux survives the flight.) Jason secures the Fleece, after
a quest for power ironically designed to distract him from
the throne, with the princess Medea's assistance. He later
leaves her to marry another princess, ostensibly to assure
security for Medea--whom he cannot marry legally--and their
children. Medea, symbol of power and knowledge, revenges
herself, killing the princess she once was and the bride she
never could become, killing the children* and escaping in the
winged chariot of her grandfather the sun god. It is a tragic
tale, wrought as a tautology; the winged ram is sent to rescue two children from their stepmother by their mother. In
the end two children die at their mother's hand with a stepmother and security imminent; the children, however, rise
in the firmament, as on the ram but as the perpetual Dioscu-
ri. Medea is a woman outside the law from the moment she
takes up the quest, and unnatural happenings follow her wake.
Education for women, in the eyes of its detractors, is just
as unnatural, in effect outside the law of nature, and sure to
distract women from their ordained duties. Thus the quest
for woman's education is a dangerous one. Should woman
immerse herself entirely in her own mental operations, she
will be distracted from the position which good sense and
feeling assign her; should she submit totally to the mind of
all, she will be removed from the law of nature and in the
end, her own law. The problem is profound and far-reaching.
Only those like Mary Lyon who find the middle way can expect to avoid the dangers which surround the quest for the
Golden Fleece.

The authors of the Declaration of Sentiments throw
caution to the wind when it comes to education: man has
denied woman the means for obtaining a thorough education.
They charge, mistaken in their zeal, that all colleges are
closed to women. 67 They note woman's limited occupational
opportunity, most particularly with regard to teaching theolo-

---

*Actually the children's deaths are imposed upon the tale
retrospectively by the Greek tragic poet Euripides. I am
grateful to Elaine Heffernan for calling this to my attention.

gy, medicine and law. Their charges do not elicit great
sympathy among prominent women educators of the day.
Willard's lack of support already has been mentioned. Catharine Beecher, who with Willard and Lyon "deserted the
fashionable sands to build on the rock of self-respect" in
founding the short-lived Hartford Female Seminary, [68] also is
unsympathetic with those "bewailing themselves over the fan-
cied wrongs and injuries of women."[69] Women are subordinate in position, according to Beecher, because their own
best interests are to promote those of men. If there is any
barbarity in this, it will be removed when woman learns of
it or lends her influence to set it right. [70] Woman's education will assure the interests of her family as well as her
own, where man's education determines only his welfare. [71]

For Beecher, the problem in the past has been that
women were not educated regarding the importance and difficulty of their duties. Questions about their intellectual abilities are beside the point, if not unanswerable. [72] What is
relevant is the lack of appreciation given woman's duties and
her poor performance of them. [73] Woman's education, for
Beecher, should be calculated to improve her performance of
duty and with it appreciation of those duties. To that end,
scientific habits of system and order in housekeeping need to
be developed. Among the principles Beecher advances are
the preference for social and intellectual interests over gratification of appetite, religion as more consequential than
worldly concern and the importance of woman's health. [74]
The first two are endemic to the literature of the time; the
last is something new and compelling. Now nothing that sacrifices health is to be allowed. Furthermore, women need
knowledge and experience to cope with their families' health
problems. [75] Woman's poor health, her nervous distress and
the ravages of her sometimes overwhelming responsibilities
during this stage of her history are well known. As often as
not, these afflictions are treated as the sacrifice she makes
in fulfilling her duties. To date, concern about her body
largely is voiced about her appearance and frivolous dress.
Now, however, the emphasis changes; woman still is to fulfill her duties, but she is not to sacrifice her bodily well-
being in doing so. This change, combined with concern for
her mental status and training, constitutes an important step
toward self respect for women.

Sarah Josepha Hale, a forthright supporter of woman's
education, sees it in its widest sense as "the full development
of all her personal, mental and moral qualities."[76] The

changes she foresees are not radical; they provide for increasing the power of existing good influences and banishing old ones. Women must be trained adequately to care for their children's minds. Medical science, too, is appropriate for woman, the preserver. [77] At this point, two thrusts to prefeminist thought about woman's education can be seen. The first has to do with the education itself, its institution and its curriculum. The second has to do with woman's capacity, her genius and intellect and ultimately her occupation with the domestic sphere, whether in the home or the world. The concern for establishing and endowing schools is reflected in the first thrust as is domestic and medical science. These concerns, however conservative they may be in form, constitute the groundwork for discussions about woman's capacity and occupation. Their realization offers the laboratory in which woman's capacity and occupational scope are tested.

Hale notes that only one endowed institution, Vassar College, provides for educating women in the widest sense. [78] The college was endowed by Matthew Vassar and opened in 1866 with a full curriculum and a preparatory program as well. In his will, Vassar states:

> It having pleased God that I should have no descendant to inherit my property, it has long been my desire ... to make such a disposition of my means as should best honor God and benefit my fellow-men. ... The more carefully I examined [the subject of erecting and endowing a college for the education of young women], the more strongly it commended itself to my judgment and interested my feelings. It seemed to me that woman, having received from her Creator the same intellectual constitution as man, had the same right to intellectual culture and development.... [79]

Vassar College also offered organized physical as well as intellectual training for women and had very extensive facilities for the time: 15 courts for lawn tennis, cycling, a lake for boating and skating, a skating rink, a gymnasium with a tennis court and theatre and a swimming tank. [80]

Physical training is only one manifestation of the concern for woman's bodily health. Harriot Hunt, a medical practitioner, writes in 1856 that it is only a short time until women and men will share the medical profession. She suggests the female physician is the physician for the female pa-

Vassar College: (top) Calisthenic Hall, 1865; (bottom) Field Day, 1913 (courtesy Vassar College Library).

tient. The attribution of a false position to woman is partially the result of her ill health. "As both sexes [are] suffering, both sexes must come to the rescue: masculine women and feminine men, if you like that order;--I do not; but
I like to see men and women helping men and women. "[81]
Elizabeth Blackwell, a medical doctor, writes along the same
lines about intelligent cooperation between sexes beginning
when women and men both study human nature. [82] Hunt also
refers to woman's underdeveloped, unappropriated and useless
intellectual power, and she asks rhetorically whether woman
is likely to use these means to any worse end than man has.
In her humaness, woman is entitled to an education just as
much as man is. Woman's ill health and false position seem
related as much to intellectual development as physical pa-
thology. Furthermore, men have a problem here as well.
It is as injurious to "allow a boy to exercise power over his
sister, to quote the perverted usages of society to justify his
selfishness, " as it is "to educate girls in dependence, timi-
dity, sentiment--with the feeling that strength of character is
inconsistent with feminine delicacy--the development of mental
power with refinement. "[83]

Mary Dodge suggests study can be healthful in doses
appropriate for the student. It contributes to both mental and
bodily peace. Just because women are classed with idiots
does not mean they are idiots. Those who so classify women
say more about themselves than about women. [84] A true education for girls, according to Dio Lewis, takes into consideration both mental and bodily needs. It praises nature through
the natural sciences, English training, composition, conversation and manners, but it also includes physical exercise such
as the New Gymnastics and amusement such as dancing and
games. Lewis' discussion of true education encompasses
girls' boots and shoes, the language of dress, outrages upon
the body (fashionable sufferings), woman's torture of her body, idleness among girls, false tests of gentility and the home
gymnasium. His is not a school for young ladies; it is for
girls and young women, most specifically those of the "Yankee" class. He believes the future rests with them and the
great woman revolution. To that end, the school conducting
this true education will provide for communication between its
resident teachers and students to enhance the development of
a vigilant, earnest public sentiment. [85] Furthermore, "my
dear girls, think for yourselves this time. Don't simper and
giggle when fools sneer at 'woman's rights. ' They don't know
what they are talking about. "[86] Better his girls should say
nothing than criticize or ridicule the means used by woman's

rights advocates. "I wish I dared tell you how we men almost despise you, sometimes, for this abandonment of each other. "[87]

The mental and bodily needs of girls and women definitely include dress reform. The dress reform movement is in full swing by now. It includes the introduction of what comes to be known as the "Bloomer" costume: long full Turkish trousers of broadcloth under a short skirt, with a Spanish cloak. The costume is introduced to Seneca Falls, New York, by Elizabeth Cady Stanton's cousin, Elizabeth Smith Miller. [88] In March 1851, it is adopted by Amelia Bloomer; who is enthusiastic about its merits. She publicizes it in The Lily, an early temperance journal which she publishes, and The Lily becomes the semi-official dress reform communication. [89] The costume proves adaptable enough for use by women gymnasts, skaters, farmers and feminists such as Lucy Stone; as Bloomer puts it, "there is nothing in the Bible to show Adam's fig leaf was bifurcated and Eve's was not. "[90] Yet it is adopted by only a handful of women in the end.

Abba Gold Woolson asserts that the bodily weakness woman exhibits is the result of her attire. Overcoming this weakness combats the main premise on which limitation of woman's intellectual development is based. [91] Women increasingly are going to ask the source of their disease, and women physicians are going to inform them about the problems which fashion engenders. This in combination with more liberal education for women in the future will lead to better understanding all around about nature's requirements for health. [92] These are not congruent with fashion. To understand this, women must be taught hygiene to become aware of the harm done them by stylish attire. [93] Women of the age are making new demands of their clothing, however. They must be able to work in it, look beautiful in it and be strong, comfortable and happy in it. Aesthetic qualities still are important, the fulfillment of woman's God instilled finer need. Thus woman will not adopt man's more utilitarian mode of dress, but she will expect her clothing to serve as "a valuable coadjutor" in her work. [94] No longer will women "consider it their first duty to mortify the flesh, and to render themselves and all humanity belonging to them as frail and uncomfortable as possible. "[95]

This self-help program confronts the patriarchal protective system which assumes woman's inability to take care

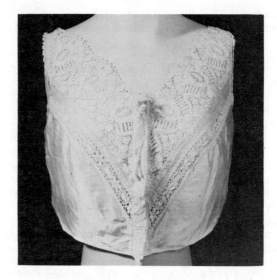

Woman's brassiere, ca. 1917, labeled "Nature's Rival.
Made in U.S.A. " (courtesy Smithsonian Institution).

---

of herself. Woman is learning "that not self sacrifice but
self development is her first duty in life that she may become fully herself. "[96] Rather than letting man think for her
as the church thinks for him, in the future woman has to be
her own judge. She is bringing her own practical reason to
bear on man's theoretical reason by questioning man's infal-
libility, his laws and his interpretation of her place in creation.[97] This involves an attack on religious teachings that
woman's condition is preordained as well as attack on custom and law. "As the most ignorant minds cling with the
greatest tenacity to the dogmas and traditions of their faith,
a reform that involves an attack on that stronghold can be
only carried by the education of another generation. "[98]
Those "whose blood has flowed to the higher arches of the
brain" are consecrated to a higher purpose, to "Pure children of the brain, " which admits "an ideal world of Beauty. "[99]
This is not wholly consistent with the idea that women are
characterized by practical reason and men by theoretical
reason; it does express simultaneous emphasis in feminist
thought on, first, woman's potential and, second, its realization by destruction of the barriers erected against it.

To that end, women and men must have the same education. M. Carey Thomas, a woman who is elected president of Bryn Mawr in 1894 by a majority of one, believes this is justified. There is only one best education; women and men live and work together, and their happiness and welfare generally will increase when they are educated similarly. [100] Sex really has no bearing on the question of professional and technical preparation. Thomas makes her case compelling:

> Given two bridge-builders, a man and a woman,
> given a certain bridge to be built, and given as
> always the unchangeable law of mechanics in ac-
> cordance with which this special bridge and all
> other bridges must be built, it is simply incon-
> ceivable that the preliminary instruction given to
> the two bridge-builders should differ in quantity,
> quality, or methods of presentation because while
> the bridge is building one will wear knickerbock-
> ers and the other a rainy day skirt. [101]

The burden of proof rests on those who argue otherwise. [102] The same case might be made for all women setting out after the Golden Fleece. They are bridge builders, every one, and knowledge of the dynamics of bridge building is essential to their quest.

For Charlotte Perkins Gilman, thinking with M. Carey Thomas in the context of Darwinian struggle, the question is not so much the burden of proof as it is one of mental reconstruction. Unquestioning assumptions must be examined carefully by the sociological observer. "Education is collective, human, a social function." [103] Education always has been part of maternity, but this function has been transferred first to widely experienced elders and then to systematic teaching of factual accumulations. Lost in the transfer is the power of analysis. As valuable as experience and facts are, the process of education is more valuable still. It is thinking about things which enables "self conscious creatures" to bypass sentiment and emotion. [104] To do this, they must be able to live life on a "plane of separate interest or industry," in "a personal home." For most people and especially women, this is not feasible. [105] Those who achieve such a state of personality development are marked by "loneliness and privation." Only bachelor men enjoy this temporary privilege. Woman's increasing individuation and her coming economic independence mark the beginnings of possibility for her personality as well. When this change is realized, the abnormal economic relations which stand in the way of humanity or being together will be overcome. "We shall need each other more, not less, and shall recognize that social need of one another is the highest faculty of this highest race on earth."[106]

Gilman suggests that social as opposed to physical evolution adds education and mutual help to heredity and natural selection; it transmits individual progress to collective action. Social intelligence is a "rational, efficiently acting, common consciousness."[107] By arresting the development of the brain as a "medium of social contact," the progress of the home and with it woman's position is discouraged, despite the state of civilization. Woman remains "a social idiot"; children receive a primitive education; man's social conscience is handicapped. Material gain in wealth, power, knowledge, production and distribution, as well as political, religious and educational superiority are not matched by progress in personal health and happiness. Social consciousness will be forthcoming only when "the habit of acting together necessarily develops in the brain the power and desire to act together."[108] Advance in private good will lead to developing common consciousness among members of society; civilized life and a vital nation depend upon it.[109]

The greatest step being taken by institutionalized education in America toward development of common consciousness is coeducation. Its first systemic manifestation is the opening of Oberlin in 1833. Oberlin educates women and men, although not along the same lines. Women and men also are educated in affiliated colleges such as Harvard and the "Harvard Annex" (1879). The final phase in the development of coeducation brings women and men together for the same education. The land grant colleges, for example the State University of Iowa in 1858, are among the first to admit women to this end.[110] A U.S. Bureau of Education brochure of the time suggests that:

> coeducation of the sexes is preferred because it is Natural, following the ordinary structure of family and of Society; Customary, being in harmony with the habits and sentiments of everyday life, and of the laws of the State; Impartial, affording one sex the same opportunity for culture that the other enjoys; Economical, using the school funds to the best advantage; Convenient, both for superintendents

Suffrage cartoon, Blanche Ames Ames 1878-1969 (courtesy Sophia Smith Collection, Smith College).

and teachers, in assigning grading, teaching, and
discussion; Beneficial, to the minds, morals, habits and development of the pupils. [111]

Sarah Burstall, a British educator reporting on women's education in the United States, finds the New Education characterized by development of a child's power of concentration.
(Burstall also finds women's colleges offering the opportunity
for thought and individual development.) She thinks existing
disputes about coeducation in higher institutions of learning
peculiar in the face of its acceptance for public primary and
secondary schools after 1870. [112]

G. Stanley Hall writes in 1907 that ideal schools always
will be radically different for girls and boys, however, and
perhaps increasingly so with the sex specialization that advancing civilization brings. Hall pleads that he joins feminists in their belief in and desire for women's higher education. No one can claim any longer that women are intellectually inferior to men; women's education nevertheless must
become more liberal and humanistic, more favorable to motherhood. Women are losing their womanly ideas in the
public schools and adopting those of men. This is not in the
best interests of the race. For women to leave their perpetual adolescence to become completely developed individuals
would be, in effect, to overdraw their account with heredity. [113] Women must be true to their generic nature and avoid
premature specialization in order to maintain their freshness,
charm and humanism. They pluck the "apple of intelligence"
only at the cost of their health or of a life adjusted to independence and self support. [114] In the latter case, the result
is a bachelor woman, who, despite her magnificent mind, il-
lustrates Spencer's law of the inverse relationship between
individuation and genesis. She foregoes wifehood and motherhood, the greater of these being motherhood, and thereby becomes the last representative in her line of descent. This
woman passionately desires happiness. She alternates between
excessive respect and distrust for men and turns to other
women, entering into "innocent Platonic pairing-off relations"
with one of them. She dreams of forbidden subjects and the
relations of the sexes generally. [115]

For Hall, the fact is that womanhood is incomplete until "the gradual blossoming of wifely into motherly love."
The "college of life" accepts wives but graduates only mothers. [116] The world's greatest work is done by "strongly
sexed men and women in the period of their maturity and

vigor. " Women and men need to be educated to this propensity; there must be a "pedagogy of sex. "[117] This argument is diametrically opposed to Gilman's. Where she is encouraged by woman's increasing individuation and specialization, Hall is alarmed by it. For him, it is man who is the "agent of variation" naturally tending to expertness and specialization, not woman. [118] Hall agrees with Gilman that women who individuate are lonely and deprived. This does not stem from an abnormal sex relation between women and men overall; it is because such a woman is abnormal; this is what attaining independence and self-sufficiency leaves her. Where Gilman argues that the sexuo-economic relationship of women and men keeps them apart, Hall argues that eliminating it will keep them apart. Rather than woman's independence marking progress and advance as Gilman suggests, it means the end of human descent for Hall.

Preoccupation with human descent and fragmentation also is notably present in The Education of Henry Adams. Adams is the great-grandson of Abigail and John Adams. His wife kills herself in 1885. By 1907 his class and heritage are displaced in mass society, centralized economics, mechanistic science and emerging skepticism; Adams is in effect at the end of his line of descent. He "was a Darwinist because it was easier than not"; what difference could it make "to an American in search of a father. "[119] He begins his quest by quoting Rousseau who, in offering his confessions, proclaims himself a better man for it. Adams' grandfather, John Quincy Adams, acquired an education through his eighteenth-century heritage, an education affected by the seasons. Summer is "tropical license" and "sexual living"; winter is "the effort to live" and "school. "[120] Henry Adams aches to absorb knowledge but is helpless to find it. Meditating chaos and finding force instead of will behind it, he adopts the dynamo and its valuable "occult mechanism" as a symbol for infinity. The new universe, "a supersensual world" of force, affords no comparable scale of measurement to that of the once New World. Men, society, time and thought yielding nothing of sequence for him, he must take causal relations on faith, in the attraction they have for him. [121] What is the force opposite the dynamo? Here a new but hazardous education opens up for Adams.

Adams recalls that woman once constituted a potent force, a goddess worshipped for the energy inherent in her reproductive powers. Woman in America, however, is confined to the magazine; she is a source of shame rather than

superiority, lost in an accumulation of inert facts. America's
puritanic tradition teaches sex is sin. American society is
sexless and sentimental. "An American Virgin would never
dare command; an American Venus would not dare exist."[122]
Yet it is woman's genius and force which constructed the art
of the cathedral, the Virgin at Chartres. "Symbol or energy,
the Virgin has acted as the greatest force the Western world
has ever felt...."[123] Unity, the synthesis of "love of God
and lust for power," is multiplicity. The new education is
the result of the dynamo and the Virgin, science and love,
accounting for direction of change where natural selection does
not, insisting that the unknowable remain unknown.[124] There
is at least some certainty in the honesty of the Virgin, more
interested in her own perfection than any other, a wholly
feminine trait.

A comparison of Gilman and Adams' thought makes
vivid Stow Persons' assertion that the gentry tradition ultimately is represented best by its women. One senses in
Adams quiet resignation at his displacement, "assent to dis-
missal. It was time to go."[125] In Gilman there is great
hope, even excitement for things yet to come. She finds in
woman's individuation the key to specialization and multiplicity; therein lies ultimate social unity. The fears Hall expresses, that the end to human descent could come in woman's independence, do not exist for Gilman. She finds in
woman's economic independence the path to a regenerated
world. The twentieth century will be the century of women.
This faith is expressed again and again in feminist literature
of the period. Looking back on the time, Sophonisba P.
Breckinridge documents the intensification in woman's organizational, occupational and political relationships and activities
which occur in the move toward emancipation.[126] Even with
a limited range of employment opportunities and the disappointing and disillusioning aftermath of suffrage, the home increasingly offers less opportunity for women. J. Stanley
Lemons points out that the involvement of women and their
organizations in a broad civilizing, democratizing and humanizing reform movement advances woman's own cause and links
the Progressive era with the New Deal period.[127] Gilman
suggests that "the woman's club movement is one of the most
important sociological phenomena of the century--indeed, of
all centuries,--marking as it does the first timed steps
toward social organization of these so long unsocialized members of our own race."[128] She and other feminist thinkers
have good empirical reason for their anticipation and high
hopes for womanhood.

This is more reason for feminist thinkers to concern themselves with the needs of girls and women when it comes to discussion of educational aims and methods. Marion Talbot writes that there is democratic and social power forthcoming for educated women from their natural relationships and the problems of everyday life. The home now is a permanent human institution, and woman's education must take this into account. Women must receive a hygienic education, over and beyond physical training, in keeping with the broader health and vigor which human welfare demands. The body thus can become an efficient agent of the mind in larger social service. [129] Woman's hygienic education should include: free and full development of her body through physical exercise and for the sake of physical liberation, courage and self-reliance; information about nutrition, the function of food and principles of dietetics; instruction in the laws of health and sanitary practice for individual protection, community health and promotion of a private and public moral sense; personal hygiene; and social hygiene and eugenics in order to train girls as wives and mothers and boys as husbands and fathers. [130] Through the college's corporate life, women can make "principles of right and righteous living" habitual. As a substitute home, college must facilitate both the efficiency of the larger group and the development of the individual. [131]

Anna Garlin Spencer introduces a cautionary note; the most important education comes through work rather than books. The currently existing pathological industrial conditions which surround woman's work injure her "work sense" and demoralize her "faculty of true service." The new feminine ideal demands that women not only develop as persons but also as serviceable functionaries in family life. This stands in marked contrast to the burden woman has borne through time, sustaining her own life to be of use to others and her offspring to continue the structure of society. The new ideal raises certain problems for woman's education. Education must begin to prepare women to provide their own personal needs and their special social function efficiently; it also must prepare them more specifically for work or a trade by which to support themselves suitably and safely. Finally, education has to prepare women for social leadership through home and profession. [132]

Ida M. Tarbell issues another cautionary note. American women are concerning themselves conspicuously with self-discussion (not to mention with wearing apparel). This suggests a state of "chronic mental ferment" which limits their capacity for happiness and efficiency. In breaking with the old order to rebel deliberately against "man and his pretensions," women express their dissatisfaction with the manner in which their brains are trained, time employed and influence directed. The problem is that some women now are taking to man's path. Yet women's mind still is uniquely her own. As a result of her experience with coeducation, woman is taking her own work more seriously than her masculine competition. Woman's greatest work is training citizens, her children; education along with freedom, organization, agitation and suffrage are means to this end. Woman's work is realized in a socialist home, one which facilitates free speech, neighborhood ties and a democratic spirit. Woman's domestic service, performed in accordance with democracy, is respectable, dignified employment.[133]

All of these thinkers are working toward resolution of the tension noted earlier. Tarbell is concerned that excessive mental ferment may deter women from the ostensible goal of their education: training to fit themselves better for rearing offspring in a democratic spirit. Talbot delves deeply into the curriculum which will enhance women's democratic and social powers through their natural relationships and everyday lives. The other aspect of the tension is represented by women who submit to a perceived communal mentality. Here Tarbell expresses an anxiety that women may take on man's more competitive attributes and slight their own qualities of perception. Talbot stresses the means by which colleges may facilitate woman's adaptation of principles of right and righteous living. Spencer encompasses the tension by contrasting the new feminine ideal with woman's older stipulated burden. Both ideal and burden stress the individual and the larger social unit, woman's social position and natural law. They do so from quite different perspectives, however. The task feminist thinkers face is not so much a transition from the old to the new order in their ideas and ideals as it is a transition in the new ideal from women as serviceable functionaries to women as developed persons. If feminist thinkers are to synthesize the dualism, they must resolve the tension or face, with Henry Adams, chaos and multiplicity. The unity Adams postulates in the attraction of science and love does not hold the kind of promise for him and his line that it does for Charlotte Perkins Gilman and hers. Gilman is systematizing individuation and specialization to a social end. Talbot, Spencer and Tarbell indicate that problems of method and application still remain for feminist thinkers concerned with women's education. Anne C. Brackett writes in 1877 that the

majority of young women, along with young men, will use the
opportunities of coeducation rightly, controlling their lives
rather than yielding to undisciplined impulses.[134] Feminist
thinkers in the second decade of the century of women want
to be sure this is the case.

As Ellen Key puts it, "we face the results of the fact
that women neither have been, nor are yet, fully liberated."[135]
Woman's real renaissance must come through education of her
feelings. Woman's intuition must be respected and active
again, if humanity is to advance ethically and aesthetically as
well as materially, intellectually and technically. Women are
adopting the value men assign utility when they yield the education of their children to "born educators." As man's external sphere of power widens through science and desire for
gain, "gain has been God, and man this God's prophet."[136]
Women have a choice between gain and intuition; they can
either accept institutionalized child-rearing or regard motherhood as social work. This is not to say that some fathers
do not have a capacity as educators. The point is that there
must be some division of labor, and men simply cannot replace women in the home. "Can the heart in an organism be
replaced by a pumping engine, however ingenious?"[137] The
answer for Key is no, it cannot be; woman constitutes society's heart. Each child, a growing soul, needs its own mother's direction.

For Key the question has to do with occupational
choice. Is woman to support herself in man's external world
or in her own home? Were woman to educate her feelings,
in effect be in touch with her instinct, she would prefer
meaningful work in her home over lust for power in the external world. Olive Schreiner's discussion of woman's "labor
in the new world of social conditions" has some bearing here.
Schreiner is referring to critical attempts to define woman's
work solely by the child-bearing function. At the core of this
effort is the reward which attaches to woman's work as, for
example, a doctor, legislator or professor of Greek. Man
"is as a rule contented that the women of the race should
labor for him ... provided the reward they receive is neither
large nor in such fields as he might himself desire to enter."[138] In many ways, Key makes the same argument that
Schreiner criticizes. In Key's case, however, she believes
a reward should attach to woman's work as mother and educator of children and further that woman will choose that work
instinctively once she is educated to it.

The fact is that education in the United States is more or less permanently institutionalized by the first quarter of the twentieth century. Parents, and of these perhaps mothers, will continue to have the greatest impact on their children's socialization, but schools are here to stay. John Dewey, America's philosopher of education (more properly, of schooling), has a great deal to say about education which reflects the concerns of feminist thinkers and of the time. For Dewey, civilization begins with vast innate wisdom which now has descended to the level of practice. (This corresponds to Tocqueville's early warning). The educational process is the most effective means by which to promote social progress and change in the face of maintenance of current practices. Through this process, individuals delve into their own needs and conflicts in a context of social responsibility, emerging to formulate individual ends-in-view. Ends-in-view are intellectual in terms of experience and valuation and existential in terms of either reinstating satisfactory ongoing activity or forming new ends-in-view. Value is the adoption or not of the end-in-view. Ends become means to further aims. Means must be criticized in relation to the results they achieve. There can be no means distinct from ends, because otherwise they would be without meaning to the individual. It would be empirically harmful to society for ends to justify means. Means and ends necessarily interpenetrate.[139]

In this context, it seems reasonable to suggest that there is some divergence among feminist thinkers' ends-in-view. Granted, there is a conscious effort to bring science and love together through mental reconstruction. Charlotte Perkins Gilman takes immense strides along this path. For her as for Dewey, education as a social function contributes the analytic power to advance beyond sentiment and emotion, in short, to change existing practices. Most feminist thinkers can tolerate a certain amount of diversity in this regard. None of them denigrate motherhood; they object to woman's potential being defined solely in terms of her biological function. They also want woman to have more control over that function, for example through sex education and access to means of birth control. All these are intellectual value judgments that they make: defining woman biologically is bad; motherhood, sex education and birth control measures are good. Existentially, feminists see woman continuing to have babies, instituting a new element of choice as to when and how many into motherhood. They diverge, however, when it comes to the occupational end-in-view. Motherhood has social connotations, they agree, but will woman do her social work in the home, or, by institutionalizing the home, do her social work in the world? For women already in the gainfully employed work force, the problem is to be able to institutionalize the home more than technology already has. Most women still are not employed gainfully, however. Feminist thinkers are anxious that women fulfill their individual potential in a social context. The question is, how are they to do this best? Here there is considerable divergence among ends-in-view.

There also is the old problem of what ought to be for women and what really is. There is much to excite the feminist observer in the century of women. The new ideal is being implemented in some respects, enough so that feminist thinkers can concern themselves with attendant educational problems. Nevertheless, there still is enough of the old order in existence to distract feminist attention from adopting new ends-in-view. As Alice Ames Winter puts it,

> nothing is finished. The most ancient of processes seem to be just at their beginning. ... That old, old lesson of self-immolation is by no means mastered. If one is sentimentally inclined, one might call it the mother-lesson, the willing acceptance of anguish for the sake of someone else, or some ideal. ... The great difference is that now ... [o]ur hearts and our stomachs are approximately where they ought to be, instead of pushed about by tight clothes. [140]

Of what use are new ends-in-view to these women? Dress reform is a cogent result, but the aim was ever so much wider.

Virginia Woolf hits upon the problem when Mary Beton-Seton-Carmichael (whatever name she is given is not important) is asked to speak about women and fiction. "All I could do was to offer you an opinion upon one minor point-- a woman must have money and a room of her own if she is to write fiction; and that, as you will see, leaves the great problem of the true nature of woman and the true nature of fiction unsolved."[141] She only can offer her opinion and explain why she has it; her readers must draw their own conclusions. Thus it is for all feminist thinkers. They are not the sole determinants of society's aims and needs. Feminist discretionary powers are not the only powers with which feminist thinkers have to contend. Furthermore, if they project their norms as the one and only true end, they obliterate the educational process and its promise by promoting their norms to the place of innate wisdom. They lose their ability to analyze the past and, therein, to plan for the future as well. All feminist thinkers can do is offer their opinions and explain them; they must let women draw their own conclusions. Women do have illusions about education, Mary Beton-Seton-Carmichael muses as she asks herself what is truth and what is illusion.[142]

Mary ponders with a friend funding women's educational institutions and the small endowments forthcoming from women (with none from men). If only women's mothers and grandmothers had accumulated great sums of money to endow women's education, Mary and her friend might be enjoying any number of worthy and exciting intellectual adventures--but then they never would have been born at all. One cannot bear and rear a family and make money as well; the question of their forebears' making money is useless anyway because there were no means for them to do it and, had they done it, they legally would not have possessed the money they earned. "To raise bare walls out of the bare earth was the utmost they could do."[143] Yet the ages of faith and reason yielded great sums of money for the universities to preserve "rare types" who seem obsolete in the face of the current struggle for existence. Even if the cathedral at "Oxbridge" was inspired by the Virgin, by woman's instinct, as Henry Adams would have it, precious little was expended for reflection on that instinct by women.

Truth about questions arising from the difference in endowments for women's and men's education and their impact surely will be encountered at the British Museum. "If truth is not to be found on the shelves of the British Museum, where, I asked myself, picking up a notebook and a pencil, is truth?"[144] In fact, truth but for one drop runs between Mary's fingers like so much water. In discovering that many men write about women, and no women about men, and upon reading through certain examples of her discovery (for want of a more rigorous Oxbridgean method), Mary learns that the professors are angry with women. The anger is disguised and complex, but it is there. Mary in turn is angry with reading that she is considered mentally, morally and physically inferior. Upon reflection, she wonders if perhaps the patriarchal professor is not anxious about his own superiority; after all, "his was the power and the money and the influence."[145] Women reflect as looking glasses, even magnifying glasses, man's violent and heroic action. "Without that power probably the earth would still be swamp and jungle. "[146] Telling the truth would reduce the vision, and that would explain why men are uncomfortable with criticism by women. (One deludes oneself to imagine men would wither and die without it, however.)

Mary recalls how her entire disposition toward the other sex, even toward the patriarchal professors, changes remarkably in the glow of the security of a fixed income. Of the vote and money, money seems the greater. The question of value is a relative one, however, and in a century women no longer will be the protected sex. "Anything may happen when motherhood has ceased to be a protected occupation"; women will act and exert themselves as they never could before, just as men do now. (Then to say that one saw a woman may become as unusual as it once was to say one saw an airplane.) "... what happens when ... this organism that has been under the shadow of the rock these million years--feels the light fall on it, and sees coming her way a piece of the strange food--knowledge, adventure, art. "[147] Having been confined for so long, women must have "overcharged the capacity of bricks and mortar" by their creative force. In perhaps 100 years, woman will speak her mind and be a poet. She will write artistically and with integrity and genius, rather than as a method of self-expression alone, holding her looking glass to life. [148] She will not think of her sex, though; "some marriage of opposites has to be consummated. "[149]

Woolf concludes, speaking for herself,

For my belief is that if we live another century
or so--I am talking of the common life which is
the real life and not of the little separate lives
which we live as individuals--and have 500 a year
each of us and rooms of our own; ... if we face
the fact ... that we go alone and that our relation
is to the world of reality and not only to the
world of men and women, then the opportunity
will come and the dead poet who was Shakespeare's
sister will put on the body which she has so often
laid down. Drawing her life from the lives of the
unknown who were her forerunners, as her brothers did before her, she will be born. [150]

With Shakespeare and Jane Austen, woman's mind will over-

come its impediments. Her chastity, so often related to her
education and her past achievement, and her anonymity will
give themselves to creation. She will, at last, be able to
"think of things in themselves. "[151]

Virginia Woolf, in one short book, says perhaps all
there is to say about feminism and education. She is retro-
spective and futuristic; she is full of hope and sorrow. She
meets the great questions--how? why? when?--and leaves
them both answered and open. She reaches back to Tocqueville's perception of the association between woman's chastity
and education and to Henry Adams' Virginal force at Chartres.
She understands Abigail Adams' fancy "for a closet with a
window, which I could more particularly call my own, " and
Charlotte Perkins Gilman's call for a "personal home. " The
question of sexuo-economic dependence is broached by its
conclusion, a fixed income. Self-support and a room of one's
own constitute living in the presence of reality. With these,
woman may be less self-conscious and thus capable of the
act of creation. There is an implicit suggestion that in woman's anonymity and lack of learned method lies genuine promise, a promise little fulfilled by men since Shakespeare.
Men somehow have lost their literary powers, their ability
to perceive reality; their confessions and autobiographies
make this all too clear. Woman, however, is characterized
by a freshness which lends itself to creativity, given the
proper opportunity for realization.

Mary Beard introduces America Through Women's
Eyes, a collection of writings by American women and a
sort of intellectual history in itself, with the statement that
an intellectual revolution is in progress. In this revolution,
separate categories of thought, "such as economics, politics,
war, art, literature, education and feminism, are being dis-
solved as separate entities" to incorporate woman and her
contributions to life. [152] If the chaotic economy has had any
impact at all, it is in the awareness that man alone cannot
make a better world. Cultural resources and powers must
supplement political and economic structures. Here woman
always has been at life's center, in "its continuance, care,
and protection. " Economics and politics must be adapted to
life, and woman's primordial force, her image of herself and
her role in cultural and civilized processes hold the key to
this effort. [153] While the "Decline of the West' ... marks
the twilight of the era of mother goddesses, god-kings, ora-
cular wisdom, castes, and reliance on force as the prime
mode of acquisition, " the "Rise of the West" may mean a

return to woman's primitive concerns with life. This quest may be carried "to romantic lengths and altitudes. "[154] Wherever one looks, woman may be found fulfilling her responsibility to life. Sex is only one aspect of her responsibility, and even as the education and nurture of children is institutionalized, woman will continue as before to be alive to the world and its activities. "Feminism as sex antagonism" and "masculinism as sex monopoly" will yield to merit as a standard. At the center of that standard will be "the eternal feminine ... the care of life. "[155]

Beard suggests a new conceptual mode which effectually transcends feminist or masculinist self-consciousness. At its center she sees the eternal feminine, as do many feminist thinkers. There are others, however, such as Woolf, who see in it androgyny, clusters of blossoms which are female and male both. Woolf introduces a sense of equilibrium which Beard really does not deny when discussing cultural resources and power supplementing political and economic structures. Beard is not so explicit, but the sense of her words is very similar to Woolf's. She is kinder to men than perhaps Woolf is, but neither thinker rejects them. With Gilman, they both aim for mental reconstruction on this point. With all feminist thinkers, they realize that man has not used the benefits of science and technology to their fullest, and they believe women have something to contribute here. Woman's education, the development of her thought processes, will make this possible. In this development, woman will find and lose herself, gain a personal identity and yield it for a more collective or social one. Women will be individuals, but they will not behave as individuals ultimately. In coming in touch with their ancient, creative force, they will use it to its fullest for the benefit of all.

The question of identity is a most important one. Feminist thinkers are well aware that woman's identity has been stifled. They seek to enhance it but not at the expense of woman's own law. Thus, in enhancing it, they seek to overcome it as well. Man's experience with his identity provides a serious lesson not to be repeated by woman. Gertrude Stein makes the lesson graphic in "Identity--A Tale" (1935).

> Since there are no men in existence anywhere
> except here on this earth being men is not an easy
> thing to happen.
> Sweet William had his genius and so he did

not look for it.   He did look for Lilian and then
he had Lilian.
    There is any day in what they say there is
a man there and it is well done.   If he likes it
or not it is well done.   They like to know it is
well done.   That is what a man is they like to
know it is well done.   What is it that a man is
a man is that they like to know that it is well
done.   If it is not well done he is dead and they
like to know that he is dead if it is well done.
That is the one thing that there is that there is
now that he is dead and that it is well done. [156]

Being men naturally is made all the harder, all the
lonelier, by putting humans into the context of a vast universe.
Yet the male, Sweet William, has inborn genius, the power of
origination, to guide his destiny.   Through foppish bonding,
he lets it descend to the level of practice rather than spontaneously combining ideas with it.   He looks to woman--ir-
regular ridge on the surface of man's brain, ornamental
fleur-de-lis that she is--as to a looking glass for compensa-
tion.   In easily capturing Lilian, Sweet William's conventional
definition of her dominates her.   Man too is dominated by
his own standard of superiority.   It is expected of him,
whether he likes it or not; it is comforting to know man has
everything under control.   One might wonder what it is about
man that he likes to know "it is done well."   That is what
there is about man. Without it, he no longer exists; with it,
he no longer exists either.   He permanently is configured by
his superiority.   If anything can be known with certainty, it
is this: "that he is dead and that it is well done."

Compare Stein writing on human identity through the
male with Helene Deutsch writing on female intellectuals or
sportswomen nine years later.   Here the "intelligent, brilliant and promising" girl lets personality values which spring
from masculine elements expand about her essential center,
the "eternal feminine."[157]   The imagery in Deutsch having
to do with personality components stemming from overlays to
an essential core is reminiscent of what Stein uses for man,
Sweet William.   Sweet William the flower is made up of um-
bel-like clusters in which the pedicels spring from a common

---

*Dulcinea is Don Quixote's sweetheart but Dulcinea means
sweetmeat.   Compare Sweet William; William means helmet
of resolution.   Sweet William thus is Lilian's sweet Helmet.
This seems to suggest woman is man's source of compassion.
Man in turn is stifling that compassion.

center. Women of the Dulcinea type* have a feminine center, but their personality is dominated by masculine rays stemming from wrappings about the center. These women sacrifice their subjective experience to develop their intellect or strength exclusively. Their affective life is seriously injured. "Modern education unfortunately neglects this truth, and girls are very often intellectually overburdened."[158] Feminist thinkers would not be likely to suggest that modern education excessively weighs down woman's intellect; however, they would express concern that her intellect not overshadow her instinct, the care of life--which Beard and Deutsch both label the eternal feminine. One does not reach equilibrium by ignoring an essential component to it; rather one brings opposing force into balance. Henry Adams labels those forces the Dynamo and the Virgin, science and love. He looks for unity in multiplicity. Deutsch with Woolf sees the forces as male and female. Deutsch would stress one or the other force consistently. Virginia Woolf, however, says "it is fatal for anyone who writes to think of their sex. It is fatal to be a man or woman pure and simple."[159] Stein makes the same assertion. For Woolf, "one must be woman-manly or man-womanly."[160] For feminist thinkers generally, the active or masculine "layers and wrappings" of the female personality with which Deutsch concerns herself now are as essential to wholeness as is the essential feminine core.

There is a tendency among American thinkers of the period to seek synthesis, to combine the dualisms which so distressed Henry Adams into complex wholes. Woolf discusses such formulation in terms of the novel, a perception of reality, as "a structure leaving a shape on the mind's eye, built now in squares, now pagoda shaped, now throwing out wings and arcades now solidly compact and domed like the Cathedral of Saint Sofia at Constantinople." It begins in an appropriate shape and mixes with others, not "stone to stone" but human relation to human relation.[161] It is not so much the question of sequence (as in Henry Adams) as it is the question of construction (as in arcades and domes).[162] Charles A. and Mary R. Beard exhibit the tendency to synthesis in their quest for the American interpretation of life in its essence and scope. The Beards find this world view for America, the American spirit, in the idea of civilization. The idea of civilization forms a common foundation for self-possession in America's future and has behind it the power of acquirement. In this American synthesis, an irreversible but dynamic historical heritage contributes to a practical and activistic/idealistic new American philosophy. This ethic seeks to advance the good life for individuals in a social context.[163]

The Beards' delineation of an uniquely American philosophy or ethic is interesting in relation to feminism. Several years before publication of The American Spirit, Mary Beard suggests feminism as a separate body of thought is ceasing to exist as it becomes apparent woman's culture is needed to supplement man's politics and economics. All bodies of thought feed into this new American philosophy, just as streams of prefeminist thought feed into feminism as an identifiable body of thought in the 1870s. American philosophy accepts progress in human affairs, and it accepts the perpetuation of custom and habit. It stresses human intelligence as creative as well as routine in nature. It posits that the study of creative intelligence at work yields truths as valid as those derived from the study of habitual experience.[164] The difference or similarity between feminist thought and the new American philosophy is not unlike that between Virginia Woolf and Mary Beard. Virginia Woolf and Mary Beard are both feminist thinkers. Each maintains her own identity as she nonetheless contributes to a single body of thought. So it is with feminist thought and the new American philosophy. Feminist thought aims to synthesize certain opposing elements, just as American philosophy does. It is part of American philosophy in this sense, but it retains its own identity and integrity as a separate body of thought. Logically, feminist thought must aim one day to yield its identity for the sake of a more collective one. By 1942, it has not done so, however.

Dualisms such as those in feminism and the new American philosophy are not brought into balance easily. Ellen Glasgow, writing autobiographically illuminates the dilemma.

> Science has failed me. One could not build one's home in a skeleton. Religion has failed me. One could not build one's home in a phantom. From the beginning, I had harbored a dual nature, for my reason and my emotion were perpetually in conflict. Emotionally, I was a believer; intellectually, I was a skeptic.[165]

Early in the twentieth century, science offers great promise for women. Robert Lowi and Leta Hollingsworth discuss feminism and science in 1916. They assert that it is not natural to restrict woman's sphere and that there are no scientific grounds on which to base any artificial limitations of woman's activities.[166] J. Piaget is demonstrating that boys and girls begin life with the same variable intellectual capacities.[167] Yet in <u>Virginia</u>, written in 1913, the first book of Glasgow's maturity, knowledge shatters the little and large beliefs in Virginia's life. The triumph of actuality looms over her last stand for idealism. Law is on Virginia's side, but life is not.[168]

The fact is, actuality does not triumph for feminist thinkers at all. The century of women is almost half completed, but woman's liberation is not. It is ironic that Glasgow can believe emotionally but not intellectually; it was the development of intellect which offered so much hope from the beginning, even with regard to woman's emotion. The scale is not in equilibrium. It is tipping back and forth precipitously for women, for feminist thought and--one hazards to suggest--for the new American philosophy as well. Margaret Mead attests to this in her observation that few cultures have devised the means to encourage women to quest as well as to bear children. On the other hand, most cultures have devised ways to satisfy men in their constructive activities without distorting their sense of masculinity. Mead believes the only way to encourage such "divine discontent" in women is to educate them.[169]

One wonders how successful education will be, reading through Mead's <u>Male and Female</u>. Institutionalized education is widely and fairly uniformly available to girls and boys and young women and men in the United States by now. The crucial factor in their socialization seems to be their parents; it is the primary experiences in childhood which provide the systematic transition to adulthood on which civilization depends. This important and seemingly kind function yields "culturally approved elaborations." Culture is a predetermined phenomenon for children. They have no part in its creation. Culture is transmitted to them through a process they cannot comprehend. This is true for girl and boy children. Children encounter their own feelings about themselves and significant others, and they encounter their parents' feelings about them.[170] In one way or another, they must accommodate both sets of feelings. Human beings have the capacity to adjust as part of their evolutionary heritage. "But we have yet to prove that we can develop an insight that ... can economize on the wastefulness of the ages of innocence and still build ... a new innocence that will never have foundations in human sacrifice."[171]

David Riesman's <u>The Lonely Crowd</u> is published in 1950. Riesman suggests education and enculturation have un-

dergone a profound historical change in emphasis from morality to morale. Children are perceived not as Lockeian
blank slates but as "partially plastic receivers" of the social
character of the future. This conceptual shift is apparent in
Mead and stems from the progressive education movement.
Its most fluent spokesperson is John Dewey. Teachers and
other factors outside the home have taken on more responsibility for character formation. According to Riesman, where
Puritan or inner-directed parents looked for indications of
predestined grace in their children, modern or outer-directed
parents look for indications predicting upward mobility in a
status hierarchy. Where once a person's ability to cope with
and get on in the world was of prime importance, now a
person's image in the eyes of the world is preeminent. A
person must be able to manipulate others and in turn be
manipulated. Rather than being taught to internalize the discipline necessary to pursue and compete for clearly defined
goals, children are involved in personality production and
veiled competition. Children must define what is good; they
are judged by the effect of their definition on others. Children and their parents are increasingly self-conscious. They
manipulate each other now; no longer, are children fighting or
succumbing to parents.[172]

Schools originally were sex segregated; now they are
sex integrated. Early schools focused on an impersonal intellectual curriculum; now they focus more on children and
developing their individuality. Sex no longer is inhibited or
taken for granted within certain limits. "It is viewed as a
consumption good not only by the old leisure classes but by
the modern leisure masses."[173] Women are not objects for
consumption any more; they are knowing consumers.
"... [T]hey must foster aggressiveness and simulate modes-
ty."[174] Direction in either an inner- or other-directed context is external and not a matter of informed choice at all.
Furthermore, the other-directed person is troubled deeply by
the difficulty which proper group adjustment poses. She or
he is confronted with "barriers of false personalization and
enforced privatization."[175] Here more than anywhere else
it is apparent how far astray woman's (and man's) liberation
has gone. Intellectual development and the hopes feminist
thinkers have for it have not yielded the expected results at
all. The transition from an inner-directed society which
stifles woman's potential is not to one in which sexuo-economic independence for women can contribute to humanity or
being together. The transition is from a society in which
nature as prescribed by the book of Genesis directs human

activities to a society in which the normal as prescribed by one's peers directs human activities. Women still are stifled and men with them.

Riesman sees the answer in consciousness of a more utopian environment which stresses autonomy as a human goal. Of this much he is sure: "the enormous potentialities for diversity in nature's bounty and men's capacity to differentiate their experience can become valued by the individual," enough so that she/he will be able to overcome the need to adjust.[176] Riesman gives up the attempt to balance dualisms by seeking an alternative, autonomy. He does not escape the problem, however, any more than John Stuart Mill did. What the state or society must do and what the individual may do is still going to be a dilemma in the years to come. Questions about woman's status are embroiled deeply in the dilemma. That human beings, women included, should have some say in their life's direction, that women shall be the absolute monarchs of their own bosoms, is a historical issue. Feminist thinkers believed, and still do, that education is part of the issue's solution. Yet concrete advances--both in thought and actuality--have not resolved the issue. It is a continuing one.

The ideal of coeducation--helping "John and Mary to understand each other," as Marshall McLuhan expresses it-- is no more than "the classroom and campus version of [the quaint old New England theory and practice of] bundling."[177] Women expend ambivalent years on their schooling only to become aware of and attracted to their male classmates. The acquisition of knowledge, essential to the civilized mind, is shunted aside as in a dream. In the end, women and men are prepared only for "neuter and impersonal routines of production and distribution." Sex becomes increasingly sterile. Perhaps Mary McLeod Bethune, more than anyone else in the twentieth century, reinstitutes the quest in her 1953 legacy to the black people of this nation: "I leave you a thirst for education. Knowledge is the prime need of the hour."[178]

Two hundred fifty-two years have passed since Mary Astell advanced A Serious Proposal to the Ladies. One hundred sixty-six years have passed since Mary Wollstonecraft applied herself to Thoughts on the Education of Daughters. The quest for the Golden Fleece is not over. It goes on, much as Wollstonecraft would continue her search where she here today.

> ... [F]or her, life had no axioms; its geometry
> was all experimental. She was forever testing,
> probing; forever dominated by an utter unwilling-
> ness to accept ... the convention in place of the
> reality. She reasoned because ... a passionately
> intellectual attitude toward living was her essential
> tool.[179]

Ideas and ideals remain the tools of feminist thinkers. For
them as for women generally, educating is an end-in-view.

References

1   See Carol Addams, "She Wrote as One Who Loved Her
    Sex," Quest, 3 (Summer 1976), 70-79.
2   A Serious Proposal to the Ladies, 4th. ed. (1701) (New
    York: Source Book Press, 1970), pp. 9, 7, 1-2.
3   Ibid., pp. 4, 6, 20, 129-30.
4   Ibid., p. 159.
5   Ibid., pp. 10, 15-16, 18-19.
6   L'Emile (1762), trans. Barbara Foxley (New York:
    E. P. Dutton, 1911), p. 327.
7   Ibid., pp. 340, 350, 316.
8   Ibid., pp. 326, 333, 328, 348-49, 214, 218.
9   Thoughts on the Education of Daughters with Reflections
    on Female Conduct in the More Important Duties of Life
    (1787) (New York: Garland, 1974), p. 56.
10 The Rights of Women (1790) (New York: E. P. Dutton,
    1929), pp. 155-156.
11 Wollstonecraft, Education of Daughters, pp. 93-95, 58,
    83, 91.
12 Ibid., pp. 11-12. Here she mentions "Mr. Locke's
    system." She is referring to John Locke's Some
    Thoughts Concerning Education (1690). Locke stresses
    the influence in later life of children's early education
    and the necessity for their minds to submit to discipline
    and bend to reason. In this way, their education be-
    comes habitual and part of their very nature.
13 Wollstonecraft, Education of Daughters, pp. 1, 3-4, 11.
14 Ibid., p. 22; Wollstonecraft, Rights of Women, pp. 126,
    168, 188. This is especially important training for wo-
    men who do today what they did yesterday merely be-
    cause they did it yesterday and because they do not
    generate matters of fact (p. 26).
15 Wollstonecraft, Education of Daughters, pp. 26-27.
16 Ibid., pp. 41, 47, 49, 194, 118, 120-21.

17 Eleanor Flexner, in her biographical Mary Wollstone-
    craft (New York: Coward, McCann and Geoghegan, 1972),
    p. 149, concludes the ideas of Mary Astell were unknown
    to Wollstonecraft as Astell's ideas.
18 Thomas Woody, A History of Women's Education in the
    United States (1929) (New York: Octagon, 1966), vol. 1,
    pp. 197, 93.
19 "On the Education of Her Family" (1732), in Child-Rear-
    ing Concepts, 1628-1861, ed. Philip J. Greven, Jr.
    (Itasca, Ill.: F. E. Peacock, 1973), p. 51.
20 Morris R. Cohen, American Thought: A Critical Sketch,
    ed.. Felix S. Cohen (Glencoe, Ill.: Free Press, 1954),
    p. 25.
21 See Greven, Child-Rearing Concepts, p. 4.
22 John Locke, "An Essay Concerning the True Original,
    Extent and End of Civil Government," Second Treatise
    on Civil Government, in Social Contract, ed. Ernest
    Barker (New York: Oxford University Press, 1960), pp.
    30-45.
23 June 29, 1778, Familiar Letters of John Adams and His
    Wife Abigail Adams During the Revolution (1875) (Free-
    port, N.Y.: Books for Libraries Press, 1970), p. 339.
24 Judith Sargent Murray, "On the Equality of the Sexes,"
    The Massachusetts Magazine (March 1790), 132-35,
    (April 1790), 223-26.
25 The Excellency of the Female Character Vindicated (New
    York: Arno, 1972), p. 101.
26 Ibid., pp. 119, 160, 33, 31, 81.
27 Ibid., pp. 125, 156, 214-15.
28 Paul Kurtz, ed., American Thought from 1900: A
    Sourcebook from Puritanism to Darwinism (New York:
    Macmillan, 1966), pp. 18-19.
29 Morris Cohen, American Thought: A Critical Sketch ed.
    Felix Cohen, p. 40.
30 Ibid., see discussion at p. 40.
31 Women in the Nineteenth Century, in The Writings of
    Margaret Fuller, ed. Mason Wade (New York: Viking,
    1941), pp. 109, 176, 211.
32 Ibid., p. 216.
33 Southern Literary Messenger, 2 (September 1836), 659-
    62, reprinted in Kenneth Walter Cameron, Philothea or
    Plato Against Epicurus--A Novel of the Transcendental
    Movement in New England ... (Hartford, Conn.: Trans-
    cendental Books, 1975), p. 169.
34 Rights of Women, p. 160.
35 Education of Daughters, pp. 117, 113-14.
36 Elizabeth Cady Stanton, Eighty Years and More: Remi-

niscences 1815-1897 (1898) (New York: Schocken, 1971), p. 4.

37 Ibid., p. 20.
38 Ibid., pp. 21-22.
39 Ibid., p. 23.
40 Ibid., pp. 21, 23-24.
41 Barbara Welter illuminates the plight of such women in "The Cult of True Womanhood: 1820-1860," American Quarterly, 18:2 (1966), 151-74. Sarah Grimke, another "woman of superior cast," on adulthood reveals her bitterness that she was unable because of family disapproval to achieve her dream of becoming a lawyer. "With me learning was a passion.... My nature [was] denied her appropriate nutriment, her course counteracted, her aspirations crushed." "Education of Women," quoted in Gerda Lerner, The Grimke Sisters from South Carolina: Pioneers for Women's Rights and Abolition (New York: Schocken, 1971), p. 29. Linda Grant De Pauw tells the sad story of Phillis Wheatley, an educated, African-born, Boston-bred black woman, who was a freed house slave. Wheatley wrote and published poetry but died at 31 in abject poverty. Founding Mothers: Women of America in the Revolutionary Era (Boston: Houghton, 1975), pp. 91-95.
42 Stanton, Eighty Years, pp. 37, 40.
43 "An Address to the Public Particularly to the Members of the Legislature of New York Proposing a Plan for Improving Female Education" (1819), reprinted in Willystine Goodsell, Pioneers of Women's Education in the United States: Emma Willard, Catharine Beecher, Mary Lyon (New York: McGraw-Hill, 1931), pp. 55, 46, 59.
44 Ibid., pp. 61, 64, 77-79.
45 Ibid., p. 45. In the first Ladies Magazine (1828), Sarah Josepha Hale comments that legislatures still have not endowed women's colleges, but much is being done through individual enterprise. Hale's daughters attended Troy Female Seminary--Ruth E. Finley, The Lady of Godey's: Sarah Josepha Hale (Philadelphia: Lippincott, 1931), p. 225.
46 Lutz, Emma Willard: Daughter of Democracy (Boston: Houghton, 1929), p. 238. See also Harriot K. Hunt, Glances and Glimpses or 50 Years Social, Including 20 Years Professional Life (1856) (New York: Source Book Press, 1970), p. 296: "the interest [Willard] has evinced in education of girls, many of whom she has trained for teachers, claimed my respect. It matters not whether such women avow themselves as coadjutors of woman reform--it is enough that they live it out."

47 "Woman," in Benjamin Lundy, The Poetical Work of Elizabeth Margaret Chandler with a Memoir of Her Life and Character (1836) (Miami: Mnemosyne, 1969), pp. 177-78.
48 Lundy, Poetical Work, p. 36.
49 "To Prudence Crandall," in Lundy, Poetical Work, pp. 177-78.
50 Gerda Lerner says Wright is the first woman in America to lecture publicly. Maria W. Stewart, a black woman who became a teacher, is the first American-born woman to lecture; she preceded the Grimke sisters in this regard by five years--Black Women in White America: A Documentary History (New York: Vintage, 1972), p. 83.
51 Frances Wright D'Arusmont, Life, Letters and Lectures, 1834/1844 (1844) New York: Arno, 1972), pp. 19, 24, 15, 32.
52 Ibid., p. 20.
53 Ibid., p. 5.
54 Stanton makes this distinction vivid when she discusses the aged person and his musty books and papers, the preacher speaking from above the heads of his congregation, the chorister droning David's Psalms and the congregation wandering along behind, all this without "attractions for the youthful mind," in Eighty Years, p. 25. See also her characterization of the shriveled mistress of the parsonage and her blind sister, "more like ghostly shadows than human flesh and blood," p. 24.
55 Wright, Life, Letters and Lectures, p. 5.
56 Society in America (London: Saunders and Otley, 1837), vol. 3, pp. 145-46.
57 Ibid.
58 Society in America, vol. 1, pp. 340-41, 206.
59 Tocqueville, Democracy in America, ed. J. P. Mayer, trans. George Lawrence (Garden City, N.Y.: Anchor Books, 1969), pp. 590-92.
60 Ibid., p. 429.
61 Ibid., p. 435.
62 Ibid., p. 460.
63 Beth Bradford Gilchrist, The Life of Mary Lyon (Boston: Houghton, 1910), p. 5.
64 Ibid., p. 172.
65 Ibid., pp. 202, 200.
66 Ibid., p. 12.
67 For comprehensive histories of women's education, see Elene Wilson Farello, A History of the Education of Women in the United States (New York: Vantage, 1970),

and Thomas Woody, History of Women's Education. For a series of short biographies of early prominent women educators, see Mary S. Longan, The Part Taken by Women in American History (1912) (New York: Arno, 1972), pp. 706-37.

68 Gilchrist, Life of Mary Lyon, p. 96.
69 A Treatise on Domestic Economy for the Use of Young Ladies at Home and at School (1841) (New York: Source Book Press, 1970), p. 9.
70 Ibid., pp. 9-10, 4. This statement is ironic in light of Hartford Seminary's decline in 1853 for want of adequate endowment and support.
71 Ibid., p. 13.
72 Ibid., p. 142.
73 Catharine E. Beecher and H. B. Stowe, The American Woman's Home: or, Principles of Domestic Science, Being a Guide to the Formation and Maintenance of Economical, Healthful, Beautiful, and Christian Homes (1869) (New York: Arno, 1971), p. 13.
74 Treatise on Domestic Economy, pp. 144-47.
75 Catharine Beecher and H. Stowe, American Woman's Home, p. 104.
76 Ruth Finley, Lady of Godey's, p. 237.
77 Hale, Manners; or, Happy Homes and Good Society All the Year Round (1868) (New York: Arno, 1972), pp. 356-58.
78 Ibid., p. 357.
79 Reprinted in Marion Talbot, The Education of Women (Chicago: University of Chicago Press, 1910), pp. 109-11.
80 See Sara A. Burstall, The Education of Girls in the United States (1894) (New York: Arno, 1971), pp. 152-53.
81 Harriot Hunt, Glances and Glimpses, pp. 153, 157, 159. See also Sophia Jex-Blake, "Medicine as a Profession for Women," in Woman's Work and Woman's Culture, ed. Josephine E. Butler (London: Macmillan, 1869), pp. 78-120.
82 Pioneer Work in Opening the Medical Profession to Women (1895) (New York: Source Book Press, 1970), p. 253.
83 Hunt, Glances and Glimpses, pp. 328-29, 394.
84 Grace Hamilton [i.e., Mary A. Dodge], Woman's Wrongs (1868) (New York: Arno, 1972), pp. 62-63, 111. Women are only half-educated, but this is no indication they cannot be fully educated. They suffer more from the practical inability forced upon them than from an education once it is acquired.

85 Lewis, Our Girls (1871) (New York: Arno, 1974), pp.
    353, 10.
86 Ibid., p. 179.
87 Ibid., p. 180. Elizabeth Cady Stanton is making a simi-
    lar observation at this time. "Women have crucified the
    Mary Wollstonecrafts, the Franny Wrights and George
    Sands of all ages. Men mock us with the fact and say
    we are ever cruel to each other. Let us end this ig-
    noble record and henceforth stand by womanhood"--Letter
    to Lucretia Mott, April 1, 1872, in Elizabeth Cady Stan-
    ton, ed. Theodore Stanton and Harriot Stanton Blatch
    (New York: Arno, 1969), vol. 2, p. 137.
88 Alma Lutz, Created Equal: A Biography of Elizabeth
    Cady Stanton 1815-1902 (New York: John Day, 1940),
    p. 63.
89 E. Douglas Branch, "The Lily and the Bloomer," The
    Colophon, 12 (1932), n.p. The Lily also becomes de-
    cidedly feminist in other aspects. For example, Branch
    quotes from the third volume: 'OLD MAID--a lady who
    has attained the age of 24 or 5, without having married
    a fool, a knave, a gambler, or a drunkard. "
90 Lutz, Created Equal, pp. 64-65.
91 Woolson, ed., Dress Reform (1874) (New York: Arno,
    1974), p. 175. Constantia in 1780 was willing to con-
    cede animal strength to those who argued man's superi-
    ority but not mental strength. A century later the two
    were being linked together.
92 Ibid., pp. 169-70. Mary Walker, a medical practitioner,
    was one of those active in the dress reform movement,
    both on her own and other women's account. See
    Charles McCool Snyder, Dr. Mary Walker: The Little
    Lady in Pants (1962) (New York: Arno, 1974), passim.
93 Abba Woolson, Dress Reform, pp. 126, xiv.
94 Ibid., pp. 134, 148-49, xii.
95 Ibid., p. 132.
96 Matilda Gage, Woman, Church and State (1893) (New
    York: Arno, 1972), p. 531.
97 Ibid., p. 528-39.
98 Elizabeth Cady Stanton, Susan B. Anthony and Matilda
    Joslyn Gage, eds., History of Woman Suffrage (Roches-
    ter, N.Y.: Charles Mann, 1889), vol. 1, p. 23.
    Keeping in mind the interdependence of all reform and
    the need to establish one principle throughout, a commit-
    tee composed of Stanton, Gage and 23 others set out to
    revise the Bible. The result is The Woman's Bible,
    published in 1898.
99 Ibid., p. 22. Among the examples of these lofty souls
    are George Eliot and Maria Mitchell.

100 "Should Higher Education of Women Differ from That of Men?" (1901), in The Educated Woman in America: Selected Writings of Catharine Beecher, Margaret Fuller, and M. Carey Thomas (Classics in Education 25), ed. Barbara M. Cross (New York: Teachers College Press, Columbia University, 1965), p. 154.

101 Ibid., pp. 147-48.

102 Ibid., p. 152.

103 Gilman, Women and Economics: A Study of Economic Relations Between Men and Women as a Factor in Social Evolution (1898) (New York: Harper Torchbooks, 1966), p. 283.

104 Ibid., pp. 284-85, 240.

105 Ibid., pp. 258-59. Abigail Adams longed for her own room over 100 years before Charlotte Perkins Gilman wrote Women and Economics.

106 Ibid., pp. 260, 265, 305.

107 Gilman, The Home: Its Work and Influence (1903) (Urbana: University of Illinois Press, 1972), pp. 309-10.

108 Ibid., pp. 311-13, 315, 300, 303.

109 Ibid., p. 306.

110 See Elene Farello, History of Education of Women, p. 182; Joan Roberts, "Creating a Facade of Change: Informal Mechanisms Used to Impede the Changing Status of Women in Academe" (Pittsburgh: Know, 1975), pp. 2-4.

111 Quoted in Sara A. Burstall, Education of Girls, pp. 162-63.

112 Ibid., pp. 8-9, 174, 164. In fact, coeducation was the norm for early dame schools, Dutch elementary schools, schools of Quaker communities and some academies. See Elene Farello, History of Education of Women, p. 182.

113 Hall, Youth, Its Education, Regimen and Hygiene (New York: Appleton, 1907), pp. 321, 283-84, 277-78, 286, 293, 304.

114 Ibid., pp. 293, 290. The primary flaw with the training of women's colleges is this tendency to self support. See pp. 303-04.

115 Ibid., pp. 290, 304, 297, 301.

116 Educational Problems (New York: Appleton, 1911), p. 475.

117 Ibid., pp. 390-91, 397.

118 Youth, p. 294.

119 Henry Adams, The Education of Henry Adams (1907) (New York: Modern Library, 1931), pp. 225, 229.

120 Ibid., pp. 7, 9.

121 Ibid., pp. 377, 379-83.

122 Ibid., pp. 384-85. Edward S. Morgan challenges Adams' equation of the Puritans with American squeamishness about sex in "The Puritans and Sex," The American Family in Social-Historical Perspective, ed. Michael Gordon (New York: St. Martin's Press, 1973), pp. 282-95; see especially pp. 282-83.
123 Education of Henry Adams, p. 388.
124 Ibid., pp. 427-28.
125 Ibid., p. 505.
126 Women in the Twentieth Century: A Study of Their Political, Social and Economic Activities (New York: McGraw-Hill, 1933), passim.
127 The Woman Citizen: Social Feminism in the 1920's (Urbana: University of Illinois Press, 1973), passim.
128 Women and Economics, p. 164.
129 Talbot, The Education of Women (Chicago: University of Chicago Press, 1910), pp. 233, 56, 205.
130 Ibid., pp. 209-10. Social hygiene and eugenics include instruction in normal sex health. Cf. G. Stanley Hall's pedagogy of sex.
131 Ibid., pp. 233, 226.
132 Spencer, Woman's Share in Social Culture: The Family and Its Members (Philadelphia: Lippincott, 1923), pp. 121, 130, 182, 176, 186.
133 Tarbell, The Business of Being a Woman (New York: Macmillan, 1912), pp. vii, 12, 32, 35-42, 81-82, 88, 144-45.
134 "Liberal Education for Women," Harper's New Monthly Magazine (April 1877), 695-96.
135 The Renaissance of Motherhood, trans. Anna E. B. Fries (New York: G. P. Putnam's, 1914), pp. 83-84.
136 Ibid., pp. v, 92, 126-27.
137 Ibid., pp. 333, 135-46. Cf. Olive Schreiner, Woman and Labor, 5th. ed. (New York: Stokes, 1911), pp. 226-27. "As no sane human concerns himself as to whether the right or left ventricle of his heart works most satisfactorily, or is most essential to his well-being ... so no sane man or woman questions over the relative perfections of male and female."
138 Olive Schreiner, Woman and Labor, pp. 207-13.
139 See John Dewey on Education, ed. Reginald D. Archambault (New York: Modern Library, 1964), passim.
140 The Heritage of Women (New York: Minton, Balch, 1927), p. 287.
141 Virginia Woolf, A Room of One's Own (1929) (New York: Harbinger Book, 1957), p. 4.
142 Ibid., p. 15.

143 Ibid., pp. 21-23.
144 Ibid., pp. 25-26.
145 Ibid., pp. 25-34.
146 Ibid., p. 35. And there would be no cathedrals, I dare say.
147 Ibid., pp. 40-41, 88-89.
148 Ibid., pp. 91, 98, 74-75, 83. At last, a meaningful use for woman's Glass!
149 Ibid., p. 108.
150 Ibid., pp. 117-18. See also Mary Johnston, Hagar (Boston: Houghton, 1913); Francine du Plessix Gray, "What Are Women Doing," New York Times, sec. 7 (April 24, 1977), p. 3.
151 Woolf, Room of One's Own, pp. 71, 67, 69, 115.
152 Mary R. Beard, ed., America Through Women's Eyes (New York: Macmillan, 1933), p. 2.
153 Ibid., pp. 4-8.
154 Mary R. Beard, On Understanding Women (New York: Longman's Green, 1931), pp. 401, 404-05.
155 Ibid., pp. 513-14, 521-22.
156 Painted Lace and Other Pieces (1914-1937) (New Haven, Conn.: Yale University Press, 1955), p. 69.
157 Deutsch, The Psychology of Women: A Psychoanalytic Interpretation (New York: Green and Stratton, 1944), p. 142.
158 Ibid., p. 143. Anon once again makes an appearance, this time only briefly. Inscribed on the margin here is one word. (Expletive deleted.) Virginia Woolf ventures "to guess that Anon, who wrote so many poems without signing them, was often a woman," in Room of One's Own, p. 51.
159 Woolf, Room of One's Own, p. 108.
160 Ibid.
161 Ibid., p. 74.
162 Ibid., p. 80.
163 The American Spirit: A Study of the Idea of Civilization in the United States, vol. 4, The Rise of American Civilization (New York: Macmillan, 1942), pp. i, v, 166-67, 661, 665-76.
164 Ibid., pp. 671-72.
165 The Woman Within (New York: Harcourt, 1954), pp. 167-68. Glasgow, with reference to Virginia Woolf's thesis, was a successful and well-known novelist in the first part of the twentieth century; she did her writing in an austere office and study and before that in any room which had a closed door. She was financially independent by virtue of family inheritances.

166 Lowi and Hollingsworth, "Science and Feminism,"
Science Monthly (September 1916), 277-84.
167 He was criticized later for ignoring emotional development, underestimating social and cultural factors and
overestimating the efficacy of a child's activity--D. W.
Hamlyn, "Epistemology and Conceptual Development,"
in Cognitive Development and Epistemology, ed. Theodore Mischel (New York: Academic Press, 1971), pp.
3-24.
168 Virginia (1913) (Garden City, New York: Doubleday,
Page, 1923), pp. 478, 505, 514.
169 Male and Female: A Study of the Sexes in a Changing
World (New York: Morrow, 1949), p. 160.
170 Ibid., pp. 58, 61, 105.
171 Ibid., p. 127.
172 David Riesman with Nathan Glazer and Reuel Denney,
The Lonely Crowd, abr. ed. (New Haven, Conn.: Yale
University Press, 1961), pp. 37-38, 42, 45-58, 52.
173 Ibid., pp. 59-61, 146.
174 Ibid., pp. 145, 148, 258.
175 Ibid., pp. 159-60, 304.
176 Ibid., p. 307.
177 The Mechanical Bride; Folklore of Industrial Man (New
York: Vanguard, 1951), p. 53.
178 Dorothy C. Massie, "The Legacy of Mary McLeod
Bethune" (Washington, D.C.: National Education Association, 1974), n.p.
179 Ruth Benedict, "Mary Wollstonecraft," in An Anthropologist at Work: Writings of Ruth Benedict, ed. Margaret Mead (Boston: Houghton, 1959), p. 491.

PART II
Ideological Undercurrents

THE PATH OF DUTY:
FEMINISM AND LIBERTY

Among the ideological undercurrents to feminism is
liberty. Feminist thinkers who espouse a libertarian creed
concern themselves with woman's continuing search for a
meaningful existence. Such an existence is characterized by
fulfillment of duty rather than license. The emphasis is on
individuality, responsibility and inner self-development.
Imagine feminist thinkers once again outside time and space;
one by one they ponder their libertarian creed.

Mary Wollstonecraft sees liberty as the mother of virtue. Perfect freedom comes in doing service to reason, in
the possession of which women will discharge their duties
and thereby earn their subsistence. Mercy Otis Warren says,
certain it is that the noble life is forthcoming from freedom's
genius, nourished in schools of law and liberty. Freedom is
heaven's bright progeny, adds Phillis Wheatley, in tune with
nature and peace. Ah, smiles Frances Wright, how well
Mercy and Phillis show us the dual traits of American women: confidence born of national freedom in manner and innocence born of national moral purity. Then Mary Griffith
earnestly begins to speak: in the future American women will
eliminate the disgrace of war forever and by their moral influence create a beautiful, orderly world. Yes, says Ezra
Heywood, it is liberated, self-loyal womanhood who builds a
bridge from isolation to society with her intelligent moral

sense. Perfect freedom for women and men, though, will be characterized by their enfranchised souls and purified intelligence, asserts Margaret Fuller. These will develop within inherited limits and decorum. Harriot Hunt inserts the thought that freedom is neither male nor female; it is the law of individualism and growth. Yes, Margaret Fuller agrees, the liberty the nation now enjoys will be enjoyed by individuals. Then women can develop their strength and beauty.

Someone recalls the Declaration of Sentiments proposing that women as well as men have an inalienable right to life, liberty and the pursuit of happiness. Beatrice Forbes-Robertson Hale reminds those about her that democracy, by translating theory into practice, is the mother of feminism. When democracy matures, it will be realized in collectivism and happiness; until then, it is individualistic and demands freedom. Now, says Hunt, we must have freedom to think our own thoughts and to utter them, freedom to live out the promptings of our inner lives. Hope and perfection follow these freedoms. John Stuart and Harriet Taylor Mill nod in agreement, their arms linked. They describe the sphere of human liberty in terms of inner consciousness, taste, planning one's life and combination with others. No interference-- individual, collective or magisterial--is warranted here except for self-protection or to prevent harm to others.

The Mills go on to say that individuals are not accountable to society for personal matters affecting only their own interests. Victoria Woodhull begins speaking about perfecting human beings by combining freedom and love. Most of the individuals standing about her turn away. The Mills speak softly. Impulse and restraint must be related positively by socially cultivating strong susceptibilities to virtue and self-control. Heywood adds that without woman's moral rule,

liberty soon would become libertine. George Eliot speaks of
the conflict between woman's duty to her birthright and to
love. Frederick Engels thinks aloud of the contradictions inherent in monogamous marriage alone: woman's labor is
privatized, while man has socially useful labor; she is enslaved, and he is free. This is the first historic class opposition and oppression. The conflict between natural and
revealed rights comes to Matilda Gage's mind as Engels
talks. She speaks of progress which overthrows tyranny
based on the revealed rights of church and state. She smiles;
woman's freedom is increasing as woman learns her first duty is self-development rather than sacrifice.

I have learned, says Julia Ward Howe, that such freedom is compatible with true womanliness. With progress
comes freedom and with freedom a cooperative force among
women. I think so too, says Ellen Key. Women share a
common dual purpose by virtue of womanhood, creation of
children and development of humanity. As woman asserts
her liberated power for emotional perception in the face of
war, she will fulfill national moral and political duties as
well. No, Ellen, I disagree--it is Suzanne LaFollette speaking. Woman's freedom must be obtained on her own behalf,
not because of her child bearing function. Freedom for women, continues LaFollette, is part of a larger issue. And
its price is self-control, adds Alice Ames Winter. Its
struggle is of the earth, says Agnes Smedley. But we can
do nothing to change the world, regrets Ellen Glasgow. We
can create an individually perfect world which can be a refuge
for others, insists Anaïs Nin. Woman will be last to find
independence because of her past ties. The process of insight is so slow, but it does permit deep growth and change.
Anne Morrow Lindbergh nods; woman comes of age in growth,

fluidity and freedom.   Nin goes on: hope lies in keeping the
dream alive.   It takes patience and faith, says Lindbergh.
Nin speaks again.   We must transform destruction into creation and everlasting continuity.   Simone de Beauvoir turns
to her and speaks: woman needs an apprenticeship in liberty, abandonment and transcendence.   She can never know her
essential self until she is emancipated.

* * * * *

Mary Wollstonecraft posits liberty, which entails submission to reason and not man, as the mother of virtue.
Once sound politics diffuse liberty, humankind will become
wiser and more virtuous.   Man will enjoy natural freedom
only when governed by reasonable laws in which woman
shares, however.   Presently, women have surrendered the
natural rights to which use of reason would entitle them.
Only by submitting to reason does one submit to the nature
of things.   "I do not wish women to have power over men;
but over themselves."[1]   The real definition of independence
has to do with earning one's own subsistence by discharge
of duty, rather than depending upon another for existence.
Those who will be free are free, given sufficient enlightenment to forego prerogative.

Reliance on blind impulses must become a thing of
the past.   For this to take place, men must resign their
tyranny; women, their place as love object.   In place of impulse comes a rare privilege indeed, reflection on the past
and contemplation of the future.   In beginning to act for oneself, old habits of thinking take on new force.   Right use of
reason will make woman independent of everything but un-
clouded reason, "whose service is perfect freedom."[2]   Once
women are freed from restraints upon their natural rights,
they will fulfill their duties.   The problem is, "who can tell,
how many generations may be necessary to give vigor to the
virtue and talents of the freed posterity of abject slaves?"[3]

For Wollstonecraft, it will take time, who knows how
long, but once liberty is achieved, women and men will begin
to fulfill their duties in the state of virtue which is ultimately
perfection.   Political theorists, Wollstonecraft included, commonly depict liberty as synonymous with freedom and inde-

pendence. The implication is one of free-wheeling activity
and absence of compulsion. Closer examination suggests
common usage may be only the tip of the iceberg--an optical
illusion, so to speak. The underside of the iceberg is inde-
terminate, its outline refracted by play of light rays through
air and water. A paradox is at work. To understand this,
first it is necessary to reach beyond Wollstonecraft to the
thought of three Western political theorists: Thomas Hobbes,
John Locke and Jean-Jacques Rousseau.

For Hobbes, liberty is the absence of any external
impediment of motion to man's natural right to everything.
It is consistent with necessity--which stems from God, the
first of all causes--and constitutes the naturally just use of
power for self-preservation. Natural rights, however, may
be renounced voluntarily and transferred by contract to the
leviathan, a state or artificial man which will protect and defend natural man. The subject's liberty lies in those things
the leviathan neglects, each subject in effect authoring every
state act. The liberty of the leviathan is that which man
would have had he not transferred it. Both liberty and obligation are inferred by submitting to the state. The family,
in which the father gains dominion by generation and by
marital contract with the mother, could be a little monarchy
were it not part of the leviathan which has sufficient power
to protect it. [4]

Locke states that the state of nature is one of liberty
but not license, subject to the dictates of reason and conscience. Within these limits each man may do to all others
what he chooses. Women and men set up a conjugal society
by voluntary compact to perpetuate the species in the care of
their children. Man's power in this relationship by virtue of
ability and strength is limited, and the relationship is based
on mutuality and common concern. Men unite in a community
by individual consent, empowering that community with the
consent of the majority. Entry into the state, a second step,
entails commitment of law-making and war and peace powers
to the preservation of the life, liberty and property of members of society. [5]

For Rousseau, even though the noble savage may work
as a peasant and think as a philosopher, the state of nature
becomes intolerable. Thus, man renounces it, but to re-
nounce liberty is to give up the essence of one's being.
"Man is born free, and everywhere he is in chains, " having
become a slave against nature. Social order can be legiti-

mated, however. True happiness lies in an equilibrium of desires and powers. The shared liberty which is its characteristic is the result of man's nature. Men enter into a social contract which represents the free or general will of all, losing natural liberty but gaining civil liberty as well as the right to whatever is theirs. Natural liberty is subject to the continuance of enough strength to defend it; civil liberty is subject to the general will. Anyone who will not recognize the general will can be compelled to be free. In this way, justice and social order replace instinct and bondage in human association. [6]

For these theorists liberty in its essence is not necessarily desirable. Even man, the embodiment of strength and ability for Locke, cannot cope with natural liberty. Mutual association among men and women, arrived at voluntarily, can help to institute a more civil liberty within which people are guaranteed the right to life and property. Hobbes, Locke and Rousseau each discuss the relationship of man and woman, with all its implications for perpetuating the species and self-preservation. Wollstonecraft is drawing heavily on this body of thought, particularly Rousseau and Locke, by implication Hobbes. She basically is dissatisfied with woman's position in natural rights theory, but she is influenced by that theory nonetheless. Her focus is on a potentially perfectible civilization, and her point is that it is obtainable only when women as well as men become virtuous through the use of reason. She disclaims any intention to reverse the current state of affairs in which men exercise tyranny over women. In fact, she holds that women can be tyrants in their position as well. She expresses confidence that, after an unknown period of time elapses, this situation will be put to rights. There is an existential dilemma here, however: how to free the impetus to reason in women and men alike that both may fulfill duties essential for the right ordering of society.

Wollstonecraft, with Hobbes, Locke and Rousseau, agrees unbridled liberty will not do. To be free requires certain choices be made. Choice requires some things between or among which to choose. For Wollstonecraft, women must resign their place as love object and men their tyranny in favor of reason, in whose service lies perfect freedom. Wollstonecraft intends the key to the dilemma of how this will come about to be ability to earn one's own subsistence by discharge of duty. This will not take place before women are loosed from restraints upon their natural rights, however, and one suspects the restraints will not be slackened before discharge of duty takes place. On the other hand, even if the choice to be free results in irresponsibility for an unknown period of time, making the choice could be construed an act of responsibility. Hobbes, Locke and Rousseau all seem to assume this to be the case. Locke stresses the voluntary nature of the compact; Hobbes and Rousseau attribute a degree of compulsion to the choice. All, however, stress the role the ultimately undesirable state of the natural environment plays in coming to this choice. Wollstonecraft finds woman's environment to be an undesirable one, affecting women and men unfavorably enough to constitute a kind of compulsion toward choosing the more perfect end state of civilization.

For Wollstonecraft, making the choice to be free requires submission to reason; for Hobbes, to the leviathan; for Locke, to majority consent; for Rousseau, to the general will. As Locke puts it, "liberty is to be free from restraint and violence from others," which cannot be where there is no law," and "he that is not come to the use of his reason cannot be said to be under this law."[7] Woman must share in these laws, according to Wollstonecraft, and to do so she must submit to reason. Law which binds and liberty as the absence of restraint from others are opposites, but for most political theorists, liberty is not worth having without the voluntarily accepted mutual self-restraint which law implies.* Thus making the choice to be free in a civil context is an act of responsibility, even though irresponsibility may follow for an unknown period of time. A responsible act is something for which the actor is going to be accountable. This bespeaks something to which the actor is accountable for the choice made as well. The object of accountability variously is described as reason, the leviathan, majority consent, the general will.

There is something more to these objects than a convenient fiction. Accountability posits restraint. This is not immediately compatible with the free-wheeling activity that common usage of the concept liberty implies. Common usage suggests something very basic, known immediately upon contact and not to be passed over lightly. Some sort of accommodation between common usage and its logical underside is needed. As binding practice, law has an element of compul-

---

*I am grateful to Carl Linden for his valuable insights about this distinction.

sion to it. As an expression of an invariant relation, it encompasses the past, the present and potentially the future. Human beings concern themselves with the future and try to understand it by means of what has taken place in the past. The problem of deciding once and for all what controls are necessary remains, however.

Alexander Hamilton poses the question, "Whether societies of men are really capable or not of establishing good government from reflection and choice, or whether they are forever destined to depend for their political consequences on accident and force." James Madison offers an answer: "There is a mean, on both sides of which inconvenience will be found to lie."[8] Whether a feminist mean can be located precisely between potentially perfectible civilization and woman's current position as abject slave, to put it in Wollstonecraft's terms, remains to be seen. The feminist thinkers discussed in this chapter observe particular sets of circumstances and represent different portions of the political spectrum. Each feminist thinker nonetheless is part of an all encompassing whole, something usually referred to as truth. What liberty amounts to depends on the circumstances in which it is pursued.

Feminist thinkers' prescriptions about woman's position result from their reflection on the facts of human existence. As Wollstonecraft points out, women generally have a rather narrow experiential base and their powers of observation are limited accordingly. In the meantime, however, reason will know what it has the opportunity to learn, and women will continue to create life itself. Feminist prescriptions will adapt to each other and in doing so will maintain the semblance of truth. Liberty, it seems, will be pursued by feminist thinkers into the future as it has been from the past, but the track on which the chase takes place is part of the present. Who is there to compel them to participate in the license of the chase? Which of them can escape the restraint of the track on which they choose to run? It may be instructive to ponder if the choice involved is not an existential one. Women, and men, necessarily are restrained by the need to make choices for which they will be held accountable, and making choices has an element of responsibility to it, but in making choices women and men are irrepressibly free. Freedom lies in participating. Liberty is in the pursuing.

The New World, fighting for its independence, rings with liberty. Yet there are disquieting notes for women.

Abigail Adams writes John, "I have sometimes been ready to
think that the passion for liberty cannot be equally strong in
the breasts of those who have been accustomed to deprive
their fellow creatures of theirs." Certain it is that such behavior is not founded upon the Golden Rule.[9] In the face of
war, however, women in America devote themselves to the
cause. They long have been involved in political discussion
clubs, their minds free to engage serious issues while their
hands spin, knit and sew. Beginning in 1766, their clubs
take on more formal organizational structure throughout
America. Many of them are known as "Daughters of Liberty." Their contributions to the war effort are considerable.[10]
Women's homes and very lives are at stake, and they meet
the crisis with energy and activity.

One fancies Mercy Otis Warren thinks of these women
in the person of Donna Maria in The Ladies of Castile: A
Tragedy in Five Acts (1790). The play is set during the last
struggle for liberty in Spain before Ferdinand's tyrannic rule.
Donna Maria is wed to the commander of troops raised by the
Spanish states. In his eyes, her "undaunted soul/ Reflects a
lustre on her feeble sex;/ By strategem, she's gained an
ample sum/ To quiet mutiny and pay the troops." Donna
Maria scorns life lived on ignoble terms. The truly noble
life is touched by "freedom's genius, nurs'd from age to
age,/ Matur'd in schools of liberty and law,/ On virtue's
page from fire to sun convey'd...." Donna Maria struggles
not to become "less than woman" by yielding to wifely and
maternal impulses which would level her with her sex. She
calls upon her friend Donna Louisa, the regent of Spain's
daughter who loves Donna Maria's brother, to shun "weak
compassion" and "pity's tears" for her personal plight. Justice must be done. The king must learn his people "will be
free/ And ... the duty that a monarch owes,/ To heaven--
the people--and the rights of man." Better Donna Louisa
had lived "in the lap of peace," but for Donna Maria, she
never will submit or be a slave.

There is much at stake indeed, and liberty and peace
are at the center of it all. Phillis Wheatley, in one of her
finest efforts, captures the meaning of liberty and peace for
the times in 1784.

Lo! freedom comes. Th' prescient muse foretold,
All eyes th' accomplish'd prophecy behold:
Her port describ'd, "She moved divinely fair,
Olive and laurel bind her golden hair."

> She, the bright progeny of Heaven, descends,
> And every grace her sovereign step attends;
> For now kind Heaven, indulgent to our prayer,
> In smiling peace resolves the din of war.
> . . .
> Now sheath the sword that bade the brave atone
> With guiltless blood for madness not their own.
> . . .
> With heart felt pity fair Hibernia saw
> Columbia menac'd by the Tyrant's law:
> On hostile fields fraternal arms engage,
> And mutual deaths, all dealt with mutual rage:
> The muse's ear hears mother earth deplore
> Her ample surface smoke with kindred gore:
> The hostile field destroys the social ties,
> And everlasting slumber seals their eyes.
> . . .
> Descending peace the power of war confounds;
> From every tongue celestial peace resounds:
> As from the east th' illustrious king of day,
> With rising radiance drives the shades away,
> So freedom comes array'd with charms divine,
> And in her train commerce and plenty shine.
> . . .
> Auspicious Heaven shall fill with fav-ring gales,
> Where'er Columbia spreads her swelling sails:
> To every realm shall peace her charms display,
> And heavenly freedom spread her golden ray. [11]

Liberty is a fair bright woman, divine in issue and attuned to mother earth's lament. Liberty is at one with mother earth's love for nature and life. The menace of tyranny, hostility and death is confounded by her prophesied coming on the path of peace. Destruction, whatever its source, first must be restrained for freedom, commerce and plenty to commence.

Facing monarchical despotism which places the free-born colonists in bondage, American women fervently espouse libertarian principles. They are not radical--Mercy Warren later writes John Adams of her "dread of the result of dissemination of Voltaire's work"[12]--but they are libertarian. Civil liberty cannot exist for those in bondage; the bonds must be severed. War's devastation is no fit habitat for liberty either. It is akin to the state of nature which natural man finds so inhospitable. Family and social ties are never stronger than when their preservation is in doubt. With peace

Statue of Liberty (Tyrone Dukes/The New York Times).

comes liberty, and commerce and plenty follow after. The
cause is as much woman's as man's. What woman herself
lacks in legal status is not at issue here. Later the libertarian cause will take on more personal connotations for her.
Now life and hearth's preservation demands her attention.
Liberty in Puritan America is above all a moral concept.
There is natural liberty, which is absolute, unlimited and
sometimes troublesome, and federal liberty, which constitutes
freedom of motion as covenanted with God. Federal liberty
exists independently of society or any legal entity. [13] The
colonists are committed morally to maintain life, family and
federal liberty.

In 1918, Frances Wright recalls that much of America's struggle for liberty issued from its women. Women encourage this same strength in their daughters, that their sons
might remain freemen and patriots. In American women,
confidence born of national freedom in manner and innocence

born of national moral purity are "twin sisters." Wright observes woman's position to be that of a thinking being and attributes it to the American man's liberal largesse.[14] It seems, though, that much credit is due the women themselves. Their commitment to liberty and peace is tested and found strong. The War for Independence is fought for immediate ends but on broad principle. As time passes, women will find that principle applicable to their own situation as well and will begin to apply it accordingly. The seeds of feminist libertarian thought are sown in fertile soil.

The years 1820 to 1860 bring an ideological atmosphere which seems to exclude the libertarian spirit of colonial women. Barbara Welter labels it "the cult of True Womanhood." True women are characterized by piety, purity, submissiveness and domesticity.[15] Women are believed to be naturally religious, and religion is attuned to the home, woman's sphere. Purity is both natural and feminine, flowing from woman's religiousness and virtue. Woman understands her position and submits to it with the correct air of dependency and gratitude. Since her place is in the home, she is domestic. There she can fulfill her functions of beauty and usefulness. Her patriotism is displayed best at home, inspiring patriotic sentiment in her sons.[16] Middle-class women dutifully try to be true, and when they fail, they are distressed.[17] In trying, however, they broaden their sphere. Activities in missionary societies open up a whole new world, and temperance activities follow soon after. For the bravest of them, abolition is a further step. Women assert their moral law unto themselves and begin to expect men to follow it. Woman's position as guardian of the home and keeper of morals entitles her to man's submission in this regard.

The promise of woman's fulfillment of her moral duty is large, indeed. Mary Griffith's Three Hundred Years Hence prophesies an improved world which begins by improving the education of poor women. The "superior delicacy and refinement" of the female sex becomes a most important influence. Women first unite to eliminate the disgrace of war forever, teaching their children to refrain from bloodshed except in self-defense. Through woman's influence, war becomes a crime. With the means of moral reform in their power, women next teach their children to reverence religion. Drunkeness among men becomes a thing of the past when women receive the right to divorce their husbands for it.[18] Cities are characterized by hygienic conditions and the markets are immaculate and beautiful. It is a world which could

never be without the influence of the true woman. Freedom
and peace are linked to prosperity, an important end state in
a material culture. Prosperity is reached through industry
and application. Mary Griffith's utopia is based on such principle. The purveyors of change and improvement are women,
empowered by fulfillment of their moral duty.

In this intellectual setting, Margaret Fuller writes
about liberty as a condition of enlightenment which in turn is
a condition of progress.[19] She is not a Puritan/Yankee ma-
terialist, but she is a moral product of the New England
gentry nonetheless. Women, she writes, want the freedom
not only of religion but of the intellect so as to enable them
to comprehend the meaning of religion. In this way only can
they develop their strength and beauty. Woman's essentially
electrical, magnetic element never has been developed fully;
yet she is born for the universal energy of truth and love.
"... The law of right, the law of growth, speaks in use and
demands perfection of each being in its kind--apple as apple,
Woman as Woman."[20] This expansive intellectual consciousness is typified by the Spartan-like matron, Madame Roland.
Women and men assist one another to attain this "sublime
priesthood of nature." In perfect freedom, they will be as
"enfranchised souls" and "purified intelligence." Freedom is
not fearful, but the acknowledged slavery of women and men
is. As slaves, women and men are but "work tools" and
"articles of property."[21] Inevitably every member of this
nation must achieve the external freedom won for the nation
itself. Thought will stimulate action in this regard, and action will flow into the evolution of even higher thought, with
reverence for inherited limits and decorum all the while.

Fuller links the implications of national freedom to the
lives of women and men. In doing so, she stresses the restraint of inheritance and decorum. She focuses upon a mystical intellectual element. American mysticism is not Puritanic in derivation--it is Quaker--but the focus on intellect
is gentry-like, and the gentry were Puritans. She does not
discuss success, and she explicitly denies license. Freedom
of religion and intellect in the context of woman's strength
and beauty is not wholly radical. Americans are accustomed
to thinking about women in terms of religion and beauty, at
least. Fuller cautions that such thinking must not stop with
"the vulgar error that a love to woman is her entire existence."[22] Woman has a quality of energy about her which
transcends such narrow definition. God is the guide and
judge of woman's use of this birthright.[23] Woman's energy

is at once spiritual and magnetic, drawing unto herself as her understanding of that energy is propelled inevitably onward. In Fuller's eyes, woman is the same fair bright personage that liberty is in Wheatley's.

When the organizers of the Seneca Falls Convention issue their own Declaration of Independence, the Declaration of Sentiments and Resolutions, among their first assertions is the proposition that women and men "are endowed by their Creator with certain inalienable rights; that among these are life, liberty, and the pursuit of happiness." Enlightenment and progress have not advanced to a stage which wholly admit liberty for women. There is, however, enough enlightenment and progress to stimulate action by a select group of women and men. Their action shows that something can be done and defines what that something is for others. For Harriot K. Hunt, it is "freedom to think our own thoughts, freedom to utter them, freedom to live out the promptings of our inner life." Such freedom includes education, remuneration and taxation. It is the "legitimate outbirth of the eternal law of progress," and its demands are made in the name of justice. "All nature speaks of freedom. Thy childish thought, thy first ray of intelligence, thy first perceptions of cause and effect, led thee in harmony with nature, which is free and unfettered to ask freedom for thyself."[24]

For Hunt, as in the sciences, great truths cluster together about humanity's future. Human hope centers on it alone in a most healthful sense.[25] The central question about freedom is sex, yet freedom is neither male nor female. It is "the law of individualism ... and growth." Woman is as human as man and shares with him a birthright of education and freedom. She must gain freedom to follow her mind's natural direction. Hunt and Fuller closely link freedom and inner life for women and men alike. Whatever benefits may flow from freedom, and Hunt introduces some material ones, will be forthcoming from the mind's natural proclivities. Give individual intelligence free rein, and hope and perfection will follow after. Most importantly, hope and perfection are for humanity and not men alone. For Hunt, they are attained through a life in which a profession plays a large role. She recalls, "my medical life has trained me to an individuality which I have never regretted."[26] Home and profession are married in her life.[27] The possibility that humans may not have access to equal intelligence is not at issue here. The point is that women and men must have the freedom to pursue their natural inclinations in this regard. Fuller suggests women possess unique attributes when it comes to truth and love. Hunt is more concerned with the attributes women bring to the medical profession. Hers is the more narrow focus, but her discussion of inner freedom presumably is applicable to everyone.

The most systematic and comprehensive statement about liberty by a prefeminist thinker is John Stuart Mill's On Liberty, published in 1859. It is known that Harriet Taylor Mill helped to compose the treatise before her death in 1858. Currin Shields points out that John Mill's best work is done in association with Harriet Taylor.[28] Alice Rossi quotes from Mill's biography an attribution of joint production to On Liberty.[29] The treatise's dedication has the last word on the matter: "Like all I have written for many years, it belongs as much to her as to me...." John goes on to regret that Harriet did not live to assist with revision and re-examination, but first and foremost offers the book to the "memory of her who was the inspirer, and in part the author, of all that is best in my writings." The book itself does not address specifically the question of sex and liberty, one must assume because the question is neither female nor male--as Hunt puts it. It makes woman's inclusion explicit by reference, however. In discussing to whom the doctrine does not apply, it states "we are not speaking of children or of young persons below the age which the law may fix as that of manhood or womanhood."[30]

Much of On Liberty is concerned with freedom of thought processes. It begins citing the importance of enforcing restraints upon action, especially with regard to majority tyranny. This tyranny has much to do with predominant opinion and feeling.[31] It might be added that the cult of True Womanhood is one example of such tyranny. For the Mills, the problem is that societal should's and personal preferences often supersede concern for individuals. The Mills advance the principle that individual, collective or magisterial interference with liberty of action is warranted only for self-protection or to prevent harm to others. Liberty itself is applicable only when mankind is able to benefit by free and equal discussion.[32] The appropriate sphere for human liberty includes inner consciousness, taste and planning one's life in combination with others.[33] Fuller and Hunt's concerns are represented well here.

For the Mills, rational assurance that an opinion is correct for purposes of action can come only upon confronting

the opinion. One must hear all sides of an issue. At the
same time, following a thought to its conclusion contributes
much to the mental stature of both great thinkers and average
human beings. Truth likely is to be found in balancing these
thoughtful conclusions. The more certainty there is to a conclusion, the greater the need to pursue it further. Truth is
largely a question "of the reconciling and combining of opposites" in a process of struggle. An assumption of human
fallibility plays a large role here as well as the possibility
that any opinion may include a modicum of truth. The truest
of opinions, however, can descend to the level of prejudice and
be deprived of its vitality as a result. [34] Human energy is capable of good but can turn to evil when tied to a weak conscience.
Impulse and restraint must be related positively by socially cultivating strong susceptibilities to virtue and self-control.

According to the Mills, genius flourishes only "in an
atmosphere of freedom," for people of genius seldom fit social molds. They are above all individuals. Unfortunately
individuals largely are lost in the collective mediocrity of
mass public opinion. For America, this refers to the white
population; for England, the middle class. Progressiveness
ceases when people no longer possess individuality. People
generally desire progress but react negatively to individuality. [35] For liberty to exist among people, two general maxims
must be observed: first, individuals are not accountable to
society for personal actions affecting only their interests;
and second, individuals are accountable to society for actions
which prejudicially affect others' interests. Social or legal
sanctions may be enacted where social protection is in order.
"The principle of freedom cannot require that [one] should be
free not to be free," but it is consistent with certain limitations on freedom. The practical principle by which these are
enacted has to do with disseminating power as efficiently as
possible, while centralizing information and its diffusion.
There is tension within this principle, as there is between the
Mills' two general maxims. [37] This problem is discussed
briefly in the feminism and family chapter. The greatest
problem On Liberty introduces for feminists is how women
are to realize the benefit of their experiences and natural
aptitudes in the context of majority tyranny. The majority
includes women as well as men. Applying the Mills' thought,
those who would improve woman's position must cultivate their
own individuality, wedding conscience firmly to individuality.
They then must cope with mass public opinion, the effect of
which potentially is stifling. They must be willing to reconcile and combine their opinions with opinions antithetical to
their own.

It has been noted that women generally have rather
narrow experiential spheres, allowing for some slippage in
their missionary type activities. Their aptitudes largely are
undeveloped, although education for women is beginning to expand and woman's moral aptitude is conceded widely. The
practical answer to the dilemma seems to lie in using woman's experience, however narrow, and her aptitude, however
undeveloped, as a basis for asserting the justice of her
claim to liberty. In fact, this is what women's advocates
are doing. Examining feminist thought about two key issues,
family and education, strongly suggests this is the case.
Combining such advocacy with a wait-and-see attitude seems
the logical approach to take. The other alternative would be
to overthrow the existing state of affairs entirely. Historically this does not take place. It is a recognized alternative,
however, and it will be discussed further with feminism and
equality. Stressing liberty is a pacific solution stressing development of women's and men's inner selves. It posits restraints which may be social or legal but which also may be
individual, as in the case of conscience. As in early liberal thought, restraint is warranted only for self-preservation and perpetuating the species. Perpetuation of the species and preservation of woman, frail being she is believed
to be, are advanced most often as arguments against changing
woman's position. Feminist thought confronts these arguments in terms of family and education. At the same time,
it argues for woman's liberty in liberal and transcendental
formats.

Female liberty, as a result, is tied inextricably to the
path of duty. Women in the family setting have duties they
must fulfill. Educated women undertake responsibilities to
their children and society which must be met. Liberty must
not interfere with these and, more, must enhance their performance. This difficult theme is presented and elaborated
by feminist thinkers many times over. It is a way of linking
past and custom with future and change. Woman's past may
be undesirable in many aspects, but it is irreversible.
Feminists seeking future change must contend with it. Writing in 1867, George Eliot--an English author well known to
American feminists--deals with the irreversible past in the
context of duty in The Spanish Gypsy. The result is a tragedy.

Fedalma, who does not know her past, is betrothed
to a Spanish nobleman, Don Silva. She ponders her forthcoming wifely duties:

That very thing that when I am your wife
I shall be something different--shall be
I know not what, a dutchess with new thoughts--
For nobles never think like common men,
Nor wives like maidens (oh, you wot not yet
How much I note, with all my ignorance), --
That very thing has made me more resolve
To have my will before I am your wife. [38]

Zarca, Fedalma's father, reveals himself to her, and her
past becomes apparent. She is of the Zencala, a tribe of
Spanish gypsies. Her future is to dedicate herself to the
tribe's regeneration. She is born to reign. "'T is a compulsion of a higher sort,/ Whose fetters are the net invisible/
That holds all life together."[39] Her hereditary duty demands
that she not marry Don Silva. "Enslave yourself to use your
freedom?" asks Zarca.[40] The duties of wife and queen are
irreconcilable. Fedalma's freedom is determined by her
birth. She is at once right and law. It is a crown of thorns
for Fedalma, the woman, whose crown is love, however.[41]
She muses sadly about her gypsy attendant who "knows no
struggles, sees no double path;/ Her fate is freedom, for
her will is one/ With the Zencala's law, the only law/ She
ever knew." For herself, "For me--oh, I have fire within,/
But on my will there falls the chilling snow...."[42]

Freedom unsheathed has a double-edged blade. For
the woman in love, it promises freedom within right and law.
For the woman born to reign, womanly duty is superseded by
her existence as right and law. Both positions require voluntarily accepted restraint, and both positions compel freedom.
One cannot occupy them both simultaneously. Fedalma cannot
be subject to her husband and exist as right and law. She
cannot yield to her birthright and wear the crown of her love
for Don Silva. A choice must be made. She is accountable
to her people before Don Silva. The restraint of her heredity
is upon her. The compulsion is of a higher sort. Fedalma's
future can be understood only in terms of her past. Woman's
sphere and aptitude is appropriate for woman; it is not appropriate for a queen. Fedalma is compelled to be free. The
regeneration of her tribe depends upon it. The path of duty
is marked by struggle.

Ultimately and logically, the irreconcilable requirements of duty must be confronted and taken to their conclusion.
In fact, this does not occur. Feminist thinkers do as humans
are wont, take reality as they find it and deal with it. They

show that something can be done and define that something
for others. The requirements of family and education are
foremost in their minds and to them they must and do respond. Feminist thought is shaped to meet these issues in
the discussion of liberty. The tragedy of irreconcilable duty
is circumvented but not solved, remaining ever-present behind feminist thought. By adhering to liberal and transcendental formats, feminist thinkers avoid meeting the problem
head-on. They confine their thought about liberty to developing the inner self of women and men and to giving intelligence
free rein. The final consequences go unexplored except in
the most immediate sense.

Frances Wright speaks earlier about the necessity of
knowledgeable opinions, which will be just in their virture
and truth. Such opinions require both freedom of the mind
and teachers of fact rather than opinion. As such, they constitute individual conclusions reached "in the sacred and free
citadel of the mind and there enshrined beyond the arm of the
law...." If civil liberty is based on ignorant opinions unfounded in fact, then "better the wild freedom of the wild
hunter."[43] One could apply these remarks, although not
specifically addressed to the cause of female liberty, to the
cult of True Womanhood. They would seem to justify extreme
individualism, even anarchy, as a response. On the other
hand, the Mills suggest the more practical response: following such opinions to their conclusion and then reconciling and
combining them with their opposites. If the question of how
to accomplish this is overlooked, the rationale seems ideal.
It is a relatively easy case, however. A much harder case
is the very unpopular opinion which may be altogether rational
and which even may be presented in a public forum and hence
open to debate. When that opinion is offered in the name of
female liberty, the response is more difficult. One expects
public opinion to condemn that opinion, however unjust its action may be. What about feminist opinion, however?

The difficult case in point is Victoria Woodhull's advocacy of free love within the principle of social freedom. In
a lecture delivered at New York's Steinway Hall in 1871,
Woodhull begins by asserting that freedom means to be free.
Freedom can occur only when government's true function is
realized; that is, to protect an individual's exercise of right
as determined by the individual. No interference with an individual is warranted unless someone's rights are being in-
fringed by another's exercise of right. Where the individual
is governed by others, despotic government exists. In de-

manding social freedom, Woodhull asks that government be administered in the spirit of free and equal women and men's inalienable rights. These include life, liberty and the pursuit of happiness, "nothing more, nothing less."[44] Only freedom offers safety and happiness, everything that is pure and good. It is a concept even more beautiful than love. The perfect and harmonious interrelationship of freedom and love, the practical antithesis of lust, promises a perfected human being. Woodhull attests, 'I believe in love with liberty; in protection without slavery; in the care and culture of offspring by new and better methods, and without the tragedy of self-immolation on the part of the parents."[45]

Woodhull's name probably is guaranteed infamy the moment she suggests freedom and love could or should be interrelated. Elizabeth Cady Stanton gives one example of this in her autobiography when she tells about Dr. Patton of Howard University, who preached a sermon on "Women and Skepticism" in 1885. He suggested that freedom for women leads to skepticism and immorality. He cited as one example Victoria Woodhull. She is in good company, however, with Mary Wollstonecraft, Frances Wright, George Eliot, Harriet Martineau and Madame Roland, among others.[46] The impact of Woodhull's suggestion within the woman's movement is devastating. Without recounting its history, suffice it to say that most condemned and few made the effort to reconcile or combine her thoughts with their own. Stanton is among the few who refuse to stoop to recrimination. After Woodhull involves herself in personal scandal beyond the lecture in Steinway Hall, Stanton writes Lucretia Mott that no one should pry into Woodhull's private affairs. She suggests individual experience is too sacred to stoop to exposé. "This woman stands before us today as an able speaker and writer. Her face, manner, and conversation all indicate the triumph of the moral, intellectual and spiritual."[47] It must be said that the feminist call to liberty is not entirely consistent. It is noteworthy, however, that one of the great feminist thinkers does decline to stoop to exposé. The Mills make it clear analytically what a difficult position this can be. One expects nothing less of Elizabeth Cady Stanton. Woodhull makes her choice but exercises little restraint in doing so. In flaunting woman's law unto herself, she ensures her own downfall.

Thus the family is to retain its place, at least--as Ezra Heywood puts it in 1877--in the narrow sense. "Enlightened liberty will eliminate its defects and universalize its merits."[48] The citizen rather than the family is to be considered the social unit, with each "individual moral being a law unto itself. " Woman holds her citizenship by virtue of God's will; it is a fact of her existence. Furthermore, "liberated, self-loyal womanhood" will build the bridge from isolation to society with her "intelligent moral sense. " Otherwise liberty is not the fair bright woman commonly portrayed. Liberty out from under woman's rule becomes libertine--male and incontinent. Women and men must come to know truth and honor and entertain an intelligent interdependence. In possession of their rights, they should be impelled to the corresponding duties. [49] Holding woman in political servitude no more constitutes republican government than compelling dissenting men to political fidelity does. In civil liberty, each individual acts as he/she will, limited only by the right of others to do the same. Institutions and individuals who would deny woman her rights and citizenship must face woman's judgment. [50]

The sanction is a preordained one. Man is only half himself without woman, and woman only half herself without man. What they require is a love relationship which is "select, intimate and refining. " This less formal and less promiscuous mutuality will come about through growth and historical progress as democracy leaves its embryonic state. In determining what basic right is, diversity ensues; the whole acknowledges its parts and its sources. To forestall such growth would be revolutionary. Arguments against woman suffrage are no more than an attempt to maintain an outgrown order; they could be used as well to justify slavery or imperialism. [51] In stating women and men cannot become total individuals without one another, Heywood hearkens Fuller and Rousseau before her. The remainder of his analysis belongs to Wollstonecraft and Locke's lineage. He moves from woman's law unto herself, through mother right up to the fringe of a higher evolutionary law. He looks to revision of woman and man's love relationship but does so well within the bounds of social mores.

Advocating female liberty is not without its problems. It is largely a pacific solution assumed to have natural compulsion about it. Liberty will develop naturally, and with its development, society will recognize it necessarily entails women as well as men. Prefeminist thinkers acknowledge that the attainment of liberty can entail a struggle. Liberty, however, typically is associated with peace. In fact, peace is essential to the enjoyment of liberty. Without peace, liberty exists at best tenuously. One who wants to enhance liberty's development needs to support peaceful means and times.

Near the turn of the century, a work appears which strongly suggests liberty's natural development is not the smooth process it appears to be. This work suggests that attaining liberty may not be as peaceful a solution as is believed. Frederick Engels, in The Origin of the Family, Private Property and the State (1891), traces the transition from hetaerism to monogamy and from mother right to father right. Hetaerism is an early state of sexual promiscuity which--because it excludes certainty about paternity--requires descent through the female line according to mother right. As men become indispensable because of their activities outside the home and as the concept of property evolves, sexual relations become contractual and monogamous. Descent now is reckoned by father right. Woman is reduced to servitude, enslaved by man's lust, within the boundaries of her reproductive function. [52] The state arises to moderate the conflict wrought by cleavages between rich and poor, free men and slaves. [53] Woman is confined to private domestic labor. Her emancipation is impossible as long as she remains alienated from socially meaningful productive labor. [54]

According to Engels, the basal cell of civilized society becomes monogamous marriage. It is characterized by serious contradictions, sanctioning an institutionalized form of adultery for man but not woman. The formerly communistic household provides women with public, socially necessary labor. Once this labor is privatized, woman becomes man's possession, and sexual love is a thing of the past. Woman's enslavement constitutes the first historic class opposition and oppression. Marital freedom requires abolishing capitalistic production and its contractual relations. Economics then will not determine woman's choice of a marriage partner. Mutual inclination will replace economics, and persons will be free to love and return love. [55] Abolishing capitalistic production and contractual relations is not likely to be accomplished peacefully. In fact, Engels states increasing violence will be manifest as contradictions inherent in this system necessarily assert themselves. Engels' theory will be dealt with further in terms of feminism and equality. For now, the important point is the problematic nature of woman's attainment of liberty.

As stated earlier, many American thinkers do not know Marxist thought as such, but they are influenced by it pervasively. [56] Engels himself discusses published work which is known: that of J. J. Bachofen (1861), John Ferguson McLennan (1886) and Henry Morgan (1871). It may be

assumed that there is growing awareness of the problems discussed above, even as feminist ideals are being cast in a social Darwinist evolutionary context. Feminist thought, despite its anthropological and sociological overtones, remains
idealistic, however, and awareness of the problematic nature
of attaining female liberty never is made explicit. Matilda
Gage, for example, discusses the pronounced conflict between
natural and revealed or divine rights in America and predicts
it will develop fully and finally. She expresses confidence
that church and state tyranny will be overthrown by progress,
resulting in a regenerated world. [57] Gage is reacting to the
patriarchal influence of the Five Books of Moses which de-
lineate what Engels labels the bourgeois family, if discussions
about polygamy are eliminated. Engels deplores the mysticism
characteristic of religion when it becomes a mechanism for
determining the direction of history. [58] On this much, Gage
and Engels are agreed. With Engels, Gage also foresees
elongated and heightened conflict based on inherent contradiction. For Gage, the end to conflict and the resumption of
progress will be forthcoming through the political doctrine of
individual sovereignty, however. The fact that woman enjoys
increasing freedom is because civilized forms such as the
printing press, education and free thought are advancing. [59]

For Gage, the very progress which is going to overthrow church and state tyranny is being impeded by conflict
between natural and revealed rights. The political doctrine
of individual sovereignty, which is being realized by woman's
increasing freedom, can bring an end to conflict and the resumption of progress. Gage seems to be aware of some problems in liberty's natural development along with progress
(or, civilization), and she introduces a Marxian type of explanation for them. She concludes, however, with a rather
lame statement about the fact that woman's freedom is increasing and this in the context of individual sovereignty will
end any delay. She sees the War for Independence as striking a blow against tyranny based on belief in woman's inability to care for herself. [60] One assumes this blow exacerbates
conflict between natural and revealed rights. According to
Gage, however, it also should help end conflict that progress
may resume. Gage suggests neither church thought nor legal
conception recognizes that woman is created for herself as
an individual being to whom all opportunities should be open
because of herself. Further, the family is not yet founded
on this premise. [61] If this is so, how then is the political
doctrine of independent sovereignty being accomplished through
woman's increasing freedom? Gage would answer woman is

learning for herself that her first duty in life is self-development and realization rather than self-sacrifice. [62]   Even if
church and state do not know woman's duty, woman increasingly does.   She knows because she is better educated, because there is more printed matter for her consumption, because printing makes it possible to communicate new ideas
more rapidly and because freedom of thought is more and
more the norm.   How will this new-found knowledge bring
an end to conflict between natural and revealed rights?   That
much is far from clear.   Supposedly it will destroy the protective spirit which typifies revealed rights, but how this is
to take place is not apparent.

It might be added that not all women, according to
Gage, know their duty lies with self-development.   Unknowing
women, enslaved as they are by self-sacrifice, declare against
their own freedom and attempt to hinder such declaration by
women who would end the bondage.   Furthermore, men are
influenced by revealed right and do not accept women as part
of humanity.   They do not know that whether woman's influence on life is good depends upon the extent of her freedom. [63]   The question of how woman's new-found knowledge
will conclude conflict between natural and revealed rights is
complicated by the facts that not all women share this knowledge and that men do not accept women as part of humanity.
The only thing certain about liberty, beyond its expression
by a person's innermost self, seems to be that feminist
thinkers revere it.   Matilda Gage's gravestone reads: "There
is a word sweeter than Mother, Home, or Heaven; that word
is Liberty. "[64]   Women are believed to love liberty as much
as men, such love being a justifiable extension of the right
to consent to one's government.   All national progress is
concerned with extending and applying this proposition.   Reform in harmony with it must be right. [65]   Women trained to
think, write and speak discover they have a stake in liberty;
new individualistic ideas are heavy with hopes for female
liberty; woman, at the proper point in the progress of civilization, spontaneously will begin to insist upon a broader
sphere of action. [66]   The argument may be problematic, but
the sentiment behind it is clear.

It also seems clear that the classical liberal ideas on
which feminist thought about liberty is based preclude in-
depth Marxist analysis.   This is so even though Marxist
thought at least implicitly influences feminist thinkers.   They
sense, as a Marxist would, that conflict somehow holds the
key to change but continually refer to the unidirectionality of

change as a classical liberal would. That is, they believe
society inevitably is progressing to a perfect end state in
which women will attain liberty rather than about to erupt
because of contradictions inherent in existing conflict. Those
of transcendental and Rousseauian persuasion, for example
Fuller, see paradox or dualism as a central fact of existence;
harmony rather than struggle based on the dualism is of
central importance to them, however. Feminist thinkers, in
embracing a socioanthropological perspective, undertake a
kind of Marxian materialism, but their consciousness is non-
Marxist given its reliance on idealism. They begin to make
what they believe is the economic nature of woman's enslavement explicit, as in Charlotte Perkins Gilman's Women and
Economics, and they appreciate how this molds institutions
as a Marxist would. Essentially, though, they suggest institutional organization is evolving toward a more civilized end
state, as a classical liberal would. If they had a Marxist
perspective, they would expect institutional change to occur
when economic contradiction becomes most acute. Thus,
while it can be said there is much about Marxism which over-
laps with feminist libertarian thought, there is much which is
not Marxist at all in feminist thought. A rather incomplete
feminist discussion about liberty is the result of a predominantly liberal/transcendental concept influenced partially by
Marxist ideas.

Thus Julia Ward Howe can write, at the age of 83 in
1901, that "true womanliness must grow and not diminish in
its larger and freer exercise."[67] For her and for feminist
thinkers generally, progress is inevitable and with it the extension of freedom to women. The past is irreversible, however, and inevitably will have its own impact on the future.
Even though true womanhood and liberty may appear contradictory, in the end they somehow will be harmonized. Howe
suggests woman's duty no longer can be defined precisely,
but barbaric obstructions to her progress must be removed.
With progress comes the ideal condition of freedom now attractive to women as well as men; womanhood no more can
prosper in tyranny than manhood can. With freedom comes
a cooperative force among women based on identical interests.
These interests for Howe probably best are described in
terms of worthier views of marriage, parentage, culture and
commonality.[68] Womanhood possesses a dynamic power of
movement as well as traditional creative but static power as
mother of the race and homemaker.[69] This is not a revolutionary creed. Liberty is conceived within traditional, albeit revised, perimeters. Problems which could require con-

sideration of thorough change are bypassed. This probably
is not so much deliberate as it is necessitated by the primary
analytic framework. It constitutes a distinct intellectual limitation within this body of thought.

G. Stanley Hall observes that unmarried American women by the age of 30 feel a passion for happiness as intense
as that experienced by French revolutionaries and suffragists. [70] Hall, as discussed earlier, does not find this desirable because of the danger such a choice poses to perpetuating the species. Christopher Lasch suggests retrospectively
that social critics in the early part of the twentieth century
fail to develop theory which potentially could guide social behavior. [71] As a result, Hall's concern probably is not well
founded. Neither suffragists nor feminist thinkers produce a
rigorous body of interlinking generalizations which could be
labeled theory. However much they extol the desirability of
life, liberty and the pursuit of happiness for women as well
as men, they themselves do not provide the means or the
logic by which to institute far-reaching change in woman's position. At times their thought is quite suggestive in this regard, but it never is concretized. Lasch believes the personalized nature of the generalizations dilutes their usefulness
as the basis for more theoretical constructs. [72] Libertarian
thought in feminist literature is tied to inner states, as has
been discussed. Twentieth-century feminist thought about
liberty becomes highly inner-directed. In surveying it,
Lasch's comments should be kept in mind.

That said, one also needs to consider the role ideas
play in American thought. Feminist thought is very much
part of this tradition. If this be a limitation, it is quite an
understandable one. Henry Steele Commager notes the "intense practicality" of American thought which is, as a result,
little given to recondite philosophy. [73] If anything, American
thinkers are suspicious of such abstruseness. In this context, feminist assertion that "the tendency of woman's mind,
at this stage of her development, is toward practical rather
than toward speculative science" makes sense. [74] It is a
statement about potential and reality, as discussed in the education chapter, but it also is a product of typical American
intellectual processes. As Paul Kurtz puts it:

... One characteristic then seems to distinguish
the American tradition: Ideas are evaluated prag-
matically, and their significance is most frequently determined by reference to their practical con-

texts, their political, religious, moral or social
purposes. Thinking is a form of activity: and
there is great confidence and optimism in the ability of knowledge to solve the problems of men. [75]

Thus feminist thought about liberty considers what is feasible
in the context of the past and present. There it makes its
stand. A thinker such as Victoria Woodhull never could hope
to survive in such a situation. Advocating free love within
social freedom contradicts social mores and woman's law unto herself. The advocacy of free love may be a logical extension of liberty, but it is not a practical idea. It is not
an appropriate or useful solution for women's problems.

One recalls Ida Tarbell's insistence that freedom is
but a tool to an end. [76] Scott and Nellie Nearing stress the
constant responsibility of choice which freedom entails. [77]
These are two sides of the central concern with practicality.
If freedom is only a means, it must not become an end in
itself. Thus Mercy Warren fears widely disseminating Voltaire's thought. Citing the responsibility that freedom carries with it also is a cautionary note. Responsibilities must
be fulfilled; best they not be too overwhelming. Liberal
theorists focus on the horrible burden absolute freedom imposes. For the Nearings, only slaves have the freedom to do
whatever they will. With woman's emancipation comes the
duty to make choices about the use of liberty. Rather than
implying license, liberty requires that women accept the duty
it imposes on them. [78]

Response to feminist thought about liberty indicates
the critical intellectual environment with which feminist thinkers must cope. Ethel Maud Colquhoun, for example, writes
that change and progress are not necessarily the same thing.
For her, feminist demands that women have the right to bodily realization on their own terms and in their own ways
amount only to a shibboleth based on individualism. [79] Mr.
and Mrs. John Martin are even more devastating in their
criticism. Mr. Martin charges that in seeking a new freedom
for women, freedom from maternity, feminism actually adds
to the burdens of motherhood. Most women will become
mothers anyway; in addition to their already heavy responsibilities, feminists would add the necessity of earning a living.
Woman's bondage thereby is doubled rather than lightened. [80]
He goes on to contrast feminism with humanism. Where
feminism is individualistic, humanism is socially oriented.
Feminism is anarchistic; humanism is family oriented.

Feminism is "centripetal"; that is, a force impelling women
into themselves. Humanism is "centrifugal," impelling women
outward. Feminism believes women are inferior, where humanism believes they are superior. Humanism welcomes
maternity and would make it as painless and carefree as possible by exempting women from earning their own living.
For the humanist, unlike the feminist, motherhood is a natural right. [81]

Mrs. Martin composes a dialogue among Commercial-
ism, Necessity and Feminism which is particularly damning.
With Mr. Martin and Ethel Colquhoun, she sees freedom as
the watchword of feminism. Feminism does all its work in
the name of freedom, ignoring woman's natural tastes. [82]
The result is that even Mrs. John Martin must cultivate an
artificial taste for politics and go out into the world to combat feminism. That statement is inconsistent with Mr. Martin's assertion that humanism is the centrifugal force, feminism the centripetal one. Furthermore, feminist thought
does not demand that woman be freed from maternity altogether. It demands the means, for example birth control,
to loosen the bondage of motherhood. Feminist thinkers
stress individualism in a libertarian context, but they also
stress social ties, as has been discussed. Feminist thought
has some anarchistic implications, but above all it is family
oriented. Finally, feminist thinkers criticize those whom
they perceive as suggesting woman is inferior; they seek a
broader, more socially useful sphere for woman which includes motherhood and which may include material reimbursement.

Feminist thinkers believe their plan is founded on love,
with happiness the end-in-view. Nevertheless, their plan is
misapprehended seriously by the Martins. This strongly suggests the potentially incendiary nature of the subject matter.
It also helps to clarify the practical impetus in feminist
thought. Volatile subject matter is bound to generate intense
criticism. Approaching it as practically as possible by instituting careful limitations on a concept such as liberty is
quite possibly the only way feminist thinkers will be heard at
all. To do otherwise is to risk flat rejection by nearly everyone, just as Victoria Woodhull does. The Mr. and Mrs. John
Martins may not hear what feminist thinkers actually say, but
there are others less extreme in viewpoint who might be more
receptive. Perhaps the really remarkable thing is that feminist thinkers manage to be as radical and futuristic as they
are. They work in a primarily liberal/transcendental frame-

work well within American intellectual tradition and risk
grave misunderstanding as it is.

One of feminist thinkers' strongest strategic points,
despite its limitations, may be the part feminism plays in
the progress of democratic freedom. Beatrice Forbes-Robertson Hale believes democracy is the mother of feminism.
The women's movement is born in the ideal of individual liberty. The failure of democracy to destroy the domination of
men over women is not being rectified. Hale quotes Madame
Roland: "O Liberty, what crimes are committed in thy name. "
In its adolescence, democracy begins to translate its ideal into accepted practice. The maturity of democracy rests not
in individualism and demands for freedom but in collectivism
and demands for happiness. [83] Freedom, however, offers
sentient beings the opportunity to display their capacities.
Hale finds this a strong base on which to build the feminist
position. [84] The problem is to make the transition from individualism to collectivism. Thinkers such as Gilman believe
the transition takes place in evolutionary process. This adds
a scientific overlay to belief in inevitable progress. It does
not necessarily solve the problem of how obstacles to progress
will be removed.

The assumption throughout this body of thought is that
once women gain control of their individual capacities the
problem will take care of itself. Given liberty, women will
develop their inner selves and thereby take control of their
lives. Florence Guertin Tuttle discusses this in terms of
psychic awakening. Feminism is a matter of spiritual initiative and impulse which is both natural and scientific. As a
social and spiritual question, feminism ultimately is a race
problem existing on three planes: body, mind and spirit. [85]
The libertarian stream in feminist thought applies itself to
awakening women's minds. Ellen Key discusses this in terms
of educating feelings. Women always have applied existing
laws and morals to life. They better will be able to do this
once they are in touch with their feelings, many of which
stem from their maternal capacity. Morals are a fund of human experience and actions possessing life preserving and enhancing value for individuals and society. The relation between women and morals is a pacific one. [86]

Key acknowledges that throughout history woman's will
is directed toward fulfillment of her eternal destiny in wifeliness and motherhood at home. Woman's will, however, is
turning gradually to the liberation of her womanly power for

personal development and activity within and without the home. The spector and reality of world war make this an inevitable necessity. Women's experiences in war are heart-rending. Their sons and husbands die or are mutilated. Their families are separated, perhaps never to reunite. Young women's hopes of marriage and family are destroyed. Women understand only too well war's horrors and in their understanding experience a general increase in their self-esteem which makes their "helplessness as citizens intolerable." Those women who support war and hatred experience "an unbalanced state of mind." It is fortunate that women are not among the strong sent off to war. Spared from destruction, their social work as life conservers gives them the opportunity to perceive through their emotions. By virtue of motherhood, women share a common dual purpose: the creation of a child and the development of humanity. "The thoughts and feelings of women may become an undercurrent that breaks the ice formed by the habit of thought over man's feelings for, and opinions about, war." [87]

According to Key, war renders woman's fulfillment of her natural duty, motherhood, unlikely. Furthermore, it destroys the strongest members of the male sex, defeating the evolutionary mandate that only the fittest shall survive. Thus it is that women must "arise and hold together in the will to make an end to this state of affairs that has for century after century made the goal of their mother love and mother labours so meaningless." Women in effect must wage war against war, enter into holy revolt. They will do this pacifically, teaching their children that there is a natural law of mutual help between individuals and nations as well as a natural law of competition. Mother and earth, through their renewal powers, will gain an honored position in the community, but it is through woman's fulfillment of her natural duty that this will come about. Woman will forego her patience and passivity, her untiring giving. (Man already has learned this is too much to expect of the earth.) She will rely on the "inmost strength" of her nature, translating it into "the great strength-giving feeling of one-ness with our kind." [88]

For Key, peace on earth is generated only from within. Its spirit is awakening in woman, even if it is only presently half conscious. More active pacifism by women will contribute to political reorganization. These thoughts must be expressed in "upbringing and education, in every speech and at every election, in every home, and in public

<u>life.</u> " In this way, woman will strengthen the bridge between past and future, showing the way to both. No more will woman be deceived by man's false beatitude of motherhood; no more will woman be the means to mass produce children who die for want of vitality or who are sapped in industry. [89]

> Something is about to happen to the wrong thinking
> to which mankind has been confined as in a herme-
> tically sealed glass bell. In the same way as a
> too-high tone of an instrument can break a glass
> so has the cry of suffering from the world agony
> made a crack in the glass bell. [90]

Thinking women precede the host of women and working men who will institute the conception of the state's duty to the individual, in place of the state's right over the individual. They advance the cause of international rights and duties. [91]

Key asserts that by influencing public opinion and gaining and using the vote, thinking women can accomplish a great deal in this direction. Yet one must not be overly optimistic about these means. Woman's suffrage may not have the influence it should have on world peace. Should woman sanction war as a means to settle national misunderstandings, she will defeat the very things she once claimed she would accomplish with her vote. "The 'militants' in the woman's movement have now, if ever, placed themselves in the position of self-contradiction that their false premises in the question of their own methods of combat were bound to bring them. "[92] Key begins to develop the answer to the hard question of how obstacles to progress will be removed from woman's path. Women's minds are awakening to the agonies and suffering which war brings to their lives and humanity. Though the spirit of peace is but half conscious within them, there is an inevitable necessity about liberating womanly power for emotional perception through the exercise of will. The duty of motherhood is expanding to include national political and moral responsibilities. Woman will fulfill her eternal destiny by means of a holy revolt which is both spiritual and moral and which begins within her. The thinking woman must lead the way to war's end once and for all by asserting the natural law of mutual help. She can do this by properly educating her children, by speaking out and by voting, in the home and in public life as well. Should woman sanction the natural law of competition by her actions, however, she will contradict herself, and her powers will be diluted. Collectivity and happiness are within woman's grasp, if only

she will use her individuality and freedom to fulfill her
duty.

Key, with other feminist thinkers, still is tied to the
notion of inevitable necessity, but she posits war as the
stimulus to woman's inner development and gives concrete
examples of how liberated womanly power can exercise its
will.   This in itself is a large step forward.   Her work on
war and peace has a more specific change orientation than
her work on the renaissance of motherhood.   This author
commented earlier that the latter work concedes to feminism's critics the biological bases for woman's position.
One also might note, however, that the critics are not any
kinder to Ellen Key than they are to feminist thinkers generally.   To give an example:

> The Professional Politician ... the popular preach-
> er ... can always and easily be bullied by the
> shrieking sisterhood.   Meanwhile, the soul of Su-
> san Anthony, like that of Old John Brown, goes
> marching on.   It goes marching on toward the
> Feminist goals of blatant infidelity, rejecting the
> religion of Christ and Him Crucified and repudi-
> ating the man-made Bible of Moses and the pro-
> phets in favor of Elizabeth Cady Stanton's 'Wo-
> man's Bible,' which teaches the religious here-
> sies of Voltaire, Paine and Ingersoll, along with
> the Free Love theory of Mary Wollstonecraft,
> Victoria Woodhull and Ellen Key. [93]

If nothing else, this demonstrates the serious pitfalls
faced by those who call upon women for collective action.
Not all women are going to be inclined to offer their support.
Key partially circumvents this by suggesting that right-thinking women will lead the way.   Right-thinking women are in
touch with their feelings and cognizant of their duty.   It is
their enhanced ability to perceive emotionally which sets them
apart from other women.   Women as a whole nevertheless
possess womanly power which they can use effectively once
their feelings are educated.   By learning the natural law of
mutual help, for which they presumably have an inclination,
women will mobilize to implement the holy revolt.   Gage and
Engels explicitly would add patriarchal law, the Five Books
of Moses, to a list of things against which to revolt.   Key,
however, really subsumes this into her thought. The point
for her, as for Harriot Stanton Blatch, is that women mobilize to conserve civilization and to direct the race more eco-

nomically. This they can do only by the broadest cooperative action.[94] For feminist thinkers, women are both conservative and liberal, static and dynamic. They would sustain humanity, to which they give birth, but they would change the conditions which make human life unbearable. While this is logical enough, the ultimate question of how to pass from one state to another is unsolved. One just does not expect individuals of a predominantly conservative orientation to be transformed into a liberal host over night. Perhaps it can and does take place, but the burden is upon feminist thinkers to demonstrate how the transition will come about. Their critics not only press that burden upon them, they make the problem itself more vivid.

In disbanding the suffrage movement after the Nineteenth Amendment is ratified, Carrie Chapman Catt looks forward to women "informing the whole field of public life with the woman spirit" rather than granting rewards to ammunition-making women. Members of the suffrage movement now must move on to translate for society the inner meanings which were their concern all along.[95] One recalls, however, that Catt leaves the Woman's Peace Party, the result of a 1915 alliance between Jane Addams and herself, after committing suffragists to the forthcoming war effort. She does this to improve chances for ratifying the suffrage amendment. In the end only U. S. Representative Jeannette Rankin's vote against the war in Congress stands as an expression of woman's pacific spirit.[96] The reality which feminist thinkers must confront is hard indeed. Women who should be their natural allies do not consistently support feminist ideas and ideals about liberty and peace. Perhaps in calling for woman's mobilization to end war, feminist thinkers breach the American tradition of practicality and diminish their opportunity for support. As Charles and Mary Beard point out in 1942, the American spirit admits to one invariable, war.[97] If one can support peace only in the absence of war, it is not a practical concern at all. If ever feminist thinkers need to develop overarching theory as a guide for concrete action, it is in the area of liberty and peace. Liberty and peace are essential to feminist thought, but they go begging for want of answers to hard questions. If womanhood is to shake off its bondage in favor of a liberated morality through which it can transmit the qualities which make for a greater race,[98] then it must know how this is to be accomplished. Giving women freedom to choose may not be enough.

The fact is that women can be aware of their problems

and yet unable to cope with them. Charlotte Perkins Gilman's The Yellow Wallpaper gets inside a woman who is angry about the impertinence and everlastingness of her existence. Her relief comes from expressing herself by ripping away the wallpaper which is a repellent, irritating and provocative reminder of her confinement. Amber Lee writes a possibly autobiographical statement which parallels Gilman's in its emphasis on mental instability. The insights of The Woman I Am are considerable. "A woman's life is so short. The best of it pressed into the shallow measure of 20 years. From 20 to 40 ... we women whom men buy cannot look forward to 50 or even 45 with optimism."[99] Yet there must be other means than madness to achieve a future and freedom.* Gaining inner awareness of the problems of one's existence without the means to achieve their solution is a hollow victory indeed.

Attempts at complete fulfillment in job and love life, which Elizabeth Breuer attributes to American feminists, are a big order. The choosing and dividing of self which such attempts entail have an aesthetic aspect to them, the key to which Breuer finds in a state of inner aliveness. Inner aliveness may be manifest in self consciousness as well.[100] Feminist thinkers would not want to suggest they are different from or superior to women as a whole. Feminist thought is premised on the potential that women harbor within. The feminist thinker's role is more that of intellectual catalyst than leader. If some women progress further than others, the assumption is that they will reach out a hand to assist others along the way. Attempts at inner self-development, if madness be one possible result, may call for something more than a catalyst. It is a paradoxical situation.

Whatever that something is to be, Suzanne LaFollette makes it clear that something is not the state or any kind of monopoly. Furthermore,

> Freedom implies the right to live badly, but it also implies the right to live nobly and beautifully; and for one who has faith in the essential goodness of the human spirit, in the natural aspiration toward perfection which flowers with touching beauty even in the bleak soil of that hardship, degradation and crime to which injus-

*Death is a kind of freedom but one without a future.

tice condemns the mass of humanity--for one who
has this faith in the human spirit, there can be
no question what its ultimate choice would be. [101]

She is implying that freedom to choose is enough for naturally
good human beings.   Freedom's essential nature is forthcoming from the abolition of monopoly, especially monopoly
of natural resources; thus individuals are free to apply their
productive labor wherever they will.   In this way, woman's
freedom is part of the larger question of human freedom, and
legal equality between women and men is not enough.   "How
this freedom is to be obtained is not for me to say." It is
more important that the nature of freedom be established
clearly. [102]

For LaFollette, current belief--that living, behaving
and desiring as the majority does is freedom--is mistaken.
It bespeaks coercion and intolerance, not freedom.   Women
must obtain freedom on their own behalf.   Until books about
women are of historical interest only, women cannot be assumed free.   The important thing is to get beyond arguing
woman's right in terms of her child-bearing function.   Woman's emancipation in the largest sense rests with abolishing
all restrictions on natural human rights.   The mass of humanity must not be subject to a privileged class.   Thus feminists must choose whether to join with humanists and pursue
the larger issue or to "play at political and social make-be-
lieve while the issue is being decided." [103]

The question for LaFollette is not how freedom is to
be reached, but what freedom means.   For her, as for Hunt,
freedom is neither male nor female, but part of a whole
sphere of natural human rights which must not be restricted
by any privileged class.   Human goodness assures that ultimately freedom will be used nobly and beautifully; thus LaFollette need not concern herself with women faltering in freedom.   The price of liberty then, as Alice Ames Winter
writes, must be self-control.   When women no longer are
coerced to live as custom dictates, they must force themselves to do things.   Inner compulsion to self-control is a
highly personalized mechanism in a broad context of natural
human rights. [104]   Every human bears the responsibility for
the use of freedom, however it may be reached.

There are many disappointments ahead for feminist
thinkers who subscribe to this creed.   Dorothy Parker makes
this bitingly clear in "Now at Liberty." She tells the tale of

one whose little white love deserts her, using her badly in
the process, while her heart is dying. Now that she is at
liberty, albeit suffering, her thoughts turn in asides to:
"(Whom shall I get by telephone);" "(Nevertheless, a girl
needs fun);" "(Which of the boys is still in town);" "(Nevertheless, a girl must eat);" "(Who'd like to take me out to-
night);" "(Nevertheless, a girl must live)."[105] The woman
is given her liberty in summary fashion by a man and seeks
to give it back to someone as soon as she possibly can.

The women about whom Parker writes are of one class
only and in that sense hers is a limited perspective. Feminist thinkers are not all as restricted in their libertarian
outlook, however. Fuller writes about women in prison;
many prefeminist thinkers are abolitionists and concerned for
black women, children and families; Willard, Addams and
Sanger work with poor women; Goldman is a member of that
class. Sometimes their thought is within a gentry framework; sometimes it is not. Agnes Smedley is among those
whose thought is presented in a working-class framework.
Her Daughter of Earth is a tragic statement about the meaning of liberty for a poor woman. Beside a Danish sea, she
writes in desperation and unhappiness about a ruined human
life, her own. "There have been days when it seemed that
my path would better lead into the sea. But now I choose
otherwise." She recalls the adventure of gazing upon her
mother's crazy quilt and resolves to make such a quilt of
the fragments of her life, "unity and diversity." She will
die for a cause someday, but for now she and her struggle
are of the earth.[106]

Marie Rogers, the focus of her tale, is born to extreme poverty, and her childhood is marked by deprivation
and beatings. She struggles throughout her life to gain an
education. She refuses duty. "'Dooties!'" Protection she
does not need because she can take care of herself. She is
driven to avoid the fate of women she knows, all of whom
marry a working man, bear many children whose fate is uncertain, and die early. She painfully shuns love. "I threw
up fortifications to protect myself from the love and tenderness that menace the freedom of women; I did not know then
that one builds fortifications only where there is weakness."
She believes she would rather become a prostitute than a
wife, although she never sells her body but marries twice
and enters secret love affairs.[107] Her life leads her to socialism and to prison. In prison a priest tells her, "It is
women like you who land in prison--you women who believe

in study instead of in a home or children. " She undergoes
two abortions and deserts her two small brothers--one of
whom later dies, one of whom lives to write her of the hopelessness and horror of World War I--but she salvages her
sister. 'I longed for tenderness, for love, but these I
feared. When one loves, one can easily be enslaved; and I
would not be enslaved. Freedom is higher than love. At
least today. Perhaps one day the two will be one. "[108] She
will not become private property; sex exists for her, but love
does not. Her public life is a good one. Still she longs for
understanding, tolerance and freedom. [109]

Smedley writes as one who consciously seeks freedom
but believes she never finds it. She rejects duty and responsibility but exercises control over her life nonetheless. Her
courage is great; her unhappiness profound. Somehow one
admires Agnes Smedley immensely; yet she herself seems to
find a liberal creed ultimately disappointing. Despite the
disappointment, Smedley is willing to pick up the pieces,
patch them together and move on with the struggle that life,
the earth itself, has in store. For her, liberty lies in its
pursuit, in her very existence, even though she believes she
never finds it. On one hand, it seems that few lives could
hold less potential than Smedley's for freedom. Her circumstances are dire, and her suffering is immense. Opportunities are few for her. On the other hand, it may be that her
life affords more potential than most in this regard. Her
will is strong, and her self-control is remarkable in many
ways. Beyond these, her awareness of the issue is clear
and fertile. This stands out, fair and bright, in Daughter of
Earth. Perhaps making the choice to be free, as LaFollette
suggests, is enough after all, even though freedom eludes the
chooser. Perhaps failure lies only in choosing not to be
free, although that in itself is a choice to be made.

Ellen Glasgow's autobiography, written from the standpoint of a gentry woman, is in some ways similar to Daughter
of Earth but not entirely. The libertarian issue for Glasgow
and Smedley is, in Glasgow's words, "the great discovery
that my own identity, that I myself, could triumph over brute
circumstances, [that discovery] destroyed and then re-created
the entire inner world of my consciousness. "[110] Glasgow
never marries, convinced she is unfitted to marriage, partially because she faces increasing deafness, and lacks a
maternal instinct. Further, she knows the close possessive-
ness of marriage is not what she needs in life. She loves
and is loved in return, but none of the relationships are last-

ing ones. One senses this is a relief for her. Most importantly, "what I wanted was not to know, but to live. To
live in the mind, it is true, but to live with certitude and
with serenity, with reason in the ascendant, but still in sympathy with all animate nature."[111] Much of this thought is
reflected in Smedley as well with some variation. Both women face divided selves, yearning on the one hand for love
and on the other for freedom. They both know struggle, and
in the end their longing for freedom prevails. Rather than
choosing and dividing themselves, they choose wholeness based
on the pursuit of liberty.

There is one essential difference to their stories.
Smedley perceives herself as an agent for change, Glasgow
does not. Glasgow tells how, as a small child, she saw an
old Negro man struggling as he is taken off to the poor
house. Her thoughts at that moment are that nothing she can
do will change the world. After 60 years, she discovers
there is nothing to be done about her own life any more than
the world in which she lives.[112] Smedley does not believe
she can change everything; thus she leaves her little brothers
behind. Her own life is an adventure, however, and there
are certain injustices in the world which she addresses as
well. Glasgow writes to release mind and heart; Smedley
to gather unity in diversity. Glasgow seems to have a far
more static or conservative libertarian posture in contrast to
Smedley's dynamic or liberal one. Here again there does not
seem to be much possibility for transition between one posture
and the other. Despite similitude in espousing a libertarian
creed, the two postures are worlds apart. Yet for those who
would move from individualism and freedom to collectivism
and happiness, it is important that the relative differences
here be bridged.

The schism for women between being static and being
dynamic is an old one; Ruth Herschberger suggests in "Anent
the Apple" that it is as old as Eden. There with Adam, Eve
finds her spirit choked.

> The Peace is a real but convalescent good,
> In Greenrushed Eden was its ancient bed.
> I loved it well, and followed where it led,
> Spoke when I dared, but listened when I should.
> Yet tired I, o weary of the green
> That I must be, I grew not, nor devoured
> What I would, but where blue cowslips flowed
> I lived discreet and full, not young nor keen.

...
No single fruit could do what knowledge did,
Show me diversity in bough and twig,
Give reason that was more than legal must. [113]

For Eve, life in perfect freedom is a static state. The
transition to knowledge and diversity is abrupt but worthwhile.
It takes an exercise of will to encounter knowledge and diversity and perhaps a lapse of duty as well.

One recalls Elizabeth Breuer's attribution of aestheti-
cism to the choosing and dividing of self which feminists undertake. Eve chooses and divides herself in a manner which
is condemned almost universally, leading as it does to a fall
from grace. For the religious, she raises the question of
morality; for the practical, the question of the usefulness of
her actions. For those aesthetically inclined, the question
has to do with the beauty of life itself. In America, women
control moral life through a law unto themselves. Their law
is structured within the American tradition of practicality and
given breadth by feminist thought. In Smedley and Glasgow,
especially the latter, an aesthetic aspect which transcends but
does not necessarily preclude considerations of morality and
usefulness appears. It is traceable to the paradoxes of Fuller
and Rousseau. The feminist aesthetic expression of liberty
is expressed most comprehensively by Anaïs Nin in her diaries. The diaries are chronological; over time Nin's art develops, and the themes become more explicit. Because the
libertarian issue raises important questions about how inner
self-development is begun and directed, the following discussion focuses on an early seminal diary.

Nin has been "humanly the least lonely of women, ...
surrounded by family, friends, all those I love, but there is
a world into which I go alone, a Tibetan desert." This world
she must enter boldly, with her feelings and insight alone, for
she is not bound to it as in human earthly marriage. Yet the
diaries are kept first in "an Arabian wedding-chest, violet
velvet with gold nails," and later in a locked bank vault among
others' valuables and legal papers. Art is Nin's only religion;
she does not believe in politics, living as she does at a time
of dissolution and disintegration. "I thought I too would dis-
solve. But my diary seems to keep me whole." She maintains her belief in people but never believes in systems. Her
creations are as woman's creation of children, of flesh and
different from man's abstractions. She creates an individually
perfect world which can be a refuge for others. Liberty must
come from within, not from outer systems. [114]

Facing page: "Christina's World" (1948), by Andrew Wyeth. Tempera on gesso panel, 32 1/2"x47 3/4" (collection, the Museum of Modern Art, New York.)

The beginnings of freedom are imitative for one such as Nin who does not lead a life of license. She obtains her hunger for life and freedom, her emotional freedom, from friends. She is happiest in her selfless days, but once personal growth and expansion begin, they cannot be halted. Woman, however, will be last to learn independence and to find strength in self. Her potential is tied to past loyalties, commitments and promises and human responsibilities, in the midst of which the self cannot develop.[115] Such personal patterns have deep roots and are slow to change in the face of insight. One can accelerate the process through psychoanalysis, but too much consciousness and awareness may be a dangerous shortcut. It is better to grow in depth, sublimating an intoxication with freedom and love of adventure. For Nin, this involves a search for a continuous life form such as the sea in one's subconscious. In flowing, drifting, living naturally, "I am always true to life, as woman is." Fantasy and reverie are interwoven with realism and action, as she makes her own world.[116]

For Nin, as man's world disintegrates into war, woman's world gives life, "as it is in this book, as it shall forever be." The absolute thus must be sought in flight, as life is given as much meaning as possible. This is a contribution to the whole, but it is not total unity, which is wrong. Happiness lies in what is aroused within and in what is created for it. Before happiness comes a prolonged struggle for fulfillment, a struggle against chaos, through the constant pursuit of mirages. Hope lies in keeping the dream alive; danger lies in awakening. The monster of reality is destructive indeed, but through meeting its attacks comes the transformation which turns destruction to creation and which produces everlasting continuity.[117] "Parts of my life, parts of my energy are passing into others. I feel what they feel. I identify with them." In this way, human writers empathize with victims such as themselves, uniting against agressors rather than becoming them.[118]

In creating without destroying, "I almost destroyed myself," for to create is to take sides. This is relativity instead of "destructive contrariness." Rebellions attract only weaklings who destroy because they cannot create. Revolution is not necessary for those who can transform life and thereby free themselves. Such contrariness would be death for Nin. Better to give selflessly until something personal is destroyed, then to stop. For Nin, except for what can be given individually, the world's suffering seems without remedy. "I can

only fill the diary, " and by filling it, record through necessity her 1000 years of womanhood. [119] Humanity is impo-
verished when it is reduced to a struggle for bread alone.
Not all the world's problems are economic. Women would
rather destroy aloneness and recover the original paradise.
For Nin, this entails asserting the possibility of an individually perfect world, personal loves, personal relationships, creation, in the face of a crumbling world. ("I may be trying
to place an opium mat atop a volcano. ")[120]

No matter how rapidly she lives, there are the voices
of those who fall behind. Yet, "Part of me remains always
Anaïs Nin." There is duality here, as in herself, wanting
creation and faithfulness as well. She needs to split up, to
do something apart. Thus her destiny is to live "drama of
feeling and imagination, reality and unreality, ... drama
without guns, dynamite, without explosions." Her madness
lies in perpetually identifying with human beings. Her intense
feelings for others are partly duty, but also for herself, the
divine pleasure which is the natural function of the pleasure
lover. To defeat such desire would be to destroy part of
life. [121]

Nin's libertarian statement is not a political one. It
is personal, and it comes from within herself. It is not
born of the ego, that caricature people mistake for self, [122]
but of subconscious and of consciousness of others. How does
it begin? It begins imitatively, among her friends, until personal growth and expansion take over. After that, it flows
along on its own of necessity. The independence born of
awareness will come late for woman who is so tied to the
past and to responsibility, but with insight it will develop
slowly. It is a continuous, fluid process, like the sea, and
it entails transforming the destruction of reality into the creation of a mirage. How is independence to be directed? In
creation lies empathy with others and their suffering, in it
lies relativity, selfless giving-up to the verge of personal
destruction but no further. Without such consciousness of
others, part of life would be destroyed. Without placing oneself apart from it, part of self will be destroyed. Only
through giving personally and individually can the world's suffering find any relief. Revolution is for those who cannot
create and who thus must destroy. It is not for those who
seek an individually perfect world, who would be at once
creative and faithful. The attempt at direction flows naturally, but the duality is open and evident.

The dualities which so distressed Henry Adams are ever present. There is an attempt to flow from one aspect of them to another, not into total unity, but by contributing to a complex whole. As noted before, dualities are not brought into balance easily. In fact, Nin seems to deny expressly the kind of equilibrium characteristic of the system. Her emphasis rather is upon slow development and continuity in which woman's deep personal roots have time to change. Thus, "time kills nothing in me, even though I tried to deliver myself of all possessions through art."[123] Time is always present and even irreversible, and Nin is faithful to it. At the same time, she seeks to split herself apart in order to create an individually perfect world for herself. In this way, change is possible, but it is not destructive revolutionary change. There is still religion, still morals, but they are transformed into the aesthetic, into art which knows no limitations. Nin's thought is paradoxical, but it flows naturally as she would wish. People mingle within her, and there is a flow between them and an absence of the separateness of Martha Quest's trinity of selves.

The problem observed earlier in Fuller's thought is evident in Nin's as well. In thinking and acting according to her own needs, woman seems more likely to maintain the status quo. How is woman to flow from deep personal roots into the ability to set oneself apart from consciousness of others when it becomes personally necessary to do so? Independence is deeply personal, but--in Nin's case, at least-- it begins imitatively among friends and then continues to develop of necessity. There is an attempt to cope with awareness and the problems it may bring by slowing the process down to a lifetime, by surrounding the new consciousness with friends and loved ones. Assuming necessity does take over the developmental process, then the question is how will the ability to set oneself apart from these important others, before they destroy the emerging self, develop? For Nin, the answer lies in her diary, in the naturalness it records and creates. It is the dream that if she can do it, others may as well. By keeping the dream alive, everything is kept alive, if only one does not awaken too soon. Nin's libertarian thought beautifully fills the feminist's intense desire that women should be free; it does so perhaps dutifully, perhaps to fill a personal need for divine pleasure. In its personalization, her thought somehow misses the reality of struggle. True, in struggle Nin finds hope, and hope is important. As with a mirage, however, hope is evanescent, and paradise can be invented for only so long. The reality of loneliness and

hopelessness may develop with increasing consciousness in
such proportions that friends and self alike cannot chase them
away, that one becomes dependent upon friends or friends upon
self. Nin realizes destruction could lie in either instance.
How deep and how strong can a dream of liberty be?

For Anne Morrow Lindbergh, the mind will awaken
and come to life again.

> It begins to drift, to play ... like those lazy
> waves on the beach. One never knows what
> chance treasures these easy unconscious rollers
> may toss up, on the smooth white sand of the
> conscious mind....
>
> But it must never be sought for or--heaven for-
> bid!--dug for. ... That would defeat one's
> purpose. The sea does not reward those who
> are too anxious, too greedy, or too impatient.
> To dig for treasures shows not only impatience
> and greed, but lack of faith. Patience, patience,
> patience, is what the sea teaches. Patience and
> faith. One should lie empty, open, choiceless
> as a beach--waiting for a gift from the sea. [124]

Lindbergh learns there are other women, and men, different
but struggling as well. She is not alone or unique at all.
There will be a coming of age for women in growth, fluidity
and freedom. These cycles, small and large, recede and
return forever. [125]

Liberty is, essentially, a conservative creed. It embraces the potential of becoming, and it is fluid, but for all
that it is static. It is a most paradoxical situation. The
emphasis on inner development increasingly becomes personalized, until the individual is left to dream of what might be
for others. Individuality is reinforced by the assurance that
there are others, different but nevertheless the same, who
dream and struggle as well. One heeds their suffering by
living one's own life as perfectly as possible. Therein human
suffering will be relieved in some small way. Liberty is a
continuous process of insight which is slow yet driven by necessity. It is first and foremost preservative of the very
roots which bind those who seek independence from enslavement.

Simone de Beauvoir suggests that women must undertake an apprenticeship in liberty, in abandonment and trans-

cendence.[126] Women's civil liberties are theoretical, lacking in economic freedom. Transcendence of the vain pursuit of woman's true being, a being which is the curse of her parasitism, comes only through active productivity in gainful employment. The vote and job are not enough, however, so long as female destiny contradicts woman's vocation. To overcome the duality of professional and sexual life, the social structure must be modified. Until it is, the concept of femininity will continue to be imposed upon women from without. (In the gradual transformation woman is undergoing, even trousers become feminine.)[127] Thus it is that today's independent woman has no taste for adventure unless she is given to artistic expression. At that, she often descends to self-worship, and spontaneity is "often confused with the direct presentation of the subjective impression." Woman's essential reality becomes her own self. The question, however, is woman's situation, the historical fact of which is taken as eternal truth. The free woman only now is being born. Once she gains possession of herself, attaining man's situation, she will be emancipated. Only then can one begin to speak of difference and essential reality.[128]

The chase continues. The broad insight of a de Beauvoir flows quite naturally through and beyond its feminist forebears. The libertarian thought which precedes it mingles therein. De Beauvoir strives to introduce a dynamic note, and perhaps she does to a certain extent, but the wait-and-see attitude persists. The question of beginnings is circumvented by the assertion that the process of independence for woman has begun already. Direction is instated in terms of economic freedom and social modification, but emancipation is posited in terms of man's situation. It is a path which is well traveled. Economic freedom is an old theme largely agreed upon; most feminist thinkers do not agree, however, that man's situation is for woman. The dualities de Beauvoir sets forth are familiar ones. Hers is a penetrating and comprehensive analysis of woman's situation. Yet is is more a summing up than a creative assertion. The chase seems to slow to a painfully burdensome pace at this point as patience and faith become synonymous with the feminist watchword of liberty.

References

1   Wollstonecraft, The Rights of Woman (1790) (New York: E. P. Dutton, 1929), pp. 41, 44, 50, 61, 171, 25, 69.

2   Ibid., pp. 96, 159, 193, 110-11, 166, 128, 132.
3   Ibid., pp. 193, 84.
4   Hobbes, Leviathan (Indianapolis: Bobbs-Merrill, 1958), pp. 170-74, 163, 165, 167.
5   Locke, "An Essay Concerning the True Original, Extent and End of Civil Government," Second Treatise on Civil Government, in Social Contract, ed. Ernest Barker (New York: Oxford University Press, 1960), pp. 5-6, 10, 45-46, 48-49, 51, 57.
6   Rousseau, The Social Contract, in Social Contract, ed. Barker, pp. 179, 169-70, 172, 175, 184-85, 187.
7   "Essay," p. 33.
8   "The Federalist No. 1, No. 10," in The Federalist Papers, 2d ed., ed. Roy P. Fairfield (Garden City, N.Y.: Anchor Books, 1966), pp. 1, 22.
9   March 31, 1776, Familiar Letters of John Adams and His Wife Abigail Adams During the Revolution (1875) (Freeport, N.Y.: Books for Libraries Press, 1970), p. 148.
10 Linda Grant De Pauw, Founding Mothers: Women in America in the Revolutionary Era (Boston: Houghton, Mifflin, 1975), pp. 150-73.
11 "Liberty and Peace," in The Poems of Phillis Wheatley, ed. Julian D. Mason, Jr. (Chapel Hill: University of North Carolina Press, 1966), pp. 93-95.
12 August 1, 1807, Correspondence Between John Adams and Mercy Warren, ed. Charles Francis Adams (1878) (New York: Arno, 1972), p. 396.
13 See discussion in Charles Edward Merriam, A History of American Political Theories (New York: Macmillan, 1921), pp. 23-24.
14 Views of Society and Manners in America, ed. Paul R. Baker (Cambridge, Mass.: Belknap Press, 1963), pp. 215, 220-21.
15 Welter, "The Cult of True Womanhood," in The American Family in Social-Historical Perspective, ed. Michael Gordon (New York: St. Martin's Press, 1973), p. 225. Linda Grant De Pauw adds delicacy to a list of the true woman's attributes.
16 Ibid., pp. 226-27, 231, 233-34, 241.
17 That they do fail should not be surprising. See Anne Firor Scott, The Southern Lady: From Pedestal to Politics 1830-1930 (Chicago: University of Chicago Press, 1972), pp. 22-44, for a regional example of the reality of woman's existence.
18 Griffith, Three Hundred Years Hence (1836) (Philadelphia: Prime Press, 1950), pp. 64, 88, 98-102, 116.

19 Mason Wade, Margaret Fuller: Whetstone of Genius (New York: Viking, 1940), p. 60.
20 Fuller, Women in the Nineteenth Century and Kindred Papers Relating to the Sphere, Condition and Duties of Women, ed. Arthur B. Fuller (Boston: John P. Jewett, 1855), pp. 63, 103, 177.
21 Ibid., pp. 74, 72, 63.
22 Ibid., p. 177.
23 Ibid., p. 63.
24 Hunt, Glances and Glimpses or 50 Years Social, Including 20 Years Professional Life (1856) (New York: Source Book Press, 1970), pp. 257, 330.
25 Ibid., pp. 330, 394, 328-29, 257.
26 Ibid., p. 171.
27 Ibid., p. ix.
28 Mill, On Liberty, ed. Currin V. Shields (Indianapolis: Bobbs-Merrill, 1956), p. xii.
29 John Stuart Mill and Harriet Taylor Mill, Essays on Sex Equality, ed. Alice S. Rossi (Chicago: University of Chicago Press, 1970), p. 40.
30 Mill, On Liberty, p. 13.
31 Ibid., pp. 7-8.
32 Ibid., pp. 7, 10, 12-14.
33 Ibid., p. 16.
34 Ibid., pp. 24, 29, 41-42, 44, 52-53, 58, 64.
35 Ibid., pp. 73, 79-80, 86-87.
36 Ibid., p. 114.
37 Ibid., pp. 125, 139.
38 The Spanish Gypsy, in Complete Works of George Eliot, 15 (New York: Merrill and Baker, n.d.), p. 93.
39 Ibid., p. 140.
40 Ibid., p. 134.
41 Ibid., p. 147.
42 Ibid., p. 226.
43 Frances Wright D'Arusmont, Life, Letters and Lectures 1834/1874 (New York: Arno, 1972), pp. 88-90.
44 Madeline B. Stern, ed., The Victoria Woodhull Reader (Weston, Mass.: M and S Press, 1974), pp. 24, 11, 4, 6.
45 Ibid., pp. 30, 25, 40, 42.
46 Stanton, Eighty Years and More: Reminiscences 1815-1897 (1898) (New York: Schocken, 1973), p. 382.
47 April 1, 1872, in Elizabeth Cady Stanton, ed. Theodore Stanton and Harriot Stanton Blatch (New York: Arno, 1969), vol. 2, pp. 136-37.
48 "Uncivil Liberty: An Essay to Show the Injustice and Impolicy of Ruling Woman Without Her Consent," in Sex and Equality (New York: Arno, 1974), p. 23.

49 Ibid., pp. 10, 23.
50 Ibid., p. 4.
51 Ibid., pp. 23, 9-10, 4.
52 Engels, The Origin of the Family, Private Property and the State: In Light of the Researches of Lewis H. Morgan (1891) (New York: International Publishers, 1972), pp. 76, 120.
53 Ibid., pp. 229, 223.
54 Ibid., p. 221.
55 Ibid., pp. 129-30, 137, 140, 144.
56 Stow Persons, American Minds: A History of Ideas (New York: Henry Holt, 1958), p. 324.
57 Woman, Church and State (1893) (New York: Arno, 1972), p. 545.
58 Origin of the Family, pp. 74, 77.
59 Woman, Church and State, pp. 531, 526.
60 Ibid., p. 530.
61 Ibid., p. 531.
62 Ibid.
63 Ibid., pp. 536-37, 528.
64 Paul S. Boyer, "Matilda Joslyn Gage," in Notable American Women: A Biographical Dictionary, 1607-1950, ed. Edward T. James (Cambridge, Mass.: Belknap Press, 1971), vol. 2, p. 5. See also Matilda Joslyn Gage, "The United States on Trial; Not Susan B. Anthony," in An Account of the Proceedings of the Trial of Susan B. Anthony, on the Charge of Illegal Voting at the Presidential Election in November, 1872 (1874) (New York: Arno, 1974), p. 180.
65 Clara Bewick Colby, "The Philosophy of Woman Suffrage," in History of Woman Suffrage, ed. Susan B. Anthony and Ida Husted Harper (Indianapolis: Hollenbeck Press, 1902), vol. 4, pp. 254-55.
66 Elizabeth Cady Stanton, Susan B. Anthony and Matilda Joslyn Gage, eds., History of Woman Suffrage, 2d ed. (Rochester, N.Y.: Charles Mann, 1889), vol. 1, pp. 50-51.
67 Florence Howe Hall, Julia Ward Howe and the Woman Suffrage Movement (New York: Arno, 1969), p. 223.
68 Ibid., pp. 153-55, 225, 178.
69 Ibid., pp. 223, 158.
70 Youth: Its Education, Regimen and Hygiene (New York: Appleton, 1907), p. 301.
71 The Agony of the American Left (New York: Knopf, 1969), p. 44.
72 Ibid., p. 46.
73 The American Mind: An Interpretation of American

Thought and Character Since the 1880's (New Haven, Conn.: Yale University Press, 1961), pp. 7-8.

74 Stanton, Anthony and Gage, eds., History of Woman Suffrage, 2d ed., vol. 1, p. 50.

75 American Thought Before 1900: A Sourcebook from Puritanism to Darwinism (New York: Macmillan, 1966), p. 16.

76 The Business of Being a Woman (New York: Macmillan, 1912), p. 82.

77 Woman and Social Progress: A Discussion of the Biologic, Domestic, Industrial, and Social Possibilities of American Women (New York: Macmillan, 1912), pp. 272-73.

78 Ibid.

79 The Vocation of Woman (London: Macmillan, 1913), p. 205.

80 Feminism: Its Fallacies and Follies (New York: Dodd, Mead, 1916), pp. 170-71.

81 Ibid. But see The Woman Voter, official communication of the Woman Suffrage Party, "Open Letter to Mr. John Martin," (January 1915), p. 20.

82 Mr. and Mrs. John Martin, Feminism: Its Fallacies, pp. 341-59, 329. See also Weir Jepson, Feminism vs. True Capitalism (Sioux City, Iowa: Hoyt-Purcell, 1932).

83 Hale, What Women Want: An Interpretation of the Feminist Movement (New York: Frederick A. Stokes, 1914), pp. 3, 8, 35, 263.

84 Ibid., p. 167.

85 Tuttle, The Awakening of Women: Suggestions from the Psychic Side of Feminism (New York: Abingdon, 1915), passim.

86 Key, The Renaissance of Motherhood, trans. Anna E. B. Fries (New York: G. P. Putnam's, 1914), pp. v., 4-5, 18.

87 Key, War, Peace and the Future: A Consideration of Nationalism and Internationalism and of the Relation of Women to War, trans. Hildegard Norberg (New York: G. P. Putnam's, 1916), pp. 141, 262, 255, 85, 241, 169, 84. See also Kate Richards O'Hare, "The Wounded Who Do Not Fight," Social Revolution, 11 (October 1914), 7.

88 Ibid., pp. 90, 87, 97, 92, 85, 94, 99-100, 103.

89 Ibid., pp. 102, 109, 114-15, 104-05, 184-85.

90 Ibid., pp. 147-48.

91 Ibid., p. 241.

92 Ibid., pp. 200-01. Aileen Kraditor discusses the problem of contradictory tactics further in The Ideas of the

Woman Suffrage Movement 1890-1920 (New York: Columbia University Press, 1967), pp. 219-48.

93 The Woman Patriot: A National Newspaper for Home and
National Defense Against Woman Suffrage (April 27, 1918),
p. 4.

94 Harriot Stanton Blatch, Mobilizing Woman-Power (New
York: Woman's Press, 1918), ch. 12; see also her A
Woman's Point of View: Some Roads to Peace (New
York: Woman's Press, 1920).

95 Catt, "Introduction," in The Woman Citizen, Mary Sumner Boyd (New York: Frederick A. Stokes, 1918), passim.

96 See Marie Louise Degen, The History of the Woman's
Peace Party, John Hopkins University Studies in Historical and Political Science, 58:3 (Baltimore: John Hopkins
University Press, 1939), for a chronological and detailed
account of this aspect of women's history.

97 The American Spirit: A Study of the Idea of Civilization
in the United States, vol. 4, The Rise of American Civilization (New York: Macmillan, 1942), p. 674.

98 See Margaret Sanger, Woman and the New Race (1920)
(Elmsford, N.Y.: Maxwell Reprint, 1969), ch. 13.

99 Amber Lee, The Woman I Am (New York: Thomas
Seltzer, 1925), p. 183.

100 "Feminism Is Awkward Age," Harper's Magazine (April
1925), 545-52.

101 Concerning Women (1926) (New York: Arno, 1972), pp.
155-56.

102 Ibid., pp. 237, 207.

103 Ibid., pp. 271, 7-9, 117, 306.

104 Winter, The Heritage of Women (New York: Minton,
Balch, 1927), p. 288.

105 In The Collected Poems of Dorothy Parker, (New York:
Modern Library, n.d.), p. 42.

106 Daughter of Earth (1942) (Old Westbury, N.Y.: Feminist
Press, 1973), p. 8.

107 Ibid., pp. 111, 114, 123, 156, 189.

108 Ibid., pp. 331, 361.

109 Ibid., pp. 361, 371-72, 367.

110 The Woman Within (1944) (New York: Harcourt, 1954),
p. 160.

111 Ibid., pp. 153, 230, 172.

112 Ibid., pp. 11, 283.

113 In A Way of Happening (New York: Pellegrini and Cudahy, 1948), pp. 22-23.

114 The Diary of Anaïs Nin 1934-1939 (New York: Harcourt,
Brace and World, 1967), pp. 317, 265, 99, 102, 144,
233, 293, 310.

115 Ibid., pp. 308, 10, 6, 46, 21.
116 Ibid., pp. 22-23, 34, 41-44, 69, 51, 65.
117 Ibid., pp. 145-56, 257, 265, 293, 314.
118 Ibid., pp. 35, 15.
119 Ibid., pp. 31, 63, 272, 321, 68, 103, 92, 252-54.
120 Ibid., pp. 93-94, 131.
121 Ibid., pp. 156, 242, 185, 110, 233, 252, 188, 213, 269.
122 Ibid., p. 20.
123 Ibid., p. 329.
124 Gift from the Sea (New York: Pantheon, 1955), pp. 15-16.
125 Ibid., pp. 10, 96, 108, 110.
126 The Second Sex, trans. H. M. Parshley (1952) (New York: Bantam Books, 1970), p. 670.
127 Ibid., pp. 639-42.
128 Ibid., pp. 660-62, 664-65, 672-73.

4

AND AR'N'T I A WOMAN?
FEMINISM AND EQUALITY

The second ideological current to feminism is equality.
Feminist thinkers in America before the twentieth century do
not develop a notable egalitarian creed, however. They largely are preoccupied with libertarian concerns. Most feminist egalitarian thought is not American in its derivation before the twentieth century. As egalitarian thought unfolds
after the turn of the century, it stresses equality of opportunity which in many ways is a libertarian emphasis. It already is apparent, however, that equality and liberty are essentially inapposite. As a result, feminist egalitarian thinkers often stress revolution or at least militancy and civil disobedience as a means to attain equality for women with men.
The components of a spiritual community as a basis for re-
sisting woman's oppression begin to appear. Feminist thinkers start espousing socialist measures to the end of economic
equality. They stray from the path of self-imposed duty and
their libertarian creed in doing so. Once again feminist
thinkers convene outside time and space to try to discuss
feminism and equality mutually.

Mary Wollstonecraft reminds everybody of women's
and men's equal souls, and sensing consent, moves on to assert that virtue rests with equally developed and exercised
minds and bodies for both sexes. She prefers that equality
come about through systematically managed reform in which

men and the attainment of liberty will play a large part.
Here George Sand recalls the problems which changing society as it already is constituted presents.   Wollstonecraft
agrees that revolution may be necessary to restore order and
to blow away clouds on the face of truth that women may reform themselves.   But women do not show the physical
courage this may require, Sand reminds her; women show
great moral courage, though.   Frances Wright insists that
equality lies in educational reform.   Jane Grey Swisshelm
protests, but Wright goes on to state that women are not
rendered more useful by their subordination.   Tennie C.
Claflin suggests that herein lies the difficulty.   Women are
committed to being useful and doing service instead of being
committed to accomplishment--to the noble development of
their powers and faculties.   Yes, agrees Swisshelm, and
women cannot compromise usefulness and accomplishment
successfully.

Everybody murmurs about the profound changes install-
ing equality for women with men may require.   Constantia
speaks out about her dislike for doctrinaire equality and the
despicable excesses of the French Revolution.   Emma Goldman points out that to her way of thinking political violence
is the product of intensely felt indignation over social wrong.
Abigail Adams speaks of the rapid changes revolution presents
to her generation.   She can neither fathom nor comprehend
them.   Alexis de Tocqueville reminds everybody that women
in America may not be socially equal to men, but they are
morally and intellectually equal with them.   Harriet Martineau
answers him with some feeling: currently, women enjoy what
rights they have by man's dispensation; until they are entitled
to consent, they cannot be equal.   Catharine Beecher agrees
with Tocqueville: in America, women hold a position separate

from men but nonetheless equal, and highly respected. Sojourner Truth rises, and everybody is still. "Nobody eber
helps me into carriages, or ober mud puddles, or gives me
any best place, and ar'n't I a woman?" Claflin nods vigor-
ously. For her, women must become aware of the falsity of
their position if equality is to prevail, but at the same time
she suggests women must be true to themselves.

Elizabeth Blackwell looks doubtful. Only socialism as
an expression of Christian consciousness can control and guide
selfhood to an enlarged sense of duty. Helen Keller indicates
that social blindness and poverty stand in the way of equal
rights. Susan B. Anthony speaks wistfully: I had hoped the
Constitution would be interpreted broadly and liberally when
I was tried for voting illegally, but it was not. I believed
then that I had to urge women to resist tyranny, but in the
end I could only believe that equal voting rights would come
inevitably. Ah, Susan--Ida B. Wells speaks--I cautioned you
that the millennium would not come with the ballot.

Harriet Taylor Mill nods briskly: the question is one
of equal admission to all social privileges. Alice Paul adds
that equal rights should not depend on sex. Ellen Key says
that woman's equality must include rights to her earnings,
freedom of action, perfect equality in marriage and authority
over her children. John Spargo turns to Key in agreement.
Actually what we're talking about is equality of opportunity;
with it, the right to vote and equality in the labor force will
become the foundation for freedom of motherhood. August
Bebel addresses himself to Paul. I don't think attempts to
attain merely equal rights for women and men will change
woman's general condition; the future belongs to socialism,
to the worker and the woman.

Keller makes it clear that rights are obtained by those who are strong enough to claim them. She thinks women must become an aggressive enough political factor to try revolution. Charlotte Perkins Gilman hastily reminds everybody that woman's newly gained social condition still is in the process of development. Just remember, muses Gertrude Stein, that things never can be the same for everybody. Ruth Herschberger adds that wisdom such as Eve gained does give a kind of rude equality, but it is a mixed blessing. B. F. Skinner sums things up by stating that economic freedom yields equal opportunity which will not eradicate gross physical differences but which will allow women to exist on a par with men. Somebody recalls that Hannah Arendt once said brotherhood is no substitute for equality. For her, only mutual thought and meaningful combination yield lasting institutions in touch with principle.

*   *   *   *   *

Mary Wollstonecraft asserts that the more equality exists, the more social virtue and happiness there will be. This is because virtue has only one external standard, and since both women and men have souls, there is only one way to attain virtue or happiness. The way lies in a strong body and exercised mind. Women and men must be able to reflect on causes, in conjunction with observation of natural effects, throughout the important years of life. This activity is preferable to matters of sensation, love, lust or corporeal accomplishments. It is by reflection that rules are deduced from pure reason which apply to the whole species and which contribute to the order of creation. With reason comes the power to discern truth, and truth is the same for women and men. [1]

Twice Wollstonecraft refers to a forthcoming revolution in female manners. Revolution will restore lost female dignity and inspire worldly reform as women reform women. Revolution well might precipitate salutary effects tending to improve mankind. As things currently stand, wealth and female softness equally debase women and men. Furthermore, the most respectable women are the most oppressed, subject to male tyranny which produces female cunning. This will change only when society is constituted differently through submission to reason instead of habit. The problem of re-constitution lies in widespread fear of innovation. With great men, great revolutions occur to restore order and to blow aside clouds which obscure the face of truth. Revolutions are not necessary, however, where reason and virtue prevail. [2]

For all her focus on liberty and domestic duty, Wollstonecraft's egalitarian statement is a radical one. It was radical for her times, and it still is radical. She does not claim that women and men are the same, but their souls are equal and subject to the same eternal standard. Until this principle is recognized and acted upon, women and men equally are debased. "... I not only tremble for the souls of women, but for the good natured man, whom everyone loves." [3] As to how the principle will be enacted, she entertains the thought of revolution as a means to restore order. She does not fit revolution explicitly into her projected pattern of change, however. Order there must be, and order by implication is egalitarian, but she stops short of calling for a revolution to impose order. Wollstonecraft speaks out for the French Revolution and is in France during the revolutionary surge of the 1790s. She and others of her international circle of friends are disillusioned "with the revolution as it moved from Jacobin 'excesses' to Thermidorean opportunism (what Mary called the 'aristocracy of riches'). "[4] Furthermore, some of her positions decidedly are not Jacobin, for example, her belief that her thought enhances property relations. [5]

One supposes Wollstonecraft's ambiguity here is a combination of, first, her realization of the enormity of woman's problem and, second, her own experiences in a revolutionary context. In addition, her own incorporation of rationalism and mysticism, her professed love for Rousseau's paradoxes, all probably play a part in the ambiguity. Thus, while the necessity of equality is a given for her, its revolutionary achievement is only one possibility. Order is at the center of her egalitarian creed. To understand what equality means to her, one must understand it in the context of her thought and that of her theoretical forebears. This requires specification of certain fundamentals, namely: equality of what and for whom? Equality for whom seems very clear; it is for women and men, who already possess equal souls. Equality of what is not so clear. It seems she is referring to body and mind, not as to sameness, but as to development and exercise of strength and reflective power. Here her language becomes decidedly inflammatory, and this is especially note-worthy because it is an exception to her usual dialogue. 6 She speaks both of woman's oppression and man's tyranny. Here as nowhere else does the reader experience the enormity of the problem as Wollstonecraft perceives it.

Part of the conceptual difficulty Wollstonecraft faces stems from the fact women are not treated as equals in cur-rent affairs. Even given their inherently equal souls, their ability to reflect the eternal standard that Wollstonecraft be-lieves exists is compromised. Some women complicate mat-ters further by reacting to man's tyranny with devious, tyran-nous ways of their own. Furthermore, women who do this tend to be those who garner the most respect. "On this scheme of things a king is but a man; a queen is but a wo-man; a woman is but an animal, and an animal not of the highest order!--All true, Sir; [she is addressing Edmund Burke] if she is not more attentive to the duties of humanity than queens and fashionable ladies in general are."7

This is where a revolution in female manners comes in; women have to reform other women, and it may require a revolutionary wind to remove the clouds which obscure truth for them. Were woman to attain reason and virtue, however, such revolution would not be necessary. Wollstone-craft seems to believe men could play an important role here--perhaps because they currently are more in possession of reason than women are--by removing the chains which restrain woman's impetus to reason. Liberty could play an important role in this regard too. Should men or the insti-tution of liberty fail, however, a revolution may be required to reveal the sorry truth about women to women in order for them to reform themselves.

It is all very problematic, as has been noted else-where. Nevertheless it is a beginning. A brief review of Wollstonecraft's liberal forebears will be useful to understand the context in which the beginning is placed. For Hobbes, human beings in the state of nature are starkly equal. "Na-ture has made men so equal in the faculties of the body and mind as that, though there be found one man sometimes, manifestly stronger in body or of quicker mind than another, yet, when all is reckoned together, the difference between man and man is not so considerable as that one man can thereupon claim to himself any benefit to which another may not

pretend as well as he. " From this equality of ability arises
an equality of hope which inevitably leads to quarrels with
others for purposes of gain, safety or reputation. The result
is a state of all-out war. Life is "solitary, poor, nasty,
brutish, and short, " and nothing is unjust. [8]

The move into the leviathan already has been traced.
It is important to note the nature of Hobbes' proclamation
that fathers and mothers are equally parents having equal dominion over the child. The child is subject equally to both
parents, but this is impossible in fact. The assumption of
dominion by the man is not by reason of his excellence.
"For there is not always that difference of strength or prudence between the man and the woman as that the right can
be determined by war. " Dominion by civil law usually rests
with the man by virtue of his role in building the commonwealth. Dominion by natural law is between the parents who
may dispose of it by contract. Hobbes here notes the contractual relations the Amazons have, regarding disposal of
dominion over offspring, with men of nearby lands with whom
they couple. [9] In other words, human beings are equal to one
another in a state of nature, and they are on equal footing
when they enter the contractual state which is the leviathan.
The same holds true for women and men when it comes to
parental dominion. They are equal to one another when they
enter the contractual state through which they dispose of dominion over children. There are distinct disadvantages to
natural equality in both cases, and for this reason it is foregone in favor of a contractual relationship.

For Locke, the state of nature is one of equality and
reciprocity which can be set aside only by an explicit appoint-
ment of dominion and sovereignty in another. Men live by
the rule of reason and common equity, or they transgress the
law of nature. Women, by reason or revelation, have equal
title with men to parental power. Furthermore, the power
of husband over wife is not the same as the political power
a magistrate has over a subject. It must be understood,
however, that natural equality does not embrace all forms of
equality. Human beings may be distinguished by reason of
age, virtue, excellence, merit, birth, alliance or benefits.
Still every human being enjoys an equal right to natural freedom. Thus the in effect blank slates that all women and men
are naturally may be inscribed by a number of events which
ultimately may transfigure their natural equality. [10]

Rousseau also sees human beings as naturally equal.

Each existence has an absolute value. However corrupt individuals may become, it is the result of institutions which cause them to become slaves against nature. Institutions must become responsive to the general will. A social system thusly based is characterized by "moral and legal equality which compensates for all those physical inequalities from which men suffer." Whatever bodily or mental differences exist among individuals, they are "equal in the eyes of the law and as a result of the compact into which they have entered."[11] Inequality is linked closely to the injustice inherent in the artificial system of private property which originally Locke laid down for purposes of right and convenience. Social equality is based on morals and law.

The social equality Wollstonecraft seeks for women and men, based on their already equal souls, is to be attained by bodies and minds developed in accordance with an eternal standard. This standard is divine, and it has strong moral overtones, ergo the concern for women's manners. Law plays a part here as well, and all of this is traceable to Rousseau. The part reason plays is distinctly Lockeian, as is the reciprocity for good or ill evident between women and men. Hobbes and Locke both have set the stage for asserting women's inherent equality by their analyses of the dominion of parenthood. Locke's notion of individuals as blank slates to be inscribed by the play of certain events leaves open the possibility for manipulating those events in order to change woman's position to a more equal one. Finally, as individuals contract with the state, so do women and men contract with each other in marriage. The terms of the contract can be changed should circumstances dictate.

According to Locke, should the body politic fail to provide for the safety and security of its members and seize absolute power over life, liberty and property, then it forfeits its power. The people shall be the judge of when this breach of fundamental social rule occurs, at which time power reverts to them. In other words, the people may revolt. This has happened historically but not often, and if anything, the right to revolt serves as a deterrent against tyranny.[12] Revolution, for Locke, then is a real but remote possibility, an extraordinary means where all others have failed. It rests with the people, and the people determine when it is warranted. Wollstonecraft's view of revolution seems very Lockeian. Wollstonecraft states that "nature having made men unequal, by giving stronger bodily and mental powers to one than to another, the end of government ought to be, to

destroy this inequality by protecting the weak. "[13] Where
government does not meet this end, and where its degeneracy
has advanced to a state of dominance over the weak, then
people are justified in revolting, using coercive means to re-
peal a coercive state.

This apparently is what Wollstonecraft has in mind as
a possibility for women to right their relation to the existing
order. Wollstonecraft does not seem to take this possibility
lightly. In her history of the French Revolution, she sadly
reflects upon the precipitate events which follow the magnani-
mous conduct of those involved.[14] She also discusses the
gradual improvement which might be forthcoming with systematic management of reform, and one gathers that this is
the preferred means by which to attain change. Only when
things are utterly out of hand would people determine "to
strike at the root of all their misery at once. . . . "[15] Only
when a person's very birthright, "such a degree of liberty,
civil and religious, as is compatible with the liberty of every
other individual with whom he is united in a social compact,
and the continued existence of that compact, is at stake would
one turn to revolution. "[16] For Wollstonecraft, then, liberty
is essential to the attainment of equality in well developed
and exercised bodies and minds for women and men. Liberty
is associated with peaceful means, systematically managed
reform and gradual improvement. Revolution is justified only
in the extraordinary case, but it is a possibility. Should women and men remain degraded and their birthrights be curtailed, then a revolution in female manners may be necessary
for truth and right order to prevail. In the meantime, moral
and civil reform should suffice.

In the New World during the Revolutionary era, liberal
ideas are assimilated widely. At the time they are applied
to the attainment of liberty and self-determination for the colonies. The doctrine of equality is not extended to women,
except as regards their comparative status with European women. In other words, upper-class women such as Abigail
Adams generally do not demand political, legal or educational
equality for themselves, but they do expect to be considered
equal to their European counterparts.[17] In personal correspondence, Abigail does remind John saucily:

> that arbitrary power is like most other things
> which are very hard, very liable to be broken;
> and notwithstanding all very wise laws and
> maxims, we have it in our power not only to

> free ourselves, but to subdue our masters, and,
> without violence, throw both your natural and le-
> gal authority at our feet.... [18]

She specifically states that the means of this overthrow of
arbitrary power will not be violent. She hints at rebellion
elsewhere, but this does not seem to be a serious challenge.
Years later she writes her long-time friend Mercy Otis Warren of her own seeming bewilderment at the age's revolutions:

> If we were to count our years by the revolutions
> we have witnessed, we might number them with the
> antedeluvians [sic]. So rapid have been the changes,
> that the mind, though fleet in its progress, has
> been outstripped by them; and we are left, like
> statues, gazing at what we can neither fathom nor
> comprehend. [19]

Revolution simply is not considered a viable means to change
woman's position in the revolutionary era.

Constantia, as already noted, asserts the equality of
women and men's souls and bases her proposal to reform
woman's education on this premise. In the Gleaner, she
views doctrinaire equality with disfavor. While she originally
admires the fervor of the French Revolution, she comes to
despise its excesses. [20] All of this is in line with Wollstonecraft's thought, although much of it lacks her assertiveness
and forthright advocacy. Colonial prefeminist thinkers are
at the fountainhead of revolutionary ideas and propaganda.
They have some inkling that these ideas apply to their own
position as well. They are not prepared, however, to re-
adjust their priorities to include women's rights explicitly
among the concerns of the time. Preservation of their homes,
families and lives, liberty and self-determination for the new
state and getting ahead in the world hold their attention instead. American revolutionary maxims will come to be very
important in future assertions about women's rights, however.

With the rise of Jacksonian democracy, roughly 1829-
1837, comes what Page Smith refers to as "the Great Repression" of women. [21] Women are constrained sexually,
economically, politically and socially. Sexually, although
they are having fewer children, they are expected to devote
more time to them and take more responsibility for them.
Where they help to earn a living as well as maintain a home
in the colonial era, now they increasingly are consumers of

the output of a more industrialized economy. Politically the
climate is egalitarian, but women constitute a status-deprived
class. Socially women are experiencing ever-widening class
distances among themselves, with women of the upper class
expected to be ladies. The quality of woman's existence
seems to be declining. As French author George Sand puts
it, in discussing her heroine Indiana, "Indiana is a type; she
is woman, the feeble being whose mission it is to represent
passions repressed, or, if you prefer, suppressed by the
law; she is desire at odds with necessity; she is love dashing
her head blindly against all the obstacles of civilization."[22]

As Wollstonecraft does, Sand regrets the lack of extant social virtue, the decline of honor and heroism. Society
is merely necessary. Sand defines what seems to her an
insoluble problem: asserting the welfare and dignity of those
persons whom society oppresses without changing society.
Woman's unhappiness, far from being trivial, involves men
as well as women. This is the cause Sand defends in Indiana.
She also regrets that "women rarely have the physical courage
which consists in offering the resistance of inertia to pain or
danger, but she is heartened that "they often have the moral
courage which attains its climax in peril or suffering."[23]
The problem of changing the quality of woman's existence,
her oppression, is a real one for Sand. She seems to indicate a certain amount of disillusionment with the feasibility
of reform; that is, affecting change within society as presently
constituted. Elsewhere she speaks of the need for complete
reformation of marriage. Woman's physical inequality may
reduce the likelihood of revolt, but her moral equality or even
superiority seems to have the staying power which could overcome misery.

Frances Wright notes all people are born free and
equal but do not so live. Equal rights for her are based
upon equal education. Without such instruction, people cannot be equal, and if they are not equal, they cannot be free.[24]
In Wright and Sand, two intellectual thrusts are present which
will be evident in feminist thought about equality. Both of
these stem from an assumption about women and men's intrinsic equality and recognition of the fact such equality does not
exist in real life. The primary question is one about changing reality to better reflect essential equality. There are
two possibilities in this regard: reform and revolution.
Wollstonecraft discusses them both. Sand discusses reform
but seems to suggest the impossibility of changing woman's
oppression without changing society itself. This implies only

revolution can bring about needed changes. Such revolution
will not be violent; woman has not the physical courage for
violence. It will be a moral revolution, for which woman
has ample courage. Wright, on the other hand, discusses
equality solely in terms of one specific and practical reform:
education. "Equality! where is it, if not in education?"[25]
She directs her argument to woman's utility, which is not increased by ignorance and resulting subordination. [26]

Harriet Martineau discusses equality in terms of politics and politics in terms of morals. For her, democratic
principle requires that the political relations of all rational
beings be equal. "Politics are morals, universally implicat-
ing the duty and happiness of man."[27] In discussing the morals of slavery in the economy, she finds women in America
are held as property by men. Women are but domestic
managers of man's estate. [28] So long as they lack will or
liberty and property, they are going to be excluded from representation. As things now stand, whatever protection woman
enjoys is a dispensation at the discretion of those men to
whom she belongs: father and/or husband. Only when woman's sphere is broadened so as to require both women's and
men's consent will the principles of equal rights be instated.
Here Martineau invokes the well-known proposition of the revolutionary era; governments can derive their just powers only
from the consent of the governed. In the meantime, woman
can expect to be confined. Martineau approaches equality as
a political principle which is ultimately a question of morals.
As discussed earlier, she does not question woman's moral
purity; she believes, however, that woman is degraded morally by the behavior of men about her. Society in America establishes the political nature of woman's degradation and sees
the solution as a moral one. It does not offer a program for
change, however.

Alexis de Tocqueville, it will be recalled, sees women
in America as social inferiors, but moral and intellectual
equals. As a result, women control mores which in turn are
maintained by an equality sweeping away differences between
the sexes. Mores, according to Tocqueville, are much harder to change than law. In his observations about democracy
in America, he notes a tension between love of equality and
the urge to freedom. The latter is nurtured by concern for
natural rights and limitations placed on authority but is not
dependent on democracy and is lost easily. The former constitutes an inevitable force stemming from destruction of the
aristocracy and is a distinctive, long-lasting characteristic of

democracy. Yet only in democracy do equality and freedom
meet. The democratic tendency is toward an ideal in which
people are perfectly free and perfectly equal because they
are entirely equal and entirely free. [29] The problem is that
liberty may present immediate burdens with its benefits
realized only gradually through sacrifice and effort, pleasing
but a few. Equality presents few burdens immediately; its
benefits are realized right away on a daily basis by everyone
as a part of existence. Democratic people "want equality in
freedom, and if they cannot have that, they still want equality
in slavery. "[30]

According to Tocqueville, Americans do not ascribe the
same duties and rights to women as they do to men, but they
believe women and men are beings of equal worth, entitled to
equal regard for their activities. The relationship of women
and men is conditioned by strict mores which are aided and
increased by their equality of condition. By engaging in separate but necessary activities--women as managers of the domestic economy and men as politicians or the gainfully employed, women and men enjoy a healthier relationship in
America than elsewhere. Men solicit sexual favor less, and
women have an easier time of resistance. Man's authority
in marriage and the family still is intact, but neither sex in-
fringes upon the other's sphere of activity. [31] In considering
the type of sexual equality Tocqueville describes, it is crucial
to refer back to his analysis of liberty and equality generally
in America. Recollect that he sees in equality a sort of irresistible impulse characterized by short-run benefits for
everyone and in liberty, a state which must be nurtured yielding benefits only in the long run and then not necessarily for
everyone. Equality, as Tocqueville understands it, is a
source of potential concern for him. For woman, liberty
exists in the right to choose the marital state and a marital
partner and in the separate nature of her sphere. Equality
consists of the respect afforded that sphere.

Tocqueville thus relegates equality to a question of respect rather than the comparative nature of the spheres themselves. He suggests that the sexes consent to this arrangement in the marital contract, a choice made possible by the
relaxation of class barriers to marriage. Martineau clearly
disagrees. In a way, the type of analysis being made depends
upon what the observer is observing: the effect of the situation (Martineau) or the respect accorded the situation (Tocqueville). The linkage Martineau ascribes to politics and morals
is quite unlike the mutually exclusive treatment Tocqueville

gives them. Both these perspectives are extremely important in feminist thought, as will become apparent in the last two chapters of the book. Martineau is part of a stream of thought passing through Locke and Wollstonecraft; Tocqueville is part of a stream of thought passing through Rousseau and Fuller. Both streams of thought converge in what comes to be known as feminism later in the nineteenth century. There is tension between them, however, just as there is between liberty and equality.

It is worthwhile to note that none of the previous thinkers is American. Sand and Tocqueville are French; Wright and Martineau are English. Equality is not an indigenous theme in American feminist thought. Liberty receives far more attention with regard to woman's position. Considerations about equality up to this point are introduced to American prefeminist thinkers by non-Americans. Explicit references to equality are few and far between in American prefeminist thought, and detailed discussions of it are even rarer. Catharine E. Beecher's thought on the subject, for example, replicates Tocqueville's observation but not his analysis, in fact lacks any analysis at all:

> It is in America alone, that women are raised to
> an equality with the other sex; and that, both in
> theory and practice, their interests are regarded
> as of equal value. They are made subordinate in
> station only where a regard for their best interest
> demands it, while, as if in compensation for this,
> by custom and courtesy, they are always treated
> as superiors. [32]

Beecher asserts the above is the case in every social class, with women being given precedence in all life's comforts, conveniences and courtesies.

It is interesting to speculate why liberty receives so much intellectual attention and equality so little. Perhaps it is because prefeminist thinkers believe, as Tocqueville notes, that liberty is hard to come by and must be nurtured if it is to flourish. Perhaps they also believe, with Tocqueville, that equality is as inevitable as they believe change is. Or perhaps their inclination to pacific means, including reform, is not appropriate for the institution of equality. Sand suggests women have moral but not physical courage. Clearly there is a moral overlay to all the changes prefeminists are seeking. Furthermore, woman's existence in America after

the revolution does seem to revolve around activities which
largely require moral but not physical courage. Prefeminist
thinkers take woman's moral law unto herself very seriously
and expect it actually to be heeded. While they are beginning to apply woman's law to political matters, they generally
do not suggest--as Martineau does--that morals and politics
are linked. Instead they suggest morals are needed to reform
politics. Express linkage of morals and politics would facilitate constructing an ideology to guide change-oriented activities. In fact, such an ideology is not constructed, and activities become increasingly inner directed and personalized.
Gradual (slow) development toward independence is taken as
desirable, and the importance of woman's moral law is emphasized with reference to reforming man's unjust law.

The Declaration of Sentiments refers to the self-evident truth of the equality of women and men. Through its
close relation to the Declaration of Independence, it is Lockeian in scope, citing woman's duty to throw off the despotic
government she heretofore suffers patiently. "Such is now
the necessity which constrains them to demand the equal station to which they are entitled." One would not classify this
as a revolutionary document, however. Its authors insist
upon woman's "immediate admission to all the rights and
privileges which belong to them as citizens of the United
States," listing in justification woman's disenfranchisement,
her social and religious degradation, unjust laws and woman's
feelings of grievance, oppression and deprivation. How are
the rights and privileges due a citizen to be obtained? The
authors intend to "employ agents, circulate tracts, petition
the State and National legislatures, and endeavor to enlist the
pulpit and the press in our behalf." They also call for a
series of meetings such as that at Seneca Falls to be held
across the country. They outline in the resolutions several
reforms by which to rectify the situation they describe.

The most revolutionary of the resolutions is the assertion that all laws which limit woman's sphere and render
her subordinate are of no force or authority. There is no
call, however, for even civil disobedience in this regard.
All of the means called upon are well within existing law, for
example the right to petition. Gerda Lerner discusses the
lessons petitioning for abolition teaches women, including
methodicalness, reliability and perseverance. She also discusses the uselessness of these petitions with respect to their
recipient: the U.S. Congress. She suggests, however, that
use of petitions broadens the base of the abolition movement. [33]

Petitioning thus appears to be a reasonable, systematic means for improving women's organizational skills and encouraging women to participate in meaningful social activity. It is scarcely indicative of revolution. Apparently woman's degradation is not yet that unendurable.

Presumably the Declaration's reference to disenfranchisement falls within the category of laws without force or authority, although actually the U.S. Constitution does not limit voting to males until passage of the Fourteenth Amendment in 1868. Here Henry David Thoreau's "On the Duty of Civil Disobedience," published one year after the Seneca Falls convention, is particularly interesting. For Thoreau, voting is a kind of game played with right and wrong or with moral questions. Voters (or would-be voters) are not so much concerned that right should prevail as they are that the majority should decide the question. The obligation entailed thus is one of expediency rather than of right. [34] To extend Thoreau's discussion to woman's disenfranchisement, the problem seems to be that women begin to seek enfranchisement as a validation of their inherently equal status rather than as a means of doing right by it. Seen over the long run, despite campaign rhetoric to the contrary, the suffrage movement does just this. The Declaration of Sentiments intellectually sets the tone for what takes place. The libertarian and reform focus of prefeminist thought contributes to this tendency. A more overtly egalitarian orientation and less commitment to woman's law unto herself might have resulted in quite a different emphasis.

Prefeminist egalitarian thought might have remained in this unsatisfactory conceptual state were it not for the appearance of the woman who is described best as the high priestess of feminism, Sojourner Truth. Her egalitarian statement, related by Frances Gage and transcribed by Olive Gilbert, is delivered in 1851 to one of the meetings which follow the Seneca Falls convention. Woman's rights is not a popular cause, and the presence of a black woman on its behalf engenders disapprobation among those present. Truth's tall gaunt figure, plainly clothed but for a turban beneath her sunbonnet, is described as queenly nonetheless. When she speaks in deep, modified tones on the second day of the meeting, silence falls before her "almost Amazon form, which stood nearly six feet high, head erect, and eye piercing the upper air, like one in a dream":

'Well, children, whar dar is so much racket dar

must be something out o'kilter. I tink dat
'twixt de niggers of de Souf and de women at
de Norf all a talkin' 'bout rights, de white men
will be in a fix pretty soon. But what's all dis
here talkin' bout? Dat man ober dar say dat
woman needs to be helped into carriages, and
lifted ober ditches, and to have de best place
every whar. Nobody eber help me into carriages, or ober mud puddles, or gives me any
best place [and raising herself to her full
height, and her voice to a pitch like rolling
thunder, she asked], and ar'n't I a woman?
Look at me! Look at my arms! [And she
bared her right arm to the shoulder, showing
her tremendous muscular power.] I have
plowed, and planted, and gathered into barns,
and no man could head me--and ar'n't I a woman? I could work as much and eat as much
as a man (when I could get it), and bear de
lash as well--and ar'n't I a woman? I have
borne thirteen chilern and seen 'em mos' all
sold off into slavery, and when I cried out with
a mother's grief, none but Jesus heard--and
ar'n't I a woman? Den dey talks about dis ting
in de head--what dis dey call it?' 'Intellect,'
whispered some one near. 'Dat's it honey.
What's dat got to do with women's rights or
niggers' rights? If my cup won't hold but a
pint and yourn holds a quart, wouldn't ye be
mean not to let me have my little half-measure
full?' And she pointed her significant finger
and sent a keen glance at the minister who had
made the argument. The cheering was loud and
loud.

'Den dat little man in black dar, he say women
can't have as much rights as man, cause Christ
want a woman. Whar did your Christ come
from?' Rolling thunder could not have stilled
that crowd as did those deep wonderful tones,
as she stood there with outstretched arms and
eye of fire. Raising her voice still louder, she
repeated, 'Whar did your Christ come from?
From God and a woman. Man had nothing to
do with him!' Oh! what a rebuke she gave the
little man.

Turning again to another objector, she took up

the defense of mother Eve. I can't follow her
through it all. It was pointed, and witty, and
solemn, eliciting at almost every sentence
deafening applause; and she ended by asserting
that 'if de fust woman God ever made was
strong enough to turn the world upside down,
all 'lone, dese togedder [and she glanced her
eye over us], ought to be able to turn it back
and get it right side up again, and now dey is
asking to do it, de men better let 'em!'[35]

There is nothing expedient about Sojourner Truth's
egalitarian creed. It is based on earned right, pure and
simple. She does not rely on inalienability or woman's moral law. The change of which she speaks--turning the world
right side up again--is all-encompassing. Relative intellect
and class have no bearing here, but physical strength does.
There is no appeal to reason or civil law. The appeal is
based on her ability as a woman to cope with life and its experiences equally as well as anyone else. She speaks from
strength. There is an ominous tone to this statement: white
men are going to be in a fix before long, and they had better
not stand in woman's way--with regard to either abolition or
women's rights. Sojourner Truth implicates and compels the
participation of other women by glance, word and inference.

Sojourner Truth is not a lady, and she is not inclined
to become one. She earns her way in life and takes her
share of its hard knocks; she expects to receive her measure
for it and is not going to wait for men to break her chains.[36]
It also might be said that at her point in time hers is the
only genuinely egalitarian American prefeminist creed. It
doubtlessly is important that she has no formal education and
hence is not constrained by the mostly libertarian thought
structure of the gentry. Truth's education is experiential,
and her background includes evidence of mysticism. Her
adopted name reflects her education and her life very well.
Maria Stewart's words in 1833 anticipate Sojourner Truth:
"brilliant wit will shine from whence it will...."[37] The fact
Truth is not of the gentry class is important with regard to
her expectations about what women should be doing. In short,
there is no struggle between potential and reality for her.
They are one and the same.

Two years after the Akron meeting, Truth explains
women are not asking for half a kingdom. They want their
rights, pure and simple. "[Y]ou can't stop us from them;

see if you can. "[38] In other words, she is not interested in dividing the spoils equally, any more than she is interested in mere recognition of the justice of her demands. In 1867, she puts the plight of the black woman into striking perspective. "There is a great stir about colored men getting their rights, but not a word about colored women"; and if "men get their rights, and not colored women theirs, you see the colored men will be masters over the women, and it will be just as bad as it was before. "[39] She speaks as a person doubly oppressed: by race and by sex. She has good reason to appreciate the burden of oppression. Most importantly, she has the ability to put the burden into realistic, cogent perspective. Hers is a call to action, and the call is not couched in conventional reform terminology. It is all the more effective for its singularity.

In 1851, Harriet Taylor Mill--an Englishwoman--publishes a particularly apt and rational defense of equal political, civil and social rights for women. In it, she notes a growing political movement by women to enfranchise women in the United States. She criticizes those who attempt to link women and men's equality with "enforced distinctions in their privileges and functions." She points out that the issue is "equal admission to all social privileges" rather than separate but equal privileges and functions. [40] Although inequality historically and customarily is the basis for society, it is being outgrown. Physical force as a justification for dominion of the strongest ceases with the coming of democratic revolutions. Regarding questions pertaining to an aristocracy of sex or color, presumption should rest with equality. Of the justice of the movement for women's equal rights, she believes there can be no doubt; the movement also is based firmly on grounds of expediency. In asking whether women should live in coerced subordination to men, one must note first the presence of correlative obligation between them. In addition, their characters both are demoralized by the dependence of women. With Wollstonecraft, Mill observes that whatever moral influence women have over men, it is promoted either by using dependence as a means to power or by artifice; women and men both are corrupted by these means which have no relation to a sense of public duty. In addition, many women--lacking moral courage--submit to subordination to please their masters, having been taught from childhood on that in submission lies their greatest charm. [41]

Taylor's insights reproduce those of Wollstonecraft and Martineau. Demands for equality cannot rest on demands for

special consideration by virtue of woman's law unto herself.
This, in effect, is no more just than the privilege men have
had all along by virtue of civil law. To make such a demand
only is to reinforce the cleavage Tocqueville notes between
American women's and men's spheres. This does not constitute social equality. In addition, Mill describes the movement for equal rights for women as political in character.
At best, arguments pertaining to the woman's sphere, particularly economic ones, are irrelevant when it comes to the
public rights and duties which political equality implies.
This helps to explain why equality does not achieve the importance liberty does in American prefeminist thought. The
large conceptual investment prefeminist thought makes in
liberty precludes a similar investment in equality. Most
prefeminist thinkers pay equality lip service and little more.
Were they to do more, they soon would find themselves involved in serious conceptual difficulty. This also helps to
explain why Sojourner Truth is equality's sole fervent spokesperson up to this point in time. As a former slave, she is
committed to liberty, but she is not committed to the conceptual overlay of woman's law onto herself or to conventional
reform mechanisms. Woman's sphere and domestic duties mean nothing to her. She is free to speak out for
equality as an earned right.

Oftentimes the questions of those charged with investi-
gating the appropriateness of equal rights for women are directed to the issue of earned right. There is an example of
this in Elizabeth Cady Stanton's collected correspondence.
Stanton is writing about a question put to her by Horace Greeley, then chairing the New York State Constitutional Convention Standing Committee on the Right of Suffrage. Greeley:
'"The ballot and the bullet go together. If you vote, are you
ready to fight?' 'Yes,' I replied, 'we are ready to fight,
sir, just as you did in the late war by sending your substi-
tutes.'" Stanton believes she deals Greeley "rather a crushing
blow" with her reply. [42] She does point out that some men
are not so eager to fulfill their public duties in return for
public rights. The remark intimates that some women expect
the same prerogative. Stanton circumvents the issue of women's earned right to equal enfranchisement. In fact, the
ballot and the bullet are not linked for women in the years
that follow ratification of the suffrage amendment. The issue
is far from dead, as is evident in discussion in the 1970s of
the equal rights amendment. The gradual acquisition of liberty gives women the opportunity to engage in self-reliant
activities which supposedly could earn them equality. Femi-

nist thought, however, directs efforts inward. As a result, liberty, which lies in its pursuit, perpetuates a waiting attitude for feminist thinkers. The chase slows, as patience and faith become synonyms for the feminist watchword of liberty. Answers to questions about earned right suffer accordingly.

Tennie C. Claflin poses the dilemma in terms of a distinction between accomplishment and usefulness. Woman exists in a state of servitude which confines her to being useful to others and limits her ability to accomplish anything for herself. For Claflin, the equality being sought entails a noble development of powers and faculties, such as that of which Wollstonecraft speaks. Even though women are born equal, their relative position changes because of difference in education. Men learn self-reliance, but women do not. Women are taught to expect dependence in the future, the consequence of which is their servitude. Men limit women to semi-individuality. Such a state negates external world affairs and, as a result, women are not conscious of the false pretenses on which their position depends. The problem for Claflin is that women are not necessarily willing to shoulder the burden of becoming individuals.[43] Women and men should be equal in the eyes of society and the law; this means man will be subject to woman's moral law and woman will enjoy man's choices of occupation and action. Only when women become conscious of the falsity of their current position will they cease to live miserable and unprofitable lives. Then they will expect joint and perfect equality and mutuality in marriage, its aims, purposes and pursuits.[44]

At this point, the direction of Claflin's discussion shifts, from the question of accomplishment and earned right to equality, to woman's need to be true to herself. This seemingly is a logical focus for one who advocates emphasizing accomplishment instead of usefulness. Claflin points out that once woman demands her independence, she will undertake individual responsibility and begin to live for the same ends that man does. She then asserts that in demanding freedom, woman does not wish to use it in the same direction man uses his. She apparently means that woman must find and be herself. In doing so, virtue surely will follow, and woman will be competent to fill the duties of sister and wife that she owes man in the same proportion he owes her as brother and husband.[45] What seems a logical progression from accomplishment to woman's need to be true to herself actually yields rather illogical results. Given

freedom of self, woman will behave differently from man.
One expects that woman's need to be true to herself would
lead her away from woman's sphere with its implications of
usefulness to man's sphere and the ends of accomplishment.
In fact, Claflin suggests woman will not behave as man does
at all. Taken in the context of the American feminist libertarian creed, this is wholly reasonable because it supports
demands for liberty. Taken in the context of the non-Ameri-
can feminist egalitarian creed, it is not reasonable at all because it defeats demands for equality.

Although lucid conceptual arguments on behalf of woman's equality in American prefeminist thought are few and
far between, they are being supplemented by less conventional
activist tactics. There now is evidence of some militancy behind egalitarian demands. Susan B. Anthony, Elizabeth Cady
Stanton and Parker Pillsbury begin to publish The Revolution
in 1868. It is mailed out under the frank of U.S. Representative James Brooks (a Democrat from New York), but its
slogan is "down with politicians; up with people." Several
women--Abby Kelly Foster, Harriot Hunt, Julia and Abby
Smith, Lucy Stone--refuse to pay their taxes in a Thoreauian
exercise of civil disobedience under the American revolutionary maxim, no taxation without representation. A Women
Tax Payers Association appears in Rochester, New York.
Carrie Nation is wielding her ax in saloons. Victoria Woodhull runs for the U.S. Presidency with Frederick Douglass
as her running mate (without his acquiescence) in 1872 and
again in 1876. In 1872, Susan B. Anthony and 13 others
cast their votes, albeit illegally, in Rochester, New York; in
the same year, Virginia Minor tries to exercise the right to
vote in St. Louis County, Missouri.[46] All these activities
are alternatives to systematically managed reform and gradual
improvement. They are off the path of duty which feminist
libertarians are traveling, although some feminists such as
Harriot Hunt pursue both equality and militancy on one hand
and liberty and the path of duty on the other.

Essentially feminist thinkers are becoming disillusioned
with conventional reform tactics. In 1873, Elizabeth Cady
Stanton calls upon women to help themselves as never before:

> Let the churches alone; don't carpet churches,
> don't have fairs to deck them with painted win-
> dows, don't give your ministers donation par-
> ties. Put all your energies into earnest work
> for your own emancipation. Make a social revo-

lution. ... When [men] find out their comfort
depends on allowing us the ballot, they will
wheel into line and give it to us. Women have
too long petitioned and begged of men; let them
now make siege and carry the war into their own
homes. ... We are going to vote, peaceably if
we can, but with war if we must. [47]

She does not abandon her libertarian creed in calling for a
social revolution, however. In fact, she seems to suggest
that women are to withhold the special services which so en-
dear them to men until men grant them the right to vote,
after which women will resume their duties.

When Susan B. Anthony is brought to trial before the
U.S. Circuit Court for the Northern District of New York in
1873 for "knowingly, wrongly and unlawfully" voting for U.S.
Representative without the lawful right to do so ("the said
Susan B. Anthony being then and there a person of the female
sex"), she is charged with doing so "against the peace of the
United States of America and their dignity. "[48] When she responds to the question as to why she should not be sentenced
by the Hon. Ward Hunt, presiding judge, she replies, "I
hoped for a broad and liberal interpretation of the Constitution
and its recent [fourteenth] amendment ... that should declare
equality of rights the national guarantee to all persons born
and naturalized in the United States. "[49] Since such is not to
be, she asks that the judge impose "the full rigors of the
law" upon her. Her remarks are made amidst judicial or-
ders that the prisoner take her seat and be silent. When a
fine plus costs is levied, she refuses to pay it, promising
that 'I shall earnestly and persistently continue to urge all
women to the practical recognition of the old revolutionary
maxim, that 'resistance to tyranny is obedience to God. '"[50]

Anthony is the only one of the 14 voting illegally who
is brought to trial, because a nolle prosequi* is entered for
the other indictments. She must argue through her male
counsel that she made an honest mistake, believing herself
entitled to vote, and that she is being denied her right to a
jury trial by the directed verdict. The Slaughterhouse cases,
decided by the U.S. Supreme Court in 1873, hold that under
no construction of Fourteenth Amendment "due process" could

---

*Formal acknowledgment by the prosecution that the proceed-
ings will go no further in some respect.

"Susan B. Anthony," by Suzanne Benton, $46\frac{1}{2}$" (cast of original in the collection of Mr. and Mrs. David Mishkin).

restraint imposed by Louisiana upon exercise of the butchers' trade in New Orleans be considered a deprivation of property within the meaning of that provision. They also hold that the privileges and immunities clause of the Fourteenth Amendment could have no implication independent of the contents of the U.S. Constitution.[51] In other words, the Constitution protects only the rights of U.S. citizens as they are enumerated in the Constitution. These are distinct from the rights of state citizens, which the Constitution does not protect. The same year the Supreme Court holds in Bradwell v. Illinois that the privileges and immunities clause of the Constitution does not entitle Myra Bradwell to a license to practice law in Illinois contrary to judicial rule.[52] In 1874, the Court holds in Minor v. Happersett that the privileges and immunities clause likewise does not entitle Virginia Minor to vote in Missouri contrary to state law.[53] Enfranchisement effectively is controlled by the states, not the Constitution.

Thus, even though Anthony engages in civil disobedience on behalf of woman's equal right to vote, she is tried within conventional judicial boundaries. Her pleas are addressed to the only defenses permitted the charge, and those defenses do not address the issue of woman's equal right to vote. The decision is rendered within existing case law. The issue itself never really is heard by the Court, and the decision as to issues actually before the Court is predetermined by precedent.[54] Her hopes for broad and liberal interpretation of the Constitution by the Court are not well founded. She writes Stanton after voting and before her trial that "[i]f only now all the woman suffrage women would work to this end, of enforcing the existing constitution, supremacy of national law over state law, what strides we might make this very winter."[55] These hopes are not well founded either given the precedent of the Slaughterhouse cases. Years later she gives evidence of discouragement with means such as her own illegally-cast vote in response to a question about whether women ever will be given the vote. "It will come, but I shall never see it.... It is inevitable.... It will not be wrought by the same disrupting forces that freed the slave, but come it will."[56] In fact, civil disobedience is not indicted by the disappointing aftermath to Anthony's illegally-cast vote; the judicial system is.

Most feminist thinkers do not put all of their eggs in the suffrage basket, as noted before. Anthony is an exception to this rule. She fervently believes that suffrage is the answer to equal rights for women. In vain her colleagues

try to change her mind. Ida B. Wells reports such an instance. Anthony tells Wells that with the ballot, women no
longer will be subject to wrongs, injustice, inequality and
maladministration of the law. Wells replies, "Miss Anthony,
do you really believe that the millenium is going to come
when women get the ballot? ... I do not believe the exercise of the vote is going to change woman's nature nor the
political situation."[57] Once again a black woman offers cogent insight with respect to equality for women. As Anna J.
Cooper puts it in 1892, women of her race are in a unique
position, facing as they do questions of sex as well as race.
"To be a woman of the Negro race in America, and to be
able to grasp the deep significance of the possibilities of the
crisis, is to have a heritage, it seems to me, unique in the
ages.... Such is the colored woman's office."[58]

There are white women as well who embrace an egalitarian creed in this period. Jane Grey Swisshelm is one of
them. She is not impressed by proposed reform measures
which are believed widely to be the means for achieving
equality for women. She learns early in her married life
that compromising accomplishment with usefulness is not the
answer. She speaks of spending her "best years and powers
cooking cabbage. 'A servant of servants shall she be,' must
have been spoken of women, not negroes."[59] She disapproves
of what she regards as issues tangential to the exclusive interests of women, among them the bloomer: for her, "pan-
taloons were not the real objective point, at which all dis-
contented woman [sic] aimed." She is frustrated by women
seeking to publicize their grievances without distinguishing
between the legal and personal nature of them. She despairs
at the rush of small women-owned and -edited papers, which
disappear overnight but which attempt to meet the demand
for publicity. "Not one [woman] in a hundred thought of
merit as a means of reaching [her full allowance of nobility]."
She attends the woman's rights convention in Akron, Ohio,
and vehemently protests the introduction of a resolution stating
"that the difference in sex is one of education."[60]

Swisshelm's criticisms at times are well taken, but
her behavior appears at times to be dilettantish. She herself becomes a well-known journalist and must know the value
of visibility for an issue.[61] She disparages the suggestion
that education is the sole difference between women and men,
which seems reasonable, but she scorns women who cannot
make distinctions having to do with the legal basis for their
grievances--something education could help remedy. She is

critical of the woman's rights conventions but admits to at-
tending only a few and declines requests that she preside at
them--a position which would enable her to facilitate some
concrete direction for them. In short, she lacks the commitment to develop her criticisms constructively and comprehensively and to implement them in the woman's rights movement. Her thought has little impact as a result.

The concept of equality still is not a well-developed
one in feminist thought. June Sochen suggests that the period's reformers--she labels them "moral crusaders"--sim-
ply do not appreciate the revolutionary implications of their
demands. The reliance on natural rights theory with its libertarian overtones translates into moral imperatives in need
of legal sanction for most of them. Reformers believe their
cause inevitably must triumph in the end by virtue of its
rightness. They ultimately fail because they are unwilling to
advocate and work for radical change. Their successes lie
in advocating modest and nondisruptive changes. Their cultural commitment to traditional ends and means ensures both
their success and failure. As Sochen points out, and Harriot
Hunt as well, women reformers "are aware of moral flaws
in the accepted values of their peers," and they do act on
their awareness. [62] Limitations on their accomplishments in
the end are the product of commitment to the very longstand-
ing values and procedures they are trying to reform.

The point is made earlier that social change in this
area of American history is seen in terms of institutional
change. Feminists know the injustice being done by virtue
of their own life experiences. They feel the injustice acutely.
Some of them, Sojourner Truth for example, experience
greater injustice than others. These feminists realize the
interconnection of race, sex and economics, among others.
For them, things are far enough out of hand to seek to eradicate misery all at once rather than piecemeal. They grasp
the possibilities of such crisis. They number too few and
some of them are not committed enough, to impress their insights about equal rights for women on most feminist thinkers, however. On the whole egalitarianism goes begging for
want of serious advocates.

When feminist thinkers and their forebears do speak
of revolution, they qualify their statements either with implicit references to the disadvantages revolution entails or by
specifically stating revolution will be accomplished without
violence. Physical resistance per se is not advanced as an

alternative. Eugene D. Genovese's comments about such resistance in the context of the slave community are applicable
to feminism as well: for black people held in slavery, flee-
ing bondage or participating in insurrection may have been
the only genuine means of political action. Less far-reaching
activities of accommodation, i. e. lying, dissembling, or sui-
cide, represent prepolitical or even apolitical resistance.
Short-term resistance could be indispensable in constructing
a basis for political action, however, for it "contributed to
the cohesion and strength of a social class threatened by disintegration and demoralization. "[63] Here Genovese refers to
activities such as religious emphasis on love and dignity and
mutual support in the marital relationship which produce a
collective spiritual life. The importance of this life finally
lies in its linkage to political response.

According to Genovese, those members of the black
slave community who take the step to political action do so
as a result of their underlying collective spiritual life. Harriet Tubman is one of these. Earl Conrad shows that early
in Tubman's life she turns to prayer, "the same kind of religion that Nat Turner and Denmark Vesey had acquired ...
[i. e. ,] applied religion, a religion premised on the need for
a tremendous social change. "[64] The profoundness of Tubman's religious experience is evident when she successfully
flees her bondage. "When I found I had crossed that line,
I looked at my hands to see if I was the same person. There
was such glory over everything. The sun came like gold
through the trees, and I felt like I was in heaven. "[65] Her
own liberation is not enough, however. Others must have the
same opportunity. She returns to the South time and again
assisted by worthy others to lead her people from bondage.
Her strength, courage and morale are legend. In addition
to her work on the underground railroad, she plays an active
part in the Civil War as a soldier and scout and in the reconstruction aftermath. She is plagued by poverty but remains self-reliant and goes on to help develop the African
Methodist Church and to work in the temperance and suffrage
movements.

Few feminist thinkers advocate such dramatic means
for achieving women's equality. They evidence moral courage,
however, in confronting social moral flaws. In this sense,
they do the groundwork necessary to develop physical courage
among their kind. When a person such as Sojourner Truth
appears, they make it possible for her to inspire others by
her own physical courage. In this regard Truth is the priest-

ess of feminist thought. There also is the influence of
Quaker thought and Fuller's mysticism. The collective spiritual life characteristic of the slave community is a long
time in coming for feminist thinkers, but the elements necessary for its development are fully present by the time feminist thought acquires an identity of its own. Feminist thinkers will go on in the twentieth century to develop further the
implications of the bonds of womanhood of which Angelina
Grimke speaks earlier. They emphasize woman's growing
love for woman and the need for collectivity and what hinders
it, as well as seek to draw men into their cause. In doing
this, however, they are faced with their own burgeoning libertarian creed and its individualistic premises. The path of duty points in a direction not readily congenial to an egalitarian
creed.

For the meantime, the suffrage movement eclipses
feminist thought. In the eyes of the world, suffrage ideas
and ideals are feminism. This is an inaccurate perception,
but the time for suffrage comes, and attention focuses on it.
The Puritan ethic is crucial to its enactment, and feminist
thinkers have a partially Puritan heritage. The application
of Puritanism in the suffrage case leads to ends which are
not entirely feminist, however. Part of the explanation for
this lies in the importance of the West in woman's enfranchisement. As Alice Rossi shows, the moral crusade in
which prefeminist thinkers play such an important role is
centered in New York.[66] The Eastern moral crusaders include both economic reformers and social conservatives whose
lines are not well defined in relation to suffrage. Mormon
social doctrines represent a renaissance of the Puritan ethic.
Efforts to maintain the Puritan ethic contribute to the establishment of woman suffrage. In Wyoming, suffrage is enacted
partially by ironic chance, partially by political chicanery.
Once enacted, however, it becomes the means by which largely Republican community builders seek to establish civilization and counter more Democratic saloon advocates. The effort in Wyoming thus is to achieve the Puritan ethic as a
controlling political force.[67]

Populism is identified with woman suffrage throughout
the 1890s. Populism stresses a Puritanic, rural and traditional life style. A values struggle is in progress, with Populism on one side of the struggle and a capitalistic, urban
and modern life style on the other. Prohibition and immigra-
tion restriction are at the forefront of Populist reforms, and
it is believed that woman suffrage will help guarantee them.

Woman suffrage appears an effective way to maintain native-born Caucasian political supremacy to Western constituencies. Suffrage loses its momentum when the Populists are subsumed by the Democrats in 1896; it is accomplished in the context of the Progressive reform movement, but it still might be seen "as a by-product of the western Puritan revival."[68] In short, according to Alan Grimes, suffrage is part of a secular reformation committed to less than equal social ends. It represents an attempt to change the locus of political power, leaving its base undisturbed, through a kind of Puritan purification.

Bertrand Russell suggests the renaissance of Puritanism in America is tyrannic, relying on vindictive means to constrain naturally sinful acts, among them obscenity defined as birth control and white slavery. The acquisition of power to prevent others from doing what the Puritan condemns becomes an integral part of enforcing Puritan moral indignation.[69] Perhaps the renaissance of Puritanism is discussed more precisely in terms of application of the Puritan ethic as it is perceived by later-day Populists. Be that as it may, the problems of secular reformation and Puritan purification are real ones for feminist thinkers. Feminists are opposed to white slavery, and Emma Goldman for one devotes a fair share of her thoughts and efforts to its eradication. Birth control is another question. The passage of the Comstock laws in 1873 represents acknowledgment of the dominance of the Puritan morality of the masses and of prevailing orientations toward sexual matters, this in "an age of skepticism, pragmatism, discovery, and change."[70] Margaret Sanger's prosecution under the Comstock laws is a very good example of the kinds of problems the renaissance of Puritanism brings for feminists. Furthermore, once again a feminist uses civil disobedience to gain access to the courts to air an issue, and once again the court rejects the issue as irrelevant.[71]

As Elizabeth Sheldon Tillinghast puts it in 1900, "without political expression woman's economic value is at the bottom of the scale. She is the last to be considered, and the consideration is usually about exhausted before she is reached."[72] Political power is in the hands of those who advocate women's rights only when they serve as means to ends not of feminists' choosing, ends often unrelated to any change in woman's position. Carrie Chapman Catt and Nettie Rogers Shuler comment that "Superimposed upon [the] biological foundation of male resistance to female aggrandizement was the failure of political leaders to recognize the inescap-

able logic of woman suffrage in a land professing universal
suffrage. "[73] The point is, however, that such logic is
bound to escape those who do not begin with democratic premises in the first place. The suffragists accept the presump-
tions of American power politics throughout the Puritan revival; they simply interpret some of its components differently. [74] Then they are perplexed when the expected change in
woman's position does not follow. They accept the premise
that woman is separate but equal, recalling Tocqueville's
analysis[75]; however, they narrow the list of appropriate reforms to adapt the premise to suffrage. When political expression is not forthcoming, in either the immediate enactment of suffrage or its aftermath, they turn to existing political procedures to rectify the situation. All the while, they
are the last to be considered in power politics, and when they
are considered, they really never benefit from it.

As already noted, at this time feminist thinkers are
turning in increasing numbers to evolutionary justification for
their thought. Robert Riegel suggests this is their substitute
for revolution. [76] Change still is believed to be inevitable,
but now there is scientific verity to it. Removing environmental obstacles to woman's development is the end-in-view.
The most important of the obstacles is economics. Charlotte
Perkins Gilman analyzes women and men's sexuo-economic
relationship and concludes it is running its course; with woman's increasing individuation and specialization will come
the impetus to collectivity and humanity. Were feminists
more in tune with Marxist thought, they would find Gilman's
assumptions born out up to a point. For Frederick Engels:

> to emancipate woman and make her the equal of
> man is and remains an impossibility so long as
> the woman is shut out from social productive
> labor and restricted to private domestic labor.
> The emancipation of woman will only be possi-
> ble when woman can take part in production on
> a large, social scale, and domestic work no
> longer claims anything but an insignificant amount
> of her time. [77]

Were feminist thinkers to read further, however, they
would discover that Engels suggests an oppressed class which
is not self-liberated validates the existing order and is politically part of it, however radical it may be. Thus, according
to Engels, enfranchisement of an oppressed class within the
modern state is no measure of maturity. Over time, enfran-

chisement will become a measure of the intensity of an oppressed class's awareness of the true nature of enfranchisement. Of historical necessity, the class structure and with
it the state superstructure must fall. Then free and equal
association among producers will prevail. Before this takes
place, there will be elemental violence. [78] In this context,
nonviolent revolution appears nothing more than a pipe dream.
Furthermore, reform activities are only an extension of existing power politics, and they contribute to inherent contradiction which will culminate in the overthrow of the class structure and state superstructure.

Given the pacific overview of feminist thinkers' libertarian creed, one really does not expect a commitment to
violent overthrow of class and state. Beyond that, many
feminist thinkers are of the very merchant class which will
be caught in the middle of the tumult. To accept Marxian
revolutionary thought would be to accept the eradication of
themselves and their mercantile heritage. It is not surprising then that they seek other alternatives. There is an exception to this rule: Emma Goldman. Much later she is to
discuss the Attentäter* as analogous to nature's destructive
forces. She sees appreciation for political violence as a
product of intensely felt indignation over social wrongs. Political violence itself is sparked by "degrading, soul-destroy-
ing economic struggle." Goldman asserts that any social
theory which presents human beings as conscious social units
can infuse rebellion. [79] This suggests that even the feminist
libertarian creed could play a role here. Additionally, Goldman asserts that factors other than heredity shape the human
character, which suggests that the feminist mercantile heritage is not necessarily a bar to revolutionary violence. In
fact, feminist thought for the period under consideration does
not develop this natural intensity of feeling. For Goldman,
"That so few resist is the strongest proof of how terrible
must be the conflict between their souls and unbearable social inequities. "[80]

There is some feminist militancy during the suffrage
campaign, but it scarcely qualifies as political violence.
Compared to suffrage activity in England, it is decidedly low-
key. [81] Harriot Stanton Blatch, Ernestine Rose and Alice
Paul observe the English suffragettes firsthand and return to

---

*A revolutionist committing acts of political violence (German:
"assassin" or "assailant").

this country determined that their own movement will benefit
from their observations. Blatch and others found the Equality
League of Self Supporting Women (Women's Political Union),
notable for its appeals to working women and their trade
unions as well as for some imaginative tactics, for example
a trolley tour in Massachusetts. Alice Paul founds first the
Congressional Union under the auspices of the National American Woman's Suffrage Association and in 1916 the National
Woman's Party. The Woman's Party has access to funds, organization, will power and votes. [82] More than that, it engages in militant activities which are controversial and dramatic.

     The Woman's Party pickets President Woodrow Wilson,
is subject to arrests, administrative terrorism and intern-
ment in the Occoquan workhouse, engages in riots and prison
episodes, undertakes hunger strikes, burns President Wilson's
portrait in effigy, maintains Watchfires of Freedom in front
of the White House. Many of its members risk their jobs in
doing so, and some lose them. Some women are injured.
Catherine Flanagan for one suffers gashes on her hands when
the police dig their nails in to tear away her banner pole; the
insides of her hands are cut by her own nails as she struggles
to maintain her hold. [83] No substantial feminist egalitarian
thought, with one important exception, is forthcoming from
these activities, although Inez Haynes Irwin and Doris Stevens
produce detailed histories of them from the standpoint of participant observer. The twentieth century is underway, and
still feminist thought lacks an egalitarian creed. As is the
case in early American history, egalitarian feminists largely
are not Americans. If they are American, then they mostly
are too eccentric or radical for acceptance. Historical analyses of militant activities are solely in terms of freedom, [84]
and egalitarian implications go unexplored.

     The exception so far as egalitarian contribution to
feminist thought is an equal rights amendment proposed to
the U. S. Congress by the National Woman's Party in 1923. [85]
It states that "Men and women shall have equal rights throughout the United States and in every place subject to its juris-
diction. "* It is not well received in or out of Congress.

---

*The equal rights amendment passed by the U. S. Congress in
1972 (but requiring ratification by three-fourths of the states'
legislatures) states that "Equality of rights under the law shall
not be denied or abridged by the United States or by any state on
account of sex. "

Along with the proposal of the amendment comes opposition to the enactment of protective labor legislation for women which does not apply to men as well. The Woman's Party carries its opposition to numerous state legislative committees as well as to the International Labor Organization's annual conference in 1936.

Frances Perkins, U.S. Secretary of Labor, uses the Department's resources to oppose not only enactment of the amendment but the Woman's Party itself on as many fronts as possible. Resentment on both sides burgeons into an open feud. Woman turns against woman in the ensuing melee; accusation follows accusation. For one commenter:

> Annoying to a budding feminist, were those anti-suffragettes who by keeping their faces nicely mended while their fellow females were scrapping for the vote, were now in positions of power. ... [This] group is led today by Secretary of Labor Frances Perkins; Mary Anderson, Director of the Women's Division, Manpower Commission ... and others who proclaim that 'woman must assume equal responsibility with men' but turn thumbs down on proposals for real equality. [86]

Actually Perkins does not oppose suffrage at all. Her biographer, George Martin, suggests "she was only in her thirties whereas the leaders [of the suffrage movement] for the most were a good deal older. She was a member of the ranks." [87] She enlarges on her commitment after ratification of the Nineteenth Amendment by working to inform women about their newly won right and to encourage them to use it. The greater share of women and their organizations agree with her when it comes to passage of the equal rights amendment. They best are described as on the offensive in the battle. Despite Perkins' skirmishing behind the scenes, she can afford to offer a subtle exterior approach:

> It is with great regret that some of us recognize that the small group of women in the National Woman's Party who were in favor of suffrage and who worked with us for suffrage, should have taken this doctrinaire position which makes more difficult the passage and maintenance of legislation armed to improve the conditions of their working sisters, which was one of the primary reasons why many women wanted to vote and many wanted to have them vote. [88]

The stand of Perkins and others on protective legislation is not hard to understand within the context of their lives
and times. Perkins herself sees what working conditions are
through her surveys and investigations. She has two intense
personal encounters with the results of those conditions. She
is involved in the settlement movement. Her own belief in
autonomous principles of social justice mingles with the
settlement tradition of "protective walls."[89] The crisis orientation of the Roosevelt administration encourages short-
term solutions. Perkins is acquainted with what will and will
not be acceptable to Congress. Congress is not ready for
equal rights. Neither is she. In this context, equal rights
seem doctrinaire.

In the meantime, there is a growing commitment to
socialism in feminist thought which begins at the turn of the
century. The new emphasis on economics as the basis for
woman's oppression encourages this commitment. It also is
traceable to Rousseau's assertion of the injustice of the private property system. Socialism in and of itself implies economic equality. Elizabeth Blackwell is among those who advocate transition to a more socialist economy. She does not
base her argument on equality per se, however. Her concern is that in trusting individuals to do what is right, one
does not obtain the enlarged sense of duty on which most
libertarian thought depends. Blackwell suggests the basic social element is man, woman and child, not the individual.
She lists as possible applications of the principles of Christian
brotherhood (socialism) the following: (1) repurchase of land
by Christian joint stock companies, with control and management vested in those who live upon and use the land; (2) rational economy in distribution and management; (3) allotment
of a fair share of profits to all workers; (4) a form of in-
surance funds to secure aid to every worker in sickness and
old age; (5) arrangement of dwellings to facilitate communication, domestic service and supply, sanitary arrangements,
children's education and municipal government; and (6) abolition of all trade in the human body. For Blackwell, only
such Christian consciousness has the power to control and
guide selfhood.[90]

One recognizes Charlotte Perkins Gilman in Blackwell's suggestions as well as utopian thought generally. The
underlying Puritan-Populist assumptions are evident. Also
evident is the influence of the settlement house movement
philosophy. Notable, however, is the asexuality of her remarks. Women are not placed in a special class. What

might apply to women applies to men too. Nowhere does
Blackwell mention equality. Essentially she is attempting to
adapt individualism to a Christian principle of brotherhood.
She does not advocate overthrowing the capitalist economy.
She tries to adapt it to more Christian principles which she
describes as socialism. She anticipates Ellen Key's discussion of the need to move from competitive norms to those of
mutual help. Her focus here is on economic security. The
implication is one of a more collective society, organized
around spiritual principles.

When compared to extant socialist literature, especially that dealing with women and socialism, Blackwell's normative essay is incomplete. There is no discussion here of woman's position in marriage or her economic dependence.
There is no program by which to reach the ends Blackwell
prescribes. August Bebel in the late nineteenth century suggests that attempts to attain equal rights for women and men
will not change women's general condition.[91] Blackwell does
work within the existing social order, even though she would
alter it rather drastically were her suggestions implemented.
She would remove the economic barriers which make one human being dependent on another, but this would not necessarily propel woman into the work force. Whether she expects
motherhood and housewifery to become socially useful labor
tantamount to participation in the work force, there is no way
of telling. She does mention domestic service and supply and
children's education. What she means by these in the wider
sense is not known.

Bebel asserts, "The future belongs to socialism, that
is, primarily, to the worker and to woman." Blackwell talks
about man, woman and child. Bebel discusses the irresistable demand which will arise among most of the population
for transformation of unbearable evil. Here "the quickest
help will be considered the most appropriate."[92] This is
not the impact of Blackwell's essay. It is reform oriented.
She is advocating the systematically managed change which
Wollstonecraft prefers. Blackwell's socialist feminist thought
is a beginning. It is not well developed, and at best it is only
suggestive. It does promise things to come, and this promise
implies the development of a feminist egalitarian creed.

Ellen Key goes somewhat further in her thought, although it too lacks a systematic discussion of equality. She
posits that there must be perfect equality in marriage between spouses for the sake of women's and men's ethical

ennoblement. This includes the right to one's earnings and
property as well as authority over children and personal
freedom of action.[93] John Spargo goes even further and is
more explicitly egalitarian. For him, the right to vote and
equality in the labor force are the very foundation of freedom
of motherhood. He conceptualizes equality in terms of opportunity. In this regard, mothers of the race must have equal
freedom with fathers. The message of socialism for him is
life, liberty and love.[94] Thus the principle of equality, as
it develops in feminist thought, is being linked to the dominant but inapposite principle of liberty. It is equality of opportunity, of freedom of action, which is important.

Helen Keller's socialist feminist thought, which is
contemporary with Key's and Spargo's, is an exception here.
She is tied neither to liberty nor to pacific means. So far
as she is concerned, whatever educational and political opportunities women have gained are the result of "a march of
conquest with a skirmish at every post." She disclaims demands based on inalienable rights. Reminiscent of Sojourner
Truth, she declares "rights are things we get when we are
strong enough to make good our claims to them." To her
way of thinking, there can be no women or men's rights until the fair demands of working people for ownership and
control of life and livelihood are recognized. It is the close
relationship between social blindness and poverty which stands
in the way of equality of rights. Her indignation at the ill
treatment and abuse which meet those who would change degradation, enslavement and tyranny is profound. Her response
to such neglect is openly confrontational. "First of all, we
must organize. We must make ourselves so aggressive a political factor that our natural protectors can no longer deny
us a voice in directing and shaping the laws under which we
live."[95]

For Keller, the Woman's Party is a symbol of woman's solidarity, standing for allegiance to the ideal of sex
equality and responsibility. When it comes to decisive action,
reality--however sad--is preferable to illusion. There can be
no education for reality without revolution. "Let us try revolution and see what it will do now."[96] Keller is certain that
love will triumph in the end, but she is sympathetic with the
need oppressed peoples have for force to gain their rights.[97]
"I too hear the voices that say 'come,' and I will follow, no
matter what the cost, no matter what the trials I am placed
under. Jail, poverty, calumny--they matter not."[98] Once
again the spiritual voice rings out in feminist egalitarian

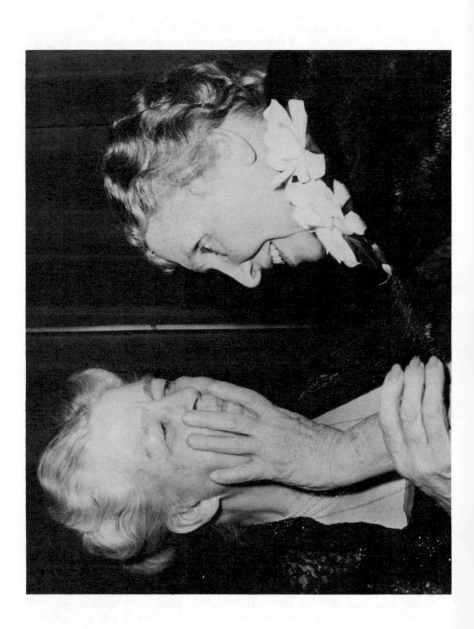

Eleanor Roosevelt and Helen Keller, 1955
(courtesy United Press International).

thought. Once again the voice belongs to a woman who has borne more than most, who has had to struggle against almost insuperable odds to gain her place in the world. Keller has a strong heritage in Sojourner Truth and Emma Goldman as well as in socialist thought generally. Her commitment to change is a broad one, and it emphasizes social injustice, economic inequality and physical resistance. Her commitment does not stop with opportunity; it is premised on concrete results. To that end, she joins the International Workers of the World and for her effort earns the label of "uncompromising radical,"[99] all this for a woman who is blind, deaf and mute.

Generally speaking, critics of feminist thought see equal rights for women as an abrogation of male and female biological, moral and mental differences. In this regard, feminism constitutes rebellion against the limitations and duties of sex.[100] The critics believe the 1923 equal rights amendment proposes to make a man a woman and a woman a man by applying the same laws to both of them. "If this Amendment passes, there will no longer be any such thing as sex in the United States...."[101] Here Havelock Ellis would make a critical distinction between artificial sex differences, which are abolishable by social change, and natural characteristics and predispositions, which no equalization of social conditions can remove totally. He suggests women and men never can be absolutely alike as long as they differ in primary sex characteristics and reproductive functions, but some sex differences are amenable to social change.[102] Rather than seeing the Woman's Party as a symbol of woman's solidarity with regard to sex equality and responsibility, the critics suggest a separate organization is not consistent with the equal rights amendment's spirit. This is so even if the extreme feminists who comprise its membership will not tolerate sex discrimination.[103] More feminist critics are concerned with the movement toward government paternalism which socialist equality entails for them. They attribute this tendency to a herd instinct in women which compels them to move through Uncle Sam to obtain desired ends.[104]

The concerns voiced about socialism are attributable to deep-seated commitment to liberty. No matter how piecemeal, changes with socialist import rub against individualism. Concerns about the absolute abrogation of sex differences partly are related to the "period of escape and revolt"[105] evident after World War I. The Flapper Age, about 1904-1915, constitutes changes in manners and morals which deeply trouble many individuals from all walks of life. The changes often are attributed to the increase of women in the paid labor force, although the high point there is reached in 1910 with no further substantial increases forthcoming until 1940. For Charlotte Perkins Gilman, newly enfranchised women--she calls them "freed slaves"--are experimenting with the indulgences, e.g. smoking, men heretofore call their own. Thus "we learn unsuspected weakness in their newly exposed characters, as we learn unsuspected anatomical errors in their newly exposed knees." Women exist in a man-made world in which social relations are excessively masculine; sex relations, excessively feminine. For Gilman, the important thing to remember is that woman's newly gained social condition is in the process of development. [106] In other words, when all is said and done, a more natural state of affairs will prevail.

The concern that women's equality with men will mean abrogation of sex differences, sexual sameness, continues. Among those who broach the topic is Gertrude Stein in her "A Plan for Planting" (1933).

> When I came away that is when I came to stay she
> said. I will be alike. And she was alike so much
> alike that there was no doubt about it. She might
> have been taken for her sister.
>   Only this was due to the fact that there was
> no reason why anybody should be different or just
> history.
>   ... And now what am I talking about, I am
> talking about how if there were a history it
> would be the same and in a kind of way there
> can not be a history because indeed it can never
> be the same. And so question me say that you
> like and you look like me and that you look at
> me.
>   And so every week almost every week we
> have some one who does not look alike but who
> does look like somebody else.
>   All this is not a puzzle it is a true story of
> anybody. [107]

One might infer from this that when woman leaves her former social condition, she means to stay with her newly gained one. She means to be equal to man. Her alikeness ironically leaves her similar to her sister, her heritage. The reason for this is that there never was a need to be different from men or a need to be only traditional. In fact, Stein seems to suggest that if there really were a tradition in this regard, it would be the same for women and men. There never can be such a tradition, in a way, because it never can be the same for women and men. In short, alikeness and equality are not equivalent to sameness and identical. Here Stein uses a personal play on the word "like," first as attraction toward and second as a state of being alike, concluding with a statement about an attempt at external perception. Frequently there is some individual who does not appear equal but who looks to be in a state similar to some other physical being. This is no mystery; it is a fact of physical existence. Things are not always what they seem. The past is not necessarily prologue, but one must be careful about what one attributes to the past. The problems of alikeness and equality are inherent to physical existence for women and men.

This is the selfsame issue Locke addresses with regard to equality. Human beings, although naturally equal, may be characterized by social inequality for any number of reasons. Thus, for Stein it seems that while one can make plans to sow the seeds of equality, one should be forewarned about the yield. Human beings vary from one another. Women vary from men, and women may vary from other women; men, from other men. Some individual may appear not to be equal and yet be similar to another. In the end, the concern that equality will make a man a woman and a woman a man may be much ado about nothing. To revert to Gilman's example, women may smoke as men do and appear manly to onlookers, but appearances can be deceiving. Woman may be attracted to smoking, perhaps because it is man's indulgence, and hence she is equal to him when she smokes--with regard to smoking. Not all men smoke, however; men are not equal to one another in this regard now or by tradition. Granted they may have the prerogative to smoke, which woman heretofore has not had. Yet if woman really chooses to smoke, what is there to stop her ultimately? She could filch tobacco and retire to the backlot to smoke it, if need be. She is not identical to man in doing so, but she is equal to some men with regard to the act of smoking only.

Equality in some minds is equivalent to the very license which those who espouse a libertarian creed are so anxious to deny. Gilman hastens to attribute license to a passing phase. Application of Stein's thought would suggest it is not worth all the excitement, given the variability of

physical existence. Still the concern continues. Ruth
Herschberger finds its roots in Eve's crime:

> Sad Eve, the crime all hers and mankind cursed
> When she deserted reason for delight,
> Seeing in evil, flavor, and an appetite
> Delirium and diet not the worst.
> Her mind unequal to her spouse and head,
> She thought to gain equality, though rude,
> Allaying custom's tyranny of blood,
> And ate of liberty though it was dread.
> Wisdom is risky, law saves but denies.
> Eve pondered, seeing pleasure at the swallow,
> And first of rebels, dared the apple bait.[108]

Eve exerts her will to choose pleasure in place of
revealed reason. She would gratify her taste in what is defined for her as evil. Sampling of liberty in this fashion
constitutes rude equality to the man God sets over her. The
forbidden fruit of knowledge yields but risky wisdom, for Eve
is assigned the crime and all mankind is cursed for it. Law
denied Eve an equal mind, but adhering to law would have
saved her from blame and mankind from the curse. Yet
Eve, first of rebels, perceives delight in a taste and meets
temptation. She resists custom's tyranny--which may be
merely expedient and no tyranny at all--by an exercise of
free will. Her motive is to attain that pleasure for herself
which, it seems, Adam already enjoys. With pleasure comes
equality of sorts and a fearful burden as well. Liberty and
equality are linked closely here, but the exercise of liberty
is intentional; attainment of equality seems to be a contingency. Eve rebels from her state of perfect but stifling freedom. To what end? She rebels for the sake of pleasure,
which is a mixed blessing. One gathers that the rude equality which goes with it is a mixed blessing as well.

Yet, as one actor in B. F. Skinner's Walden II puts
it, "you've got to experiment, and experiment with your own
life." Perhaps this is the test of an idea's goodness and internal consistency. If political action--the sort which reforms an existing structure--will not build a better world,
then other measures should be explored as soon as possible.
Rather than choose conspicuous unconsumption (of delight itself, as an example, or smoking or voting), one could sacrifice personal options for the sake of community, economic
self-sufficiency and behavioral engineering. In doing so, one
would abandon a leisure class for physical work whose final

value is determined by the whole community. Economic
freedom here translates into equality of opportunity with at
least the assurance of answers to the questions equality of
opportunity raises. Original sin--the interests of an individual which conflict with those of everybody else--is overcome by communicating means of self-control, a sort of social conscience. In return for this, people "get the satisfaction of pleasant and profitable social relations on a scale
almost undreamed of in the world at large."[109]

Gross physical differences--intelligence quotients, abilities, skills, physical prowess--all are part of Walden II,
where the community accepts its members as they are.
"[I]ndividuals are seldom compared." As for freedom--in
the words of Frazier, Walden's alter ego, "Freedom is a
question, isn't it? But let's not answer it now. Let's let
it ring, shall we? Let's let it ring."[110] Women in Walden
complete childbearing at an early age, still young in body
and spirit, and spend their adult life on a par with men, having "made the special contribution which is the either duty or
privilege of woman...." They then assume their place, and
it is not distinguished by sex. There is complete equality
of women and men in the community, with few types of work
not shared equally. Walden replaces the family, economically and, to a certain degree, socially and psychologically.
"Other things being equal," community members at Walden
simply do what they know is good without searching out a
rational basis for their decision. They agree to abide by
Walden Code, rules of conduct which are changed occasionally according to the dictates of experience, and receive a
constitutional guarantee of a share in the community's wealth
and life. This constitutes a kind of conversion process for
new adult community members, who agree to exercise necessary self-discipline in exchange for benefits of community living. Agreements about the common good are developed by
experimental ethics.[111] The community exists by virtue of
its motto: "Experience is the mother of all certainty."

Walden, as a cooperative community, values skill and
strength. It has no competitive sports but chess. Hero worship is discouraged. The important thing is to grasp current
forces. Progress is not determined by political action. "An
efficient state culture must be discovered by experimentation." In this context, religion, drinking, smoking--all fall
by the wayside. The only method of conquest is to set an example by offering "a full and happy life to all who go and do
likewise." This is expected to yield permanent results.

"[T]he only effective technique of control is unselfish. " Love
and positive reinforcement are regarded as interchangeable. [112]
Thus Skinner offers a truly egalitarian idea, even if an imperfect one--that of a community based on mutuality of purpose and effort.   It is the result of a nonviolent cultural revolution which eschews politics so far as possible.   Existing inequality, such as it is, is bypassed.   Members of the Walden
community are not given to comparisons, to hero worship, to
competitive games.   Women, once they complete their child-
bearing years, are equal to men with regard to their employment.

        The implication seems to be that the fact of childbear-
ing is an inescapable inequality.   This is incontrovertible if
by equality one means sameness.   If one means alikeness,
then even pregnancy should pose no barrier to equality, since
both sexes participate in the reproductive function.   Skinner
offers a curious treatment of sex equality.   He echoes Stein
with respect to the results of sowing seeds of equality.   In a
community based on cultural cooperation, however, it is hard
to understand why an exception to social equality should be
made at all for woman's childbearing years.   In many ways,
Walden is Eden revisited.   The law is that of reason revealed, in this case, by experience.   Women and men are
basically equal--but there is a contingency, woman's child-
bearing years.   Walden has its own forbidden fruit, and as
in Eden, only self-discipline stands between community members and immorality.   Here science and religion are as one.
If there is tyranny in Walden, it is expedient.   Compared to
the good life, to perfect freedom, any other choice is for
the sake of momentary pleasure.   Just as momentary pleasure is a mixed blessing, however, so it appears is imperfect
equality.   In the end, both entail a balancing of priorities by
those who must choose between them.   Seemingly there is no
middle way.

        It appears that equality is to be achieved more readily
through revolution than reform.   For feminist thinkers, equality is a political statement, but it is not likely to be attained by political means.   Revolution, when and if it comes,
will not be violent, although it will stress a kind of physical
resistance--whether through civil disobedience or bodily toil.
There is a spiritual note to feminist egalitarian statements.
Community and mutuality are essential to their expression.
Egalitarian statements contradict most libertarian statements
in this regard.   Liberty implies individual license; equality
implies community constraint.   Libertarians attempt to cir-

cumvent this by emphasizing the path of duty. Close scrutiny
reveals the impossibilities this entails for women, but that
kind of scrutiny is not forthcoming from feminist libertarians.
Equality does not present this problem, but it offers one with
respect to control and authority. Women are subject to many
limitations which smack of authority: paternal, religious,
economic, social. Feminist thinkers generally focus on independence from authority and impose an overlay of self-imposed
duty on independence. The few feminist thinkers who focus on
equality are more apt to see things in terms of earned right
or merit and opportunity than in terms of restraint. The
question for egalitarians largely is one of method, something
sorely lacking for libertarians. While reform is posited as
preferable to revolution, revolution appears to be the only viable means by which to obtain equality.

The case for revolution is not open and shut, as feminist thinkers are well aware. This, in addition to their overall intellectual orientation, helps to account for the inordinate
amount of effort devoted to reform. Hannah Arendt brilliantly
discusses the meaning of revolution and contemporary loss of
revolutionary spirit.[113] Her analysis offers some applicable
insights to the genuine difficulties revolution poses for feminist thought. She begins by stating that "revolutions ... are
not mere changes." For astronomers, revolution originally
means the regularized, recurring cyclical motion of the stars,
in accordance with scientific law. In modern times, revolution refers to the emergence of something new, its major
schema being freedom.[114] One can judge intuitively the vast
difference in early and modern treatments of this concept.
According to Arendt, eighteenth-century gentry and Jacobins
alike as revolutionaries are acquainted with the philosophy of
revolution, but their interest dims once revolution is achieved
through their deeds and specific events.

For Arendt, remembering concepts is a crucial part
of mental activity. By losing touch with their conceptual
base, the revolutionaries also lose touch with the spirit which
antedates their revolution. Spirit is represented by three
principles: public freedom, public happiness and public spirit.
In America, loss of spirit leaves civil liberties, majority welfare and public opinion as the prime ruling forces. Thus
principles which are originally political become socialized.
In the loss of revolutionary spirit, the tension between stability and beginning is accelerated to the point they become mutually exclusive. If spirit is to be regained, it must be through
mutual thought and meaningful combination.[115] This is strong-

ly reminiscent of Charles and Mary Beard. Loss of spirit.
is predated by failure to establish a lasting institution. In
short, "Brotherhood ... was no substitute for equality."
Freedom can exist only among equals, and equality too is the
product of certain limitations. Revolution originally is conceptualized as a means to achieve total control over violent
means, over power; actually control over violent means is
lost, as old power fragments and new power is based on
people's organizational motives.[116]

The above description does not begin to do justice to
Arendt's thought. The brief points made can be discussed in
terms of revolution as a means to achieve equality for women and men, however. For revolution to be meaningful, it
must establish something lasting which, for Arendt, is political and not social. That something needs to be linked closely
to principles which antedate revolution. It cannot be tied to
specific revolutionary deeds and events, to mere organizational impetus. It will be forthcoming only through mutual
thought and meaningful combination. Stability and beginning
must be one and the same. As such, they will incorporate
freedom among equals. The spiritual community that Genovese notes among slaves, the applied religion that Conrad attributes to Tubman and others of her ilk, become even more
crucial in this light. Without them, mutual thought and
meaningful conclusions scarcely would be possible. The
feminist libertarian creed will not reach its goals of inner
development and woman's subsequent liberation--will not attain freedom among equals--without such thought and combination.

Yet, for Arendt at least, spiritual community is not
enough. It must give birth to a lasting institution which she
believes is political. Feminist egalitarian thinkers at times
exhibit an aversion to the polity, although they are not generally anarchistic. This aversion is by no means universal
among them. The counter-tendency, however, is in many
respects a civil libertarian one, emphasizing equality of opportunity. Arendt finds this to be socially oriented as well.
One must move beyond organization--whether a National Woman's Party or a Walden II--to the creation of a stable political institution which assures remembrance of essential
principle. Short-term solutions, for example in the nineteenth amendment or the proposed 1923 equal rights amend-
ment--are not likely to be successful here. Further-reaching revolution will not be successful either should it lose
touch with equality in its attempt to introduce freedom. The

lasting establishment of something new which is firmly in touch with principle is a ringing challenge indeed. Feminist egalitarian thinkers face an arduous task if they are to meet the challenge.

References

1   Wollstonecraft, The Rights of Women (1790) (New York: E. P. Dutton, 1929), pp. 19, 31, 25-26, 34, 37, 53, 57-58.
2   Ibid., pp. 51, 213, 57, 163, 196, 171, 176, 179.
3   Wollstonecraft, A Vindication of the Rights of Men (1790) (Gainesville, Fla.: Scholars Facsimiles and Reprints, 1960), p. 115.
4   Margaret George, One Woman's "Situation:" A Study of Mary Wollstonecraft (Urbana: University of Illinois Press, 1970), p. 12.
5   Ibid., p. 90. See Wollstonecraft, Vindication of the Rights of Men, pp. 25-28, 50-52, 142-51, where she criticizes the private property system and points the way to its reform and extension.
6   See also George, One Woman's "Situation," p. 90.
7   Wollstonecraft, Vindication, p. 54.
8   Thomas Hobbes, Leviathan (Indianapolis: Bobbs-Merrill, 1958), pp. 104-05.
9   Ibid., p. 164.
10 John Locke, "An Essay Concerning the True Original, Extent and End of Civil Government," Second Treatise on Civil Government, in Social Contract, ed. Ernest Barker (New York: Oxford University Press, 1960), p. 4, pp. 30-31.
11 Jean-Jacques Rousseau, The Social Contract, in Social Contract, ed. Ernest Barker, p. 189.
12 Locke, "Essay," pp. 128-31, 143.
13 An Historical and Moral View of the Origin and Progress of the French Revolution and the Effect It Has Produced on Europe (1795) (Delmar, N.Y.: Scholars Facsimiles and Reprints, 1975), p. 7.
14 Ibid., pp. 70, 300.
15 Ibid., pp. 302, 68.
16 Wollstonecraft, Vindication, pp. 7-8.
17 Linda Grant De Pauw, "The American Revolution and Rights of Women: The Feminist Theory of Abigail Adams," paper prepared for the Annual Convention of the Organization of American Historians, Boston, 1975, pp. 1-2.

18   May 7, 1776, Familiar Letters of John Adams and His
     Wife During the Revolution (1875) (Freeport, N.Y.:
     Books for Libraries Press, 1970), p. 169.
19   March 9, 1807, in Correspondence Between John Adams
     and Mercy Warren, ed. Charles F. Adams (1878) (New
     York: Arno, 1972), pp. 493-94.
20   For a discussion of these writings see Chester E. Jor-
     genson, "Gleanings of Judith Sargent Murray," American
     Literature, 12 (March 1940), 73-78, especially 75-77.
21   Daughters of the Promised Land: Women in American
     History (Boston: Little, Brown, 1970), pp. 57-76.
22   Indiana (1831), in The Masterpieces of George Sand,
     trans. G. Burnham Ives (Philadelphia: George Barrier,
     1900), p. xii.
23   Ibid., pp. xiv, xvii, xix, 128.
24   Frances Wright D'Arusmont, Life, Letters and Lectures,
     1834/1844 (1844) (New York: Arno, 1972), p. 25.
25   Ibid.
26   Ibid., p. 32.
27   Society in America (London: Saunders and Otley, 1837),
     vol. 1, pp. 200, 61.
28   Ibid., 2, p. 340, 338.
29   Alexis de Tocqueville, Democracy in America, ed. J. P.
     Mayer, trans. George Lawrence (Garden City, N.Y.:
     Anchor Books, 1969), p. 503.
30   Ibid., pp. 505-06.
31   Ibid., pp. 603, 595, 598, 601.
32   A Treatise on Domestic Economy for the Use of Young
     Ladies at Home and at School (1841) (New York: Source
     Book Press, 1970), p. 9.
33   The Grimke Sisters from South Carolina: Pioneers for
     Women's Rights and Abolition (New York: Schocken,
     1971), pp. 270-75. See also Aileen S. Kraditor, The
     Ideas of the Woman Suffrage Movement 1890-1920 (New
     York: Columbia University Press, 1965), pp. 219-20.
34   "On the Duty of Civil Disobedience" (1840) (New York:
     Milestone Editions, n.d.), pp. 300-01.
35   Olive Gilbert, Narrative of Sojourner Truth: A Bonds-
     woman of Olden Time ... (1875) (Chicago: Johnson
     Publishing, 1970), pp. 103-06.
36   Gerda Lerner describes Truth's self-reliance generally
     in The Woman in American History (Menlo Park, Calif.:
     Addison-Wesley, 1971), pp. 67-68.
37   In Gerda Lerner, ed., Black Women in White America:
     A Documentary History (New York: Vintage Books, 1973),
     p. 565.
38   Ibid., p. 568.

39 Ibid., p. 569.
40 "Enfranchisement of Women," in Essays on Sex Equality, ed. Alice S. Rossi (Chicago: University of Chicago Press, 1970), pp. 93, 120.
41 Ibid., pp. 95-96, 99-100, 107, 113-15, 118.
42 Letter to Martha C. Wright, June 27, 1867, in Elizabeth Cady Stanton, ed. Theodore Stanton and Harriot Stanton Blatch, vol. 2, p. 116.
43 Constitutional Equality: A Right of Woman (New York: Woodhull, Claflin, 1871), pp. 3, 5-6, 55, 57.
44 Ibid., pp. 5, 57, 7.
45 Ibid., pp. 75, 78-80.
46 Discussion of much of the foregoing is to be found in Alma Lutz, Created Equal: A Biography of Elizabeth Cady Stanton 1815-1902 (New York: John Day, 1940), pp. 157, 231.
47 Ibid., p. 233.
48 "Indictment against Susan B. Anthony, District Court of the United States of America in and for the National District of New York," in An Account of the Proceedings on the Trial of Susan B. Anthony, on the Charge of Illegal Voting, at the Presidential Election in November, 1872 ... (1874) (New York: Arno, 1974), p. 3.
49 Ibid., p. 84.
50 Ibid., p. 85.
51 83 U.S. (16 Wall.) 36.
52 83 U.S. (16 Wall.) 130.
53 88 U.S. (21 Wall.) 162. For a discussion of constitutional tradition with regard to privileges and immunities, sex, lawyering and voting, see Kenneth M. Davidson, Ruth Bader Ginsburg and Herma Hill Kay, Text, Cases and Materials on Sex-Based Discrimination (St. Paul, Minn.: West Publishing, 1974), pp. 4-10.
54 Karen O'Connor discusses the problems of woman's rights issues in the context of constitutional interpretation in "Sex and the Supreme Court: Some Methodological Considerations," in The Study of Women and Politics: A Symposium Exploring Methodological Issues, ed. Sarah Slavin Schramm, forthcoming.
55 Quoted in Alma Lutz, Created Equal, p. 232.
56 Quoted in Alma Lutz, Susan B. Anthony: Rebel, Crusader, Humanitarian (Boston: Beacon Press, 1959), p. 311.
57 Alfreda M. Duster, ed., Crusade for Justice: The Autobiography of Ida B. Wells (Chicago: University of Chicago Press, 1970), p. 230.
58 Gerda Lerner, ed., Black Women in White America, p. 574.

59 Half a Century (1880) (New York: Source Book Press, 1970), pp. 48-49.
60 Ibid., pp. 140-42.
61 Gerda Lerner traces Swisshelm's career as a journalist briefly in The Woman in American History, pp. 36-37.
62 Herstory: A Woman's View of American History (New York: Alfred Publishing, 1974), pp. 132-33, 137.
63 Roll, Jordan, Roll (New York: Pantheon Books, 1972), p. 598.
64 Harriet Tubman: Negro Soldier and Abolitionist (New York: International Publishers, 1942), pp. 6-7.
65 Ibid., p. 9.
66 See Figure 2, The Feminist Papers: From Adams to de Beauvoir (New York: Bantam Books, 1973), p. 243.
67 Alan P. Grimes analyzes these tendencies in The Puritan Ethic and Woman Suffrage (New York: Oxford University Press, 1967), chs. 2-3.
68 Ibid., p. 118.
69 Bertrand Russell, "The Recrudescence of Puritanism," The Outlook, 52 (October 20, 1975), 300-02.
70 C. Thomas Dienes, Law, Politics and Birth Control (Urbana: University of Illinois Press, 1972), pp. 28-30, 33.
71 Ibid., pp. 84-85.
72 Susan B. Anthony and Ida Husted Harper, History of Woman Suffrage 1883-1900 (Indianapolis: Hollenbeck Press, 1902), vol. 4, p. 377.
73 Woman Suffrage and Politics (Seattle: University of Washington Press, 1969), ch. 32.
74 See Jean Bethke Elshtain, "Moral Woman and Immoral Man," Politics and Society, 4:4 (1974), 461.
75 Ibid., p. 462.
76 American Feminists (Lawrence: University of Kansas Press, 1963), preface.
77 The Origin of the Family, Private Property and the State: In Light of the Researches of Lewis H. Morgan (1891) (New York: International Publishers, 1972), p. 221.
78 Ibid., pp. 232, 234.
79 The Psychology of Political Violence (1930) (New York: Gordon Press, 1974), pp. 1, 13.
80 Ibid., pp. 28-29.
81 Rose Tremain traces The Fight for Freedom for Women in England, with some comparisons to the American suffrage campaign, in a spirited, beautifully illustrated piece of research (New York: Ballantine Books, 1973).
82 See Charles A. Beard, "The Woman's Party," The New

Republic, 7 (July 29, 1916), 329-31.

83 Inez Haynes Irwin, The Story of the Woman's Party
(1921) (New York: Kraus, 1971), pp. 468, 474; see also
Doris Stevens, Jailed for Freedom: The Story of the
Militant American Suffragist Movement (1920) (New York:
Schocken Books, 1976).

84 Janice Law Trecker, in an introduction to the recent reprint of Doris Stevens' Jailed for Freedom, p. viii, describes Woman's Party militancy as nonviolent and characterized by religion, a strong sense of discipline and
moral superiority, and an abhorrence of violence.

85 See Davidson, Ginsberg and Kay, Text, Cases and Materials on Sex-Based Discrimination, pp. 9-10.

86 Janet Grant, "Confessions of a Feminist," reprint from
American Mercury (December 1943), National Archives,
Frances Perkins' papers, GS File 1940-44.   The discussion about the equal rights amendment largely is derived
from Sarah Slavin Schramm, "Frances Perkins: Too
Soon for Equality," paper prepared for the Midwest Regional Women's Studies Conference, University of India-
na/Bloomington, April 1975, pp. 12-14.   See also J.
Stanley Lemons, The Woman Citizen: Social Feminism
in the 1920s (Urbana: University of Illinois Press, 1973),
pp. 181-208; William H. Chafe, The American Woman:
Her Changing Social, Economic and Political Roles, 1920-
1970 (New York: Oxford University Press, 1972), pp.
112-32.

87 Letter to Sarah Slavin Schramm from George Martin,
March 15, 1974.   See also Frances Perkins, The Roosevelt I Knew (New York: Harper & Row, 1946), p. 25.

88 Letter to Miss Florence A. Armstrong, chair, National
Woman's Party, July 10, 1944, National Archives, Frances Perkins' papers, GS File 1940-44.

89 Perkins, People at Work (New York: John Day, 1934),
p. 41.   See also Helen Louise Stitt, "A Study of the Woman's Party Position on Special Labor Laws for Women,"
thesis, Ohio State University, 1925.

90 Essays on Medical Sociology (1902) (New York: Arno,
1972), vol. 2, pp. 158-64, 166.

91 Woman and Socialism, trans. Meta L. Stern (Hebe) (1885)
(New York: Socialist Literature, 1910), pp. 5-6; see al-
so Olive M. Johnson, Woman and the Socialist Movement
(New York: Socialist Labor Party, 1919), p. 36.

92 Ibid., pp. 508, 366.

93 The Renaissance of Motherhood, trans. Anna E. B. Fries
(New York: G. P. Putnam's, 1914), p. 28.

94 Socialism and Motherhood (New York: B. W. Huebsch,
1914), pp. 11, 41, 68.

95 Philip S. Foner, Helen Keller: Her Socialist Years (New York: International Publishers, 1967), pp. 68, 64, 32-33, 30, 42.
96 Ibid., pp. 87, 82, 84.
97 Keller, Midstream, My Later Life (New York: Doubleday, 1929), pp. 334-35.
98 Foner, Helen Keller, p. 85.
99 Barbara Bindley, a reporter for the New York Tribune, so labels her. See Foner, Helen Keller, p. 82.
100 John William Porter, Feminism (Louisville, Ky.: Baptist Book Concern, 1923).
101 "Feminism in the Federal Constitution," World's Work (November 1922), 20-21.
102 Man and Woman: A Study of Human Secondary Sexual Characteristics, 6th. ed. (1894) (London: A and C. Black, 1926), p. 18; but see Elizabeth Blackwell, Essays on Medical Sociology, vol. 1, pp. 19-23.
103 "Feminism in the Federal Constitution," pp. 20-21.
104 See George Madden Martin, "American Women and Paternalism," Atlantic Monthly (June 1924), 744-53.
105 Charlotte Perkins Gilman, "Feminism and Social Progress," in Man and His World, ed. Baker Brownell (New York: Van Nostrand, 1929), vol. 7, p. 129.
106 Ibid., pp. 129-31, 122.
107 Gertrude Stein, Painted Lace and Other Pieces (1914-1937) (New Haven, Conn.: Yale University Press, 1955), p. 14.
108 "Anent the Apple," in A Way of Happening (New York: Pellegrini and Cudahy, 1948), p. 21.
109 B. F. Skinner, Walden II (1948) (New York: Macmillan, 1962), pp. 9, 14, 19-20, 26, 57, 53, 92-93, 130, 104-05, 151, 112.
110 Ibid., pp. 127-28.
111 Ibid., pp. 133, 138, 159, 162-63, 174, 172.
112 Ibid., pp. 237, 239, 193, 195, 199, 228, 289, 300.
113 On Revolution (New York: Viking, 1963). Arendt's discussion of the roots of revolution is crucial to an understanding of the concept. While space does not permit extensive review of her thought, the treatise is recommended highly by this author to the reader.
114 Ibid., pp. 13, 35, 21.
115 Ibid., pp. 221-23, 225.
116 Ibid., pp. 251, 279, 260.

Part III
Women's and Men's Roles

5

THE BROADER PROTEST:
FEMINISM AND COMPLEMENTARY ROLES
FOR WOMEN AND MEN

In what goes before, the importance to feminist and prefeminist thought of two intermingled issues, family and education, is discussed along with the existence of two inapposite ideological streams, liberty and equality. Feminist and prefeminist thought cannot be distinguished internally with respect to its issue orientation because the treatments these issues receive are interrelated. It cannot be distinguished internally with respect to its ideological streams either. Their inapposition might appear to offer a basis for distinction, but the fact is that--for all the inconsistency this represents--development of an egalitarian creed is accommodated to the burgeoning libertarian creed. In short, the libertarian creed is the watchword of feminist and prefeminist thought. This body of thought is of one cloth when it comes to issues and ideological creeds, despite some tension between warp and woof. There is a basis for asking about internal distinctions, however. It lies in the treatment feminist and prefeminist thinkers give to women and men's roles. By far the broader protest here is initiated on behalf of complementary roles for women and men. In this regard, women and men are believed to be by nature complements. Neither women nor men can fulfill their functions or purposes alone. This is immediately understandable in terms of reproduction, but there is far more than biology involved. From the beginning, culture and with it civilization are understood to be affected profoundly by whether women's and men's complementary roles are fulfilled.

Reciprocally enjoying the benefits of transcending time and space, feminist and prefeminist thinkers ponder the implications of complementary roles for women and men. Mary Wollstonecraft cites her well-known theme of companionship as the basis for both the relationship of women and men and the right ordering of society in a moral sense. You see, she says, women and men are possessed of relative duties for which arbitrary designations of status have no bearing. In addition, woman's fulfillment of her duties can in no way be deemed to reflect poorly on her beauty. Instead it must bring her respect and comfort. Hannah Adams reflects, though, that doing business out of what is considered the female line was a source of great discomfort and personal trial for her in her lifetime. Mercy Otis Warren agrees; I myself wondered, she says, if the female character didn't suffer from penning satire such as I did during the War for Independence.

Oh, but were women to develop their strength and beauty, they would not wish to be men or man like--it is Margaret Fuller speaking: women and men represent two sides of a great radical dualism, and they should correspond, appreciate and prophesy to one another. To that end, women need to retire within themselves to find their peculiar secrets. Women may love women, and men may love men, intellectually and spiritually, free from temporal considerations. Then individual character expansion and development can take place. Alexis de Tocqueville seems to agree. He remembers observing how Americans think man and his wife have equally firm understanding and clarity of mind and equally

possess courage, even though they don't expect them to be
applied to the same ends or to have the same character.
John Stuart Mill believes women and men will come to employ themselves with natural tasks: women, those which reflect beauty, delicacy and taste; men, those which require
muscular exertion.

A number of thinkers recall J. J. Bachofen's study
of classical mythology and his systematic establishment of
stages of lunar mother right and solar father right in early
human development. The lunar stage is characterized by
love, union and peace; the subsequent solar stage, by definite
groupings which result in an assault on women's rights. Women long for security and purification throughout the assault,
for a higher stage of existence which transcends eros. As
men do in Orphic homosexuality, Lesbian women come to love
their own kind and thereby attain purified psychic beauty.
August Bebel speaks about how socialism will reinstate in a
higher civilization the communism of the matriarchate, liberating male egotism and female service. Then women can
rise to heights of natural perfection. Women absolutely must
not adopt man's ways for her own, states Ida M. Tarbell; the
world needs the qualities and powers which differentiate women
from men. George Burman Foster replies that no human nature is man-less or woman-less. If only the woman's movement will extend great generosity to men, women and men
will enjoy the heightened harmony of intercurrent selfhood.

While women must have the right to think their own
thoughts and go their own ways, says Ellen Key, the real
nature of women collectively must be protected. Yes! Alice
Henry responds enthusiastically; thus trade women and their
own organizations must champion adaptation of modern conditions for the protection of women in the labor force. Key

nods and goes on: otherwise, the power that is motherhood, the deepest vital source of her physical and psychical being, gradually will be destroyed. Women's rights in the end must be limited by the right of the child who might be. Helen Keller suggests that women must have the right to protect themselves, freeing man from his feudal responsibilities. Women's peculiar attributes entitle them to be heard through suffrage. John Spargo speaks up quickly. This will be facilitated by a socialist communism of opportunity or equality of advantage which facilitates individual achievement and glorious inequality. Charlotte Perkins Gilman muses that the action which is life and happiness is a freely chosen fulfillment of function which will enable the world realization of woman's birth-based altruistic principle. This is opposed to man's death-based individualistic principle for the end of human improvement, the religious duty which transcends all others. H. L. Mencken responds dryly about the special feminine character which naturally functions as compassionate irony in an extension of the maternal instinct. He remembers, though, that people of talent are characterized by reciprocity between complementary feminine and masculine elements.

Amy Lowell points out that women of talent are a queer lot, "mother creatures, double-bearing, / With matrices in body and in brain," sisters of a family and yet unlike one another--unless the veils which obscure their souls be removed. Lowell ponders Sappho, the "leaping fire we call so for convenience," Ah, Amy, sighs Alice Ames Winter, Sappho's symbolic martyrdom as uncontrolled womanhood is post mortem. Inferences about loving women no longer refer to women's and men's passion alone. Women are loving other women.

Then there is Freud, someone thinks aloud. For Freud, the human tendency is to reach out to and join living substance in increasingly larger units, expressing the instinct of life before that of death without being overcome by conscience. It is the woman artist who links creation and life in her womb, says Anaïs Nin, bringing together man and life despite the masculine alchemy which masks his role. As for woman, she is a mermaid dipping her tail in the pool of the unconscious. Edna St. Vincent Millay suggests man is woven into a suit-of-mail of wit and love, while woman contends with a body that plants its muddy feet in her mind. But in unmasking themselves, says M. Ester Harding, women and men could release emotional energy not unlike that of religious experience and expend it for mutual development. Acting only for personal or ego ends will bring an end to development, however. The problem, states Simone de Beauvoir, is that woman is being posed as absolute Other which makes it impossible for authentic drama to occur. Transcendence takes place when women and men confirm each other as conscious free beings. Alterity is realized in desire, embrace, love. Lesbianism can be an authentic expression, but if it becomes exclusive, woman loses the opportunity to be torn from self in relation with man.

* * * * *

Mary Wollstonecraft normatively understands women's and men's relations in terms of companionship. Such a state currently does not exist because women are not educated for it. In addition, weak men are inebriated with their power of supreme dignity. The ultimate question behind the need for companionship among women and men is one of moral and civil interests. First, subordinating the rank of one group of people as the basis for another group's power is injurious to morality. Second, private morality cannot be translated into private virtue by way of citizenship where one's discharge of duty is based on arbitrary distinctions of station. For men to maintain women as children throughout their lives is to behave in an unphilosophic manner. Women and men both must be educated in an orderly manner by the opinions and manners of their society if their moral and civil interests are to be represented adequately. [1]

Heretofore, according to Wollstonecraft, brute force governs the world. For woman to become the friend of man, her husband, she must strengthen her body and exercise her mind. The chaste wife and serious mother will prefer respectability to dependence on a being such as man who is subject to certain infirmities just as she is. In the end, women and men should reflect knowledge and virtue which are the same in nature, if not degree, even if bodily strength renders men women's natural superiors. Women might have less power in a world governed by laws forthcoming from reason, but they would be less degraded and licentious in character. [2] In this respect, women need to be stimulated to the attainment of virtues which are their own. Society is not organized correctly if the discharge of women's and men's respective duties is not the basis for human respect and comfort. Thus, even though women may have duties different from men's to discharge, they with men have human duties governed by innate principles. Woman's beauty naturally harmonizes with the countenance which should be forthcoming upon fulfillment of her relative duties. Favor should not be a product of some preposterous distinction of rank. [3]

For Wollstonecraft, speaking largely of women, woman's first duty is to herself as a rational creature. Her second duty, in order of importance, is as a citizen, and this duty includes, among others, motherhood. Discharge here includes nursing and educating one's children, and this reflects on wifeliness. Only slothfulness and conceit in a vacuous mind could lead woman astray from this duty, for whatever disables the maternal disposition removes woman from her sphere. Woman as citizen could study politics in order to base her benevolence more broadly. First, however, she must be in possession of her natural rights; without them, her duties are nullified. [4] Wollstonecraft really does not say what men's duties are; she instead refers to the relative nature of women and men's duties. In doing so, she seems to assume and even accept difference here. The difference is not an arbitrary one, however. It is a difference necessitated by the orderly functioning of society; it is premised on what she believes to be natural distinctions. What these distinctions are explicitly, she does not say.

For Wollstonecraft, the point is the importance of discharge of relative duties to orderliness as well as the harmoniousness of woman's beauty with her discharge of duty. In other words, women and men have respective obligations which they must fulfill and which will enhance their moral state. Today these would be referred to as roles, patterns of expectations held by self and significant others about what behavior and interaction should be.[5] In Wollstonecraft's thought, fulfilling one's role and thereby gaining respectability poses no threat to womanliness or, it might be said, femininity. This is the promise of independence and the natural result of women's and men's immortality. It is the end of education and the key to rightfully ordering family relationships and society. It is all important.

Premising the roles of women and men on their relative spheres and demanding respect for their fulfillment is very much a part of feminist and prefeminist thought, as will become evident. Women's and men's respective roles are considered to be complementary. The discharge of one without the other leaves the world at large incomplete; in fact, one role probably cannot be discharged adequately unless the other is fulfilled as well. Thought along these lines is not new, and it is not original with Wollstonecraft generally. Perhaps its most comprehensive spokesperson in antiquity is Aristotle.

Without presuming to do justice to the detailed work which is The Politics of Aristotle, it may be said that the association of women and men for Aristotle is part of a larger association, the family, and a still larger association, the village, which ultimately is part of an associational whole, the polis. While the former are prior in time, the latter is prior in nature as a whole is to its parts. According to Aristotle, to understand difference among persons and associations, one must begin by analyzing constituent elements. Aristotle suggests there is a natural distinction between females and slaves, each of whom serves a separate purpose. Only among barbarians who lack a ruling element is this distinction obliterated. The union or pairing of male and female is the result of a natural impulse toward reproduction of their species. In this respect, women and men cannot exist without each other. The union of master and slave is that of ruler by virtue of intelligence and ruled by virtue of bodily power to carry out the ruler's plans. Here as well, there is a common interest in the preservation of both master and slave. [6]

The household is formed as a means of meeting daily or intermittent needs. It is made up of three relations: master/slave, husband/wife, parent/child, as well as an element of acquisition. The first three relations have moral implications, the latter an economic one. The master/slave union is like that of a superior to an inferior. With reference to mental differences, in discussing master/slave relations, Aristotle states that "the relation of male to female is naturally that of the superior to the inferior--of the ruling to the ruled. This general principle must similarly hold good of all human beings generally [and therefore of the relation of master and slaves]. "[7] He then moves to a discussion of acquisition as opposed to use, the fulfillment of household needs and a criticism of usury. At this point only does he revert to the rule of a household's head over wife and children, who are free members of the household. It seems to the author that this is a means of underscoring distinctions among slaves, wives and children and the differences in their respective associations with the head of the household. [8] While each of the former is inferior to the latter, wives and children are distinguished from slaves with respect to function. All inculcate a certain goodness relative to function, but the functions must be kept ordered and distinct. The husband/wife union or marital association is likened to that of statesman over citizen; the parent/child association, to king over subjects. The male/female union, however, is permanent where that of statesman/citizen is temporary, males always being naturally fitter to command than females (except in cases of natural aberration). It must be noted, however, that Aristotle in another passage distinguishes the authority of household head as monarch from that of statesman. The statesman has authority over freemen and equals; the household monarch, over slaves, wives and children. [9]

In distinguishing slaves, wives and children as household members, Aristotle seems to be suggesting that these have something in common in terms of the authority of the household head over them. Thus, while slaves, wives and children can be differentiated with reference to certain associational analogies, they must be understood in terms of household order as well. This is underscored in a later passage discussing Spartan women who are licentious and given to lives of luxury. Aristotle states that in "all constitutions

... where the position of women is poorly regulated, one-
half of the citizen body must be left untouched by the law. "
Women and men are essential to the family, and the polis
can be understood only in terms of the women and men who
constitute it. Without an ordering of these constituent parts,
among others, harmony will be lacking, and avarice will de-
velop.10 In this regard then, as Ernest Barker puts it, "nature and convention are not in their essence opposites, but
rather complements."11 One consciously constructs an association such as marriage in keeping with a natural impulse
such as reproduction. In this fashion, the impulse is recognized, and its fulfillment ensured, in keeping with the respective purposes of women and men.

Aristotle sees men as superior, women as inferior,
with respect to ruling and being ruled. That is not to de-
precate their respective functions; it is to institute natural
order into their immediate union and into the greater whole
of which that union is a part. Wollstonecraft really does not
make extended generalizations about superiority and inferiority, although she criticizes the results of man's superior dignity in her society. It is at least possible that she would
maintain or reinstate men as heads of household; she is suggestive but not explicit here. She would not have the relationship of women and men be arbitrary, however; she specifically states that notions of station have no bearing in this
matter. Imposing order through discharge of respective duties and awarding respect and comfort on the basis of such
discharge are most important. There is no question that Wollstonecraft is a forthright advocate for women and that Aristotle
is not. He does not consider such matters, leaving them with
the assumption that right-ordered associations, as he understands them, are for the good of the whole as well as its
constituent elements. Nevertheless, it is not inappropriate
to invoke Aristotle's analysis as a means to highlight certain
aspects of Wollstonecraft's later one. Understanding Aristotle
in this limited fashion is useful when it comes to generalizing
Wollstonecraft's thought about women's and men's relationship.
She is the seminal thinker in this regard for American feminist and prefeminist thinkers, not Aristotle. He is an important thinker, however, with respect to this particular
means of conceptualizing the relationship of women and men.

Wollstonecraft and Aristotle alike make fleeting references to sexual relationships between members of the same
sex. They seem to confine their references to men or young
boys. Page Smith asserts Wollstonecraft discusses "homo-

sexual tendencies promoted by English boarding schools and the lesbian attachments of girls forced to keep each other company."[12] Perhaps she does. On this author's reading, at least, her references to "vice and folly" among young boys in boarding school seem to indicate homosexual play. With respect to young women's "bad habits," her meaning is not so clear.[13] At any rate, she clearly does not approve of these relationships, whatever their expression may be. Aristotle's references to homosexuality are explicit, but his overall attitude toward it is less clear. He would restrain such impulses in the public square; he labels familiarity among close male relatives "the very height of indecency...." He approvingly notes, however, that people who sanction homosexuality are not likely to be ruled by their wives. Finally, he states that the question of rightness or wrongness, with regard to sanctioning homosexuality, "may be left for a later occasion."[14]

It seems that imposing order plays a large part in both sets of considerations. For Wollstonecraft, right order apparently would eliminate homosexuality. For Aristotle, it seems order implies regulation rather than elimination. Importantly, both appear to consider homosexual expression more pertinent with respect to men than women. This probably is a statement about the freedom of expression which attaches to man's position but not woman's. Whatever women's and men's respective spheres may be, however, Wollstonecraft and Aristotle seem to suggest their complementarity should be stressed and stabilized. According to Wollstonecraft, this entails elimination of situations which throw members of the same sex, especially young men, into potentially provocative relationships. It is a moral question which ultimately reflects on virtue and attendant perfection and the necessary order of society.

In the colonies, women and men's relationship is characterized by mutuality. Page Smith suggests that, "in a simple frontier society without any very clearly defined notions of the 'role' of women, able and enterprising females moved quite easily and naturally into a wide variety of jobs."[15] That they did, but even then there were certain expectations about what certain women could and should be doing. The idea of the lady is an imported one which makes its appearance by 1780-1790. It is acknowledged by upper-class women at the time of the American Revolution. Hannah Adams is a woman of some literary talent who, because she is reduced to few material means, must publish in order to

support herself. Her memoir clearly expresses her consternation about engaging in such activities.

Adams writes, for example, about how she must reconcile herself to the necessity of "doing business out of the
female line, which exposed me to public notice." She feels
deeply "the trials which attend literary pursuits." She recalls being educated in "habits of debilitating softness," only
partially balanced by her voracious reading at an early age.
She mentions the emotional turmoil attendant to compiling her
Views of Religion, being required as she is to delve in controversy "with a mind naturally wanting in firmness and decision."

> Reading much religious controversy must be ex-
> tremely trying to a female, whose mind, instead
> of being strengthened by those studies which ex-
> ercise the judgment, and give stability to the
> character, is debilitated by reading romances
> and novels, which are addressed to the fancy
> and imagination, and are calculated to heighten
> the feelings. [16]

She seems at times to attribute her difficulties to her femaleness, at times to her education. When the situation demands
it--for example, on one occasion another adopts her work as
his own, on another occasion she has difficulty with a printer
about her reimbursement, she successfully asserts herself to
right matters. Here too she relates her discomfort about
having to take such steps. She is aware that her publishing
is a matter of the utmost importance to her well-being and,
while she regrets the ridicule it may entail, she believes
those closest to her understand. [17]

Adams never marries, which gives her more leeway
than she would have were she married, but she still displays
the impact of expectations--her own and others--about what
her behavior should be. She manages to persist in her publishing, but she pays an emotional price for doing so. Women
are expected to shoulder their share of the burden of subsistence at this time, but literary pursuits and publishing are
not necessarily expected to be part of the burden. One married woman who writes, although anonymously at first, with
the encouragement and praise of the men in her life is Mercy
Otis Warren. She too bears testimony to the pangs of conscience her activity gives her.

Warren confides her doubts to John Adams, noting the unusual nature of the times but wondering if perhaps the "female character" suffers from penning the satire which is her singular contribution to the patriotic cause.[18] Throughout life, she fulfills her domestic pursuits with satisfaction, pities those who do not, loves her needlework and is garbed fashionably even in her senior years. She acknowledges women's "appointed subordination" at the same time she fosters their attempts to match masculine intellectual attainment.[19] On a reading of Warren's life, one would never want to describe colonial expectations about women's roles as inflexible, by any means. They are present nonetheless and destined to become more prominent in the nineteenth century. Women who might be described as of a prefeminist persuasion near the end of the eighteenth century are conscious of these expectations. They accommodate them to the situation and activity in question, but this largely is as far as their protest goes.

By the time the nineteenth century is well underway, "lectures on some model woman of bridelike beauty and gentleness, ... treatises intended to mark out with precision the limits of Woman's sphere and Woman's mission...," as Margaret Fuller puts it, are disseminated widely and having their effect. Fuller can only remark the inconsistency this entails, for advocates of ladylike demeanor among women are not moved by the fact pregnant black women must toil in the fields or by the terrible strain seamstresses endure. Given their independence, women would develop their strength and beauty; "... they would not wish to be men or manlike. The well-instructed moon flies not from her orbit to seize on the glories of her partner." In this respect, for Fuller, the remedy for lack of correspondence, appreciation and prophecy between men and women lies in individual character. It must be expanded and developed. Women are not whole beings when confined to affection and habit.[20]

According to Fuller, the world is more prepared than ever before for woman to develop her intellectual ability and thereby realize her naturally rapid and correct intuitions. Once woman's spiritual tendencies are balanced and regulated by her intellectual power, virtue will surpass innocence; submission, dependence. Woman excels "in an instinctive seizure of causes, and a simple breathing out of what she receives that has the singleness of life...." On the other hand, classification, recreation and the selecting and energizing of art do not come so easily for her.

In so far as soul is in her completely developed,
all soul is the same; but in so far as it is modified in her as Woman, it flows, it breathes, it
sings, rather than deposits soil or finishes work;
and that which is especially feminine flushes in
blossom the face of earth, and pervades like air
and water all this seemingly solid globe, daily
renewing and purifying it as life. Such may be
the especially feminine element spoken of as Femality. [21]

Some caution is in order here. One must read Fuller
very carefully to understand what it is that distinguishes her
from lectures and treatises which limit woman's sphere and
with which she disagrees. "Femality" is not manifested
purely anymore than masculine energy is. "Male and female
represent the two sides of a great radical dualism. But in
fact they are perpetually passing into one another. ... There is
no wholly masculine man, no purely feminine woman." Yet
speaking approximately, women predominate in intuitively sight-
ing the world of causes. This is so despite exceptions to the
rule which nature provides. What is important, however, is that
no woman or man, black or white, be bound to one and only
one form of energy. Celibacy takes on new light in this regard; to undertake union and relation, one first must be a
unit of one's own. Living largely in relations, the individual
becomes estranged from its resources and deprived of instinctive means of existence. Women must "retire within
themselves and explore the groundwork of life till they find
their peculiar secret." [22]

For Fuller, were the two sides of human nature--femi-
nine and masculine--in perfect harmony, "they would correspond to and fulfill one another." Yet, as mentioned earlier,
human nature does not admit perfect harmony. Unclear perception of truth and justice hinders the rapid development
which would grant the sexes influence upon each other and
mutual improvement. Women ultimately may take up any occupation, but most will choose what they currently have.
"Nature would take care of that...." Women who are unfit
for motherhood, however, must not be confined to it. [23] To
know what their impulses are, women must not enter into
union with men for now. Instead they must come to know
themselves. They are their own best helpers here.

Katharine Anthony--in a biography compiled from secondary sources and marred by an inadequate psychological

treatment but not without some insight--characterizes Fuller as "a woman's woman." She recalls how Fuller institutes a series of conversations for women in Boston, from 1839 to 1844, to introduce the organization which will enhance their creative genius. Thus, Fuller points the way, though not without being ridiculed, for women to help themselves on their own. [24] She herself is accepted as a peer by men in the Transcendentalists' circle, but her early life reveals her adoration for and attachment to other women. "It is so true," Fuller writes, "that a woman may be in love with a woman, and a man with a man. ... It is regulated by the same law as that of love between persons of different sexes, only it is purely intellectual and spiritual, unprofaned by any need of consulting temporal interests...."[25] Thus, in her own life, Fuller maintains the celibacy which enables her to become a unit, leading the way to union later in life with the Marchese Angelo Ossoli.

While Fuller's thought is more limited than Wollstone-craft's with respect to comprehensiveness, in some ways it takes an additional step. She recognizes with Wollstonecraft that women are degraded by their current manners, but she does not understand their potential in terms of duties. She understands it in terms first of woman's nature and second of woman's personal inclinations. She generalizes about woman's nature and man's and carefully lays the groundwork for bypassing narrow expectations about woman's sphere. She expresses wholehearted appreciation for women. Her language is romantic; it also is beautiful. She transcends an approach based predominantly on objective reason for one which communes with women on a spiritual level. Reading Women in the Nineteenth Century well over 100 years later is an experience which sweeps the reader along in a flow of deep feeling.

Alexis de Tocqueville's empirical observations about women's and men's roles in America stress rights and duties but are nonetheless compatible with Fuller's normative analysis. Here it must be remembered that Fuller believes a transition is in progress from outworn inflexible notions about the respective spheres of women and men to ideas more in keeping with nature. Tocqueville states that American women remain in the domestic sphere and may be quite dependent in this respect. Regardless, American women have a higher station than they might elsewhere. The part women play is accorded equal regard with men's part. Americans

do not expect courage of the same sort or for
the same purposes from woman as from man,
but they never question her courage. They do
not think that a man and his wife should always
use their intelligence and understanding in the
same way, but they do at least consider that
the one has as firm an understanding as the
other and a mind as clear. [26]

As with Aristotle, Tocqueville's observations are not
calculated to change or improve woman's position. They
describe the roles women and men play and relate them, in
Tocqueville's case, to the political phenomenon of democracy.
Margaret Fuller's largely prescriptive analysis draws on her
observations, but its major thrust is to suggest how women's
and men's roles should be structured. To her way of thinking, some rather substantial changes need to be made.
These are not totally out of character with traditional notions
about femininity and masculinity. Catharine Beecher, for example, might feel quite comfortable with Fuller's thought
here. The changes Fuller advocates bespeak flexibility, however. Fuller's suggestion that women forego union with men
at least temporarily for their own sakes is quite a radical
one. Here Catharine Beecher, who bespeaks the need for
greater appreciation of women's contributions to home and
family, probably would feel very uncomfortable, but Sarah
Grimke and Mary Griffith undoubtedly would be delighted.
Yet, among Fuller, Tocqueville and Beecher, there is a certain amount of solidarity with respect to the complementary
nature of women's and men's roles. All three see them as
potentially or actually quite harmonizable, even if not perfectly so. There is some difference among the three, however, when it comes to reciting more particularized expectations about what sort of behavior woman's role should stimulate. Margaret Fuller is considerably ahead of her time in
American prefeminist thought.

An essay on marriage and divorce by John Stuart Mill
12 years before the publication of Women in the Nineteenth
Century displays parallels to Fuller's work. Mill suggests
woman's "great occupation" is the beautification of life. Women will not attain their potential or right social position,
however, until they are capable of earning their own way.
Once they have this power, "The only difference between the
employments of women and those of men will be, that those
which partake most of the beautiful, or which require delicacy
and taste rather than muscular exertion, will fall to the share

of women: all branches of the fine arts in particular."[27] In
the process of natural development, woman will not actually
use her ability to support herself for this would burden the
labor force unduly. Outside the working class, woman will
perform a natural task by adorning life.[28] This in effect
complements man's earning power and makes for improved
relations between women and men.

It may be said that prefeminists conceptualizing change
in the family and woman's education to the end of change in
her overall position largely understand change in terms of
complementary roles for women and men. This is the broader protest for prefeminists thinkers. Such roles correspond
in many respects to traditional expectations about what women
and men should be doing, but they are not really traditional.
A flexibility is projected here which tradition does not admit.
Prefeminist thought about complementary roles is best represented in Margaret Fuller's work. In 1861, however, a
book is published outside America which will have considerable impact on future feminist thought about women and men's
roles. It is J. J. Bachofen's Mother Right. Bachofen draws
on classical mythology for an understanding of life in antiquity
when the harmony of nature is still intact. In mythology, he
finds system and cohesion, lawfulness unconsciously stated.[29]
Suffice it to say that anthropological and archeological findings
bear him out in several crucial respects before the nineteenth
century is over.

Briefly, Bachofen suggests that the mythical tradition
reflects an opposition between paternal and maternal systems,
between the active masculine principle and the passive feminine principle. While women's and men's relations originally
are promiscuous, the tellurian stage, eventually they become
dominated by mother right, the lunar stage. Amazonism is
an extreme example of mother right. Still another transition
takes place, however, and father right comes to dominate women's and men's relations; this is the solar stage. Later
empirical findings do not validate the existence of the tellurian
stage, but they suggest grounds for accepting the lunar and
solar stages. Essentially, the explanation for the transition
from stage to stage is discussed earlier in this book in Engels work, which derives from Bachofen and scholars who follow him. To go on, however: for Bachofen, the origin of
culture is traceable to the lunar stage and the relationship
between mother and child. In a world characterized by violence, maternity operates as a principle of love, union and
peace. The paternal principle, on the other hand, is re-

"Blessed Art Thou Among Women" (ca. 1900), by Gertrude
Kasebier (Collection, the Museum of Modern Art, New York;
gift of Mrs. Hermine M. Turner.)

strictive because of the definite groupings it engenders. It represents an assault on women's rights which provokes women to self-defense and even vengeance by means of armed resistance, leading to Amazonism. This is consistent with the law of human and especially feminine nature. Subjecting woman to degradation and abuse awakens in her a desire for security and purification. [30]

Up to this point, Bachofen suggests women and men present radically different natures which are manifested in opposed principles of maternity and paternity. When either one is dominant, it engenders resistance by the other. Yet it can be seen that each principle draws on the other implicitly. The problem is one of dominance. How is this difficulty transcended? Man reaches a higher stage of existence through Orphic male homosexuality, by means of which he effectually transcends Eros. This greatly stimulates his own cultural development. Women too have an equipoised stage which transcends sensuality in Lesbian women who take up the Orphic life, leaving their Amazonian ways behind. In loving their own sex, they transform physical beauty into purified psychic beauty. In this way, love and sexual identity are united. For Sappho, the end of all contention lies in this spiritual quality. [31]

According to Bachofen, Sappho's purification and transfiguration of the feminine maternal principle expresses nature and womanhood and constitutes a distinct developmental stage. [32] Fuller represents a similar stage of spiritual development in prefeminist thought. Her plea for a celibate period in which women may discover what in them is peculiarly feminine is not unlike Sappho's and the Lesbian women's quest for purified psychic beauty. Fuller is not advocating a separatist finale. She foresees the day when women and men will transcend currently existing barriers to natural union and in fact believes the transition is in process. In effect, she suggests a means to hasten the transitional process. With Wollstonecraft, she fastens her eye on the time when women and men can unite in a relatively harmonious state, complementing one another by their respective natures in a sort of religious pilgrimage. This is the implication of women helping women for Wollstonecraft and Fuller alike: moral transcendence of the sensual aspects of life as it is being lived in their times. For it to be realized, women must come to know and respect, even love, themselves and each other.

Matilda Gage reaps the rewards of Bachofen's writings

plus anthropological and archeological findings some 30 years
later. Her emphases in many ways are religious, although
she rejects the established church and its traditions. The
commonalities between hers and Marxist thought, which also
relies on Bachofen, and the differences between them already
are noted. Gage approaches feminism spiritually, much as
Aristotle and Wollstonecraft approach women and men's association morally. For Gage and Wollstonecraft, the evolution
of civilization has a moral or spiritual, even mystic, motif
(this in spite of Wollstonecraft's predominantly rationalistic
overview). For Aristotle, the manifestation of the polis over
time is the product of certain moral associations. For Marxist thought, however, culture necessarily evolves through economic and political exploitation. Any similarities between
feminist or prefeminist thought and Marxism must be seen
for the most part as the result of shared roots rather than
as the direct influence of Marxism itself. These streams of
thought partake of the ideal of complementary female and male
roles. They stress existing and historical opposition between
them and reach out for the means to bring them together in
a more harmonic union. Thus Gage laments man's theoretical
failure to acknowledge women as an elemental part of humanity. Such recognition for her will be forthcoming only when
woman, practically speaking, can judge woman for herself.[33]

It must be noted that there is a tension in feminist and
prefeminist thought between reason and mysticism, between
logic and transcendence. This is noted earlier. In many
ways, it is the tension between Puritanism and Quakerism,
also noted earlier. In attempting to deal, as many feminist
thinkers do, with women's and men's roles in an institutional
context with attendant rights and duties, they resign themselves
to this tension. The parts women and men should play in a
more ideal or perfect world largely are understood subjectively, where understanding about institutional change derives from
more objective cognition. One can argue that without one or
the other approach, however, there could be no feminist
thought. Its focus ultimately must be on prescriptions about
women's and men's roles if it is to discuss woman's position
at all. On the other hand, change requires an appraisal of
the world at large, even if change is believed to be an inevitable force. Thus feminist and prefeminist thinkers attempt
what many social scientists would describe as impossible:
the union of empirical observation and normative thought. One
cannot help but to notice this body of thought similarly attempts
the "impossible" in seeking more harmonious roles for women
and men. Actually feminist thinkers are relatively ingenious

here. They would in one way or another isolate the components of the radical dualism which Fuller attributes to male
and female in order to purify them, making them truer to
their respective natures. Then they would bring them together again on the assumption that complementarity will be
forthcoming.

Thus August Bebel can speak simultaneously about the
salience of the common welfare to the coming of socialism
and about the respective natures and purposes of the sexes.
He believes both sexes will maintain their natural limits in
a socialist setting because to do otherwise would nullify their
natural purposes. According to Bebel, women have a particular stake in socialism, because it would reintroduce to culture matriarchal communism which was overthrown by the
private property system of the patriarchate. Only through
the subsequent overthrow of the patriarchate can women rise
to heights of natural perfection. For Bebel, the economic and
political implications of the patriarchate degrade women and
divorce her from meaningful outlets for her natural impulses.
In effect, male egotism and female service must be liberated
for harmony between them to prevail. In this way, people
will begin to serve themselves and society as well. Male and
female union henceforth will be the result of private agreements between the sexes--in a higher civilization characterized
by social forms representative of those in existence before the
patriarchate. [34] Once again the importance of complementary
roles can be discerned. Sexual natures are conceptualized in
terms of distinct purposes which must be reinstated for harmony to prevail.

One need not look far for a twentieth-century non-
Marxist rendering of this analytic framework in feminist
thought. Ida M. Tarbell develops it in The Business of Being
a Woman. She acknowledges the validity of the impulse which
motivates woman to attack man's way of life. The problem
comes when woman begins to adopt man's ways for her own.
Yet, if coeducation has yielded anything sound, it is the
awareness that "The college cannot entirely rub femininity out
and masculinity into a woman's brain. The woman's mind is
still the woman's mind, although she is usually the last to
recognize it. "[35] The uneasy or atrophied woman who takes
up a man's life is of necessity unfeeling and egoistic. She
could not be otherwise and fail to heed the natural sympathy
a woman embodies in the face of the cruel conditions with
which her career brings her in contact. The natural and social resistance she encounters constitutes an objection to the

squander her career entails. "It is a right saving impulse
to prevent perversion of the qualities and powers of woman
which are most needed in the world, which differentiate her
from man. "[36]

George Burman Foster generalizes further about women and men's respective natures:

> Sex extends to the very core of the spiritual per-
> sonality. An old monk, at the time of the contro-
> versy over nominalism and realism, was so sure
> that the universe, rather than the particular, was
> the real, that he said he was not going to eat
> apples and peaches and pears and the like any-
> more, but just fruit! But as there is no fruit
> that is apple-less and peach-less and pear-less,
> thus there is no human nature that is man-less
> or woman-less. [37]

According to Foster, the new woman's movement is forthcoming from the invisible depths of woman's nature. Its ends
include liberated selfhood, possibly socialized motherhood,
definitely the study of eugenics. Voting is one of the means
to these ends. The movement ultimately may be characterized
by great generosity to men. If this is the case, then cultural
strife between women and men will cease in favor of the
"heightened harmony of an intercurrent selfhood. "[38]

For both Tarbell and Foster, as for other feminist and
prefeminist thinkers discussed in this chapter, it is essential
that woman come to know her own nature. This is the key to
a better world, a world in which female and male will live in
harmony. One is hard pressed to find any era in American
history in which most thinkers of the feminist or prefeminist
persuasion do not present this view of women's and men's
roles. Their expectations about possibilities for change in
woman's position are based on their expectations about how
women and men should behave naturally. What they observe
in reality is a perversion of the sexes' respective natures.
That it is even barely indicative of a transition to a more
ideal stage is probably attributable to two facts. First, sub-
sisting in the colonies and along the frontier is difficult at
best, and women as well as men must cope with these problems to survive. Second, American institutions appear to
be liberal enough in principle to accommodate change in woman's position. Add this to a belief in the inevitability of
change for the better, and transition seems at least feasible.

One even might add that the fact most feminist and prefeminist expectations about the roles of women and men bear some resemblance to more traditional expectations probably contributes to judgments about feasibility as well.

In some respects, though, projecting complementary roles for women and men is not realistic. For one thing, even given more flexibility in expectations, these roles are still similar to existing, if perverted, role models. Thus one wonders if perhaps belief in substantial change with the coming of more ideal types and resultant harmony really is warranted. One wonders if harmony even will be the result of such transcendence. The brave attempt to unite normative beliefs about women's and men's respective natures with empirical observations of the world at large raises the question of how this ultimately will take place. As observed before, for the most part feminist and prefeminist generalizations lack this operational dimension. Even given the attempt to be practical, this body of thought is weak when it comes to strategizing. So far as comprehensive ideology is concerned, it does not exist. As is noted repeatedly throughout this book, American institutions do not yield the change feminist and prefeminist thinkers project. Apparently a liberal institutional overview in company with feminist and prefeminist generalizations and tactics is not enough to implement far-reaching change. The reason it is not enough may very well be traceable to the thought outlined in this chapter.

On the other hand, there still is a certain amount of merit to this approach which should be taken into consideration. Overlooking the at least questionable procedure of translating lessons of antiquity into a later time period, there is something to be said for a sort of cooling-off stage in relations between women and men. There is no real problem in asserting that woman should come to know herself and women generally, even though an extremist view of inner development presents genuine difficulties, as already noted. How woman is to know herself, whoever she may be, when she typically exists in a close relationship with men is a problem, however. This is a genuine issue for feminist and prefeminist thinkers, especially those who espouse complementary roles for women and men, which most of them do.

That feminist and prefeminist thinkers recognize this issue is evident from their intense emphasis on the intertwined issues of family and education. Family represents the most intimate example of women's and men's relationship. [39] Education represents a serious attempt to develop woman's potential and to give her some growing space, even in a coeducational setting. Woman in the family setting faces certain difficulties which education is to help resolve. For feminist and prefeminist advocates of complementary roles for women and men, most women will realize their hopefully purified nature in the family setting--although this setting may be expanded to include society as well. Institutionalized education is very important in helping women meet their responsibilities as well as come to know themselves. In the end, however, self-education among women is a crucial factor in their development and in harmonizing their relations with men.

One feminist thinker who is particularly sensitive to the implications of feminist thought for women's roles generally is Ellen Key. Key points out that emphasis on civil rights and careers for women is primarily of importance to upperclass women. Such emphasis is opposed to the highest right women possess: the right to think their own thoughts and go their own ways. Key grants that women have the right to be transformed into a kind of third sex, which she likens to working bees, if in doing so they find true happiness. She goes on, however, to state:

> I am in favour of real freedom for women; that
> is, I wish her to follow her own nature, whether
> she be an exception or an ordinary woman. But
> the opinion held by the feminine advocates of
> women's emancipation, in regard to the nature
> and the aims of everyday women, does violence
> to the real nature of most women. [40]

One might comment on the question of class Key interjects, taking some of the thinkers discussed in this chapter for examples. Wollstonecraft is not a lady, and she does not lead a lady's life. For the most part, however, her thought can be construed as directed to relatively upper-class women. Adams and Warren are ladies, although Adams must support herself, but since their thought is merely suggestive of a prefeminist persuasion, one cannot really expect a wider-ranging focus to it. Fuller has some of the advantages of an upper-class woman, but she too must support herself. Her thought refers to women in prison, to women of the working class, to slave women; yet it would be inaccurate to suggest her thought embraces these women fully. Mill and Bachofen are men of relative means, which is not to say wealthy, and one fails to find references in their work of relevance to

working women particularly. All of these thinkers are educated extremely well in their own ways. The women may or
may not be ladies; several of them support themselves.

Somehow, despite occasional references to women of
different classes, the emphasis in this body of thought does
come down especially hard on the side of relatively upper-
class women. Even given Key's protestations, she is not
immune from this criticism either. Her appreciation of the
needs of working-class women is not optimal. That said, it
must be added that in many respects, this body of thought is
wider ranging in some of its implications than might be expected. This already is noted to some extent in the book and
will be explored further in the next chapter. For now, let
it be said that emphasizing complementary roles for women
and men is not the best way to bring working-class women into perspective. When all is said and done, they simply do
not have the time or opportunity to devote themselves to the
full realization of the maternal principle.

Key realizes this is a problem, but she believes it can
be solved by supporting protective labor legislation for women.
She suggests it is quite logical to work for such privileges,
introducing the function of motherhood for justification. Only
rank individualism could lead one to think otherwise. This
is something the women's rights organization must learn. Key
suggests that it is illogical to bring up motherhood as a justification for exempting women from military service, however,
if women's rights are to be asserted. Such service is the
final consequence of advocacy for women's rights to free woman from her natural limitations. It stands in opposition to
woman's especial vocation, motherhood. Key believes she
speaks of women and society collectively. To that end, she
attempts to demonstrate "that vengeance is being exacted on
the individual, on the race, when woman gradually destroys
the deepest vital source of her physical and psychical being,
the power of motherhood."[41]

For Key, women's rights as individuals always must
be limited by the rights of the child who might be. For one
whose nature can only mean inequality to demand equality is
to seek injustice. Women should not seek man's nature for
themselves; doing so would allow the love which is the essence of woman's being to "shrivel up as a bud that has not
blossomed...." By asserting her nature, woman can demonstrate her worthiness in her own field, that of home and family, and thus engender "the recognition that in her way she

is just as complete a being" as man. [42] Key expects men to
defend and support their families and women to care for new
lives. These quite definitely are complementary roles. If
women or men were not to fulfill expectations about what they
should be doing, then their counterparts could not continue to
fulfill expectations either. Key tries to fit working-class women into this scheme by protecting their rightful vocation,
motherhood, through the institution of privileges for them in
the labor force.

That she possibly might undermine working-class women's jobs and hence their ability to support themselves and
their children does not occur to her. In a properly ordered
society, motherhood will be recognized as woman's essential
vocation. Key admits some women may not find happiness
for themselves in this manner, and she suggests such women
are free to do otherwise. They must not eliminate the vocation of motherhood for other women by their actions, however.
This in itself is a reasonable approach. The problem is that
some women will be mothers and will need to enter the labor
force as well.

From a distance of some 70 years, it does not appear
that Key deals with this fact of life very well. She is far
from idiosyncratic in her approach to working-class women
and women's and men's roles. She represents a large body
of feminist thought in her own time and in terms of her historical antecedents. The direction this thought takes is not
without its problems. There are gainfully employed women
before 1910--Adams and Fuller among them, although they
are better placed than many other such women of their era.
Between 1900 and 1910, however, women in the work force
increase 25 per cent to the point that one-fourth of all women
are employed gainfully. [43] Thus such women, many of whom
are mothers, become a fact of life which must be taken into
account. Unfortunately Key and some others of her persuasion do not accomplish this well. They clearly are aware of
the changes taking place, but they are anxious to minimize
them in the context of women's and men's complementary
roles.

Other feminists more closely linked to working class
women than Key take a similar approach. Alice Henry writes
about Women and the Labor Movement in terms of maternity
and the matriarchate. She points out that the inhuman slavery to which women working for wages are subjected threat-
ens their future motherhood. She then traces women's history

in the labor movement, beginning with primitive woman, the
earth mother, who must be credited with the inception of
mental culture and community as well as homemaking and
agriculture. Rather than being parasitic, she is "an agent
in the process of taming man himself." Colonial woman is
a domestic producer with a sound economic base who later
participates in commercial enterprises as well. With the development of the factory system, especially the textile and
shoe industries, the history of women's trade unions begins
in 1825. Unionism takes a back seat to strike activities in
the period 1840 to 1860 but by the turn of the century women
have a humble place in the regular ranks of labor. Yet the
scope of social conscience in the Reconstruction period and
of the social advance of the working-class movement is not
perceived immediately as relevant to women. Henry discusses the resultant establishment of the National Women's Trade
Union League and its local branches as a step in the direction
of organization and education for women. The League pro-
motes legislation to lessen the oppression of gainfully employed women as well as providing organizational channels of
expression to safeguard their interests. The adaptation of
modern conditions to the protection of women is championed
by trade union women on behalf of their less well-placed sisters. [44]

Alice Henry herself is employed gainfully. She opposes
the equal rights amendment and pointedly notes its supporters
are not working women themselves. Her social philosophy is
described by one commenter as "a gentle-womanly Marxism,
with the sharp, cutting edges of class conflict dulled and
cushioned by her Unitarian moralism and humanitarianism. "[45]
This is quite in keeping with feminist expression of Marxist
ideas. Additionally, Henry's espousal of complementary roles
for women and men is associated with advocating labor unions
solely for women. This coincides with tendencies among
feminist and prefeminist thinkers of a complementary persuasion. Clearly Henry does not intend to separate women from
men altogether, given her concern for motherhood. Separatism is intended to give gainfully employed women an opportunity to explore their own needs in the labor force as well
as an organizational base for meeting them.

In the meantime, protective labor legislation with respect to hours is upheld by the United States Supreme Court
in 1908 in Muller v. Oregon. [46] Louis Brandeis, later a
member of the Court himself, is asked by the National Consumers League to defend Oregon's "ten-hour law" when it is

challenged. Josephine Goldmark, a League activist and Brandeis' sister-in-law, and Florence Kelley, who heads the League, do a hasty but prodigious job of research, and Brandeis incorporates these materials into his brief. Essentially the brief argues that limiting woman's working hours is justified because of her physical organization and maternal functions, responsibility for rearing and educating children and homemaking duties.[47] The Court takes cognizance of these materials, distinguishes an earlier holding which strikes down such a law for men, and upholds the Oregon statute. Justice Brewer, speaking for the Court, states that woman

> is properly placed in a class by herself, and legislation designed for her protection may be sustained, even when like legislation is not necessary for men and could not be sustained.... The reason [for the Court's decision] rests on the inherent differences between the two sexes, and on the different functions in life which they perform.[48]

It is interesting to note that William Chafe asserts the Court here "articulate[s] a theory of women's nature hardly designed to please feminists."[49] The Court does refer to woman's dependence on man, and this would not please feminists thinkers. The statement of women's nature generally is in keeping with most feminist thought about the roles of women and men, however. These feminist and prefeminist thinkers would hasten to add that woman's nature, purified and transcendent, will render her a complete and independent being worthy of respect. They would suggest that legislation such as the Court upholds contributes to the purification and transcendental process. Passing and implementing legislation dealing with working hours is an important part of the transitional period during which women, and men, will evolve to a higher, more harmonious stage in their relations. Legislative separatism, with organizational separatism, is a means to uniting women and men in the end.

Furthermore, arguments about separatism and the respective natures of women and men are used to assert equal rights for women by many feminist thinkers. Key has a narrower outlook here than most--one might suppose because she follows her assumptions to their logical conclusion. Logic is not totally lacking among advocates of complementary roles and equal rights too, however. Helen Keller, for example, takes a very logical approach to the matter in 1915. In asserting woman's right to protect herself and thereby free m

from "his feudal responsibilities," she differentiates women
and men in terms of family concern and individualism, strong
and weak social consciousnesses, maternity and paternity.
She acknowledges that "woman's peculiar knowledge and abilities" often are cited by protagonists of woman's suffrage but
suggests such arguments are irrelevant when it comes to citizenship. She states, "If there is a fundamental difference
between women and men ... it is all the more reason why
her side should be heard."[50] If women and men fill complementary roles, they must be permitted to exert influence from
their respective viewpoints. How else will they mutually supply what is lacking in their counterparts? The franchise must
extend choice to humanity as a whole, not to just one/half of
it; otherwise its expression will be only partial and sorely
lacking in balance.

It is worthwhile to note that feminist thinkers with
libertarian and egalitarian creeds are intermingled as advocates of complementary roles for women and men in the twentieth century. Generally speaking, before the twentieth century, feminist and prefeminist thinkers are libertarians, as
chapter three establishes. In the twentieth century, however,
a libertarian such as Key and an egalitarian such as Keller
have no difficulty agreeing on expectations about what women
and men should be doing. There is a small but important
group of feminist and prefeminist thinkers who do not advocate
complementary roles; this group too includes libertarians and
egalitarians. (It will be explored in the next chapter). One
might expect that libertarians with their stress on self-awareness and spheres of duty would be the first to advocate complementary roles. Egalitarians, on the other hand, by stressing alikeness should not tend to advocate complementary roles.
This is a misleading expectation. As pointed out before, the
broader feminist protest is on behalf of complementary roles.
It cuts right across libertarian and egalitarian creeds. It is
understandable why libertarians would support complementary
roles. It seems less clear why egalitarians would. If the
ⁿiritual aspect of egalitarianism is recalled along with em-
ˋses on community and implications about constraint, then
ˋtarian support for complementary roles becomes more
ˋe. Finally, the libertarians' influence on the feminist
ˋian creed--despite implicit inapposition here--is seen
concern for freedom of action and equality of oppor-
fills out the explanation of how feminist egalitarians
complementary roles. The surprise is that any
nd feminist thinkers espouse something other than
roles at all, given their intellectual heritage.

John Spargo is an example of a feminist thinker with an egalitarian creed who advocates complementary roles for women and men. It will be recalled that he sees the right to vote and equality with men in the labor force as key elements in attaining freedom of motherhood. By introducing through socialism a communism of opportunity which facilitates individual achievement, Spargo believes the result will be a glorious inequality which rests on equality of advantage. [51] Thus he calls for equal rights in the context of complementary roles. A reading of Spargo makes it very clear how feminist egalitarian thinkers can support complementary roles and still be consistent with their creed.

As Spargo does, Charlotte Perkins Gilman examines inequality and equality among women and men and their meanings for dependence or independence. For Gilman, human beings are modified environmentally, especially in a social context, but they also adopt to and change the environment. Yet, even with all the opportunities for human improvement this ability affords, the human race is relatively indifferent to such high efforts. This is especially evident in the Christian religion's emphasis on "the glittering or terrible possibilities" of another world in preference to reality. Religion, as it develops, is a masculine idea, and its basis in death leads to "a limitless individualism" capable of eternal extension. Were religion to develop through woman's mind, however-- and here Gilman speaks inferentially and deductively--it would be based in birth with an altruistic overview. The disproportionate religious influence man exercises is often antagonistic to human improvement, to social progress. "When the unwritten [unconscious] laws of womanhood are as potent as those we hear so much of among men, and when the written ones also are partly made by women, we may look for widely interesting changes in conduct."[52]

According to Gilman, women and men are primarily and essentially different with respect to their treatments of natural impulse. Women agree with their maternal impulses and develop through them, as reflected in their altruistic and increasingly useful services. Men, on the other hand, engage in a lasting struggle with their naturally destructive impulses, injuring social growth as they go. "We cannot reconstruct the past. We can construct a very different future." Once women become aware of the essentially humanitarian implications of their nature, they can work to maintain peace. Work can become a delightful "fulfillment of function ... freely chosen," when woman's principle is realized. Woman's principle, usually realized by her participation in man's religion, can better industrial relations and in doing so improve humanity. Such improvement "is a religious duty, the religious duty above all." Man will lose his supremacy when this comes about, but, after all, it never belonged to him anyway. 53

For Gilman, this is not an expression of "condemnation of the male sex as such," only of its disproportionate influence which is antagonistic to human improvement. With the coming of new ideas,

> Men will hold all they have gained, be praised for
> all the great, good things that they have done,
> stand foremost as the world-servants for genera-
> tions yet, but they will learn another view of
> sex.... [T]he new view of woman will change
> life utterly. Man will see her not as 'his' but
> as a fellow-creature, strong, noble, free, com-
> petent in social service. The domestic subor-
> dinate ... will rise and rise in his mind, to her
> true place, a wife for him a friend, a mother
> ... measured ... as the chief channel of social
> improvement. 54

For humanity, happiness lies in fulfillment of function. In the "conscious transmission of power" which the latter entails lies the promise of "triumphant religion. "55

Here then is a predominantly egalitarian statement, glowing in its spiritual content, which stresses the fulfillment of women's and men's complementary roles for the better-ment and happiness of humanity. Gilman's expectations about how women and men should behave are based, in the context of social Darwinism, on her observations of how they do behave. For her, one can know "the form and special distinction of any living thing" only through "the balanced total of its acts." In short, "life is action."56 Thus it is particularly important that women and men fulfill their functions. With Keller, Gilman takes the distinctiveness of woman's background and acts as the primary reason for urging their recognition: woman will balance man's viewpoint for the good of all. Gilman's emphasis on woman's need to individuate, to live life on a "plane of separate interest or industry," already is noted. With such possibility will come the beginnings of possibility for woman's personality as well; then the abnormal economic relations which fragment humanity will be over-

come, and the social need human beings have for one another
at last will be recognized as the highest of faculties.   In
other words, still another feminist thinker is suggesting that
giving woman the chance for a separate existence within which
she can begin to fulfill her nature or function is to give women and men the chance to find happiness together in the end.

Gilman is writing in the 1920s about the complementary
roles of women and men but her analysis dates back to the
turn of the century. H. L. Mencken, in a biting defense of
women, brings complementary roles into contemporary perspective. For Mencken, a person's function is the product of
natural forces which must be fulfilled in a hierarchically ordered state. Behind this structure is meaninglessness and
tragedy. Within it, at least life can be good. His is not a
democratic philosophy, and yet in some respects it reflects
the thought of largely liberal feminist and prefeminist thinkers. According to Mencken, the best proof of feminine intuition or intelligence lies in woman's awareness of man's inherent shoddiness. Women may long for their spouses' prerogatives and freedom of action, but they do so with a sense
of compassionate irony, in effect extending their natural instinct to men. Herein lies the "special feminine character."
Furthermore, Mencken states,

> Find me an obviously intelligent man, a man free
> from sentimentality and illusion, a man hard to
> deceive ... and I'll show you a man with a wide
> streak of woman in him.   ... [I]n Shakespeare,
> if the Freudians are to be believed, it amounted
> to downright homosexuality. [57]

Talent of the sort Shakespeare embodies is the result of reciprocity between feminine and masculine elements.   Thus
women of talent display masculine traits as men of talent
display feminine ones. "The truth is that neither sex, without some fertilization by the complementary characters of the
other, is capable of the highest reaches of human endeavor." [58]

As usual, Mencken bursts bubbles with his remarks,
not the least of which is the bubble of male egoism. Although he has mild words of criticism for Key later on, one
can see her reflection and Tarbell's as well in his work. He
is particularly harsh in his judgment of the "suffragettes" who
would integrate women into men's political parties, thereby
playing women's votes against each other and rendering them
purposeless. [59] For Mencken, tearing down structures or-

dered by women's and men's respective functions exposes the ultimate meaninglessness of everything. What is particularly interesting, however, is Mencken's discussion of the result of interplay of feminine and masculine tendencies in one in-dividual. These are exceptional persons in his eyes, to be sure, these individuals of talent. They are not ordinary people. He is approaching the argument of that small group of feminist and prefeminist thinkers who do not espouse com-plementary roles, but he is confining it to an exceptional sort of person. Here one recalls Wollstonecraft's allowance for women of "superior cast." Mencken generally does not see people as capable of displaying both feminine and masculine tendencies--in short, coalescence. This is something extra-ordinary for Mencken. His aside with respect to Shakespeare's possibly homosexual motivations hearkens back to Bachofen. Shakespeare is presented as a man of talent at such a high stage of cultural development that he transcends sensual do-minance. Mencken also refers to George Sand as a woman of talent, as does Fuller. (It sometimes seems George Sand is as much remembered for her masculine garb and habit of smoking cigars as she is for her novels.)

Amy Lowell takes the same approach to women of ta-lent, writing: "Taking us by and large, we're a queer lot/ We women who write poetry. And when/ you think/ How few of us there've been, it's queerer/ still." She wonders what compels such women "to scribble down, man-wise,/ The frag-ments of ourselves." For Lowell, the reason there are so few women such as these lies in their nature as "mother-creatures, double-bearing,/ With matrices in body and in brain." She likens these women to Sappho as "sisters/ Of a strange isolated little family." Pondering Sappho and what Sappho was, Lowell recollects

> I know a single slender thing about her;
> That, loving she was like a burning birch-tree
> All tall and glittering fire, and that she wrote
> Like the same fire caught up to Heaven and held there,
> A frozen blaze before it broke and fell. [60]

Perhaps, Lowell ponders, if she could have talked to Sappho she could have thrown her own reticences to the wind, so surprising Sappho's that Sappho would reveal her soul. Yet Sappho is a "leaping fire we call so for convenience...."

Lowell finds other sisters. Mrs. Browning is one of these, but unlike Sappho, she is "squeezed in stiff conven-

tions, " miraculously escaping "To freedom and another mo-
therhood/ Than that of poems. She was a very/ woman/ And
needed both. " Miss Dickinson is a sister too. "With Emily/
You're really here, or not anywhere at/ all/ In range of
mind. " Yet all are unlike Lowell, she judges, "Unlike at
least until we tear the veils/ Away which commonly gird
souls. "[61] Then they are of one family, each with different
answers. Thus women of talent seem to come in all varie-
ties, each a different person but of the same family, a family
with originating elements in body and brain alike.

Lowell is one of Mencken's individuals of talent. She
fits his description well, as Louis Untermeyer unknowingly
reveals in a memoir of her. He relates a conversation in
which the cigar-smoking Lowell relegates woman to a seemingly traditional role, displaying what Untermeyer regards as
a wild inconsistency about feminism. [62] In fact, Lowell is
not inconsistent, as her poem, "The Sisters, " demonstrates.
She believes she and others of her family embody both feminine and masculine elements, "matrices in body and in
brain, " where most women essentially have a bodily matrix.
She carries the latter theme into her "Women's Harvest
Song, " beginning "I am scattering sunflower pollen to the/
four world-quarters. " To paraphrase, the Pueblo Indian woman sings her joyfulness for her melons, beans and squash.
Her heart is happy because the Sun above her fields lifts up
the corn-ears with his fingers, fashions her melons and sets
her beans full in the pods with his hands. [63] It is a rich expression of the nature of woman as earth mother. Man's
presence is felt in the sun, recalling Bachofen's solar stage;
without man's contribution, there could be no fulfillment of
woman's purpose. Were she not to scatter pollen, man's
purpose could not be fulfilled either. Lowell is consistent,
not inconsistent, in her expression of what in feminist thought
must be described as complementary roles for women and
men.

Backing up a bit to the discussion of those exceptional
but few individuals of talent, recollect that Lowell sees Sappho
as a "leaping fire. " Sappho "is Sapho--Sapho--not Miss or
Mrs. " She is one of the exceptional few but is even more
exceptional for her singularity. Still the family is more than
Sappho. It includes Mrs. Browning and Miss Dickinson as
well. Mencken makes a similar distinction with regard to
men of talent. Shakespeare is distinguished, as noted, but
his "family"--to use Lowell's word--includes Bonaparte,
Goethe, Schopenhauer, Bismarck and Lincoln. Thus, even

though an individual reaches a high level of cultural development, further transcendence is possible.   The question of
rightness and wrongness, as Aristotle puts it, or desirability
is really not at issue here.   Lowell does refer to Queen Victoria, "all-pervading in her apogee," in "The Sisters," when
discussing Browning.   "Confounded Victoria, and all the sli-
my in-/ hibitions/ She loosed on all us Anglo-Saxon crea-/
tures!/ Suppose there hadn't been a Robert/ Browning...."
Yet Victoria too "is another sister," "an older sister."   For
Lowell, in some ways, Sappho, Browning and Dickinson all
are older sisters, "very sobering things," who leave her
"sad and self-dis-/ trustful...."[64]   From this discussion,
one might see Sappho as more unencumbered by "stiff conventions" and go on to implications about desirability.   Given
Lowell's distrust of older sisters and her earlier reference
to surprising Sappho's reticences, however, one suspects she
thinks there are soul-obscuring veils here too.

Sappho is an image, nonetheless, which appears in
feminist thought time after time.   Fuller mentions her also,
with Heloise, as a name "of threadbare celebrity."   "Across
the ages forms lean, trying to touch the hem of their re-
treating robes."[65]   Indeed, Sappho is a leaping fire called
so for convenience's sake.   Still she does represent a sort
of transcendence, and her image is very important for understanding women's women.   Alice Ames Winter, for example,
points out that in the past "love o' women" stimulates mental
inferences about women's and men's passion.   In her day,
1927, it includes love of women for women.   She shortly after
suggests that although Sappho commonly stands as the symbol
for uncontrolled womanhood, in fact her status as martyr is
post mortem. [66]

Ames' remarks are insightful.   Women's women, Lesbian women reincarnated, may attract ridicule--as Katherine
Anthony points out in connection with Fuller's conversations,
but underneath the jeers there is fear and hostility.[67] Womanhood uncontrolled!   It conjures visions of manhood repressed.   The accepting men in Mary Griffith's 300 Years
Hence desert the patriarchate entirely.   As for preservation
of the species, G. Stanley Hall presents the fears endemic
here at the mention of uncontrolled womanhood.   The assumption seems to be that love of women for women is bound to
go too far if it gets a toehold in women's lives.   Consider
Henry James' explicitly sexual description of what for him is
a neurotic friendship between two bluestockings in The Bostonians.   Many biographies of feminist thinkers and activists

in their heyday from, say, 1880 to 1920 establish at least
indirectly the extent to which feminist women love other women. As William L. O'Neill puts it, "Eminent women, feminists among them, often drew comfort and inspiration mainly
from one another, and their sororital impulses doubtless
passed over into lesbianism at times." He goes on, in the
brief and somewhat guarded passage, to suggest that between
a Victorian code denying single women sexual release and
hostility among ambitious women to obstructionist men, "it
was inevitable that some kind of homosexuality, overt or not,
would often result. "[68]

    Looking at feminist thought, O'Neill's last statement
is amiss. So far as inevitability is concerned, feminist
thinkers' attitudes toward homosexuality range from ostensibly
negative (Wollstonecraft) to apparently ambiguous (Lowell) to
possibly positive (Fuller). The ostensibly negative end of the
qualitative scale sees homosexuality in terms of sensuality.
The possibly positive end of the scale sees it in terms of
transcendence. There is a world of difference between them.
So far as hostility to men is concerned, feminist and prefeminist thinkers really are not hostile to men. There is a
period, mid-eighteenth century, in which men are believed to
be at the root of all women's problems, but this largely
changes by the turn of the century. Furthermore, even mid-
eighteenth-century prefeminist thinkers include men in the solutions to those problems, and there are a number of men
among them formulating the solutions. Furthermore, there
are male feminist and prefeminist thinkers.

    Generally speaking, viewing attitudes as a whole, it
must be said that lesbianism receives a rather favorable reception in this body of thought. Perhaps the ostensibly negative pole of the qualitative scale mentioned above should be
labeled homosexuality; the possibly positive pole, lesbianism.
Whatever, understanding lesbianism in feminist thought is important for an understanding of feminist thought overall, particularly with respect to complementary roles for women and
men. One can only deplore the fact that attempts in this direction are not widespread. Furthermore, when attempts are
made, they do not seem to be so much for purposes of understanding as they are for hostility. [69] Most often, however,
lesbianism is bypassed altogether. * The problem is that only

---

*To give an example from hearsay, apparently a dissertation
in progress a few years back about the (cont. on next page)

by monumental twisting and turning can one do this. The intrinsic importance of lesbianism to the history of feminism,
intellectual or otherwise, and to a discussion about complementary roles for women and men in feminist thought cannot
be overlooked.

Chronologically, this chapter is approaching 1930.
The overview is one of role distinctions based on women's
and men's respective natures, their instincts, female and
male principles, maternity and paternity. With the coming
of social Darwinism, however, intellectual temper overall
shifts to concern with environing conditions. Thus Key and
others ponder sweatshops and seek to control their impact
on women workers by protective labor legislation. Bebel
and Spargo go further afield with their generalizations, delving into economics and proposing the institution of socialism
to free motherhood from environmental constraints. Gilman
is examining the implications for human improvement of a
maternal, birth-based altruistic religion. It appears instinct
and environment must be brought into equilibrium if woman
is to be herself and benefit by changes in her position. Sigmund Freud moves into this climate with what may be described as earth-shaking effect. To quote Juliet Mitchell,
"To Freud society demands of the psychological bisexuality
of both sexes that one sex attain a preponderance of femininity, the other of masculinity: man and woman are made
in culture." Because psychoanalysis deals with cultural
transformation rather than biological determinism, Freud
himself turns his back on biology. [70]

Freud discusses the meanings of femininity and masculinity as passive/active, ovum/semen and existing/observ-
ing. Psychologically speaking, there is no pure manifestation of femininity or masculinity. There is instead the fact
of sexual need which is expressed in an impulse, libido.
"... Libido is regularly and lawfully of a masculine [active]
nature whether in the man or the woman, and if we consider
its object, this may be either the man or the woman. "[71]

---

life of a distinguished suffragist was to include materials
relating to a lesbian attachment in her later years. Repor-
tedly the author decided to delete them--on the advice of her
dissertation committee and on her own counsel--because
their inclusion might lead to suggestions that the author herself is a lesbian and might present problems when the time
to find a publisher for the biography approached.

Ego and object cathect for Freud in a narcissistic libido
which can become an object libido. Thus there is an instinct
to extend, "to preserve living substance and to join it in even
larger units" (eros), and a contrary instinct to retract, to
bring back a "primaeval, inorganic state" (death).

> ... [C]ivilization is a process in the service of
> Eros; whose purpose is to combine single human
> individuals, and after that families, then races,
> peoples and nations, into one great unity, the
> unity of mankind. ... These collections of
> men are to be libidinally bound to one another.
> ... But man's naturally aggressive instinct,
> the hostility of each against all and of all against
> each, opposes this programme of civilization.
> ... [T]he meaning of the evolution of civilization
> ... must present the struggle between Eros and
> Death, between the instinct of life and the in-
> stinct of destruction, as it works itself out in
> the human species. This struggle is what all
> life essentially consists of, and the evolution of
> civilization may therefore be simply described
> as the struggle for life of the human species. [72]

What does this mean for feminist thought so far as
transcendence of sensuality is concerned? First, as Mitchell
points out, narcissism--which is essential to establish the
ego--must come into relation with other objects. If the object is of one's own sex, this constitutes a form of inversion,
turning back on one's self. On the other hand, one might
come to love one's self through an attachment with a more
ideal self. According to Mitchell, "idealization ... engages
... in an overestimation of the object ... or in increased
demands on the ego to be as perfect as the subject would
like to be."[73] Secondly, the homosexual impulse of libido
is attracted to the ideal self in identifications with units such
as Freud lists above, to become part of the conscience (su-
per ego). Thus civilization overcomes individual aggression.
Such internalization of authority can become a source of anxiety for the individual, however, especially for one who is
particularly virtuous. Guilt must be seen as a conscious expression of moral amity and fear of punishment, a product of
living in close alliance with others. The emergence of civilization can only heighten this amity and fear. Some accommodation by the individual and by civilization is necessary if
the amity and fear are to be resolved.[74]

Feminist thinkers must be seen as part of the accommodative process. Their own continuing emphases on civilization bear witness to this. Perhaps their penultimate effort here lies in the love of women for women, in lesbianism, in transcendence. Sappho's "tall and glittering fire ... a frozen blaze before it broke and fell" represents a statement of the ideal, what one would be if one only could. Granted, for most feminist and prefeminist thinkers, few individuals are capable of achieving such heightened culture; most women and men must be content to seek to know themselves and their natures, to perfect them insofar as nature or the environment permits and then reach out for union with each other. The environment can be tamed somewhat, as through protective legislation, but this will not necessarily stimulate great numbers of extraculturally heightened individuals. They somehow must stand apart in their expressions of perfection. Lowell's distrust of older sisters, her suspicion that Sappho too had reticences, suggests that indeed the most virtuous have their anxieties. Perhaps perfection eludes even them. It is not so inevitable as Wollstonecraft believes.

For most feminist and prefeminist thinkers, complementary roles for women and men, a gateway to transcendence, offer the most feasible means to mitigate destructive impulses between the sexes, impulses manifested in Amazonism and the patriarchate. When women and men become units in themselves, when they are capable of attraction to more ideal selves and when they identify with other such units, then means of accommodation are feasible. Woman's law unto herself, and its codicils, for all their problems, are a manifestation of civilization and provide the means to control aggression. For feminist and prefeminist thinkers, the destructive power of aggression is present in slave keeping (blacks or prostitutes), liquor interests and drunken husbands, those who would deny education to women, sweatshop ownership and so on. Such power stands in the way of civilization and must be contained. Transcending sensuality, becoming as "a burning birch-tree," presents the highest means to this end that most feminist and prefeminist thinkers can conceive. It is not biology but culture which holds the promise of civilization. Women and men must cease to exist as purely sensual beings; perfection so far as it is attainable lies in civilization and transcendence to more idealized cultural selves.

Anaïs Nin flows into this stream of thought stating that woman humanizes or personifies ideas. When an idea coa-

lesces with a person, woman experiences it emotionally and
is transformed accordingly. Man, on the other hand, denies
the personalization of ideas, for Nin. "When I write in the
first person, I feel I am more honest than when man generalizes." In a manner reminiscent of Mencken, she refers to
the "divine joke" that men think they exist or not all for the
sake of ideas. Separate from man's Weltanschaungen, Nin
creates her diary, writing "on being the womb." She swims
"in nature," englobing, unleashing a tremendous feminine universe. [75]

There is in spite of her feminine act a secret erotic
need for man's brute force in Nin, perhaps in all women,
she notes. This need fulminates in violent images of violation which constitute a trap, which lead to forgetfulness of
freedom, which only can be overcome by self-awakening.
What Nin knows, though, is that she is right for herself. In
her ability to speak women's and men's languages, to translate women to men and men to women, lies disbelief in masculine alchemy. "Poor woman, how difficult it is to make
her instinctive knowledge clear" (which undoubtedly explains
Mencken's In Defense of Women ...). Yet woman must bring
together man and his human self. Her life role is to create,
to become woman; it is the woman artist who will link creation
and life in her own womb. [76] As Lowell has it, "my answer
will not be any one of yours."[77]

For Nin, the creation of unity--destroyed by man's
proud consciousness--rests with woman. The mermaid who
is woman wets her aquatic half-self in the unconscious. She
must create something different from what man would

> within the mystery, storms, terrors, the infernos
> of sex, the battle against abstraction and art. She
> has to sever herself from the myth man creates,
> from being created by him, she has to struggle
> with her own cycles, storms, terrors, which man
> does not understand. [78]

For the sake of interdependence, she has to be the link between man's synthetic generalizations and the elements themselves. To that end, Nin proclaims, "I have a center." At
the center is affection and friendship. Man's world lacks this
core, is impersonal, denies the source of generalizations.
His role, it seems, requires that he wear a mask. Woman's
role, on the other hand, calls upon her to remain at an "un-
transmuted, untransformed, untransposed plane,"[79] a fabled
marine creature.

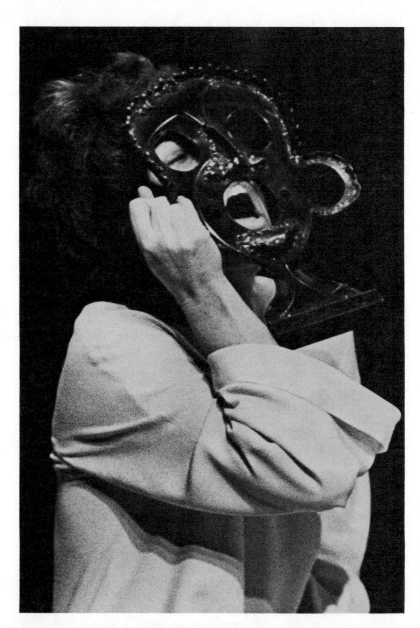

"Hagar's Mask," from the Mask Ritual Tale, "Sarah and Hagar," $12\frac{1}{2}$"; sculpture and ritual by Suzanne Benton.

Nin's is a very sophisticated rendering of Freudian
theory, in costume as it were, positing woman as the accommodative link. Woman the mermaid, fascinated, hypnotized
by violation, swimming in nature, seems less "a burning
birch-tree" in Nin's translation. She is not an earth mother,
scattering sunflower pollen. She turns inward, to her very
core, for the sake of interdependence between women and
men. Yet women's and men's roles seem opposed, man in
drag and woman treading water in the very dark and muddy
river to which Hawthorne commits Zenobia. In this state,
woman must prevail as a sort of missing link. The images
Nin conjures are primeval, full of horror. Can, one wonders,
a mermaid give birth? One looks in vain for melons, beans
and squash, for the sun's warmth. Can, one wonders, death
be far away? "The leaping fire" breaks and falls, is all but
extinguished in the confines of the womb.

The womb and nature alike have their seasons and
cycles, times of birth and times of barrenness, times of love
and life and times to discharge menses and let the leaves fall
from the tree. Heed Edna St. Vincent Millay's words in
"Menses":

> I (for I have learned more things than one
> in our few years together)
> Chafe at the churlish wind, the unseasonable
> weather.
> "Unseasonable?" you cry, with harsher scorn
> Than the theme warrants; "Every year it is the
> same!"

The speaker thinks, "('Go to/ You are unwell.')" Yet such
words cannot be spoken. Pitiful tears come to the other,
"for all the lovely things that are not and/ have been." The
speaker relents; it is all silliness after all. Its beginning
lay in a feeling. Then "Down my side/ Innocent as oil I see
the ugly venom slide...." Still, nothing pierces. The mis-
chief is over, but is it? "I see it coiling;/ The impact will
be pain." Still, it is useless; the speaker is woven about
with mail "of wit and love." As for the "Well-fanged" one,
"'I shall be better soon. Just Heaven consign and damn/ To
tedious Hell this body with its muddy feet in my mind!'"[80]

Alas, the "mother creatures, double-bearing,/ With
matrices in body and in brain" are mired in mud. Lowell
knows all along that it can occur. She recreates Mrs. Browning who, before her miraculous escape, has "all the need,/

The huge, imperious need of loving,/ crushed/ Within the body she believed so sick. " After all, words which replace action "breed a poisonous miasma/ Which, though it leave the brain, eats/ up the body. " Mrs. Browning is left with the need to bring all her strength to bear on upholding "her over-topping brain. "[81] Sappho's spirit, the reincarnation of Lesbian women, flickers dimly in the years of the Great Depression. The body which is left behind is unwell, planting its turbid feet in a mind fixed on sowing words in a diary instead of flinging pollen to the sun. Man is gracious about the delay, costumed as he is in a witty, loving web of mail. One somehow sees Cass Timberlane bringing Ginny home to recuperate after the bubble of her dream of social seduction violently bursts.

Something goes awry, siphons off the theme of love, blunts the creative act in feminist thought. Its ideas and ideals seem to cease functioning as a motive force, as moonless night comes down around the "frozen blaze" that is Lowell's Sappho. The very force which lifts feminist and prefeminist thought beyond sensual existence to a higher spiritual cultural plane now seems impotent. M. Esther Harding offers a possible explanation in her analysis of The Way of All Women. Human perception of symbols of experiential laws, which often are understood as religion, contains greater truths than most people realize. Although the means of seeking these inner values may differ from generation to generation, in seeking them, the seekers can attain "a depth and sweetness, a strength and maturity" which attracts respect and comfort. The problem is that submission to moral law historically means repression, and with the coming of the twentieth century, people begin to turn away from it. Submission to moral values is replaced by a search for consciousness and reality comprehension. The individual who acts on behalf of "personal and ego ends" undergoes no development of the soul or psyche, however. By delving into the dark unconscious for the source of difficulties, harmony may escape those who lack sincerity of purpose; misunderstandings may arise in tearing away the very veils which mask the unknown in women and men. [82] Lowell too senses the possibly frightening consequences of tearing away veils which cloud the souls of her spiritual relations. They become "frightfully near, and rather terrifying. "[83] How much worse it must be for ordinary women and men not of exceptional talent.

According to Harding, one could look beyond personal

and ego satisfactions, however, for the suprapersonal value
which lies in "real truth." This is not a simple matter.
Woman, guided by eros, confronts no relational problems
here, but there are definitional ones. These are not her
forte. Yet, outside a relationship, development comes to a
standstill, a difficulty common among Occidentals. Without
this reality, there is no test for development and no control
on introversion. In being true to themselves alone, women
can neglect what is true for others. They then are exposed
inwardly in a dangerous fashion. Life as it is usually lived
requires that people deal with the masks they and others don
for their roles. Delving into the unconscious without relational controls is not unlike opening Pandora's box. The
existence and power of evil are released. Mere recognition
of the fact will not solve the difficulties which follow the release of evil. Evil must be faced. [84]

For Harding, to do so presents distinct difficulties for
women and men, because they approach instinctual harmony
differently. "For the man sexuality is the chief power or
force which can bridge the gap between himself and the woman
he loves; it is not so at all for the woman. ...[S]he feels
that under such circumstances a sexual approach is almost a
violation." Yet, in unmasking themselves and experiencing
each other in this fashion, women and men could release
emotional energy such as that attendant on earlier religious
experience and expend it for their mutual development. The
control becomes human responsibility, and the result is self-
conscious individuality. [85] Thus, for Harding, the problem
seems to lie with singular introspection. One suspects this
is exactly the difficulty with Nin's diary. Sowing words in a
diary is not tantamount to flinging pollen to the sun. The applied religious experience of a Harriet Tubman, premised on
the need for comprehensive social change, is lost when words
replace action. As in Gilman, life is action.

The question is whether relationship must be with men
entirely. The exclusiveness of women's relations with men
in everyday life clearly is a problem. Harding does suggest
that when a woman is true to herself alone, she cannot consider the truth of others' experience, and others may be either
women or men. In fact, women may be unable to either un-
mask themselves or participate in joint unmasking with men
without deeply exploring the symbols which represent their own
experiential laws, as Millay's poem indirectly indicates. If
one believes women and men have distinctive instincts and en-
culturational processes, as many feminist and prefeminist

thinkers do, then one is going to direct women, as well as men, to seek these truths. Transcendence of purely sensual relations between the sexes is not likely to take place without such consciousness. Development, for Harding, ceases when individual acts are solely for the purpose of "personal and ego ends," however. The individual must move beyond self alone to ideal-self objects and from them to meaningful collective attachments. It seems, in the context of feminist and pre-feminist thought about complementary roles, that ideal-self objects will be found first among members of an individual's own sex. Then one is enough a unit to attempt union with persons of the presumably complementary other sex. The exceptional person of talent, according to this body of thought, will go on to find ideal-self objects among members of the other sex as well. First, however, one's own culture has to be encountered.

Nin seems to consider herself the embodiment of womanliness as well as capable of speaking both women's and men's languages. Yet, one wonders, how does she know she is womanly? She makes intuitive generalizations about herself and about other women in the framework of an artistic religion, struggling against chaos to keep the dream alive. Sometimes the very intensity of the dream, the violence which impinges upon it, forces her to a new stage of self awakening. In this way, she believes she grows in depth, foregoing the danger of too much consciousness or awareness. She gives of herself selflessly, up to the point something personal is destroyed, then she ceases. This is the extent to which she is capable of relating. She gives until she judges she can give no more, then withdraws. This she describes as perpetual identification with human beings. Yet her end-in-view, an individually perfect world, must be described as an ego end. Ultimately, as already noted, development of feminist thought slows painfully within this framework.

Simone de Beauvoir is aware of this problem. For her, what is happening is that woman is being posed as "the absolute Other, without reciprocity, denying against all experience that she is a subject, a fellow human being." Reality confronts this myth but is without power to controvert the endowment of absolute truth. She agrees "that woman is other than man ... but the real relation is one of reciprocity; as such it gives rise to authentic drama." Transcendence such as that implied when women and men mutually recognize each other as conscious, free beings, and thereby confirm their freedom, is defeated by posing. When a human being is re-

duced to mysterious essence, as woman is, the reality of the
mysteriousness of every other is obscured.   Mystery can
be understood only in terms of communication.   In woman's case, "her language is not understood; she is there,
but hidden behind veils...." She lacks definition, to be sure,
but this is necessitated by the fact there is no truth in this
realm.   "The human being ... is to be measured by his
acts" alone.   Women generally do not achieve transcendence
because they flounder luxuriously in man's false objectivity,
thinking "what they could have become, which sets them to
asking about what they are."86

Yet, according to de Beauvoir, currently women resist
"blind enslavement" in the sense that they are unable to accept the position of autonomous individualhood and womanly
destiny.   A new aesthetic is at work.   It need not deprive
woman of her intrinsic sex appeal.   Woman in her otherness
experiences desire, embrace and love.   The important point
is that in reality this is a reciprocal relation with men.
Such "alterity" could yield further myths, but hopefully men
"will unreservedly accept the situation that is coming into
existence." Woman, on the other hand, in the formative
years of her life, could attempt authentically to reconcile her
autonomy with the passivity of her flesh as a lesbian.   In
doing so, she is to be considered neither undeveloped nor superior.   In fact, women are quite naturally homosexual.   For
a woman to love another woman is to accept rather than deny
femininity.   "[Homosexuality] is an attitude chosen in a certain situation--that is, at once motivated and freely adopted."
Insofar as woman's choice reflects a positive attitude, it is
not problematic.   It is only when such choice becomes exclusive in its scope that a negative attitude is asserted.   When
women avoid the act of love with men, they lose the opportunity, "torn from self," to become other.   With women, they
are subject and object at once. 87

For de Beauvoir, lesbian women not only cannot be
"torn from self." "... [U]nconcerned with dissimilation or
self-control, a feminine couple may engage in remarkably
violent scenes," notwithstanding the mutual social condemnation and segregation they face. 88   These are the negative
manifestations of lesbianism.   A woman may assert her natural homosexuality in a positive and authentic expression of
choice.   She may become exclusive in doing so, however, and
lose other opportunities as well as face violence once the
veils are torn away.   The responsibility which Harding posits
as a control mechanism is not likely to exist in a lesbian re-

lationship for de Beauvoir. She believes homosexual women must assume masculine responsibility for their own protection in an unfavorable social climate. With few exceptions, they simply cannot live naturally. If women are to come to know other women as lesbians, then apparently--on a reading of de Beauvoir--it must be an authentic, natural expression of choice. If in making that choice, women become exclusive, transcendence will elude them. They in effect will fall back into the past, which is immanence, into a paternal definition they are forced to adopt by their very exclusiveness for their own protection. Thus are they measured by their acts, which is all anyone can be. [89]

The very immanence which confounds Nin can confound the lesbian woman as well, it appears. It is a different order altogether than Wollstonecraft envisions. Sensuality takes on a new meaning: sex appeal. It is not to be scoffed at for it is a meaningful manifestation of individual autonomy. Through the alterity of desire, embrace and love, the authentic drama in which the complementary roles of women and men are staged comes into being. Still Wollstonecraft can take comfort in that preposterous distinctions of rank are foregone for an unmasking which confirms each human being's freedom. Therein transcendence is achieved. Self definition is not at issue for de Beauvoir. It is behavior which is the measure of reality and existence. Thus Fuller ingenuously contrasts expectations about lady-like demeanor with the toil of pregnant black women slaves and the strain the seamstress undergoes. One is left with a Pueblo Indian woman flinging pollen to the sun in an abundant expression of choice. Yet one should not forget the mermaid dipping her aquatic half-self in the unconscious. Alterity still could yield other myths.

References

1   Mary Wollstonecraft, Rights of Women (1790) (New York: E. P. Dutton, 1929), pp. 10, 19, 158-59, 24-26.
2   Ibid., pp. 42-43, 34, 45, 57.
3   Ibid., pp. 57, 155, 158.
4   Ibid., pp. 159-60, 188-89, 162.
5   See Virginia Sapiro, "Gender, Gender Roles and Gender Ideology in Survey Research," in The Study of Women and Politics: A Symposium Exploring Methodological Issues, ed. Sarah Slavin Schramm, forthcoming, for a very useful discussion of this concept.

6   The Politics of Aristotle, ed., trans. Ernest Barker
    (New York: Oxford University Press, 1972), pp. 6, 2-4.
7   Ibid., pp. 4, 13.
8   See also Melissa A. Butler, "Ideology and Methodology in
    the Study of Images of Women in Political Thought," in
    Study of Women and Politics, ed. Sarah Schramm.   But
    see Jean Bethke Elshtain, "Moral Woman/Immoral Man:
    The Public/Private Split in Its Political Ramifications,"
    Politics and Society, 4:4 (1974), 453-73.
9   Politics of Aristotle, see pp. 8-38 passim, especially
    pp. 32-33.
10 Ibid., pp. 75-76.
11 Ibid., p. 1.
12 Daughters of the Promised Land: Women in American
    History (Boston: Little Brown), p. 95.
13 Wollstonecraft, Rights of Women, pp. 195, 203.
14 Politics of Aristotle, pp. 310, 46, 75, 82.
15 Daughters of the Promised Land, pp. 41, 45, 56.
16 A Memoir of Miss Hannah Adams, Written by Herself,
    in Fragments of Autobiography, ed. Leon Stein (New
    York: Arno, 1974), pp. 33, 35, 2, 4, 14-15.
17 Ibid., p. 30.
18 Katharine Anthony, First Lady of the Revolution: The
    Life of Mercy Otis Warren (Garden City, N.Y.: Double-
    day, 1958), p. 95.
19 Linda Grant De Pauw, Founding Mothers: Women of
    America in the Revolutionary Era (Boston: Houghton,
    1975), p. 212.
20 Fuller, Women in the Nineteenth Century, in The Writ-
    ings of Margaret Fuller, ed. Mason Wade (New York:
    Viking Press, 1941), pp. 120, 123, 142, 129, 150, 163.
21 Ibid., pp. 171, 167-68, 176.
22 Ibid., pp. 176-80.
23 Ibid., pp. 211-15.
24 Katharine Anthony, Margaret Fuller: A Psychological
    Biography (New York: Harcourt, Brace & Howe, 1920),
    ch. 5, see especially pp. 61-62.
25 Quoted ibid., p. 36.
26 Alexis de Tocqueville, Democracy in America, ed. J.
    P. Mayer, trans. George Lawrence (Garden City, N.Y.:
    Anchor Books, 1969), p. 603.
27 Mill, "Early Essays on Marriage and Divorce," in Essays
    on Sex Equality, ed. Alice S. Rossi (Chicago: University
    of Chicago Press, 1970), pp. 76-77.
28 Ibid., p. 75.
29 Myth, Religion and Mother Right: Selected Writings of
    J. J. Bachofen, trans. Ralph Manheim (Princeton, N.J.:
    Princeton University Press, 1967), pp. 73, 76.

30 Ibid., pp. 77, 79-80, 104-05.
31 Ibid., pp. 203-06.
32 Ibid., p. 207.
33 Gage, Woman, Church and State (1893) (New York: Arno, 1972), p. 528.
34 Bebel, Women and Socialism, trans. Meta L. Stern (Hebe) (New York: Socialist Literature, 1910), pp. 367, 245, 33, 242, 377, 466.
35 The Business... (New York: Macmillan, 1912), pp. 33, 30, 39.
36 Ibid., pp. 42-43, 46.
37 "The Philosophy of Feminism," The Forum, 52 (July 1914), 20-21.
38 Ibid., pp. 10, 19.
39 In personal correspondence with the author, April 11, 1977, Stow Persons writes, "I noted with approval that you start by discussing women's place in the family structure, which has always seemed to me to be the proper place to begin, since they scarcely had any recognized place outside of it."
40 The Century of the Child (New York: G. P. Putnam's, 1909), pp. 64-65, 70, 97.
41 Ibid., pp. 68-69, 92-93, 100, 104-05.
42 Ibid., pp. 75-77, 72, 99-100. For a similar contemporary statement, see Selma Fraiberg Every Child's Birthright: In Defense of Mothering (New York: Basic Books, 1977).
43 See William H. Chafe, The American Woman: Her Changing Social, Economic, and Political Roles, 1920-1950 (New York: Oxford University Press, 1972), p. 55.
44 Henry, Women and the Labor Movement (New York: George H. Doran, 1923), p. 30 and passim.
45 Edward T. James, ed., Notable American Women: A Biographical Dictionary, 1607-1950 (Cambridge, Mass.: Belknap Press, 1971), vol. 2, p. 184.
46 208 U.S. 412. For background materials see Clement E. Vose, "The National Consumers League and the Brandeis Brief," Midwest Journal of Political Science 1 (November 1957), 267-90.
47 See Kenneth M. Davidson, Ruth Bader Ginsburg and Herma Hill Kay, Text, Cases and Materials on Sex-Based Discrimination (St. Paul, Minn.: West Publishing, 1974), p. 12. Brandeis, interestingly, was involved in the Massachusetts antisuffrage campaign in the 1880s.
48 Ibid., p. 14.
49 The American Woman, p. 128.
50 Philip S. Foner, Helen Keller: Her Socialist Years (New York: International Publishers, 1967), pp. 65-67.

51 Socialism and Motherhood (New York: W. Huebsch, 1914), pp. 11, 40-41.
52 Gilman, His Religion and Hers: A Study of the Faith of Our Fathers and the Work of Our Mothers (New York: Century Company, 1923), pp. 34-37, 46-48, 118; see also p. 105.
53 Ibid., pp. 252-53, 256, 259, 271, 274, 278.
54 Ibid., pp. 47, 293. June Sochen, Movers and Shakers: American Women Thinkers and Activists, 1900-1970 (New York: Quadrangle, 1973), pp. 17-19, characterizes Gilman and Tarbell's thought as "polar opposite points of view" which nonetheless share a belief in woman's uniqueness. Yet the effect of their shared beliefs overshadows differences in their point of view, differences which Sochen exaggerates.
55 Gilman, His Religion and Hers, pp. 298-99.
56 Ibid., pp. 98-99.
57 In Defense of Women (Garden City, N.Y.: Garden City Publishing, 1915), p. 307.
58 Ibid., p. 8.
59 Ibid., pp. 183, 132.
60 "The Sisters," in The Poems of Amy Lowell (Boston: Houghton, n.d.), p. 459.
61 Ibid., pp. 460-61.
62 Louis Untermeyer, "A Memoir," in Poems of Amy Lowell, pp. xxv-xxvi.
63 "Women's Harvest Song," in "Songs of the Pueblo Indians," 1, in Poems of Amy Lowell, p. 588.
64 "Sisters," in Poems of Amy Lowell, pp. 460-61.
65 Fuller, Women in the Nineteenth Century, p. 131.
66 The Heritage of Women (New York: Minton, Balch, 1927), pp. 3, 29-30.
67 See also Kate Millett, Sexual Politics (New York: Equinox Books, 1971), p. 45.
68 Everyone Was Brave: A History of Feminism in America (Chicago: Quadrangle Books, 1969), p. 14.
69 T. Z. Lavine's "Ideas of Revolution in the Women's Movement," American Behavioral Scientist, 20 (March/April 1977), 535-66, presents an example of a particularly intemperate approach.
70 Mitchell, Psychoanalysis and Feminism (New York: Pantheon Books, 1974), pp. 131, 401. Mitchell's comments at pp. 408-09 about the relative places of women and men and the fact "feminist revolution has nowhere come about" are well taken for this reader of feminist intellectual history.
71 Sigmund Freud, Three Contributions to the Theory of

Sex, 2d rev. ed., trans. A. A. Brill (New York: Nervous and Mental Disease Publishing, 1916), pp. 1, 79.

72 Freud, Civilization and Its Discontents, ed., trans. James Strachey (New York: Norton, 1961), pp. 65-66, 69.

73 Psychoanalysis and Feminism, pp. 33, 35.

74 Freud, Civilization, pp. 70-73, 79-80, 88.

75 The Diary of Anaïs Nin 1934-1939 (New York: Harcourt, Brace & World, 1967), pp. 19, 25, 145, 172, 188.

76 Ibid., pp. 209, 233-34, 172.

77 "Sisters," Poems of Amy Lowell, p. 461.

78 Diary of Anaïs Nin, pp. 234-35.

79 Ibid., pp. 234, 258, 172.

80 Collected Poems, ed. Norma Millay (New York: Harper & Brothers, n.d.), pp. 345-47.

81 "Sisters," in Poems of Amy Lowell, p. 459.

82 The Way of All Women: A Psychological Interpretation (New York: Longmans, Green, 1943), pp. 294-98, 300-01.

83 "Sisters," in Poems of Amy Lowell, p. 461.

84 Harding, Way of All Women, pp. 298, 300-01, 306-07, 309, 315-17.

85 Ibid., pp. 330, 334-35.

86 De Beauvoir, The Second Sex, trans. H. M. Parshley (1952) (New York: Bantam Books, 1970), pp. 237-42, 245.

87 Ibid., pp. 246-47, 237, 398, 381-83, 391.

88 Ibid., p. 395.

89 Ibid., pp. 396, 239, 241.

6

A ROW TO HOE:
FEMINISM AND CONGRUENT ROLES
FOR WOMEN AND MEN

Feminist and prefeminist thought broadly is typified by advocacy of complementary roles for women and men. There is another stream of feminist and prefeminist thought to be considered here, however. That is advocacy of congruent roles for women and men. Congruent expectations hold that women and men will engage in coincident activities. Women and men will behave alike, in accordance with the situation at hand. American social history demonstrates numerous instances in which women and men engage in congruent roles: on the frontier of settlement, at the moral frontier of abolitionism, along the frontier of industry. Interestingly, in all of these instances, congruent behavior is undertaken more or less unconsciously because the situation demands it. Where women consciously seek to behave congruently with men, they confront conflicting expectations, and their attempts are compromised seriously. On the other hand, the congruent behavior of those who respond to situational demands does not lend itself to romanticization. This way of life often is extremely difficult. Furthermore, when attempts are made to improve the quality of such a life--by developing communities, by abolishing slavery, by improving working conditions, there often is a reversion to complementary roles. Complementary roles in this instance are somewhat modified by a continuing frontier state of mind, however.

Our feminist and prefeminist thinkers are engaged in a dialectical discussion outside time and space. The topic is congruent roles for women and men. Mary Wollstonecraft is stating that it may take generations to give energy to virtue and talent, especially in the case of woman, whose potential is so obscured by the generally oppressed nature of the female world. Still woman's destiny must not be an arbitrary force. Why should woman be kept in a prolonged state of ignorance solely for the sake of specious innocence? No, says Mary, women must experience what men do! Do you remember Anne Hutchinson, asks someone? She is an early New World rebel, holding out for the possibility that women and men may attain inner grace on their own. Certain it is, asserts Angelina Grimke, that for any moral being, sex is significant; the circumstance of sex says nothing about rights and responsibilities.

Harriet Martineau speaks rapidly: women abolitionists look to their own case, where the clergy object to their public speaking, and then continue to do their duty for the abolitionist cause. Any blending of woman and slave rights is the result of clerical interference. I always believe, though, that for every black slave freed, a white one will be freed as well. Everyone agrees that America has slaves who are not of the black race. Several sing softly the refrain to a song, about women on the industrial frontier, which becomes well known in America, "Stitch! stitch! stitch!/ In poverty, hunger, and dirt;/ And still, with a voice of dolorous pitch,/ She sang the 'Song of the Shirt'!" Dorothy Parker notes in her own inimitable way the rebirth of "Song of the Shirt" in 1941 as an ode to the lovely, charitable Mrs. Martindale. Mrs. Martindale manages to do war relief hand sewing with a great sense of sacrifice and service, despite the absence of poverty, hunger and dirt. Lucy Stone insists that even if women's hands do get harder and broader with real manual labor, they have a daily wage in them which is far better than the pittance found in the hands of most women. Harriot Stanton Blatch agrees. Unpaid work just never commands respect.

Somehow Thorstein Veblen, who is not present, makes himself heard: you see, the ideal of beauty is shifting to women of physical presence, but this is only an adaptation of physiological structure and function for invidious purposes. To understand this, we have to understand that for members of the leisure class accumulating wealth is an important means for obtaining esteem and self-respect. Women as members of the vicarious leisure class attend to nonproductive consumption of time through service to the men who make up the leisure class. Ah, but in any event--it is Antoinette Brown Blackwell speaking--sex equals sex in average males and average females. And the secondary sexual characteristics which appear so different in women and men really are the product of natural, not sexual, selection. Secondary characteristics compensate for conventional restraints on feminine physical and psychical force, restraints which are the result of assuming males to be the representative type. Veblen is heard again: however, there is a selective process at work which affects the social structure and members of society conservatively, retarding the adaptation of human nature to modern industrial life. Mrs. Martindale, Dorothy Parker murmurs, Elizabeth Cady Stanton speaks crisply: Darwinian theory has promise when it comes to understanding the human dilemma, Nette (she is addressing Antoinette Brown Blackwell), but the Bible and the book of Genesis still must be dealt with. If we read Genesis correctly, we can see that women and men evolve simultaneously, in exact equality and balance, as masculine and feminine force in the image of God, which must have existed eternally. Not many seem to approve her statement.

Well, says Elizabeth Blackwell, to go on, female and male sexual functions are exact parallels with common properties. These are regulated in like manner by two laws, that of continuity of action and that of the power of self-adjustment. Sexual functions are equivalent. In fact, adds Florida Pier, there is no difference between masculine and feminine minds either, just in what goes into them and what the world expects out of them. "We must show consideration for those poor souls who bear up under a misplaced masculine or feminine mind." Gertrude Stein flows into the conversation, considering three lives of domestic service which end unnoticed. One life is arduous; one life finds nothing but trouble; one life has but a small self regard which vanishes quickly.

Louise Bogan comments that women are using benevolence against themselves, waiting and stiffening when they should journey and bend. Theresa Billington-Grieg, in a very British manner, suggests feminism needs a program for great deeds of destruction and reconstruction, if custom is to be changed. There is no response, but she goes on: to that end, sex differences must be rejected; rights and responsibilities founded on sex must be abolished; women and men's common humanity must be recognized. It is true, says Havelock Ellis, that we cannot dogmatize rigidly about women's and men's respective spheres because women and men are indefinitely modifiable under varying conditions and within certain limits. Suzanne LaFollette cries out, we just must not reduce woman to a function. An organism's health lies in its growth, which is change. Virginia Woolf recalls her biography. Orlando participates first in one sex and then the other. This does affect the future, which changes incessantly, but not Orlando's identity or face. Orlando enters into a transaction with the spirit of her age, and ultimately, deep in other thoughts, she becomes a single, real self, successfully practicing the art of life.

Ruth Herschberger begins to speak as soon as Woolf ceases. The problem is the accommodative attitude which members of a particular caste, such as women, adopt. Even though representations of basic sex differences are constructed with calipers and glue, women become custom shrunk nonetheless. Herschberger's eyes meet LaFollette's. Women have human characteristics and must not be limited to the unique function of giving birth. We must never forget, adds Margaret Mead, how incredibly pliable human nature is. Temperament is not sex linked; it changes in response to cultural conditions. For those who appreciate the socially determined aspect of this, there are three possible courses of action. Personality can be standardized as complementary. Sex distinctions can be eliminated from personality. Or we can work to admit diverse potential. What shall we do?

* * * * *

Mary Wollstonecraft, for all her emphasis on the respective duties of women and men, hints at the possibility of something quite different in the future. For her, the generally oppressed nature of the female world obscures woman's potential. There is only the sad reality that woman has gained the follies and vices which civilization avails, just as the rich have; in doing so, woman is missing civilization's more useful products. Wollstonecraft does not project startling new images of what woman might be were all restraints on her participation in mankind's inherent rights lifted. She simply advocates that the restraints be lifted, then suggests

woman will fulfill her "peculiar duties" as a result. She
even alludes to many arguments aiming to prove that women
and men should try to develop different characters in the acquisition of virtue. The question she poses here--why should
women be kept ignorant in the specious name of innocence?--is
provocative. For Wollstonecraft, advocating innocence in an
adult is nothing more than politely recommending weakness.
Better individuals should become acquainted with the ideal of
human nature before they acquire the manners of morals and
knowledge of life. In this way, conduct could be founded on
the same principles to the same end. In fact, for Wollstonecraft, conduct should be founded thusly, unless virtue be a
relative idea, and Wollstonecraft clearly does not think virtue
is relative. [1]

According to Wollstonecraft, it may take generations to
give energy to virtue and talent, especially in the case of a
sex viewing matters through a deceptive medium. Woman is,
after all, subject to very arbitrary distinctions of destiny
with respect to family management, not to mention her mis-
management here. Woman's subjugation, however, does not
prove that she is essentially inferior to man. It seems one
must make allowance for woman's position in judging her progress. Wollstonecraft makes one very forthright demand when
it comes to woman's destiny, which happens to be her own as
well. "We must mix in the throng and feel as men feel." [2]
She is not suggesting that women be the same as men, but
she is suggesting that women must try on men's experiences.
What the end result will be is far from clear in her thought.

It is clear that Wollstonecraft believes women's and
men's duties are relative, even as they respond to an absolute concept of virtue. The point is, however, that she appears to be leaving the way open for some changes in women's and men's relationship in the future. Things may
change as civilization develops toward its perfect end state.
Ruth Benedict's assertion, quoted earlier, that for Wollstonecraft "life had no axioms, its geometry was all experimental,"
takes on especial meaning here. It will be recalled that
Benedict goes on to say "[Wollstonecraft] was forever testing,
probing; forever dominated by an utter unwillingness to accept ... the convention in place of the reality." [3] Because
Wollstonecraft does not know what reality will be in its perfect end state, because she can only observe what she perceives to be most women's folly and vice in her own time,
she must be experimental in her outlook. What could woman
be, what would her relationship with man be, were she not

subjugated and were she to rely on her own perceptions of
nature rather than on mere convention? Wollstonecraft does
not answer the question; she leaves it open. In doing so,
she provides considerable food for feminist thought.

By insisting that women "must mix in the throng and
feel as men feel," Wollstonecraft leaves the way open for a
rather considerable reconceptualization of women and men's
roles, to use contemporary terminology. There is always
the possibility that, in mixing with the multitudes and experiencing men's perceptions, women will discard relative notions of duty. In short, woman could find on the basis of
such experimentation that their interests and capabilities
exactly coincide with men's. They could move toward more
congruent roles for women and men and away from roles in
which women and men complete what the other does not.
This would not defeat the maternal disposition which Wollstonecraft believes is so much a part of woman's sphere.
So long as the fetus grows in woman's body, she would have
a maternal disposition. Once the child is present, however,
men as well as women could exhibit a coincident nurturing
attitude. Women could contribute to the child's subsistence
at the same time as men or on an alternative basis. The
possibilities here seem endless, if experimental.

Perhaps the grandest normative experiment ever conducted about women's and men's congruent roles is found in
The Republic of Plato. [4] Socrates is asked about the management of communal property, including wives, among members
of the ruler class who ought to be entrusted with the art of
living and pursuit of wisdom. (The ruler class is as gold to
the silver of the guardian class and to the iron and brass of
the craftsmen class. The three classes are characterized
respectively by different approaches to pleasure: intelligence,
ambition, license). Arguing by analogy to watchdogs, Socrates suggests that if women of the ruler class are to perform
the tasks relevant to their occupation, as men of the ruler
class will, then they must have the same education, no matter how harsh this may seem. This follows from the fact
that women are appointed to the ruler class as men are by
virtue of their competence and nature; "the nature to be taken
in hand is the same."[5]

To that end, in Plato's thought women will participate
in, for example, gymnastic education as men do, stripping
their bodies to prepare them for the social duties of their
class. Women's bodies, in other words, exist not for pur-

poses of sexual attraction but to be developed for the highest
end of goodness, which is responsibility for what is as it
should be. Union between women and men will be regulated
strictly, and children will be reared apart from their parents
who will never know them. Child bearing should pose no
problem for women of the ruler class. In participating, so
far as their strength allows, in the activities which befit
them, these women will not become "unwomanly"; their activities will be "all for the best and in accordance with the
natural partnership of the sexes."[6] There is a good deal
more which could be considered here, but a bare outline of
Plato's thought will suffice. Women and men of the guardian
class display characteristics suitable to their station and must
be educated to enhance these qualities. It might be noted at
this point that such an educational scheme in some ways is
antithetical to Wollstonecraft's insistence that arbitrary designations of station be abolished.

In Plato's thought, however, sexuality generally and
the reproductive process in particular are deemphasized so
that appropriate education can take place and the rulers thereby adequately fulfill their tasks. In discussing questions of
women's equality and abolition of the family, Plato poses a
metaphor--that of consecutively larger waves which must be
breasted if the swimmers are not to drown. The third wave,
whether the ideal society can exist, is the most redoubtable.
The Republic is meant to be an "ideal pattern" which is none
the worse if the possibility of its existence cannot be proved.
Essential forms, and the Republic must be considered one of
these, are absolutes, where appearances are only relative.
The former are founded in knowledge; the latter, in ignorance.
"[T]here will not be a perfect state or constitution, nor yet
a perfect man, until some happy circumstance compels these
few philosophers who have escaped corruption but are now
called useless, to take charge, whether they like it or not,
of a state which will submit to their authority...." Yet, for
all the difficulty, institutional realization of the ideal pattern
is not to be considered impossible. [7]

In the allegory of the cave, Plato goes on to discuss
the part a person of knowledge, the philosopher, must play
in the lower world of appearances. Earlier he refers to the
philosopher's need for "a single bold flight of invention"--in
other words, for a fable--to convince society to institute a
more ideal social institution. This seems to be a means of
avoiding the appearance of awkwardness and ridiculousness in

one who comes from the contemplation of divine
things to the miseries of human life ... eyes
still dazed ... compelled ... to dispute about
the shadows of justice or the images that cast
those shadows, and to wrangle over the notions
of what is right in the minds of men who have
not beheld Justice itself. [8]

Plato does not overstate the value of the cave allegory, a
single bold flight of invention if ever there was one. "Heaven
knows whether it is true; but this, at any rate, is how it appears to me." What is important is that good ultimately be
perceived by those capable of reaching such heights. These
philosophers will be women as well as men, and they alike
must be compelled onward in their ascent. [9]

Socrates suggests it is for the commonwealth that these
philosophers should be compelled, however troublesome their
responsibility may be to themselves. There is nothing individualistic in Plato's philosophy. The role of the philosopher
is instrumental, "binding the community into one." The philosopher is not left to go his/her own way. The "coping-
stone" of the entire educational structure which will place the
philosopher in a position to fill the role of community binder
is the dialectic, a technique of asking and answering questions.
Women with the necessary attributes will share equally with
men of the same attributes in the asking and answering. [10]

On a reading of Plato, one might come to the conclusion that if Mary Wollstonecraft never attains all the answers
to her own probing questions about woman's dilemma in her
lifetime, it is because the social institutions of her time are
too corrupt to fully enhance her attributes. Her thought does
not fully embody platonic virtue--that is, knowledge of society's end as well as knowledge of the good. Yet even Socrates
will not admit to such virtue. [11] Wollstonecraft uses her faculties to project a perfect civilization which she herself cannot apprehend entirely. She advocates educating women and
men to look to first causes that ultimately the end state may
be realized. She probably can do nothing more, and yet it
must be said that what she does is enough to inspire the genuinely dialectic set of ideas and ideals which becomes feminist thought. Wollstonecraft's inspiration is realized in a
series of ongoing generalizations, two of which deal with women's and men's roles. The furthest reaching of these is
found in feminist and prefeminist thought about women's and
men's congruent roles. That this particular generalization is

not widely adopted is perhaps no more than an indication of
its experimental nature. The difficulty is no barrier to its
final realization.

Wollstonecraft, it needs to be noted, is not directing
her argument explicitly to women of superior cast, as Plato
is,* although she speaks of making special allowance for
them. One can make a strong case that effectually the impact of her argument falls primarily on upper-class women.
Nonetheless, Wollstonecraft herself speaks generally most of
the time. Thus she can be likened to and distinguished from
Plato. To give a further example, liberty is important to
Wollstonecraft and with it a modicum of individualism which
is more humanitarian than self seeking[12]; here Wollstonecraft
can be distinguished from Plato, to a degree. Yet the outlines of social equality are present as well in Wollstonecraft,
and here she can be likened to Plato, to a degree. In other
words, the scope of possibility in Wollstonecraft's thought is
broad indeed. Feminist and prefeminist thinkers accordingly
respond to different cues and expand her thought in several
directions. Surely the most provocative, the most probing,
the most experimental of these directions is the ongoing
generalization made about congruent roles for women and men.
As pointed out earlier, Wollstonecraft safely can be read as
advocating complementary roles for women and men, a line
of thought which is Aristotelian in derivation. Just as Aristotelian thought derives from the Platonic tradition, however,
there is much in Wollstonecraft which derives from Plato
too. It is not unreasonable to posit her as the original thinker for feminist and prefeminist thought about both complementary and congruent roles for women and men. Wollstonecraft
is, in her own way, as paradoxical as Rousseau is in his.

One could cite Anne Hutchinson as an early advocate
of congruent roles for women and men in the Massachusetts
Bay Colony of the New World. Page Smith suggests, 'In order for Anne Hutchinson to play out her brief but intense drama she had to have a degree of confidence and self-assurance
that marked an entirely new stage in the emergence of women."[13] That she is rebellious seems clear. It also seems
clear that her rebellion is directed to theology and religious
thinking and not to the institution of congruent roles for wo-

---

*It should be noted too that Plato, theoretically at least, pro-
vides for recruiting potential philosophers from the guardians
and craftsmen as well as the rulers.

men and men per se, although she is charged with, among others, not properly fulfilling woman's role.[14] The antinomian dispute and Hutchinson's trial for heresy constitute a real crisis in American history, and they have implications for both women's and men's roles in religious thinking about the attainment of grace.[15] It fairly may be said that in this limited sense Hutchinson's activity is relevant to the idea of congruent roles and a precursor of prefeminist and feminist thought.

Given the frontier conditions of colonial America and the lack of "very clearly defined notions of the 'role' of women," as Smith puts it, in many ways any issue about congruent roles would be moot. This is so despite the facts that nearly everyone marries and that the common law poses distinct disadvantages for married women. Lower- and middle-class women do not find marriage the prohibiting state that upper-class women experience.[16] Frontier life largely supersedes older institutions or at least adapts them to the singular physical environment characteristic of the frontier. Women and men must eke out a living by farming, and they may have to defend themselves against Indians as well. In short, the frontier becomes more than just the environment; it "is a social fact created when men and women freely confront challenges of a life not dominated by established local traditions."[17]

The American frontier for 300 years represents the repeated and continuous rebirth of civilization along the western edge of settlement, nourished by ample free land and affected by the singular environment, certain traits inherited from the Old World, changing world conditions and various racial groupings prominent along different frontier locales at different times.[18] Women could live a lonely, even if productive life, along the frontier, but with the coming of at least distant neighbors, the work of forming a community would begin. Social activities come in response to very practical concerns such as raising a house for newcomers. Quilting bees provide a useful product--a strong, warm covering for a cold night--as well as the chance to socialize. The simplicity of design, the inventiveness, the often geometrical precision achieved in the finished quilt are perhaps as much a statement of the social fact of the frontier as anything could be.

It is proper to consider the quilt a woman's art form, and one also might consider the raised house man's cultural

Facing page: "The Emigrant Train Bedding Down for the Night," oil by Benjamin Franklin Reinhart. (Collection of the Corcoran Gallery of Art; gift of Mr. and Mrs. Lansdell K. Christie.)

contribution. Women and men are very much in evidence at both types of activities, however, and there are many activities which give them ample opportunity to make "congruent" contributions. As the pioneer farmer, who is the average frontiers-person, is replaced by the equipped farmer and then by the town, [19] the frontier moves on. Women on the urban frontier begin to fill more complementary roles, but the impact of the frontier on them and on the American way of life persists. One should not romanticize women's lives along the frontier for their lives are anything but romantic. Life often is, to recall Hobbes' words about the state of nature, "nasty, brutish and short." For all that is lost, however, much is gained in the way of confidence and self-assurance. This is especially evident when one compares frontierswomen to the would-be true women who are making an appearance early in the nineteenth century. The frontier is not the ideal pattern Plato prescribes, but it is a testing ground for woman's competence and strength, and woman proves fit. As one student of frontierswomen puts it, in bridging the continent from the Atlantic to the Pacific oceans to found the republic--a triumph of physical and moral endurance--the American frontierswoman must be allowed her share of the honor. [20]

The state of mind which is the frontier extends to moral as well as physical endurance. This is strikingly evident among the abolitionists, many of whom paradoxically are to be found in older sectors of American society. One should not forget, however, that even the older sectors of American society are part of the frontier of settlement in the not really too distant past. Angelina Grimke is an abolitionist on the frontier of principle. It is she who suggests that women can exert their moral leadership to help end slavery. Through her thought, among others, grows up the idea of woman's law unto herself. Yet Angelina Grimke is very outspoken when it comes to notions about sex differences. She believes human rights stem from moral being. "[T]he mere circumstance of sex does not give to man higher rights and responsibilities, than to woman. ... When human beings are regarded as moral beings, sex ... sinks into insignificance and nothingness." She owns that she knows nothing of either woman's or man's rights, "for in Christ Jesus, there is neither male nor female." While she would not wish to see woman sink to partisan degradation, she grieves that man does so: "what ever it is morally wrong for her to do, it is morally wrong for him to do." Any difference in women and men's duties is the product of "the diversity of our relations in life, the various gifts and talents committed to our care, and the different eras in which we live," not of sex differences. [21]

In corresponding with Catharine Beecher, Angelina Grimke chides her for referring to superior and subordinate sexual spheres without proof. She finds nothing in the Bible to support Beecher's thoughts. As for "Appropriate offices! Ah! here is the great difficulty. What are they? Who can point them out?" Thus, one who signs herself thy "sister in the bonds of a common sisterhood" finds the fact of sex itself insignificant in a moral sense. She is aware that woman's general character may leave much to be desired in its current manifestation. This says nothing about the way things should be, however. Angelina Grimke's thoughts about abolition are intense and principled; they do not reveal an uneasy self-consciousness. Rather, she seems altogether outside herself in her commitment to the antislavery cause. That is not to say she is unaware of the problems women as slaves and antislavery agents face. She is aware of them, but hers is an action orientation. She works toward changing the situation. She professes no sympathy for those who "earnestly desire to 'avoid the appearance of evil, '" whether they are colonizers, unionists or slaveholders. There is a deep essential principle at stake here, and Angelina Grimke is not going to be diverted from it. [22] Questions about sex differences are diversionary in this context.

Harriet Martineau treats the abolitionists as a moral aristocracy--a notion in some ways antithetical to the idea of moral frontierspeople--and undertakes a description of its prerogatives. The moral aristocracy as a

> body comprehends men and women of every shade
> of color, of every degree of education, of every
> variety of religious opinion, of every gradation of
> rank, bound together by no vow, no pledge, no
> stipulation but of each preserving his individual
> liberty; and yet they act as if they were of one
> heart as of one soul. [23]

It is a strange aristocracy indeed! Its cohesive principle, however, is that of a "well-grounded faith directed toward a noble object." In passing, she discusses women and men abolitionists, their struggle and the suffering their belief entails, making no references to sex differences. With respect to Angelina and Sarah Grimke, Martineau holds their leadership is not the result of intention "but the circumstance of their possessing the knowledge, which other abolitionists want,

of the minute details and less obvious works of the slavery
system." The Grimke sisters are called upon to put their
backgrounds to work for abolitionism, and they do it. Any
blending of women's and slaves' rights is the result of agitation by the clergy. The women involved "merely looked into
their own case and went on doing what they found to be their
duty." Activity such as Angelina Grimke's address to a committee of the Massachusetts state legislature is meant to be
advocacy for a class currently unable to act or speak on its
own behalf and not the result of injuries to women as females. [24]

Martineau makes certain inferences from the history
of the martyr age for the future. Among them are the continuation of the struggle until the abolitionists prevail; the
blamelessness of republicanism for the dilemma and the guilt
of the Old World's feudal spirit which must result in the end
of aristocracy; the generosity, patience and hopefulness characteristic of the black race's morale and attendant implications for their civilization. Martineau also asserts that with
the emancipation of the slaves, other freedom than theirs will
be forthcoming. "With every black slave a white will be
also freed." [25] Thus, while the abolitionist movement does
spawn a cause of woman's own and ultimately the woman's
rights movement, there seems to be even more involved for
prefeminist and feminist thought. There is the possibility of
principled commitment to human rights in their broadest
sense. Such commitment promises a great deal: the abrogation of imposed sex differences within a moral framework.
It does not foreclose awareness of woman's case, but it calls
for action which essentially bypasses definitions of women's
and men's respective duties.

What is evident in Angelina Grimke and Harriet Martineau's thought is the impact of Jacksonian democracy and
the continuing frontier state of mind on American society.
There is a strong reaction to vestiges of European aristocracy, best represented in this country in the colonial gentry
class. Ironically, it is being replaced by a moral aristocracy
but one which admits in principle to no distinctions on the basis of sex, color, education, religion or rank. It is well
known that among abolitionists this principle sometimes fal-
ters, but it is the object of intense commitment by many, including Angelina Grimke. Just as ironically, at the same
time all of this is taking place, American women of different
classes--and social attitudes about them--are being polarized
increasingly with industrialism. According to Gerda Lerner,

"The image of 'the lady' was elevated to the accepted ideal of femininity toward which all women would strive. In this formulation of values lower class women were simply ignored. "[26] Only those who somehow inculcate a frontier state of mind could escape the fragmentation entailed by these ironic turns of events. They are affected by it, but they also are isolated from it to a larger extent.

In their isolation, frontierswomen--farmers, abolitionists, pioneers all--find complementary roles for women and men at least impractical and most assuredly inappropriate for their activities. Undoubtedly many of these women do not even consider the idea. They do what must be done, which means taking up roles congruent with those of men. Angelina Grimke discusses the insignificance and nothingness of sex differences here, but most simply bypass the issue. One even might speculate that the broader protest on behalf of the complementary roles of women and men in prefeminist and feminist thought is overly loud, given the infinitely quieter nature of thought about their congruent roles. In fact, however, there is not a great deal of thought to cite here. In many ways, it is a not self-conscious action orientation which is committed to paper only under the exigency of circumstance. In Angelina Grimke's case, the immediate circumstance which provokes her pen is Catharine Beecher's Essay on Slavery and Abolitionism with its references to the duty of American females. Mostly, as Martineau points out, the individuals involved here simply do what they believe they must. Undoubtedly they often do not have time to commit their explicit thoughts--if they have many--to paper.

This is not to say that feminist and prefeminist thinkers of the complementary persuasion are not active, because they are. Many of them however are noted mostly for intellectual activities--to give two examples, Margaret Fuller and Anaïs Nin. There are exceptions to this rule in both Fuller and Nin's lives, but predominantly they are intellectuals. Angelina Grimke, by way of contrast, is an activist. She engages in intellectual activities, to be sure, but first and foremost she is an activist. Feminist and prefeminist thinkers of the complementary persuasion are deeply involved in analyzing expectations about women's and men's roles and discussing their implications. Prefeminist thinkers of the congruent persuasion are better described as responding to situational expectations and intellectualizing them as an afterthought. To understand how congruent feminist thought begins to develop more explicitly in the twentieth century, one needs

to look at the social history of the eighteenth and nineteenth
centuries.   In addition to women on the frontiers of settlement and of abolitionism, one also must observe working-
class women on the frontier of industry.

Lerner indicates working-class women--many of them
immigrants--are confined to gainful employment which is low
in status, pay and skill requirements.   Their opportunities
are few in number.   In the beginning, factory work is not
specialized by sex, but this changes.   With upper- and middle-
class women, working-class women are disenfranchised.   The
latter, however, do have an income and enjoy some possibility for advancement in their work and for participation in organized labor. [27]   Martineau notes their pride and lack of
"gross immorality."   To her, the "mill girls'" choice of factory work indicates a state of mind far above whatever dangers the factory may pose for their respectability.   It also is
worthwhile to recall Martineau's assertion that American women of the highest intellectual power are to be found among
those who give the least time to literary pursuits, being as it
were better educated by "Providence. "[28]

Sadly, working-class women pay dearly for their wages
and chances of advancement out of their own physical and
mental well being, especially those who do piece work at
home.   This is revealed in "Song of the Shirt, " reprinted in
this country after its original publication in England in 1843.

> With fingers weary and worn,
> With eyelids heavy and red,
> A woman sat in unwomanly rags,
> Plying her needle and thread:
> Stitch! stitch! stitch!
> In poverty, hunger, and dirt;
> And still, with a voice of
> dolorous pitch,
> She sang the "Song of the Shirt!"[29]

The song reveals the slavery of such labor, attended by
swimming brain and heavy, dim eyes as human life wears
out.   The hard-won wages are small and scarcely enough to
feed the seamstress.   They amount to but "A bed of straw/
A crust of bread, and rags;/ A shattered roof, and this naked
floor,/ A table, a broken chair,/ And a wall so blank, my
shadow I thank/ For sometimes falling there!"[30] The seamstress dreams of just one hour's release to the out-of-doors,
but she stops her tears lest they hinder her work.

Once again, whatever the advantages of working-class status may be for woman, her emancipation and equality, there are serious disadvantages as well. The situation does not lend itself to romanticization. Woman's competence and strength sees her through, but the toll taken by self reliance often is devastating. Still these women are an important part of the industrial work force. Although their jobs may be sex specialized, they are nonetheless tantamount to those performed by men. It is a hard example of congruent roles indeed, but it yields any number of self-sufficient women, some of whom go on to involve themselves in labor organizing and commit themselves to obtaining better working conditions. [31]

It is interesting that the advantages of wages received for work and even the cause of congruent roles for women and men are much referred to by Lucy Stone. Stone is a married woman, although she retains her maiden name, and she herself is not employed gainfully. She often is regarded as being among the most conservative of woman's rights advocates, and much is made of her personality differences with Elizabeth Cady Stanton and Susan B. Anthony. When it becomes apparent that women will not receive suffrage at the same time black men do, Stone advocates accepting the inevitable and working on for woman's suffrage, a position which much irritates Stanton and Anthony and contributes to the founding of two separate suffrage associations. Stone describes herself in 1855 as "a disappointed woman" and allows that "disappointment is the lot of woman." This is the case for education, marriage, religion and most assuredly wages. Still Stone goes on to state

> I have seen a woman at manual labor turning out chair-legs in a cabinet-shop, with a dress short enough not to drag in the shavings. I wish other women would imitate her in this. It made her hands harder and broader, it is true, but I think a hand with a dollar and a quarter a day in it, better than one with a crossed ninepence. [32]

Unfortunately many of Lucy Stone's utterances are lost forever. As her biographer, Elinor Rice Hays, notes--she often speaks extemporaneously and does not allot her time to preserving her remarks. Furthermore, the multivolume History of Woman Suffrage is compiled by Stanton, Anthony and women closely allied with them. As a result, while their contributions are chronicled carefully, Stone's contributions

receive less attention. It also must be said, however, that
Stone herself contributes to this lapse by declining to provide materials requested of her, although she often does not
have the items requested. "Lucy Stone's fame today rests
on a single fact--that she refused to take her husband's name.
Yet this act was no more than a symbol, and far less important than the many victories she helped to win for women
everywhere."[33] This glowing tribute by Hays cannot be denied. It stands of its own weight, so to speak, but Lucy
Stone's contributions are at times paradoxical. For example,
she withdraws from the movement for periods of time to
nurse and rear her only child, a source of great joy to
mother and daughter but great consternation to Anthony and
those who feel Stone is abandoning them when they need her
most. It is a fact that "In those moments when Lucy's commitment was not driving her, she was indeed the most domestic of women." Stones' insightful comments about working
women must be balanced with her condemnation of the labor
movement generally and her somewhat naive belief that the
ballot is a remedy for problems such as reduced wages. Yet
Stone herself is a model employer, according to her domestic
helpers, paying high wages and urging and assisting these
women to attain an education.[34]

It can be seen that so far as asserting the desirability
of congruent roles for women and men, prefeminist thought
admits only of hints and few explicit statements. Expectations
that women and men will correspond to one another in their
behavior are not explicated well or widely. Social history indicates a basis in fact for holding such expectations in certain
instances--on the frontier of settlement, at the moral frontier,
along the frontier of industry. Yet such expectations mostly
are ignored as prefeminist thinkers largely address themselves
to reconfigurating the image of the lady: woman does have
special attributes, and she can develop these for ends of respectability and independence. In Stone, one sees an activist
who in effect is caught between two sets of expectations.
She vows never to marry, and when she ultimately does so,
she exerts herself to retain her own person and to secure her
property interests. Her spouse supports her in this, and
theirs is in many ways an extraordinary marriage in nine-
teenth- and twentieth-century American history. Elizabeth
Cady Stanton, for example, does not enjoy such advantages.
On the other hand, Stone does respond wholeheartedly to expectations about woman's domestic duties. At times this diminishes both her value to the woman's movement and her
standing among former allies. She herself suffers from what

are probably migraine headaches, stemming from her early
life, as well as from obesity, and it appears these problems
are traceable to what today would be referred to as role con-
flict--tension among competing expectations. One views her
dilemma with considerable compassion and with admiration
for the extent to which she resolves the dilemma. Women
who undertake or try to undertake roles congruent with men's
roles clearly do not have easy lives.

It is Antoinette Brown Blackwell, Stone's sister-in-law
and friend of many years, who begins to analyze the question
of congruent expectations systematically. Holding that assumptions about special feminine instincts and tendencies are
testable hypotheses, she suggests that in time they will "be
experimentally decided, and settled by rigidly mathematical
tests." If average females and average males of the human
species are naturally equivalent, this too can be demonstrated.
Blackwell points out these hypotheses are far from settled but
believes they will become settled, one way or the other, beyond controversy. The problem is that physiologists generally and Darwinists particularly--social and otherwise--assume
males to be representative types; females, mere modifications. "Other things equal, children of the same parents
must begin embryo life on the same plane," however. Blackwell herself believes there are natural functional restraints
which work to balance or equilibrate human development between the sexes to the end of equivalence of physical and
psychical force among them. Interestingly, despite such equivalence, there may still be complementary characteristics between the sexes. Blackwell carefully points out these nevertheless are "equally transmitted to descendents of both sexes,
[and] may remain undeveloped in either, or may be developed
subject to sexual modifications...." Adult sexual differentiation occurs proportionately and in correlation with general development. Thus, in any species, females directly nurture
offspring; males never do. This, however, is evidence only
of secondary sexual characteristics which are the product of
natural selection rather than sexual selection. [35]

What Blackwell is discussing is a practicable division
of labor. "But this antagonism or opposition of the functions
of sex, though real and continuous, is in reality a balance of
acts--an equilibrium which requires that at all stages of development there shall be a virtual equivalence of sex in every
species." Blackwell goes on to suggest that the masculine and
the feminine in a wide sense exist in combination in every organism; "these elements and these forces are continually

changing sides, entering into indefinite arrangements in conjunction with other forces. Thus what might be distinguished
as masculine in one case, would become feminine in the
next. " In many ways, this is a restatement of certain aspects of Margaret Fuller's thought. The inferences drawn by
Blackwell and Fuller from their analyses are divergent, however. Blackwell believes a certain amount of feminine vitality will persist, even if undeveloped, but what is most important is that women learn to exercise all their functions in order to healthfully and symmetrically develop and strengthen
all their faculties. The only limitations here are matters
such as feasibility and fair divisions of labor. Fuller believes
in the end women will opt for motherhood and domesticity.
Blackwell is infinitely more tenacious about fair divisions of
labor. "If anybody's brain requires to be sacrificed to those
two Molochs, sewing-machine and cooking-stove, it is not
[woman's]!" Woman will not forego, or wish to forego, her
domestic relations, but these are due for reorganization. 36

Blackwell's treatment of sex differences is much closer
to Angelina Grimke's than to Fuller's in the end. She puts it
into an "equation" (see table). 37

In short, sex itself is--as Angelina Grimke puts it with
respect to morality--insignificant and nothing. Rather than
sex, Blackwell focuses on secondary sexual characteristics,
differentiated by natural rather than sexual selection. These
vary among members of the same as well as between sexes.
Blackwell's is a sophisticated, subtle analysis. It takes into
consideration the kind of role conflict Lucy Stone encounters.
It does not state flatly that women and men are the same;
instead it "mathematically" demonstrates that "Sex = Sex. "
One sex is the equivalent of the other. "Conventionality has
indeed curtailed feminine force by hindering healthy and varied
activity; but Nature is continually devising compensations for
that loss. "38 The way is left open for change in natural selection. Furthermore, Blackwell is discussing average females and average males, not just those of exceptional cast
or talent. This is an extremely important semiscientific analysis of women's and men's roles from the standpoint of feminist and prefeminist thought. It bespeaks a systematic reconceptualization of the basis for expectations about what roles
should be for average women and men.

Apparent in Blackwell's analysis is a distinction between appearances and essence. Essentially females and
males are equivalents. Their secondary sexual characteristics

MAN

Males.	Females.
-Structure,	+Structure,
+Size,	-Size,
+Strength,	-Strength,
+Amount of Activity,	-Amount of Activity,
-Rate of Activity,	+Rate of Activity,
+Amount of Circulation,	-Amount of Circulation,
-Endurance,	+Endurance,
-Products,	+Products,
-Direct Nurture,	+Direct Nurture,
+Indirect Nurture,	-Indirect Nurture,
+Sexual Love,	-Sexual Love,
+Parental Love,	+Parental Love,
+Reasoning Powers,	-Reasoning Powers,
-Direct Insight of Facts,	+Direct Insight of Facts,
-Direct Insight of Relations,	+Direct Insight of Relations,
+Thought,	+Thought,
+Feeling,	+Feeling,
+Moral Powers,	+Moral Powers

Result in Every Species.

The Females　=　The Males

Comprehensive Result.

Sex　=　Sex

Organic Equilibrium

in Physiological and Psychological Equivalence of the Sexes.

may make it appear this is not the case, but these characteristics are the product of natural selection, not sexual selection. Natural selection in effect is compensating for the restrictions which convention places on healthy and varied activity for women. One recalls the caution with which Socrates
approaches mere appearances in Plato's Republic. Appearances may or may not be true; they are founded in ignorance.
Only knowledge can yield essential forms. Blackwell herself
does not conduct the extensive investigation necessary to settle
beyond controversy the issues apparent in the hypotheses she
poses. She is engaging in a fruitful dialectic, however.
That goodness, as Socrates would have it, escapes her does
not diminish the monumental nature of her analysis. Blackwell must be considered a philosopher of some stature among
feminist and prefeminist thinkers.

Such inquiry, coming in a period reeling with the impact of social Darwinism, raises innumerable questions about
the most basic source of expectations for women's and men's
roles, the Bible. Elizabeth Cady Stanton and others about
her, although estranged from Stone and Blackwell, nonetheless
are affected by this stream of inquiry as well. In her introduction to The Woman's Bible, Stanton states that:

> From the inauguration of the movement for woman's
> emancipation the Bible has been used to hold her
> in the 'divinely ordained sphere,' prescribed in the
> Old and New Testaments.

> The canon and civil law; church and state; priests
> and legislators; all political parties and religious
> denominations have alike thought that woman was
> made after man, of man, and for man, an infe-
> rior being, subject to man. Creeds, codes,
> Scriptures and statutes, are all based on this idea.
> The fashions, forms, ceremonies and customs of
> society, church ordinances and discipline all grow
> out of this idea. [39]

Stanton finds Darwinian theory to be more promising
when it comes to understanding the human dilemma, but she
implies that the book of Genesis is a fact which must be
dealt with in itself. Particularly interesting are references
by Stanton and Clara Bewick Colby respectively to the allegory
of the fall and the myths of creation. [40] In short, members
of the revising committee are faced with bold flights of imagination not dissimilar in form to Socrates' allegory of the

cave. To return to The Republic of Plato, "Heaven knows whether it is true; but this, at any rate, is how it appears to me." Appearances are not ranked high on the scale of reality and truth. In her comments about Genesis i:26-28, Stanton notes that "man and woman were evolved on the sixth day, the masculine and feminine forces in the image of God, that must have existed eternally, in all forms of matter and mind." She goes on to state "that equal dominion is given to woman over every living thing, but not one word is said giving man dominion over woman." Later, with respect to Genesis ii:21-25, she adds that "the Old Testament, 'in the beginning,' proclaims the simultaneous creation of man and woman, the eternity and equality of sex; and the New Testament echoes back through the centuries the individual sovereignty of woman growing out of this natural fact."[41]

It is notable that the commentary, authored by different members of the revising committee, is not entirely consistent. For example, Lillie Devereaux Blake refers to the ascending series in creation, from creeping things up through man "and last the crowning glory of the whole, woman."[42] This is somewhat different from Stanton's comment about women's and men's evolution above. The problem in this instance is resolved by reading Ellen Battelle Dietrick's elucidation of the two creation myths or fables evident in Genesis, the Elohistic and the Ioahoistic. One encounters similar problems over and over when reading The Woman's Bible. The problems proffer a valuable lesson about appearances, however. Appearances may be interpreted one way by one individual, quite differently by another.

Reading The Woman's Bible, one encounters a further difficulty. What are the implications for women's and men's roles? Stanton is relatively equivocal here, referring to the exact equality and balance of masculine and feminine elements. Blake, however, refers to Eve as "Life, the eternal mother, the first representative of the more valuable and important half of the human race." Colby quotes Goethe with respect to the first chapter of Genesis: "The eternal womanly leads us on."[43] This too is partially explainable in terms of which chapter and version of Genesis is being discussed. It also is indicative of a certain lack of willingness to confront the apparent implications of evolutionary thought for the book of Genesis itself. Feminist thinkers are by no means alone in this unwillingness, and some of the revising committee have deeply felt religious beliefs which probably temper their powers of observation. Some too may be thinking ahead about the

impact of what they are doing, thus being pragmatic. In
fact, however, all are denounced roundly for the act of compiling a "Woman's Bible" by feminists as well as nonfeminists.[44] The important point to be made from all this is
that neither the revising committee--all women, three ordained ministers among them--nor feminists generally are
ready to espouse congruent expectations about the behavior
of women and men.

The predominant feminist and prefeminist complementary orientation toward women's and men's roles is a powerful conceptual framework not about to be dislodged easily.
Certainly Blackwell is in no political position to dislodge it.
Importantly, however, Stanton to a certain degree is hovering
on the frontier of transition here. Furthermore, taken in the
context of an evolutionary intellectual climate and Blackwell's
work, the entire project is ripe with implications about congruent roles. To use an analogy, the seeds are being sown,
but the crop essentially is not reaped. Lerner believes the
development of what she labels a compensatory ideology of
female moral superiority is a tactical ploy utilized as a rationale for woman suffrage.[45] In fact, however, beliefs about
complementary roles for women and men go far deeper than
rationale among feminist and prefeminist thinkers and apply
to far more than woman suffrage (as chapter 5 demonstrates).
Displacing these beliefs will be a formidable task indeed for
that small group of feminist and prefeminist thinkers who espouse congruent roles for women and men.

Harriot Stanton Blatch tells the 1898 National American
Woman Suffrage Association convention that

> from creation's dawn, our sex has done its share
> of the world's work; sometimes we have been paid
> for it for oftener not. Unpaid work never com-
> mands respect; it is the paid worker who has
> brought to the public mind convictions of woman's
> worth. It is women of the industrial class ...
> who have been the means of bringing about the al-
> tered attitude of public opinion toward woman's
> work in every sphere of life.[46]

Blatch is not espousing congruent roles for women and men,
but she is discussing them indirectly and probably unknowingly. When it comes to speculation about earned worth, it is
working-class women who earn Blatch's admiration. They do
so because their paychecks make the difference in social ac-

cord of respectability. Why are they paid? They are paid because their work is congruous with men's. Even though women began working at the dawn of creation, they have been respected for their labor only when they receive a pay check, the reward for doing a man's job. Blatch in effect is explicating a set of congruent expectations here: anyone who does a man's job will be paid; respect is accorded those who are paid for their jobs; therefore doing a man's job is the key to respect. To take it one step further, women who do a man's job will be paid and respected. This is a desirable goal.

It will be recalled from earlier discussion that Blatch calls for mobilizing womanpower to bind up wounds and conserve civilization in the aftermath of World War I. Her belief is that woman's maternity makes her the person for the job, which presumably will be an unpaid one. Sex here scarcely is an insignificant factor. This is a statement of a complementary role for women. Yet Blatch also can call for women to engage widely in paid work of the sort working-class women do. Generally speaking, she is of a complementary persuasion. She is subject to the industrial influences of her times, however, and this is reflected in her comments. It appears she is not thinking through the implications of her remarks for her complementary persuasion. Once again, the seeds are sown, but there is no one to reap them. It simply is unthinkable to abandon a complementary persuasion. Lapses by most feminist and prefeminist thinkers from their broader protest are bound to be unconscious ones.

Thorstein Veblen's The Theory of the Leisure Class affords an explanatory framework which is very useful in coming to terms with Blatch's remarks and Stone's as well. To summarize briefly, Veblen discusses the existence of a leisure class which enjoys a pecuniary relation to the industrial community, living by it instead of in it. Leisure refers to "non-productive consumption of time." Only those who exercise a pecuniary aptitude for acquisition will become members of the leisure class. Such a class is especially evident among the most elevated stages of a predatory culture which begins to develop with the rudiments of technology. This development is an additive process of selective adaptation to exploitive (male) activities. Industry gradually displaces everyday predatory activity, and wealth through the possession of property becomes the more important means of obtaining esteem and self-respect. The desire for wealth becomes insatiable because reputability now rests on invidious comparisons which forestall definitive attainment. Inclination toward achievement and aversion to worthlessness are conditioned by "secondary demands of pecuniary emulation," which lead to characteristic and "conspicuous exemption from all useful employment" as a requirement of propriety. Among members of the leisure class, which stands at the epitomy of the social hierarchy, observation of propriety is formulated as a code of behavior for all other classes. [47]

Veblen points out that women are members of a derivative leisure class and thus stand in a different relation to the leisure class than men, who are members of the leisure class itself, do.

> In all grades and walks of life, and at any stage of
> the economic development, the leisure of the lady
> and of the lackey differs from the leisure of the
> gentleman in his own right in that it is an occupa-
> tion of an obstensibly laborious kind. It takes the
> form, in large measure, of a painstaking attention
> to the service of the master, or to the maintenance
> and elaboration of the household paraphernalia; so
> that it is leisure only in the sense that little or no
> productive work is performed by this class, not in
> the sense that all appearance of labour is avoided
> by them. [48]

In short, many of the services women render the leisure class are ceremonial, and their performance constitutes
a vicarious leisure. Domestic servants are economic units
of some importance for their presence permits household
members to engage in bothersome but unavoidable conspicuous leisure, such as through "calls, drives, clubs, sewing-
circles, sports, charity organizations, and other like social
functions." Domestic servants further permit household members to fulfill the requirement of conspicuous consumption of
goods by sharing in it through maintenance of the goods.
Women administer men of the leisure class the honorific sti-
mulants, i.e. liquor, which are the prerogative of the man's
superior status. The women themselves largely abstain "due
to an imperative conventionality."[49]

According to Veblen, among the lower-middle class,
men do not present the appearance of leisure, having to pursue a useful industrial occupation, but their wives still engage
in vicarious leisure and ceremonial consumption with the assistance of menial auxiliaries. What beauty or comfort house-

wives achieve is the product of "the great economic law of wasted effort." Housewives, in short, bear "the abiding mark of the unfree servant." Interestingly, household articles achieve preferred status by the degree of their conspicuous wastefulness. One might assume then that this is the case for members of the vicarious leisure class. Here things are a little more complicated. Although the romantic ideal of beauty dwells on delicacy, for example of the face, hands and feet, the Western ideal of beauty--in communities at elevated stages of industrialism--"has shifted from the woman of physical presence [i. e., in the American colonial period] to the lady, [i. e., in early eighteenth-century America] and it is beginning to shift back again to the woman [as in the Stone and Blatch quotations above]; and all in obedience to the changing conditions of pecuniary emulation." In other words, beauty of form is not only intrinsic; it may involve "an adaptation of physiological structure and function as well." Costuming can be one means of achieving such adaptation. The corset is a very good example of economic mutilation which results in an overall gain in propriety. Once again the law of conspicuous waste is in control by limiting women's ability to usefully exert themselves. [50]

The sum and substance of all this for Veblen is in the fact that contemporary institutions do not fit contemporary situations wholly. There is a selective, repressive process at work which affects both the social structure and members of society conservatively. In many ways, the prescriptive example of the leisure class reduces dispositional differences among existing classes. It also "acts to lower the industrial efficiency of the community and retard the adaptation of human nature to the exigencies of modern industrial life." This can lead to a sense of grievance among those who perceive discrepancies between things as they are and as they should be. The "'New-Woman' movement," characterized by watchwords of emancipation and work, is an example here. The prescriptive example of the leisure class loses some of its force among less compliant persons. The problem is that there is little chance for such noninvidious efforts when most of society's excess energy is absorbed in an invidious struggle. Efforts toward "a less differentiated expression of human nature," which Veblen believes are typical of the "'New-Woman' movement," are placed at a distinct disadvantage given the influence of the leisure class. [51]

The problems faced by those who would espouse more congruent roles for women and men are underscored by Veb-

len's analysis of the part the leisure class plays in prescrib-
ing social expectations. Woman can expect little from her
vicarious existence--or from her parasitism, as Olive
Schreiner puts it; woman's existence is going to be a dead
weight when it comes to initiating change in her position.
There will be change, but it will lag with respect to the contemporary situation, and it will come mostly in response to
invidious desires. Assuming progress toward a more perfect
end state will occur inevitably means overlooking the nature
of social mechanisms for change. Apparently the only situations which admit of substantial change in woman's position
are those distinguished by the frontier state of mind. Veblen
seems to believe such isolation from higher culture merely
constitutes reversion to predation. [52] This does not seem to
be born out by a review of American social history with respect to women's and men's roles, however. The problem
is that as the frontier moves on--either in terms of settlement or the abolition of slavery or improved industrial working conditions--the effect of traditional role differentiation
once again is viable. Complementary roles, which are aban-
doned by necessity, can and do reassert themselves, although
they may be modified somewhat by vestiges of the frontier
state of mind.

Complementary role modifications find expressions in
the remarks quoted above by Stone and Blatch. Their remarks are at best ambiguous and not likely or calculated to
really displace expectations about the complementary nature
of women and men's behavior. Yet complementary expectations are self-defeating for one who would advocate change in
woman's position. To give an example of the futility at work
here, those who espouse complementary roles often point to
women as enhancers of beauty in life. Beauty, according to
Veblen, is conditioned by requirements of an invidious code
which in effect is more concerned with appearances than with
apperceptive form. The components of beauty--in women, in
dress, in serviceable household objects--will vary, but the
variance is manipulable and in accordance with propriety as
the leisure class defines it. Those who espouse complementary roles would argue that, by giving woman the opportunity
to come to know herself, this will change. First, however,
women must circumvent the canons of decent life which derive
from principles of emulation. As indicated above, this is
not likely to be a successful endeavor because of the canon's
pervasiveness. Furthermore, advocates of complementary
roles are seeking to revise the canon, for example to admit
of woman's independence, not abolish it. The only substantial

change they allow is in the case of the individual of superior caste or talent. Such individuals are in effect eccentric enough to be able to exist outside conventional social expectations. They are not necessarily given to working for change in woman's position generally.

This is not to say that espousal of congruent roles for women and men is without its problems. For one thing, implementation clearly is situational. With a change in the situation comes such substantial diminution of congruent roles as to constitute displacement. How to extend the life span of congruent expectations poses genuine difficulty. Additionally, the situations which give rise to congruent roles are rather dire, and often the advantages which accrue to congruent roles are overshadowed by the disadvantages. Improving the situations to achieve a higher quality of life is likely to lead to the reinstitution of complementary roles. Finally, there is the problem long noted by those who espouse complementary roles: woman's adoption of man's ways. Blackwell suggests this problem is one of assuming man as the representative type, and she accordingly readjusts such assumptions for her analysis. Angelina Grimke asserts that sex simply is insignificant. This is all well and good, but it seems to overlook a very practical problem. By engaging in work which usually is the province of men, are not women likely to begin to display traits similar to those men display at such work? Maybe this is desirable and appropriate; maybe it is not. Even though the natural selection which produces secondary sexual characteristics is a very lengthy process, it seems this is a matter ripe for discussion. Asserting that sex is insignificant really says nothing about the nature of the behavior in question. A good part of the problem here probably is the difficulty of conceptualizing what asexual and/or androgynous behavior is, given the scope of existing differential expectations about women's and men's behavior.

Elizabeth Blackwell deals with the problem of conceptualizing asexual behavior by examining the sexual or reproductive function itself. She posits a general structure which encompasses both women and men without differentiating them. Given a common natural goal of reproducing the species, each sex presents three common properties: the power of mental and physical self-balance, strictly guarded potency and a certain degree of periodicity. Elizabeth Blackwell contrasts female menstruation and male sperm emission and finds them to be exact parallels. The former is the means of securing the lasting unity of an essential reproductive structure and of providing release from excessive vitality. The latter is the means to natural release from and the outlet for steady action of a reproductive organ. Two laws regulate the human sexual function: first, the law of continuity of action; second, the law of the power of self-adjustment. To elaborate on the latter, although procreative ability is maintained in both sexes, it is subject to occasional spontaneous bursts of purposive activity which emancipates the individual naturally in a necessarily concurrent exercise of the faculty. [53]

Blackwell identifies herself as writing from the standpoint of Christian physiology. She suggests that the laws referred to above are established by the "Creative Power." The laws are healthful and "consistent with the freedom and perfection of human growth." The functions they govern are to be considered equivalent, created to help each other in the continuation of the human species. Importantly, sex is not essential to the individual's existence. It is essential for the continuation of the species. [54] Thus one can say, as Angelina Grimke does, that sex is insignificant on the moral frontier of abolitionism because the agent as agent has nothing to do with continuing the species per se. The agent is concerned with the emancipation of the black race in this country from slavery. Expectations governing behavior here have to do with what is appropriate for gaining that end. Clergy who object to agents who happen to be female speaking in public are introducing irrelevant and even frivolous concerns. If an agent must speak in public to support the cause and to encourage others to support it, the agent is justified in doing so. Sex has nothing to do with the matter.

The sexual unselfconsciousness of Angelina Grimke's thought is to be understood in terms of her intense commitment to the abolitionists' cause. Signing herself "Thy sister" in her correspondence with Catharine Beecher refers to her larger relation with Beecher. It does not sexually differentiate her in her part as abolition agent. One should expect similarly unselfconscious expression from other women in frontier situations. They have an intense commitment to survival, to earning a subsistence wage and so on. Continuing the species is not in itself immediately relevant to their behavior as frontierswomen. Women on the frontier of settlement may bear many children for purposes of helping the family survive. Here too the strictly biological notion of perpetuating the species is subsumed in something more utilitarian. As it happens, the species is perpetuated, and--given lack of knowledge about birth control techniques--the birth of the children may not be the product of planned parenthood. There is nonetheless an utilitarian aura about birth of children on the frontier of settlement which diminishes purely sexual connotations.

It can be seen that feminist and prefeminist expression on the subject of congruent roles for women and men is not well developed at this time. There are a very few explicit spokespeople, although there are aspects of social history which suggest congruent roles do exist to some extent. Following Veblen's analysis, a new approach to the topic appears. One cannot be certain that Veblen's thought is the stimulus, but at times the outlines of his analysis seem present. The new approach deals with complementary roles for women and men and stresses the pathos of women in this context. Gertrude Stein's brilliant Three Lives is an example of this approach. [55] She illuminates the lives of three women who are of the working class, bringing a multifaceted focus to the tragedy of their circumstances. In the end, each woman comes to a death which appears meaningless but somehow inevitable. Each woman's death is after the fact, living for them having ceased already.

Each woman in Stein's Three Lives in her way leads a life of domestic service--as Veblen would have it, of derivative or vicarious leisure. Stein writes of these three lives with a sympathetic eye to the diversity of human experience, not unlike Jane Addams in this regard. Stein keenly reveals expectations about how these women should behave, in their own eyes and in the eyes of important others. The good german Anna has an intense commitment to being a girl; she knows what it entails, and she accordingly attempts to take charge of each situation she encounters. Her life is hard. The mulatto Melanctha longs to understand what being a woman entails and to give what it is others want; she finds nothing but trouble. The people she tries to love and to lead gradually turn her away. Gentle german Lena can neither yield to, as Anna does, nor endure, as Melanctha does, her suffering. What small sense of being she has seems to pass from her as she continues to work in a lifeless manner after her arranged marriage. Each woman gives and gives; each woman leads a life of service; each woman lives but little. Each woman dies almost unnoticed. The life of service does not seem to mean much throughout or in the end. There is no strong statement of social value and industrial use in these lives.

Each woman in Stein's Three Lives has at one time or another strong ties with other women. Each woman receives her share of scolding and criticism about her ways. It all is for nought. Each woman proceeds inexorably down a path which seems from the beginning predetermined, and each passes on almost as if she never exists. Three Lives seems a statement of alienation. Each woman essentially is out of touch with others, for all her service. On reading Three Lives, one can feel strongly that there must be a better way and yet not find it, for all the points of view which come into play. Something is seriously wrong in the expectations, in the trouble, in the estrangement. What it is that is wrong is not immediately knowable. It is clear, however, that the three lives entail very little living.

To move on for a moment, Florida Pier addresses the topic of congruent roles with considerable vigor in 1910.

In fact--and now the matter is to be settled once and for all--there is not a jot of difference between the masculine and feminine minds: there is only a difference in what is and what has been put in them, and what the world expects to come out of them. The world gets very much what it expects. [56]

This is well said; one is delighted to hear it. Yet three alienated lives linger disturbingly. Pier suggests, "We must show consideration for those poor souls who bear up under a misplaced masculine or feminine mind." Somehow her sarcasm seems misplaced. She sees the entire matter as "just one of those annoying blinders made by education which last a longer time after our shame of them has risen, and remain to trip us up...." Yes, surely Pier is accurate, but those three lives...--what is to be done?

Theresa Billington-Grieg speaks of the necessity for a feminist program in a British journal. If feminism is to accomplish the "great deeds of destruction and reconstruction" it intends, if it is to "establish a new morality," it must have a program which bespeaks policy or purpose. What are the ends-in-view? They are the rejection of sex differences, the abolition of rights and responsibilities founded on sex, "the recognition of the common humanity of women and men as the foundation of law and custom." In the end, however, salvation will not be attained through law and politics: "the real harvest of feminism will be garnered outside politics...." Custom must be changed, and this is a large order indeed.

Feminists must create "conscious disturbance and distress where now habit blinds us to the existence of danger and evil." Only a change in outlook and opinion can bring this about. [57]

The above statement is British. The difference between British and American feminist points of view is noted in chapter four. American feminist thought does not cry out for "great deeds of destruction and reconstruction" in the face of three or many women's wasted lives. It scolds a little, however, as in Louise Bogan's "Women":

> They wait, when they should turn to journeys,
> They stiffen, when they should bend.
> They use against themselves that benevolence
> To which no man is friend.
>
> They cannot think of so many crops to a field
> Or of clean wood cleft by an ax.
> Their love is an eager meaninglessness
> Too tense, and too lax. [58]

Bogan suggests women should be more mobile, more flexible, should put their benevolence to better use. Women's minds are so limited, and their love so meaningless. Yet, what is to be done?

Feminist thought at times seems surprisingly passive, unable to "think of so many crops to a field...." It seems, even when calling for reconceptualization of the roles of women and men--as Bogan gently does, too stifled to act, even too stifled to call for activism beyond the bare minimum. One reads the life of Lucy Stone, marked as it is by virtual frenzies of activity on behalf of woman's rights or domestic duties; one reads the life of Elizabeth Cady Stanton, marked by similar frenzies. One recognizes their own suffering and role conflict, in Stone's headaches, in Stanton's at times plaintive correspondence with Susan B. Anthony. One knows these women are trying. One asks if they too lead wasted lives for reasons beyond their own grasp. Surely they do not, but just as surely the harvest of their activity still lies in the future. It lies in a future in which Anna, Melanctha and Lena can experience being and life as well and in which few women will be troubled deeply by role conflict. To reach such a future, feminist thought may be called upon for "great deeds of destruction and reconstruction" rather than oftentimes gentle scolding.

In the meantime, science and especially the social sciences are giving increased reason to feminist thinkers for espousal of congruent roles for women and men. Havelock Ellis--whose work somewhat ironically is so important to Ellen Key, Margaret Sanger and Olive Schreiner--writes in 1894 that his findings about human secondary sexual characteristics indicate the influence of external modifying conditions. "... [U]nder varying conditions women and men are, within certain limits, indefinitely modifiable...." One cannot, he cautions, "dogmatise rigidly regarding their respective spheres. "59 One recollects Suzanne LaFollette's later description of the health of any organism as its growth, growth being change. 60 It seems, however, even given women's and men's equivalency, that the modification or growth which is change is going to be a long time in coming without "great deeds of destruction and reconstruction. "

LaFollette, as noted before, sharply criticizes feminist thinkers such as Key and Schreiner for reducing woman to a function. This for her is an abandonment of the "scientific spirit. "61 Antoinette Brown Blackwell attempts to show that women's and men's sexual functions are parallel and equivalent; secondary sexual characteristics--the result of natural selection--are compensating for barriers to woman's development. Ellis suggests such characteristics are within limits subject to modification. Yet espousal of congruent roles still is not widespread among feminist thinkers. Perhaps this is the case because the lives of women who exemplify congruent expectations are not ideal role models. As G. G. Johnson puts it in 1925, the woman laborer makes paper boxes or constantly tends a machine in order to live and not because there is anything intrinsically beautiful or exhilarating in her activity. 62 Reducing woman to a function seems to have the advantage of romanticization, even if it means as Bogan states that "Women have no wilderness in them.... "63

Virginia Woolf's Orlando protests to an old man the beauty of nature after he shows her some of his fingers withered by frost and one of his feet crushed by a fallen rock. He becomes angry, but she persists in a dialogue about beauty and truth. "'She prefers a sunset to a flock of goats, ' said the gipsies. " Perhaps mention should be made that Orlando, though 30 years old and more, is become a woman only recently. This alters the future but neither identity nor face. Although an Ambassador at the time of the change, Orlando for a while throws her fate in with the gipsies--among

whom the women, "except in one or two important particu-
lars, differ very little from the gipsie men." She decides
to sail for England and purchases "the dress of a young Englishwoman of rank...."

> It is a strange fact, but a true one, that up to this
> moment she had scarcely given her sex a thought.
> ... At any rate, it was not until she felt the coil
> of skirts about her legs and the Captain offered,
> with the greatest of politeness, to have an awning
> spread for her on deck, that she realized with a
> start the penalties and the privileges of her posi-
> tion. [64]

For a while yet, Orlando partakes of first one sex and
then the other, criticizing them equally. She is not sure to
which she belongs, but she cannot take comfort in ignorance
for she knows the mysteries and shares the deficiencies of
each. She will pay for her desires as a man, knowing as
she now does that women are not what she formerly manfully
insists: "obedient, chaste, scented, and exquisitely apparal-
led." Women attain such graces only "by the most tedious
discipline." Orlando arrives home to find her estates and
titles, everything "in a highly ambiguous condition, uncertain
whether she was alive or dead, man or woman, Duke or non-
entity." Yet, "no one showed an instant's suspicion that Orlando was not the Orlando they had known." Indeed, it seems
there is not much difference between them for "they were as
like as two peaches on one branch." Orlando reflects that
she is growing up, shedding old illusions perhaps to gain new
ones. "What the future might bring, Heaven only knew.
Change was incessant, and change perhaps would not cease. "[65]

A change begins to take place in Orlando. "Certain susceptibilities were asserting themselves, and others were dimin-
ishing." Perhaps it was the change of dress; perhaps it was
something more profound. "Different though the sexes are, they
intermix. In each human being a vacillation from one sex to the
other takes place, and often it is only the clothes that keep the
male or female likeness, while underneath the sex is the very opposite of what it is above." Still Orlando enters into an intoxicat-
ing, brilliant social whirl, with lovers aplenty, while life escapes
her. "And it was not enough." Under the spell of illusion--
"the most valuable and necessary of all things, and she who
can create one is among the world's greatest benefactors... "--
and then in the company of men of genius from whom occa-

sionally come a ray of light, she still searches for life, although in time more narrowly. "She had, it seems, no difficulty in sustaining the different parts, for her sex changed far more frequently than those who have worn only one set of clothing can conceive...." Such a device yields "a twofold harvest," increasing life's pleasures and multiplying its experiences. [66]

All this while, in Woolf's biographical statement, it is the eighteenth century. The nineteenth century is born under a cloud, in chill and damp. "The sexes grew further and further apart. No open conversation was tolerated. Evasions and concealments were sedulously practised on both sides." Even Orlando finally is forced to acknowledge the change, though she has never "seen anything at once so indecent, so hideous, and so monumental." Her pen begins to blot alarmingly or wander "into mellifluous fluencies about early death and corruption, which were worse than not thinking at all. For it would seem--her case proved it--that we write, not with the fingers, but with the whole person." Orlando is broken by the antipathetic spirit of the nineteenth century. She dies and becomes engaged. Yet "each was so surprised at the quickness of the other's sympathy, and it was to each such a revelation that a woman could be as tolerant and free-spoken as a man, and a man so strange and subtle as a woman, that they had to put the matter to proof at once."[67]

Orlando enters into a transaction with the spirit of her age and escapes by the skin of her teeth. She gives her manuscript to publication and is delivered of a son. She awakens on October 11, 1928. She is 36 and looks scarcely a day older. "'Time has passed over me,' she thought, trying to collect herself; 'this is the oncome of middle age.'" Keeping track of time is difficult for those who successfully practice the art of life and synchronise the many different times which "beat simultaneously in every normal human system," partaking of the present and partly recalling the past. Others only walk through life, dead or unborn or very old. Consciously Orlando could call on a great many selves, but deep in other thoughts, she becomes "what is called, rightly or wrongly, a single self, a real self."[68] That self is Orlando--Orlando who is woman, who is man, who partakes of both, who is present, who is past, who is simultaneously part of many different times. This is the successful practice of the art of life, known to the gipsies and to Orlando.

So it is the successful practice of life which must be the end-in-view for feminist thinkers, the process of passing from woman to man and back again until one self emerges. Yet it is not a conscious process, so seeking it is not the answer. One must be it. Just how far away the successful practice of life is becomes sadly evident in Dorothy Parker's "Song of the Shirt, 1941." First remember, however, the woman in unwomanly rags who plied her needle and thread in poverty, hunger and dirt in Thomas Hood's rendition. Parker's seamstress, Mrs. Martindale, is a lovely woman of charitable impulse with a rippled flag set in rubies, diamonds and sapphires pinned to her jacket lapel; "you might have laughed to hear that she was a working-woman." She is, though, even if unskilled and even if she dislikes doing the work. 69

Mrs. Martindale does service work at Headquarters, a special office of a war-relief organization. She is hand-sewing hospital garments. She could use a sewing machine, but she secretly fears it. Besides there is "something more of sacrifice, of service in making things by hand." Mrs. Martindale is dogged in her devotion to the task, keeping on where others fall by the wayside. Headquarters is about to close for the summer, but at the last moment there is a call for more volunteer work, this to be taken home. Mrs. Martindale, feeling shameful because she identifies momentarily with those who say they are just too tired to continue, takes 12 shirts. The pieces of the garments make "a formidable bundle," which necessitates calling her chauffeur to take them out for her. Her maid unpacks the bundle, and Mrs. Martindale confronts the work to be done in "her sitting-room, which had recently been redone in the color of her hair and her eyes." She begins to sew and rip and sew, feeling "almost ill from the tussle with the hard, monotonous work." In the midst of it, an acquaintance calls to ask her to try to think of some work for "my little Mrs. Christie" who must have some employment over the summer. Otherwise Mrs. Christie and her crippled daughter "just won't be able to live!" Mrs. Martindale promises to try to think of something and returns to "the drudgery of her fingers," stitching and ripping. "And as she stitched, faithful to her promise and to her heart, she racked her brains."70

Mrs. Martindale clearly is a member of the vicarious leisure class. Her services are ceremonial and conspicuous in the largest possible sense. Her awareness of the world about her seems stifled. She cannot bring together so much

as Mrs. Christie's willing fingers and the 12 despised hospital garments, let alone Mrs. Christie and all the garments
which could be done. Mrs. Martindale knows her duty so
well that she is swallowed up by it in her pleasant and becoming sitting room. The needs of others have no meaning
to her. It might be added that this is so for Anna, Melanctha
and Lena as well. As involved as they are in lives of service, they have no conception of others' needs. There is
what they must do, and there is nothing else. It seems a
strange sort of service, most assuredly a way of using benevolence against themselves. How could love born of such
service be anything but meaningless? What is there of the
successful art of living here?

It seems that advocacy of congruent roles has much
to do with essential usefulness and little to do with appearances. It seems it is not so much what one does but how it
is done. It seems there is not much need to worry about
sexual differentiation, about women taking on masculine traits
or even about men taking on feminine ones. In the end,
these do not matter at all if one considers women and men
equivalents. Secondary sexual characteristics do not matter
a great deal either. These are subject to change over time.
One must, as Orlando does, enter into a transaction with the
spirit of one's age and live on. What is most important is
that one really live. Though Orlando often enjoys countless
advantages of wealth and status, Mrs. Martindale's wealth
and status do not seem to serve her to the same advantage.
Orlando constantly finds great pleasure among people not of
similar wealth and status, including the gipsies, to whom her
lineage evidences embarrassing poverty. It is all very well
to say in the spirit of the 1970s that one can find such pleasure so long as one has other alternatives. This, however,
is to miss the point of the transaction. Any class identification can be repressive if it is allowed to be so. Any class
situation can afford pleasure if it is allowed to do so. A
reading of Three Lives suggests this as strongly as a reading
of Orlando. There is, for Woolf, an art to living which does
not admit of sex or class. A reading of American social
history seems to suggest as much as well. The lives of
working-class people, of pioneers, of slaves, of immigrants,
of abolitionists, to give several examples, do not lend themselves to romanticization, but they do give evidence of pleasure and living at times.

What is most troublesome for one who espouses congruent roles is the accommodative attitude which figures pro-

minently in any caste, the deprived looking for patrons to
protect them from hostility. Such deferential activities, according to Ruth Herschberger, figure prominently in women's
lives. She suggests there are two deferential "traps" which
stand in the way of advocates of equal rights for women.

> One is the deification trap: woman is promised
> protection and reward if she will adopt the tradi-
> tional deference attitudes toward men. The other
> trap is a maze of logic, in which the enjoyment
> of differences between men and women, and be-
> tween individual women, is replaced by a sudden
> deification of 'real' women, that vast majority
> who are thought to prefer the kitchen to anything
> else. [71]

It appears to Herschberger that examples of basic sex differences are constructed with "calipers and glue rather than
by the shakier hands of Mother Nature." The end result is
that "Women ... are weary of being custom-shrunk."[72]

Herschberger goes on to suggest that while the ability
to have a baby differentiates women from men, the fact is
that women are not always having babies. In fact, "fertility
is not a fixed condition in women, nor should it invariably be
taken advantage of." Furthermore, the much-touted maternal
instinct basically is composed of human traits such as warm
feelings for others and for their needs and problems. Women
enjoy no monopoly of such traits, and such traits are not always displayed by women. There is tremendous diversity
among women, for all the emphasis placed on the "joyous
uniformity of women's subjective experience." Herschberger
poses a most provocative question: "Does this mean that the
similarities between women are greater than their differences,
and that these similarities are more important than any similarities they share with men?"[73] Her answer is that while
women may be unique in that they can have babies, they also
partake of reason, have an opposed thumb, stand erect and so
on. The latter are human characteristics. Must women be
limited only to the former?[74]

The ability to live well seems to encompass a great
many possibilities and differences within a human framework.
One cannot be tied to the past, although one may remember
it partly. One cannot be tied to a single function anymore
than one can be tied forever and ever to one moment in time.
Things change, and so do human beings. It may take a very

long time to modify some secondary sexual characteristics, as Wollstonecraft suggests; yet for Herschberger, one person's life span alone provides many opportunities for diversity. Reducing women to the ability to bear children, to the reproductive function, in effect custom-shrinking them, is to construct them with "calipers and glue," largely avoiding reality in the process. In the business of living life, sex is just as insignificant as Angelina Grimke finds it on the moral frontier. There is great equivalence among human beings: for Elizabeth and Antoinette Brown Blackwell, sexually; for Herschberger, physically and mentally. As for living, a wasted life is a wasted life. The greatest tragedy is that wasted lives need not be, if only a way can be found to encompass the many possibilities and differences a human framework affords. Out of living, really living, comes a single, integrated self who is neither male nor female, who is both feminine and masculine, who is essentially androgynous.

The congruent orientation is a long way from one who would translate women to men and men to women. Such translation should not be necessary for integrated selves. As for sex appeal and alterity, the line between a complementary and a congruent persuasion is a fine one. Perhaps it is nothing more than a change of dress; perhaps it is something more profound. The dilemma still is as Woolf suggests, that the sexes intermix, that dress may be only a matter of appearances. Alterity and intermixing may or may not be the same thing. In this author's mind, they are not alike. In the context of congruent roles, sex differentiation essentially is meaningless;[75] it does not seem to be so for Simone de Beauvoir in her discussion of alterity. Far more important than sexual differentiation in congruent role expectations is a willingness to experiment, to test, to probe. The person with integrative potential can come to grips with the Victorian age as well as the age of the Flapper. Some situations and some times may be more facilitative of integration than others, but the person with a capacity for wholeness should be able to strike a bargain with almost any situation or time. Once the barriers are down, there are few limitations for a human being.

It may seem that the congruent persuasion is an individualistic one. It is that, but it partakes strongly of an egalitarian creed as well. Both libertarian and egalitarian creeds cut across this persuasion, as they do the complementary one. Here, however, feminist and prefeminist thinkers who take a libertarian approach to the topic of congruent roles stress a

World War II airplane manufacture, at North American Aviation. (Courtesy Franklin D. Roosevelt Library.)

---

unselfconscious individualism, one which is more humanitarian than self seeking. Feminist and prefeminist thinkers who take an egalitarian approach to the topic of congruent roles do not stress opportunity so much as they do alikeness. Potential issues about contradictory duties are downplayed in a situational focus on usefulness. One must do what needs to be done, keeping an experimental outlook all the while. The androgynous person who happens to be female delivers a baby with about the alacrity that she delivers a manuscript. There is not a great conventional overlay to either activity. One is no more alarmed about the implications for one's life in one instance than the other. Both are part of living, and both are experiences worth having. Yet both are experienced unselfconsciously, and as a result, personhood is not at stake.

Clearly, rectifying woman's position in the family is going to be crucial for those who espouse congruent roles.

Antoinette Brown Blackwell makes much of this. One might
suppose that "great deeds of destruction and reconstruction"
bode ill for the familial grouping itself, but for American
feminist thought at least such is not the case. Plato's warning that abolition of the family is a wave which must be
breasted if the swimmer is not to drown goes unheeded.
Monogamous marriage and children born of and part of that
union remain basic assumptions here. What is essential is
that woman not be construed to be a mere function, confined
to the family context alone. Family relations in the future
must be approached experimentally. When spouses can view
each other as friends and with sympathy, then women can begin to exist in such a setting. It is interesting to note, however, the tenuous balancing which Lucy Stone undertakes in
her marriage and the stress it apparently produces. Worse
still, gentle Lena becomes lifeless upon marrying, but she
marries Herman Kreder, not Henry Blackwell. In Orlando's
case, Marmaduke Bonthrop Shelmerdine, Esquire, convenient-
ly takes to sea immediately after the union. Orlando and
Bonthrop communicate in cipher across the wire, truly an experimental marital state if ever there was one. Furthermore,
Orlando's baby boy never becomes an everyday factor in her
life, a situation reminiscent of women of the ruler class in
Plato's Republic.

On the other hand, Herman Kreder cares for the
children born of his union with gentle Lena, as Lena becomes
more and more lifeless. Herman is not without sympathy for
Lena, but they lack a cipher through which to communicate.
A great deal of experimentation and probing remains to be
done here.

Education in many ways is key to the introduction of
the experimental mind. Education must partake of a genuinely scientific spirit. So long as education does nothing but
produce annoying blinders, it is no more than that--an annoy-
ance. In the end, real education may be less formalized and
more experimental, as on the frontier, so that the scientific
method can be applied in the most natural of situations,
where appearances mean little and usefulness means a great
deal. One can come to terms with appearances. It is lack
of selfconsciousness which is absolutely crucial to the institution of congruent roles, and an experimental attitude will
do a great deal to foster such a state.

One wonders what the ultimate civilization will be in
this context. It logically seems there can be none, and yet

feminist and prefeminist thinkers who espouse congruent roles
make much of coming to terms with experience in order to
attain that which is essential. Essences are absolutes; once
they are attained, they afford a sort of perceptual end state.
In this state, emphasis can be placed on stability, on usefulness, even on happiness. Science, and technology, have a
lot of potential here, and congruent feminists are well aware
of this fact. B. F. Skinner draws on this fact extensively
in constructing Walden II. The recognition that behavior is
governed by its consequences is only a short step from manipulating the environment to alter these consequences. Operant
conditioning, which is an ethically neutral technology, offers the
means by which to change behavior. Here emphasis is shifted
away from someone's impression of the desirable components
of human nature to the environment which determines the species and its members. [76]

Walden offers a contemporarily conceived, scientifically shaped utopian end state. It is quite different from the
state that Mary Griffith projects. Rather than women's will-
fully asserting their own special attributes to improve society, controlling the consequences of people's behavior through
the environment produces Walden society. Aldous Huxley
leaps altogether out of the present in Brave New World to a
time when "truth's a menace, science is a public danger.
As dangerous as it's been beneficent. It has given us the
stablest equilibrium in history. ... [E]ven the primitive ma-
triarchies weren't steadier than we are. ... But we can't
allow science to undo its own good work." Thus universal
happiness becomes "the Sovereign Good"; science is "something that caused you to laugh at the Corn Dances...." Consciousness and knowledge are replaced by the need to maintain well-being. One of the results of this revolution is a
comprehensive eugenics system. The fertilization process,
developmental controls which produce standard women and
men in uniform batches, social predestination and conditioned
existence--all are forthcoming through mass production outside the female body. Mother becomes an obscenity; history
is foregone; children's and adults' minds are suggestions
from the state. [77]

The stability on which civilization depends is the product of a self-evident axiom: "Every one belongs to every
one else...." Anything else--"Family, monogamy, romance.
Everywhere exclusiveness, everywhere a focussing of interest,
a narrow channelling of impulse and energy"--would be virtually unthinkable. Few are inclined to opt for "[l]iberty to

be inefficient and miserable" or something more than physico-
chemical equality. Everyone is "safe on the solid ground of
daily labour and distraction, " conscripted to consume all that
mass production can offer in a world in which desire and fulfillment are nearly one and the same. [78] With the possibility
of pregnancy removed, sex relations are infantile and sensual;
people's relations to the state, on the other hand, are adult
and useful. For Huxley, all of this constitutes a "nightmare
of total organization, " pushed by nearly uncontrollable impersonal forces to a future which is only around the corner. [79]

What is to be done? For Walden II's mentor, Frazier,
the community inevitably must revise established practices
such as the family, replacing them economically as well as
partially socially and psychologically. "What survives is an
experiment. "[80] Yet, for those who would comprehend essences rather than appearances, something seems awry.
Walden is only one community and an utopian one at that.
For Huxley, sex becomes an insignificant factor in the useful
life of an adult. It is otherwise a sort of mass opiate, rendered purposeless with the relocation of the reproductive
function in the state. Here again, though, the community in
question is not a real one; it is a futuristic sketch of what
might be.

Margaret Mead suggests that to understand the origin
of variance in sex differences within and between actual cultures, one must look to overt and implicit assumptions made
about useful activities in which women and men engage. It
usually is assumed that such activities are part of sex temperament. Yet Mead's findings suggest "that human nature
is almost unbelievably malleable, responding accurately and
contrastingly to contrasting cultural conditions. " Thus, temperamental attitudes which customarily are regarded as, say,
feminine may become the norm for females and males alike
in one culture or outlawed for females and males alike in
another culture or standardized for one sex and outlawed for
the other in still another culture. Given such circumstances,
women and men's temperament cannot be regarded as sex
linked.

The knowledge that the personalities of the two
sexes are socially produced is congenial to every
programme that looks forward towards a planned
order of society. It is a two-edged sword that
can be used to hew a more flexible, more varied
society than the human race has ever built, or

merely to cut a narrow path down which one sex
or both sexes will be forced to march, regimented,
looking neither to the right nor to the left.   ...
Because it is social conditioning that is determina-
tive, it has been possible for America, without
conscious plan but none the less surely, partially
to reverse the European tradition of male dominance, and to breed a generation of women who
model their lives on the pattern of their school-
teachers and their aggressive directive mothers. [81]

   As pointed out earlier, Mead suggests all this leaves
open three possible courses for the society which appreciates
the socially determined aspect of personality. Women's and
men's personality can be standardized as complementary or
without sexual distinction or with an eye to diverse potentials.
Clearly there is a strong trend in feminist and prefeminist
thought toward complementary standardization. The small
group of feminist and prefeminist thinkers who espouse congruent roles appear to be headed toward the abolition of
sexual distinction. The fact is, however, that the way is
left open for the third possibility as well by both congruent
and complementary orientations. Presuming feminist thought
will continue to manifest itself in the future, and presuming
the congruent orientation will develop even more strongly,
one of three things could take place. The congruent orientation could overtake and engulf the complementary one. The
two orientations could attain approximately equal status among
feminist thinkers and confrontation or even fragmentation
could occur. The two orientations could be subsumed within
feminist thought as part of an orientation which would espouse
diverse roles for women and men, Mead's third alternative.
Given the ongoing nature of the generalizations which characterize feminist thought, which are feminist thought, Mead's
third alternative seems to be a likely next step.

References

1   Rights of Women (1790) (New York: E. P. Dutton, 1929),
    pp. 197, 64, 195, 23-24, 28, 30.
2   Ibid., pp. 47, 73, 42, 122.
3   "Mary Wollstonecraft," in An Anthropologist at Work:
    Writings of Ruth Benedict, Margaret Mead (Boston:
    Houghton, 1959), p. 491.
4   Barbara Tovey and George Tovey trace the rhetorical
    development of Socrates' argument in The Republic and

336 / Women's and Men's Roles

the underlying lesson being offered women in an article
perhaps unfortunately entitled "Women's Philosophical
Friends and Enemies," Social Science Quarterly, 55 (December 1974), 591-602. The Toveys include their discussion of Plato's work under a subheading, "The Feminist Viewpoint." Aristotle is discussed under "The Anti-
Feminist Viewpoint," pp. 586-88.

5 The Republic of Plato, trans. Francis MacDonald Corn-
ford (New York: Oxford University Press, 1972-3), pp. 146,
106-07, 149, 151, 153-54.

6 Ibid., pp. 154-61, 168.

7 Ibid., pp. 156, 177-78, 218-19, 224-26, 208.

8 Ibid., pp. 227-32, 105.

9 Ibid., pp. 231, 233-34.

10 Ibid., pp. 234, 255, 262.

11 Ibid., pp. 216-17.

12 See Vernon Parrington, Main Currents in American
Thought: An Interpretation of American Literature from
the Beginning to 1920 (New York: Harcourt, Brace,
1930), vol. 1, p. 272, for a background of this distinction.

13 Daughters of the Promised Land (Boston: Little, Brown,
1970), p. 40.

14 See Sidney A. Hart and John Walter Putre, "Communication," William and Mary Quarterly, 32 (January 1975),
164-69; but see Lyle Koehler, "The Case of the American
Jezebels: Anne Hutchinson and Female Agitation During
the Years of Antinomian Turmoil, 1636-1640," William
and Mary Quarterly, 31 (January 1974), 55-78; see also
June Sochen, Herstory: A Woman's View of American
History (New York: Alfred Publishing, 1974), p. 51.

15 See Parrington, Main Currents, p. 29, on the first point;
Sochen, Herstory, p. 51, on the second point.

16 Linda Grant De Pauw, Founding Mothers: Women in
America in the Revolutionary Era (Boston: Houghton,
1975), pp. 57-58; see also Page Smith, Daughters of the
Promised Land, pp. 221-23.

17 Morris R. Cohen, American Thought: A Critical Sketch,
ed. Felix S. Cohen (Glencoe, Ill.: Free Press, 1954),
p. 47.

18 See Ray Allen Billington with James Blaine Hedges,
Westward Expansion: A History of the American Frontier,
2d ed. (New York: Macmillan, 1960), pp. 1-3. This
book builds on Frederick Jackson Turner's frontier hypothesis and writings, mentioned earlier, as well as modifies his concepts and organization along lines suggested
by subsequent scholarship.

19 Billington and Hedges, Westward Expansion, pp. 4-5.

20 William W. Fowler, Woman on the American Frontier:
A Valuable and Authentic History of the Heroism, Adven-
tures, Privations, Captivities, Trials, and Notable Lifes
and Deaths of the "Pioneer Mothers of the Republic"
(Hartford, Conn.: S. S. Scranton, 1878), p. 3.
21 Grimke, Letters to Catharine E. Beecher (1838) (Freeport, N.Y.: Books for Libraries Press, 1971), pp. 114-
15, 118-20.
22 Ibid., pp. 103, 108, 30-31, 20; but see Catharine E.
Beecher, An Essay on Slavery and Abolitionism with
Reference to the Duty of American Females (1837) (Freeport, N.Y.: Books for Libraries Press, 1970). See
Ronald G. Walters, The Antislavery Appeal: American
Abolitionism After 1830 (Baltimore: Johns Hopkins University Press, 1976), for an interpretive historical account of the abolitionists' intense reaction to the slavery
issue.
23 The Martyr Age of the United States (Boston: Weeks,
Jordan, 1839), p. 3.
24 Ibid., pp. 36, 54, 81.
25 Ibid., p. 82.
26 "The Lady and the Mill Girl: Changes in the Status of
Women in the Age of Jackson," American Studies Journal,
10 (Spring 1969), 11.
27 Ibid., pp. 7, 9, 11-13.
28 Society in America (London: Saunders and Otley, 1837),
vol. 2, p. 325; vol. 3, pp. 145-56.
29 Thomas Hood, "Song of the Shirt," in Feminism: The
Essential Historical Writings, ed. Miriam Schneir (New
York: Vintage Books, 1972), pp. 58-59.
30 Ibid., p. 60.
31 See Eleanor Flexner, Century of Struggle: The Woman's
Rights Movement in the United States (Cambridge, Mass.:
Harvard University Press, 1959), pp. 134-44, 197-207,
248-55, for further details.
32 "Disappointment Is the Lot of Woman," in Feminism, ed.
Schneir, pp. 106, 108.
33 Hays, Morning Star: A Biography of Lucy Stone, 1818-
1893 (New York: Harcourt, Brace and World, 1961),
pp. 69-70, 288-89, 4.
34 Ibid., pp. 269, 253-54, 278, 271-72; see also Aileen S.
Kraditor, The Ideas of the Woman Suffrage Movement,
1890-1920 (New York: Columbia University Press, 1965),
pp. 158-59.
35 Antoinette Brown Blackwell, The Sexes Throughout Nature
(New York: G. P. Putnam's Sons, 1875), pp. 11, 51-
53, 65.

36 Ibid., pp. 67, 109, 135.
37 Ibid., p. 89.
38 Ibid., p. 122.
39 Stanton and the Revising Committee, The Woman's Bible (1895) (Seattle: Coalition Task Force on Women and Religion, 1974), p. 7.
40 Ibid., pp. 23-24, 31.
41 Ibid., pp. 15, 21.
42 Ibid., p. 19.
43 Ibid., pp. 15, 27, 33.
44 See Aileen Kraditor, Ideas of the Woman's Suffrage Movement, pp. 77-86, for a discussion of reaction to The Woman's Bible.
45 "Lady and the Mill Girl," p. 15, fn. 20.
46 In History of Woman Suffrage, 1883-1900, ed. Susan B. Anthony and Ida Husted Harper (Indianapolis: Hollenbeck Press, 1902), vol. 4, p. 311.
47 Veblen, The Theory of the Leisure Class: An Economic Study of Institutions (1899) (New York: Macmillan, 1912), pp. 246, 43-44, 1, 20, 13, 28-29, 31-33, 36, 40-41, 52.
48 Ibid., pp. 57-59.
49 Ibid., pp. 58-59, 65-66, 70-71.
50 Ibid., pp. 81-83, 126, 147-48, 151, 172, 178.
51 Ibid., pp. 190-91, 212-13, 244, 356-57, 361-62.
52 Ibid., p. 197.
53 Elizabeth Blackwell, Essays on Medical Sociology (1902) (New York: Arno, 1972), vol. 1, pp. 18, 32, 25.
54 Ibid., pp. 3, 32, 10.
55 (1909) Norfolk, Conn.: New Directions Press, n.d.
56 "The Masculine and Feminine Mind," Harper's Weekly (September 24, 1910), 21.
57 Billington-Grieg, "Feminism and Politics," Contemporary Review, 100 (November 1911), 694-95, 699.
58 In Poems and New Poems (1923) (New York: Charles Scribners' Sons, 1941), p. 19.
59 Ellis, Man and Woman: A Study of Human Secondary Sexual Characters, 6th ed. (London: A and C Black, 1926), pp. 512-13.
60 Concerning Women (1926) (New York: Arno, 1972), p. 5.
61 Ibid., p. 55.
62 "Feminism and Economic Independence of Women," Journal of Social Forces, 2 (May 1925), 615.
63 "Women," in Poems and New Poems, p. 19.
64 Orlando: A Biography (1928) (London: Hogarth Press, 1958), pp. 132-33, 137, 140.
65 Ibid., pp. 145, 143, 153, 155, 159-60.
66 Ibid., pp. 170-72, 177-78, 181, 188, 192, 200.

67 Ibid., pp. 204-05, 207, 209-10, 219-20, 225, 233.
68 Ibid., pp. 239, 268, 272, 274, 278, 282.
69 In The Portable Dorothy Parker, rev. ed. (1944) (New York: Viking, 1974), pp. 65-66.
70 Ibid., pp. 67-73.
71 Adam's Rib (1948) (New York: HAR/ROW Books, 1970), pp. 165-66, 162-63.
72 Ibid., pp. 2, 169.
73 Ibid., pp. 171-75. For one study which suggests the differences among women are stronger than the similarities, see Sarah Slavin Schramm and R. Darcy, "Sex as Dependent Variable and the Selection of Appropriate Predictors," in The Study of Women and Politics: A Symposium Exploring Methodological Issues, ed. Sarah Schramm, forthcoming.
74 Herschberger, Adam's Rib, p. 177.
75 See Abraham H. Maslow, "Dominance, Personality and Social Behavior in Women," Journal of Social Psychology, 10 (1937), 3-39.
76 Parts of this discussion are excerpted from Sarah Slavin Schramm, "The Future: Ethics and Social Change," Journal of Religious Concern, 4 (Fall 1976), 17.
77 Aldous Huxley, Brave New World: A Novel (1932) (New York: Harper, 1946), pp. 273-74, 211, 269, 1-19, 32.
78 Ibid., pp. 48, 45-46, 52-55, 67, 58.
79 Brave New World Revisited (1958) (New York: Perennial Library, 1965), pp. 6, 4.
80 B. F. Skinner, Walden II (1948) (New York: Macmillan, 1972), p. 138.
81 Mead, Sex and Temperament in Three Primitive Societies (1935) (New York: Dell, 1971), pp. 265, 259-60, 285.

YOU WILL LOOK BACK
AT US WITH ASTONISHMENT!

One .word more I should like to add, as I may
never again speak or write on this subject.   I
should like to say to the men and women of the
generations which will come after us--'You will
wonder at passionate struggles that accomplished
so little; at the, to you, obvious paths to attain
our ends which we did not take; at the intolerable evils before which it will seem to you we
sat down passive; at the great truths staring us
in the face, which we failed to see; at the
truths we grasped at, but could not get our
fingers quite round.   You will marvel at the labor that ended in so little;--but, what you will
not know is how it was thinking of you and for
you, that we struggled as we did and accomplished the little which we have done; that it
was with the thought of your larger realization
and fuller life that we found consolation for the
futilities of our own. '[1]

This intellectual history of feminism, in addition to
stipulating a special definition of feminism, asks hard questions of the ideas and ideals expressed.   Sometimes the
answers to those questions are less than satisfactory.   It is
so true, as Olive Schreiner states above, that there are obvious paths which feminist and prefeminist thinkers never
travel; intolerable evils which they do not always confront;
great truths which they bypass or cannot incorporate as part
of their ideas and ideals.   We must not suppose these thinkers too dense to comprehend their lapses, too rigid to
change.   Feminist thought is a developmental phenomenon.
Older conceptions are replaced by later choices in an intellectual process which is repeated over and over.   One might
liken the process to a painting in which, were layers of
paint removed at places, quite different images would appear.

Furthermore, one should not suppose that feminist and

prefeminist thinkers do not apprehend the difficulties which their ideas and ideals present at times. A normative theory teacher of mine always says that one must suppose great theorists do apprehend such difficulties. It seems that at any given time a thinker can do only so much. There are many things a change-oriented thinker must take into account. In the end, it undoubtedly is a question of priorities, and here choices must be made. Perhaps too, thinkers in an area as controversial as this one must disguise some of the further-reaching implications of their thought, in effect put them off for a more congenial tomorrow. There are feminist and prefeminist thinkers who are amazingly forthright, for example, Elizabeth Cady Stanton. Virginia Woolf too, in her own subtle manner, offers ideas which are almost clairvoyant in their outreach. If other examples of feminist thought do not attain such heights, they are nonetheless pregnant with implications to be reaped by still other feminist thinkers privileged to inherit more congenial byways.

Feminist and prefeminist thinkers engage in a passionate struggle indeed. Theirs is an open ended struggle in that--although it admits of ends-in-view--the ideals never may be realized fully. Part of the reason this is so has to do with the fact the ideals themselves keep changing. Thus we define feminism in terms of ongoing generalizations. These generalizations present intermingling concerns with women's family relations and education, inapposite ideologies of liberty and equality, and inconsistent images of women's and men's roles. These generalizations never reach the status of full-blown ideology; that is, an elaborate, closely woven, far-ranging structure of ideas which admits of abstraction. In its oftentimes practical overview, feminist and prefeminist thought offers tactics for achieving change and very occasionally strategic insights. Its generalizations really go no further than this, and it may be said quite fairly that perhaps for their times and places, these generalizations go far enough. They always are ahead of their times and usually very controversial.

We can take feminist and prefeminist thinkers out of their times and places and fantasize the dialogue which would take place. In this way, we obtain a more comprehensive picture of the body of thought, its ideas and ideals, than we do by examining it author by author, time period by time period, region by region. All of these analytic foci are useful, however, and hopefully there are more of them to come. This book really only hints at the intellectual potential of feminist and prefeminist thought. Yet there is very real potential here, potential which is in many ways broader in scope than is often assumed.

We follow feminist and prefeminist ideas and ideals in this study from their classical and Old World roots into colonial America and up through the 1950s. At times there is a proliferation of materials; at other times there is less to go on. There are always examples of feminist and prefeminist thought to be found, however. It never dies--not with the coming of the cult of true womanhood, not with the back to the home movements of the Great Depression and the aftermath of the Korean conflict. If anything, these events are stimuli to further thought at the time and afterwards.

We all know the 1960s saw a resurgence of feminism. Even now, as we move toward 1980, it is a highly visible phenomenon. I am writing at this moment the day after the Pennsylvania Women's Congress, held in Pittsburgh, which attracted 4000 participants. (The Utah International Women's Year conference attracted 11,768 persons; New York's conference, 7000; California's conference, 6000.) Federally subsidized, this Pittsburgh meeting and similar others will culminate in a collective convention from which a set of goals will be forthcoming. Not all of the participants would identify themselves as feminists, but those who do are making their presence known. (It might be added that among those who do not identify themselves as feminists are many whose intellectual forebears are nonetheless to be found in feminism's history.) Thus the period of activism and thought which begins partly with the John F. Kennedy administration's Commission and Council on the Status of Women continues. It continues at the very time many would pronounce the women's liberation movement dead for all practical intents. I mention this to caution those who would pursue the study of feminism and prefeminism, its thought and its action, to be wary of speculation about cycles and overhasty pronouncements of rigor mortis. Feminist and prefeminist thought, and undoubtedly action as well, do not die; they go on.

Our task now as scholars, as feminists, in addition to analyzing further the components of feminist and prefeminist thought, is to attempt to see this body of thought whole. For all the things unsaid, diversity, inapposition, inconsistency-- this is a feasible proposition. We need to bring contemporary feminist thought into the proposition as well. Given our closeness to contemporary feminist thought, this admittedly is not going to be easy. Yet it should be no more difficult than analyzing feminist and prefeminist thought from a distance of many years. The perceptual screens which make both endeavors so difficult are not absolute barriers.

It is imperative that we overcome these perceptual screens for, as Virginia Woolf puts it, "masterpieces are not single solitary births; they are the outcome of many years of thinking, in common, of thinking by the body of people, so that the experience of the mass is behind the single voice." This will entail devising "some entirely new combination of ... resources, so highly developed for other purposes, so as to absorb the new into the old without disturbing the infinitely intricate and elaborate balance of the whole." In undertaking this task as in reading this book, you the reader--and here again I shall adopt Virginia Woolf's words--

> you no doubt have been observing her feelings and foibles and deciding what effect they have had on her opinions. You have been contradicting her and making whatever additions and deductions seem good to you. This is all as it should be, for in a question like this truth is only to be had by laying together many varieties of error. [2]

By way of bringing contemporary feminist thought into the proposition, a discussion about women's studies will be particularly fruitful. The growth and increasing stability of women's studies continues to both amaze and dismay its advocates and detractors. Nevertheless, that growth is well documented, and the stability is well earned. An analysis, at this point in the development of women's studies, of its focus, idea power and promise seems appropriate to a discussion of the ongoing generalizations which are feminist thought. [3]

WOMEN'S STUDIES: FOCUS

We were teaching about women before we had a name for it. [4]

The resurgence of the women's movement with the establishment of federal and state Commissions on the Status of Women, the issuance of Betty Friedan's The Feminine Mystique, and the insertion of the class "sex" to Title VII of the 1964 Civil Rights Act all had a definite intellectual component. The works of Shulamith Firestone, Kate Millett, Alice Rossi and Naomi Weisstein exhibit this. The intellectual component extends far beyond the works of a few individuals, however.

In 1968, the Women's History Research Center at Berkeley was collecting and publicizing material by and about women. In 1969, 19 members of the National Organization for Women (NOW) came together to found Know, Inc., a publishing house directed toward the dissemination of serious feminist writing. By the end of 1970, the Modern Language Association's Commission on the Status of Women listed 110 college and university courses dealing with women. The following year witnessed a sixfold proliferation of formal, largely introductory and interdisciplinary courses about women and the availability of at least 17 formal programs. Today, seven years later, according to the latest listing in Women's Studies Newsletter, there are 151 such programs.[5] Departmental offerings, especially in English, sociology and history, continually are surfacing. High school and professional/vocational schools are also beginning to include courses in their curriculums.

Florence Howe and Carol Ahlum note the geographic coincidence of the women's movement per se and women's studies in volume three of the Female Studies series.[6] Early in 1973, in recognition of the congruence of women's studies and the goals of the National Organization for Women, Anne Grant and this author established a national Committee to Promote Women's Studies. Originally an appendage to NOW's Education Task Force, the Committee soon achieved independent status. Women's studies and the women's movement formally were united.

Simultaneously, as these events were occurring, consciousness-raising emerged as a small-scale organizational mechanism with broad implications for the women's movement.[7] The rap group was part of the experience of women activists disillusioned by the sexism of the civil rights and peace movements. Ultimately it reached into the homes of countless "uninvolved" women in every part of the country. Its impact was felt in women's studies settings as well. Gerda Lerner notes in volume two of the Female Studies series that students in her seminar at Sarah Lawrence are revealing "deep-seated doubts and problems ... concerning their roles as women in society."[8] By the time Female Studies seven is published three years later, Deborah Silverton Rosenfelt cites "self-actualization and consciousness-raising" as traditional women's studies components.[9]

Developmentally, neither the intellectual nor the affective dimension of women's studies was confined solely to the university. They flourished in continuing education settings, in storefronts and women's centers, in pre-schools and community programs and in a variety of alternative forms of education. Furthermore, women's studiers working from within formal programs often developed ties with the community. [10] Even with this environmental diversity, however, the focus of women's studies is remarkably unitary. It includes increasing the visibility of women's accomplishments, dispersing information and resources on women which ordinarily are bypassed, defining feminism for the community, contributing to the legitimacy of a movement which aims for nothing less than human liberation, facilitating consciousness expansion in others, and increasing the levels of consciousness of women's studiers themselves. [11]

Of the items which make up this focus, the first two may seem relatively intellectual in scope and the last two, relatively affective, with the middle two combining both dimensions. This impression is somewhat deceptive. Delving into the resources which contain, for example, women's history, and uncovering women's contributions to all facets of life constitute consciousness-raising experiences in themselves. Affective encounters, on the other hand, seldom are conducted apart from intellectual perceptions linking them to the past and to thought about the future. Attempts to explicate feminism and to support the women's movement rely on both dimensions and reflect the interaction between them.

These interactive dimensions, appearing as they do in widely diverse environments, essentially have three implications. The first implication is a personal one, reaching nearly all of those who engage in women's studies. These individuals, whatever their background, exhibit increased levels of assertive behavior and wholehearted applications of themselves to realizing their potentials. This phenomenon is commented on extensively throughout the Female Studies series. In addition, Kathleen O'Connor Blumhagen shows statistically significant change in ego levels of student women enrolled in a women's studies course over the length of one semester. [12]

The two remaining implications extend to the university and to the women's movement itself and are not explored widely or systematically at this time. These implications are the product of an idea power which grows to activist proportions with the diverse manifestations of the intellectual and affective dimensions. It is to the idea power of women's studies that this analysis now turns.

WOMEN'S STUDIES: IDEA POWER

What I want back is what I was
Before the bed, before the knife,
Before the brooch-pin and the salve
Fixed me in this parenthesis;
Horses fluent in the wind,
A Place, a time gone out of mind.[13]

With increasing self-awareness among women's studiers and more hard data at their disposal, they gradually learned that traditional ivory-tower structures and procedures for disseminating scholarship were not amenable to a radical change of perspective on women's roles. Universities, after all, generally are hierarchical in structure and conflict-oriented in procedure. Centering on personalities and coalitions, a conflict orientation is one in which there is continuous strife for mastery. Hostile encounters are frequent, prolonged and to be expected, as are competition and polemics.[14] The universities which set the tone for all of educationdom were not ready for a raised consciousness about women.[15]

Unlike oil and water, sexism and scholarship apparently do mix. Despite Mary Beard's assertion that women are a force in history with which to contend,[16] Simone de Beauvoir found it necessary to point out that all of women's history is man made, a sort of Caucasian masculine burden.[17] Discipline after discipline was found wanting as numerous women scholars, and some men, compiled statistics and conducted content analysis of the representation of women in person as faculty or in substance as data. Victoria Schuck and Judy Corder Tully, in a symposium issue of Social Science Quarterly, conceptualized these lapses as "masculine blinders."[18]

It remained for women's studies, like black studies and the free-school movement before it, to undertake an overt adjustment of the emphases being placed on white male accomplishments and history by the academy. The exclusionary nature of the academy in this regard was exposed by the operations of women's studiers within and without academia. Such exposure at times led to a forceful backlash against women who committed themselves without reserve to the new discipline.[19] The collective structure and procedure of women's studies were confronting an entrenched historical system

which systematically excluded women and minorities. That women's studies confronted it and survived is an accomplishment in itself. That it also was able to grow and even to flourish under such conditions is a genuine tribute to its idea power.

The important point lies with the growing recognition of the inconsistency between the academy's conflict orientation and women's studies' more collective nature. Centering on issues and consensus, a collective orientation is one which takes into consideration individuals as well as the group.[20] Mary Daly sees the prime ethic as one of attraction.[21] Marilyn Salzman-Webb discusses this aspect of women's studies relatively early.[22] At times the recognition of it is overt enough to stimulate a university affiliated women's studies program to seek an autonomous locale within that university. This was the case with Women's Studies College at the State University of New York at Buffalo. The inconsistency is apparent, and most if not all women's studiers in a university setting have to deal with it.

As time goes on, women's studiers have been verbalizing feminist assumptions in a consistent and coherent fashion. These assumptions include: that there is a historically valid women's culture which is knowable and relevant to women's lives today[23]; that the sisterhood of all women, across race, creed, religion, sexual preference, economic status and national origin, is grounded in a common oppression[24]; that there is a need to facilitate consciousness of this oppression among women's studiers, activists in the women's movement and other women, and to change the oppressed status[25]; and that there is a necessity for reaching consensus among these groups of individuals through a colloquy about the means by which to seek change in that status.[26] The explication of these assumptions has an ideological implication for the women's movement that is wide ranging and startling.

For those pragmatic activists who devote themselves almost exclusively to a legal/legislative approach to change in women's status, with a corresponding commitment to traditional political tactics, the explication of feminist assumptions creates a serious dilemma. Viewed on the basis of these assumptions, their tactics are inconsistent with them. Worse, their tactics are identifiably the same conflict-oriented

---

Facing page: "A Quilting Bee" (1950), by Grandma Moses (1860-1961). (Copyright Grandma Moses Properties, Inc., New York.)

tactics utilized by the academy to the detriment of women and minorities. [27]

The basic inconsistency between feminist assumptions and activist tactics effectively retards any impetus to develop overall organizational strategy. It also is detrimental to the development of women's movement ideology. Social movements of great scope generally embrace great ideologies, but as Jo Freeman observes, the women's movement experiences an almost total absence of coherent ideology. [28] As women's studies explicates feminist assumptions and moves closer to the women's movement rather than being subsumed within the academy, the possibility for grounding movement activism in such ideology grows much greater. [29]

Ideology offers an elaborate, closely woven and far-ranging structure which is more abstract than either strategy or tactics. Strategy is formulated with a view toward the future, incorporating tactics which are designed to capture an immediate advantage. It is strategy which propounds the broad direction within which tactics are mustered. The problem for the activist is to use tactics which are not self-defeating in the long run. Consistency among ideology, strategy and tactics affords the most efficient means for any social movement simultaneously to consolidate its gains and to project its program into the future. [30]

Without ideological, strategic and tactical consistency, it is not likely that those who devote themselves to seeking comprehensive change in women's status will attain it. An established socioeconomic and political system which changes only by increments and which responds only to those with authorized access to it is not amenable to their efforts. In fact, such a system maintains itself through the activities of the actors within it, relying on relative quietude among those not recruited to its top. The demands of those with access to the system's hierarchy are converted into policy. Access is not granted gratuitously. Ironically, those who support the system by their quietude do not necessarily gain access to it. They receive only the most minimal of rewards for their acquiescence.

Those who support the system but seek a greater share of its outputs may be shunned or punished for their deviance. If they are willing to forego their deviant behavior to return to their former quietude or if they show unusual ability to adapt to the rules of the game as it is being played, then they may not be punished. In some cases, their share of the distribution of values even may be increased, but it will not be increased wholesale. It will be increased either by granting them maximum feasible participation, which is likely to be diminished after a period of time, or an increment of some value, for example the issuance of regulations for Title IX legislation, which are not likely to be implemented extensively. [31]

On the other hand, groups of individuals who are able to create a serious imbalance in the system's environment will set into motion a dynamic process of adjustment which ultimately can accommodate their demands. The exchange here leads to an equilibrium in the system once again, but in the meantime changes are made in the system's overall components and in their combination. The only other alternative for change seems to be outright revolution in the modern sense--that is, probably violent overthrow of the entire system. This does not seem to be a likely event, and chances are it would not be a desirable one. [32] Groups of individuals who achieve such an adjustment must be organized, self-disciplined and internally consistent in their ideology, strategy and tactics. Without such consistency, neither organization nor discipline is likely to be effective or long-lived.

The solution to the dilemma of inconsistency among ideology, strategy and tactics, or inconsistency of the sort which inhibits development of one or more of them, lies with conscious attempts to create structures and procedures better suited to women's needs than those of a historical system which largely has denied them. Conscious attempts along these lines are typical of the idea power which characterizes women's studies. An example of such conscious attempts is the development within women's studies of collective structures and procedures subversive of institutions, disciplines and processes of thought which in the past ignore matters of utmost concern to women. This is where idea power has its fullest impact. It is to the framework for these alternative structures and procedures that this analysis now turns.

WOMEN'S STUDIES: PROMISE

I refuse to allow you, Beadle though you are, to turn me off the grass. Lock up your libraries if you like; but there is no gate, no lock, no bolt that you can set upon the freedom of my mind. [33]

It is a conscious perspective of women's own which is required. It is the ability to translate the freedom of their minds into the minds of others, thereby awakening what Virginia Woolf calls "the common life which is the real life."[34] This reality association, this realization of potentiality, is far from the "living AS IF ..." of which Doris Lessing writes in The Golden Notebook.[35] While Woolf sees the common life as the androgynous one,[36] women's studiers, at this crossroad at least, are using feminist assumptions to frame the future at the same time they explore the here and now. Only as ideas and actions, future and present, are fused, can women and men be capable someday, some century, of being born under an androgynous sign.

Woolf herself recognizes the immense problems presented by attempts to change an entrenched historical system. She is adamant in her response to the problem, however. As one commentator states:

> Beneath the institutional level, [she] perceived that the social system and its particular institution were maintained on the personal level, in part by the acquiescence and collaboration of those who accepted the system's values and chose to seek its rewards, and in part by the ruthless punishment, exclusion and even destruction of those who might seek to change it.... Woolf knew that this system would not be changed with the touch of a wand.... But she saw too that that system could not be overthrown by imitating it.[37]

The promise of women's studies as ideology and organizational strategy lies in its collective orientation, in effect a refusal to imitate the conflictual orientation of the prevailing system. This collective orientation is the result of women's studies' dual dimensionality, its focus on both the intellectual and the affective. The interaction and potential for integration of these two dimensions contribute to an emphasis on the group as a collection of individual women or, conversely, on individual women as members of a group. Intellectually, women's studiers collectively tap and expand resources, internalizing knowledge and its personal implications. Affectively, they explore with significant others in ever-widening circles their awareness of oppressed status and the need to change that status.

What is especially important here is the ability to work

collectively. Such a process is at least possible and practicable, given a reliance on assumptions about the relevance
of women's culture, sisterhood and its potential for facilitating change in women's status. It involves looking toward
the future aggregate well-being of a diverse class, namely
women. The attainment of consensus on how best to achieve
such well-being, and why it is to be achieved at all, is contingent on women's overall diversity. It is achievable, however, only where there is agreement that women have some
things in common with one another. [38] General agreement on
these matters is the basis on which to organize in a disciplined and internally consistent fashion as activists seeking
change in women's status.

The collective process is to a certain degree a conceptual mechanism in that it nowhere exists in pure form.
It is not absolutely attainable. [39] It could be visualized as a
goal, something to be attained so far as is possible as women transcend their externally prescribed destiny. It must
be emphasized, though, that it has been tested in women's
studies settings and found fit. It is, however, no nirvana.
Attempts to achieve it so far as is possible can and sometimes do result in failure. The widespread factionalism within the mid-1970s women's movement is evidence of such failure, just as it is evidence of the internalized inconsistency
examined above.

The ability to use a collective process implies maturity in the group of individuals working to achieve it. It consists of the willingness to seek out critical combinations of
diverse viewpoints on both the intellectual and affective levels.
It thus combines knowledge about women generally, about women's status and potential, and about feminist assumptions
with the awareness of what all this means to women personally. By gathering such knowledge and seeking such awareness
in diverse environments, women's studiers engage in the beginnings of a collective process. Their ability to organize
and to persevere, often in the midst of detractors, is tested.
This is the promise of women's studies as ideology and organizational strategy.

Such promise admittedly has its problems. To control
women's studies from within is not an easy matter. There
are various administrators, scholars, students and women's
studiers embodying particular political persuasions who seek
such control. The interaction of intellectual and affective dimensions in women's studies continues to frighten and/or ex-

asperate some individuals. Financial support is a necessary
and troublesome aspect of the promotion of women's studies.
The question whether it is better to integrate more traditional
disciplines or to strike out for separate status goes unan-
swered.

Still, women's studiers are not unfamiliar with the
problem of control; it is at the heart of every change they
seek. The supposed dichotomy of intellect and affect may in
the end be a non-issue; as Female Studies six points out,
"The pain and invigoration of being personal is no longer a
subject in itself."[40] Those who most fear "ghettoization" may
in time come around to the conclusion that women's studies is
worthy of separate status and can withstand critical scrutiny.
Isolation and excision are by no means inevitable outcomes of
such status, especially given the fact and potential of community ties.

It is the promise of women's studies that is pursued in
the release of its idea power. Through women's studies, the
broadest approach to sexism, one which inculcates feminist
assumptions and institutional change, can be undertaken. The
promise of women's studies as ideology and organizational
strategy is wholly indigenous; it is a perspective of women's
own.

The major point to be made in bringing the advent of
women's studies into a study of feminist thought is the ideological implications it proffers. Once again we see feminist
thinkers, descendants of the early gentry, deeply involved in
the formal intellectual and cultural aspects of feminism.
Through education, one of the major issues with which feminist thought always concerns itself, feminist thinkers approach
problems of women's status--outside the family. The limitations the family still poses for women assuredly are part of
any approach to problems of women's status. Now, however,
feminist thinkers are facilitating awareness of these problems
in a close relationship with women, within and yet apart from
the academy. With awareness and intellectual pursuit operat-
ing simultaneously, the possibility for developing an elaborate,
closely-woven, far-ranging structure of ideas capable of giving
direction to feminist activity is a very real one.

Perhaps time does sanction innovation, as Mary Wollstonecraft suggests. The important beginnings which, taken
in perspective, seem sometimes so humble and so astonish-
ing have a new opportunity for realization. Feminist and pre-

Look Back with Astonishment / 355

feminist thinkers heretofore plow the furrows and plant the apples but never reap the crop. Yet it seems fitting to conclude this study of their passionate struggle with Alice Paul's words: "When you put your hand to the plow, you can't put it down until you get to the end of the row." Even if the row seems never ending, even if instituting the ideas and ideals which are being sown seems well-nigh impossible, that is no cause for discouragement. This study must end on an upbeat. Frontiers move on, and so it is for the cause that is feminism.

References

1   Olive Schreiner, Woman and Labor, 5th ed. (New York: Frederick A. Stokes, 1911), p. 23.
2   A Room of One's Own (1929) (New York: Harbinger Book, 1957), pp. 68-69, 89, 109.
3   "Women's Studies: Its Focus, Idea Power and Promise," by Sarah Slavin Schramm, is reprinted from Women's Studies: An Interdisciplinary Collection, ed. Kathleen O'Connor Blumhagen and Walter D. Johnson (Westport, Conn.: Greenwood Press, 1978), by permission of the publisher. See also Social Science Journal, 14 (April 1977), 5-13.
4   Elaine Showalter, "Introduction: Teaching about Women," Female Studies, vol. 4, ed. Elaine Showalter and Carol Ahlum (Pittsburgh: Know, Inc., 1971), p. i.
5   Women's Studies Newsletter (Old Westbury, N.Y.), Winter 1976, pp. 8-11.
6   Showalter, "Introduction," pp. iv-v.
7   Richard E. Johnson, "The Future of Humanistic Psychology," The Humanist, 55 (March/April 1975), 5-7, describes the power of awareness. Juliet Mitchell, Woman's Estate (New York: Vintage Books, 1973), p. 178, outlines a potential problem.
8   "The Many Worlds of Women," Female Studies, vol. 2, ed. Florence Howe (Pittsburgh: Know, Inc., 1970), p. 87.
9   "Introduction," Female Studies, vol. 7 (Old Westbury, N.Y.: Feminist Press, 1973), p. viii.
10 Catherine Stimpson, "Women's Studies and the Community: Some Models," Women's Studies Newsletter (Old Westbury, N.Y.), Summer 1974, pp. 2-3, discusses this relationship and its potential.
11 See Sarah Slavin Schramm, "Do-It-Yourself: Women's Studies," Female Studies, vol. 8, ed. Sarah Slavin

Schramm (Pittsburgh: Know, Inc., 1975), p. 3.

12 "The Relationship Between Female Identity and Feminism," diss., Washington University, 1974.

13 Sylvia Plath, The Eye-Mote, The Colossus and Other Poems (New York: Vintage Books, 1968), p. 13.

14 See Marilyn Salzman-Webb, "Feminist Studies: Frill or Necessity?" Female Studies, vol. 5 (Pittsburgh: Know, Inc., 1972), pp. 64-76. Party politics and the U.S. government constitute other examples of this model. For instance see James MacGregor Burns, The Deadlock of Democracy (Englewood Cliffs, N.J.: Prentice-Hall, 1967).

15 Joan I. Roberts, "Creating a Facade of Change: Informal Mechanisms Used to Impede the Changing Status of Women in Academe" (Pittsburgh: Know, Inc., 1975), makes this evident.

16 Woman as Force in History: A Study in Traditions and Realities (New York: Macmillan, 1946).

17 The Second Sex, trans. H. M. Parshley (New York: Knopf, 1952), pp. 118-19; see also June Sochen, Herstory: A Woman's View of American History (New York: Alfred Publishing, 1974), pp. 3-4.

18 "A Symposium: Masculine Blinders in the Social Sciences," Social Science Quarterly, 55 (December 1974), 563-656.

19 Wisconsin, Department of Industry, Labor and Human Relations, Equal Rights Division, "Initial Determination, Dr. Joan I. Roberts vs. John Weaver, President, University of Wisconsin/Madison, et al." (ERD Case #7400847, EEOC TMK #4-1200), is an example of such a case. See also "Fact Sheet: Joan Roberts vs. University of Wisconsin/Madison," in The Newsheet: Notes from the NOW Committee to Promote Women's Studies (Cherry Hill, N.J.), November 1974, excerpted in Off Our Backs (Washington, D.C.), December 1974, p. 3.

20 Joan Borod et al., "Teaching Collectively," Women's Studies Program: Three Years of Struggle (San Diego: California State University, n.d.), pp. 42-43.

21 Beyond God the Father: Toward a Philosophy of Women's Liberation (Boston: Beacon Press, 1973), p. 198. A contemporary example here is the "think tank"--for example, Sagaris, an independent institute for the study of feminist thought--where alternatives to existing structures and procedures are being created. A historical example would be the community concept of the quilting bee, an early manifestation of women's culture in this country. See Ruth Finley, Old Patchwork Quilts and the Women

Who Made Them (New York: Branford, 1929).

22 Salzman-Webb, "Feminist Studies," pp. 64-65.

23 Evelyn Reed, Woman's Evolution: From Matriarchal
Clan to Patriarchal Family (New York: Pathfinder Press,
1975); Jane Alpert, "Forum: Mother Right--A New Theory," Ms., 2 (August 1973), 52-55; Elizabeth Gould Davis, The First Sex (New York: G. P. Putnam's Sons,
1971).

24 See Robin Morgan, ed., Sisterhood Is Powerful: An Antholo-
gy of Writings from the Women's Liberation Movement (New
York: Random, 1970); see also her "Forum: Rights of Passage," Ms., 4 (September 1975), 74-98. Deborah Rosenfelt,
"What Happened at Sacramento," Women's Studies Newsletter
(Old Westbury, N.Y.), Fall 1973, p. 1, discusses this concept under fire.

25 See Shulamith Firestone, The Dialectic of Sex: The Case
for Feminist Revolution (New York: Morrow, 1970).

26 Salzman-Webb, op. cit., passim. See also News Bulletin
(Pittsburgh: Know, Inc., September 1975), for a discussion
of the process in the context of the Know collective's
own experiences. See Deirdre English and Barbara Eh-
renreich, "Women Writing Together," The Feminist
Press: News/ Notes (Old Westbury, N.Y.), 4 (1973),
p. 2. See Kate Millett, Flying (New York: Knopf, 1974),
pp. 59-60, for a discussion of the process gone wrong
and yet viable.

27 See Warren T. Farrell, "Women's and Men's Liberation
Groups: Political Power within the System and without
the System," in Women in Politics, ed. Jane S. Jaquette
(New York: Wiley, 1974), pp. 171-201; Marin L. Car-
den, The New Feminist Movement (New York: Russell
Sage, 1974), pp. 166-171.

28 The Politics of Women's Liberation (New York: McKay,
1976), p. 10.

29 That women's studies was not subsumed stems from the
diverse environment within which it developed. Many
important contributions to it have been entirely extra-aca-
demy.

30 See Nancy Porter, with Julie Allen and Jean Maxwell,
"The Future of Women's Studies: From Portland State
University--In Three Voices," Women's Studies News-
letter (Old Westbury, N.Y.), Spring 1975, p. 5.

31 See David Easton, A Framework for Political Analysis
(Englewood Cliffs, N.J.: Prentice-Hall, 1965); David B.
Truman, The Governmental Process: Political Interests
and Public Opinion, 2d ed. (New York: Knopf, 1971).

32 It will be recalled that Hannah Arendt points out revolutions are not "mere changes." The once astronomic term

in modern usage implies an irrevocable, irresistible movement gone out of control. See On Revolution (New York: Viking, 1965), pp. 13-52. The radical experiment Shulamith Firestone proposes in her case for feminist "revolution" is not the uncontrolled momentum which Arendt traces. Experiment in and of itself implies controls. Firestone's program of simultaneous interwoven multiple options cannot be achieved by revolution in the modern sense.

33 Virginia Woolf, Room of One's Own, pp. 78-79.

34 Ibid., p. 79.

35 New York: Knopf, 1973, p. ix.

36 See Nancy Topping Bazin, Virginia Woolf and the Androgynous Vision (New Brunswick, N.J.: Rutgers University Press, 1973).

37 Berenice A. Carroll, "'To Crush Him in Our Own Country': The Political Thought of Virginia Woolf," paper prepared for the Third Berkshire Conference on Women's History, Bryn Mawr College, June 10, 1976; excerpts from pp. 29, 31.

38 Juliet Mitchell makes this point narrowly, confining it to the stage at which women become aware of their oppressed status, in Woman's Estate, pp. 73-74. In doing so, she overlooks the interconnectedness of feminist assumptions.

39 See Douglas W. Rae, "The Limits of Consensual Decision," American Political Science Review, 69 (December 1975), 1270-94, and in the same issue, Gordon Tullock, "Comment on Rae's 'The Limits of Consensual Decision,'" pp. 1295-97.

40 Nancy Hoffman, Cynthia Secor and Adrian Tinsley, eds., Female Studies, vol. 6 (Old Westbury, N.Y.: Feminist Press, 1972), p. 1.

BIOGRAPHICAL LISTING

Adams, Abigail (1744-1818). First Lady of the U. S.; wife of John, second President; mother of John Quincy, sixth President; self-educated with a mind of her own.

Adams, Hannah (1755-1831). Author and historian.

Adams, Henry (1838-1918). Author and historian, great-grandson of Abigail Adams.

Addams, Jane (1860-1935). Founder of Hull House, a famous settlement house in Chicago; social reformer, peace worker and writer. Shared Nobel Peace Prize in 1931.

Albee, Edward (b. 1928). Dramatist and author.

Anthony, Susan Brownell (1820-1906). Woman suffrage leader of old American stock, publisher of the Revolution.

Arendt, Hannah (1906-1975). Philosopher and political theorist.

Aristotle (ca. 433-384 B. C.). Classical Greek teacher, philosopher and political theorist.

Astell, Mary (1666-1731). English author and member of literary circles.

Bachofen, Johann Jakob (1815-1887). Swiss historian and student of classical mythology.

Beard, Charles Austin (1874-1948). Historian and political scientist, especially known for his economic interpretation of the Constitution and his advocacy of intellectual freedom. Husband of Mary.

Beard, Mary Ritter (1876-1958). Author and historian who specialized in study and analysis of women's rights and labor movement; established a World Center for Women's Archives. Wife of Charles.

de Beauvoir, Simone (b. 1908). French author of the existential school, and member of intellectual circles.

Bebel, August (1840-1878). German politician and author; founder of Social Democratic Party.

Beecher, Catharine Esther (1800-1978). Author and educator; founder of Hartford Female Seminary. Sister of Harriet Beecher Stowe and Henry Ward Beecher.

Beecher, Henry Ward (1813-1887). Presbyterian minister,

reformer and abolitionist. Brother of Catharine Beecher and Harriet Beecher Stowe.

Benedict, Ruth Fulton (1887-1948). Anthropologist.

Bethune, Mary McLeod (1875-1955). Educator, founder of Bethune-Cookman College, founder of National Association of Colored Women's Clubs and National Council of Negro Women.

Blackwell, Antoinette Louisa Brown (1825-1921). Author, lecturer and Congregational and Unitarian minister; member of third graduating class at Oberlin. Sister-in-law of Elizabeth Blackwell.

Blackwell, Elizabeth (1821-1910). First graduate woman physician in U.S., lecturer on hygiene and morals; founder of Woman's Medical College of the New York Infirmary. Sister of Henry Blackwell and sister-in-law of Lucy Stone and Antoinette Brown Blackwell.

Blackwell, Henry Browne (1825-1909). Editor and suffrage leader, married to Lucy Stone. Brother of Elizabeth Blackwell.

Blake, Lillie Devereaux (1833-1933). Correspondent, author, suffragist and woman's movement activist, of early American descent.

Blatch, Harriot Eaton Stanton (1856-1940). Woman suffrage leader and author, later aligned with National Woman's Party; Vassar M.A. Daughter of Elizabeth Cady Stanton.

Bloomer, Amelia Jenks (1818-1894). Dress and temperance reformer, suffragist and publisher of The Lily.

Branagan, Thomas (1774-1843). Author, itinerant traveler.

Breckinridge, Sophonisba P. (1866-1948). Scholar, social work leader and lawyer; Wellesley B.A. and University of Chicago doctorate; daughter of U.S. Congressman and granddaughter of U.S. Senator.

Briffault, Robert (1876-1948). Anthropologist.

Browning, Elizabeth Barrett Moulton Barrett (1806-1861). English poet.

Catt, Carrie Chapman (1859-1957). Suffrage leader and school teacher, of early American stock.

Chandler, Elizabeth Margaret (1807-1834). Author, Quaker.

Child, Lydia Maria (1802-1880). Author, abolitionist, correspondent, suffragist and member of intellectual circles.

Claflin, Tennessee Celeste (1845-1923). Lecturer and rather eccentric reformer.

Constantia [real name, Judith Sargent Stevens Murray]

(1751-1820). Author.

Colby, Clara Dorothy Bewick (1846-1916). Suffragist and woman's movement activist, editor of Woman's Tribune, graduate of University of Wisconsin.

Deutsch, Helen (b. 1884). Psychologist, student of Freud.

Dewey, John (1859-1959). Philosopher, educator and founder of school of pragmatic instrumentalism.

Dickinson, Emily (1830-1916). Poet and recluse; daughter of U. S. Congressman, of early American ancestry.

Dodge, Mary Abigail [pseud., Gail Hamilton] (1833-1896). Author and teacher, member of literary and political circles.

Douglass, Frederick [real name, Augustus Washington Bailey] (1817-1895). Abolitionist, writer, editor and lecturer.

Eliot, George [real name, Mary Anne (or Marian) Evans] (1819-1880). English author, editor and critic.

Ellett, Elizabeth Fries (1812-1877). Author and historian, of early American stock.

Ellis, Havelock (1859-1939). English psychologist and author.

Engels, Friederich (1820-1895). German socialist, author, collaborator with Marx and editor and publisher of Marx's work.

Farnham, Marynia L. Foot (b. 1899). Psychologist.

Foster, Abigail Keller (1810-1887). Abolitionist, women's rights advocate and lecturer.

Freud, Sigmund (1856-1939). Austrian physician and founder of psychoanalysis.

Fuller, Sarah Margaret [married Marquis Ossoli] (1810-1850). Highly educated author and critic, Transcendentalist and member of intellectual circles; daughter of U. S. Congressman, of early American stock.

Gage, Matilda Joslyn (1826-1898). Woman's rights leader, writer and organizer.

Gilbert, Olive. Friend and biographer of Sojourner Truth.

Gilchrist, Beth Bradford (b. 1879).

Gilman, Charlotte Anna Perkins Stetson (1860-1935). Sociologist, intellectual, author and lecturer who exerted considerable influence on public thinking during era in which American women gain suffrage. Of early American stock, grandniece of Harriet Beecher Stowe.

Glasgow, Ellen Anderson Gholson (1873-1945). Novelist and winner of 1942 Pulitzer Prize for fiction; of old American stock.

Goethe, Johann Wolfgang von (1749-1832). German poet, novelist and dramatist.

Goldman, Emma ["Red Emma"] (1869-1940). Anarchist, lecturer, author and editor; Russian immigrant.

Griffith, Mary (d. 1877). Author, farmer.

Grimke, Angelina Emily (1805-1873). Abolitionist, lecturer, author and early woman's rights advocate.

Grimke, Sarah Moore (1792-1873). Abolitionist, lecturer, author and early woman's rights advocate.

Hale, Sarah Josepha Hale Buell (1788-1879). Editor of the Ladies Magazine (Godey's Lady's Book) and author.

Hall, Granville Stanley (1846-1924). Psychologist and educator; established American Journal of Psychology and The Pedagogical Seminary.

Harding, Mary Esther (b. 1888). Medical doctor.

Hawthorne, Nathaniel (1804-1864). Author.

Hellman, Lillian (b. 1905). Author, playwright and editor; winner of 1969 National Book Award.

Heloise (12th century). Legendary but actual French woman known for the "hopeless love" she shares with Pierre Abelard and which they sublimate in their respective religious lives. Heloise becomes a noteworthy abbess.

Henry, Alice (1857-1943). Journalist and labor leader, of Australian origin.

Herschberger, Ruth (b. 1917). Author and editor.

Heywood, Ezra Hervey (1829-1893).

Hobbes, Thomas (1588-1679). English philosopher, political theorist and historian.

Hollingsworth, Leta Anna Stetter (1886-1939). Educational psychologist and one of the founders of the American Association of Clinical Psychology; Columbia University doctorate.

Hood, Thomas (1799-1845). English author, journalist and critic.

Howe, Julia Ward (1819-1910). Author, composer of "Battle Hymn of the Republic," suffragist and lecturer.

Hunt, Harriot Kezia (1805-1875). Medical practitioner and reformer.

Hutchinson, Anne (1591-ca. 1643). Religious rebel.

Irwin, Inez Haynes (b. 1873). Author, member National Woman's Party.

James, Henry (1843-1916). Author and critic.

Keller, Helen Adams (1880-1968). Author, educator of the blind, and lecturer; Radcliffe graduate.
Key, Ellen Karoline Sofia (1849-1926). Swedish author and sociologist, winner of 1927 Pulitzer Prize.

LaFollette, Suzanne (b. 1893). Journalist, editor, author, historian and woman's rights advocate; daughter of U.S. Congressman and granddaughter of U.S. Senator.
Lessing, Doris (b. 1919). English author.
Lewis, Diocletian (1823-1886). Author, educator and homeopathic physician; founder of Gymnastic School for Girls.
Lewis, Sinclair (1885-1951). Novelist and critic; declined 1930 Nobel Prize in literature.
Locke, John (1623-1704). English philosopher and political theorist.
Lowell, Amy (1874-1925). Poet, winner of 1926 Pulitzer Prize; of early American stock.
Lowi, Robert Heinrich (Harold). Ethnologist and educator.
Lundberg, Edgar Ferdinand (b. 1902). Historian and journalist.
Lutz, Alma (b. 1890). Author and suffragist; Vassar graduate.
Lyon, Mary (1794-1849). Educator and founder of Mt. Holyoke College; of early American stock.

McLuhan, Herbert Marshall (b. 1911). Canadian author and educator.
Martin, George Madden [real name, Georgia May] (1866-1946). Author and worker for better race relations.
Martineau, Harriet (1802-1876). English journalist and author.
Mead, Margaret (b. 1901). Anthropologist; Barnard B.A. and Columbia University doctorate.
Mencken, Henry Louis (1880-1956). Editor, critic, author.
Mill, Harriet Hardy Taylor (1808-1858). English thinker, writer and woman's rights advocate.
Mill, John Stuart (1806-1873). English philosopher, political theorist and economist.
Millay, Edna St. Vincent (1892-1950). Author, 1928 Pulitzer Prize winner; Vassar student.

Minor, Virginia Louisa (1824-1894). Early suffragist.
Mitchell, Maria (1818-1889). Astronomer and first woman
    elected to American Academy of Arts and Sciences and
    to American Philosophical Society; early member of
    Vassar faculty, of early American ancestry.

Nation, Carrie Amelia Moore (1846-1911). Prohibitionist,
    moralist and lecturer.
Nearing, Scott (b. 1883). Sociologist and socialist candidate
    for Congress from New York.
Nin, Anaïs (1903-1977). Author and diarist.

Parker, Dorothy Rothschild (1893-1967). Critic, author and
    journalist.
Paul, Alice (1885-1977). Quaker social worker, militant
    woman's rights leader and founder of National Woman's
    Party; Swarthmore B. A., University of Pennsylvania
    sociology doctorate, London School of Economics post-
    graduate work.
Plato (ca. 427-347 B. C.). Classical Greek educator, philoso-
    pher and political theorist.

Riesman, David (b. 1909). Sociologist.
Roland, Madame [real name, Jeanne Mannon Phlepon] (1754-
    1793). Member of French social and political circles
    and of the Jacobin Club, executed after the fall of the
    Girondists. Just before she was guillotined, she cried,
    "O Liberty, what crimes are committed in thy name!"
Rousseau, Jean Jacques (1712-1778). French political theo-
    rist and author.
Russell, Bertrand Arthur William (1872-1970). British philo-
    sopher, mathematician and social reformer.

Sand, George [real name, Amandine Aurore Lacie (née Du-
    pin)] (1804-1876). French author and member of liter-
    ary circles.
Sanger, Margaret Higgins (1883-1966). Birth control move-
    ment leader, author and nurse.
Sappho (ca. 620-565 B. C.). Grecian poet.
Schreiner, Olive Emilie Albertina [married name, Cornwright]
    (1855-1920). South African writer, crusader and intel-
    lectual.
Shuler, Nettie Rogers (1862-1939). Suffragist, club woman

and organizer; of early American and immigrant stock.

Skinner, Burrhus Frederic (b. 1904). Behaviorist, psychologist and scientist.

Smedley, Agnes (1890-1950). Author, correspondent and revolutionary.

Smith, Abby Hadassah (1797-1878). Suffragist.

Smith, Julia Evelina (1792-1886). Suffragist.

Spargo, John (1876-1966). Author, lecturer and socialist.

Spencer, Anna Carpenter Garlin (1851-1931). Author, reformer, nondenominational minister and associate director of the New York Ethical Society.

Stanton, Elizabeth Cady (1815-1902). Woman's rights leader, abolitionist, author, editor and lecturer; of early American stock. Mother of Harriot Stanton Blatch.

Stein, Gertrude (1874-1946). Author, poet and lecturer; Radcliffe graduate, attended Harvard Medical School; daughter of German Jewish immigrant father.

Stevens, Doris (b. 1892). Militant suffragist leader.

Stone, Lucy (1819-1893). Suffragist leader, abolitionist and lecturer; Oberlin graduate, married to Henry Blackwell; of old American stock.

Stowe, Harriet Beecher (1811-1896). Author (works include Uncle Tom's Cabin). Sister of Catharine and Henry Beecher.

Swisshelm, Jane Grey Cannon (1815-1884). Journalist, woman's rights advocate and abolitionist.

Talbot, Marion (1858-1948). University of Chicago dean and professor and founder of an organization which becomes American Association of University Women.

Tarbell, Ida Minerva (1857-1944). Historian, journalist and author; known as a muckraker to her chagrin; of early American ancestry.

Thomas, Martha Carey (1857-1935). Suffragist, educator, second president of Bryn Mawr; Cornell University B.A., University of Zurich doctorate; of old Quaker American stock.

Thoreau, Henry David (1817-1862). Author, Transcendentalist and abolitionist.

de Tocqueville, Alexis (1805-1859). French political scientist, historian and political theorist.

Truth, Sojourner [real name, Isabella Baumfree] (1797-1883). Abolitionist and woman's rights advocate; a slave who fled her bondage in adulthood.

Tubman, Harriet (1820-1913). Abolitionist, fugitive slave who led many others from bondage, Civil War Union spy and scout, and suffragist.

Turner, Frederick Jackson (1861-1932). Historian and winner of 1933 Pulitzer Prize.

Warren, Mercy Otis (1728-1814). Author, patriot and historian.

Wells-Barnett, Ida Bell (1862-1931). Journalist, lecturer and militant clubwoman; born of slave parents.

Wesley, Susanna (1669-1742). Mother of John Wesley and respected in her own right.

Wheatley, Phillis [married John Peters] (1753-1784). Author and poet; a freed house slave.

Willard, Emma Hart (1787-1870). Educator and founder of Troy Female Seminary.

Willard, Frances Elizabeth Caroline (1839-1896). Temperance leader and woman's rights advocate.

Winter, Alice Vivian Ames (1865-1944). Author, woman's club leader and artist; Wellesley graduate, of old American stock.

Wollstonecraft, Mary [married William Godwin] (1759-1797). English political theorist, author, woman's rights advocate and moralist.

Woodhull, Victoria Claflin (1838-1927). Reformer, lecturer and early muckraker; Equal Rights party candidate for U.S. Presidency in 1872.

Woolf, Virginia Stephen (1882-1941). English author and critic.

Woolson, Abba Louisa Goold (1838-1921). Dress reformer, teacher, author and historian.

Wright, Frances ("Fanny") [married William D'Arusmont] (1795-1852). Author and editor, reformer, lecturer, of Scottish descent.

ANNOTATED BIBLIOGRAPHY

Feminism is of two types: one sees women's and men's spheres as complementary, the other, as congruent. This bibliography accordingly is divided into two sections. As will be readily apparent, there is wide variation within each type. Some writings legitimately could be included under either heading, sometimes due to inconsistency, sometimes to the synthesis which takes place at the radical fringes of any dialectic. A few writings which discuss both types of feminism are included under both headings.

Writings relevant to a history of feminism fall into two categories: empirical, that is, those reporting on "real world" observations, and normative, those expressing an intellectual or emotional preference for something. The complementary and congruent sections are subdivided in this manner. Although there is some overlap between categories, this seems a useful distinction for analytic purposes.

COMPLEMENTARY FEMINISM

EMPIRICAL

Adams, Hannah. A Memoir of Miss Hannah Adams, Written by Herself. In Fragments of an Autobiography, ed. Leon Stein. New York: Arno, 1974.

Addams, Jane. "Aspects of the Woman's Movement." Survey, August 1, 1930, 384-87+.

_____. Democracy and Social Ethics. New York: Macmillan, 1911.

_____. "Larger Aspects of the Woman's Movement." Annals of the American Academy of Political and Social Science, 56 (November 1914), 1-8.

_____. Twenty Years at Hull House. New York: Macmillan, 1910.

Anthony, Katherine S. First Lady of the Revolution: The
    Life of Mercy Otis Warren. Garden City, N.Y.: Dou-
    bleday, 1958. Suggests because of her staunchly non-
    Federalist point of view that Warren was not forgotten.
    Sees her as having masculine interests and capacities but
    with no head for business. "The originality of this wo-
    man was of startling, almost Shakespearean proportions. "
    Places Warren and Abigail Adams as predecessors of Su-
    san B. Anthony and Elizabeth Cady Stanton. Bibliography
    and index.

    _____. Margaret Fuller: A Psychological Biography.
    New York: Harcourt, Brace and Howe, 1921. "Fuller's
    feminism represents socialization of part of that 'instinct-
    ive life, ' which, contrary to her Puritan upbringing, she
    had learned to recognize and value. The feminism of
    women, like the corresponding form of sex-solidarity
    among men, is based on a social impulse which is in
    turn rooted in an erotic impulse towards others of one's
    own sex. " See especially chs. V, A Woman's Woman;
    X, The Revolutionist; and XI, 1850. Bibliography and
    index.

Association for the Advancement of Women. Historical Ac-
    count of the Association for the Advancement of Women,
    1873-1893. Dedham, Mass.: 1893, transcript.

Bachofen, J. J. Myth, Religion and Mother Right: Selected
    Writings of..., trans. Ralph Manheim. Princeton, N.J.:
    Princeton University Press, 1967.

Barnett, Avrom. Foundations of Feminism; A Critique.
    New York: American Tract Society, 1870. Divided into
    three sections: Biological Foundations, Sex and Femi-
    nism; Psychological and Physiological Foundations, Sex
    Differences as a Basis for Sex Spheres; and Sociological
    Foundations, Labor and Motherhood. Discussion of the
    problems with which feminism must cope for a new type
    of womanhood (which seems assured) to emerge.

Beard, Mary Ritter. America Through Women's Eyes. New
    York: Greenwood Press, 1933.

    _____. "Feminism as a Social Phenomenon, " in Toward
    a New Role for Women, ed. Margaret Mead. New York:
    Woman's Press, November 1940.

_____ . "Lucretia Mott." American Scholar, 2 (1933),
6-12. Mott was of heroic spiritual stature, a bourgeois
by heritage whose ethics surpassed her own kind.

_____ . On Understanding Women. New York: Greenwood
Press, 1968. See especially Part III, The Rise of Intel-
lectualism; Part IV, Our Great Precedent of Acquisitive
Power and Pomp (i. e. , The Sword and Sex, The Indomi-
table Matriarchs); and Part VI, To the Conquest of the
Earth (i. e. , The Development of Modern Science, The
Idea of Progress and Critical Humanism). Women are
responsible for continuance and care of life and as such
are an elemental force in the rise and development of
civilization. Yet women of the capitalistic order are parasitic. There is an overt battle between state and family.
In technical society competence instead of sex will become
all important. "Feminism as sex antagonism bearing the
wounds of many honorable battles may then drop out of
sight. Masculinism as sex monopoly may then yield to
concepts of expertness" (p. 523). Bibliography and index.

_____ . Woman as Force in History: A Study in Traditions and Realities. New York: Macmillan, 1946. Women have been a great force historically, directing human
events such as thought and action. Bibliography and index.

de Beauvoir, Simone. The Prime of Life. Paris: Librairie
Gallimard, 1960. An autobiographical discussion of the
exhiliration of freedom and the despair of meaninglessness for one of world's prominent feminist thinkers.
Establishment of "living affirmative" in face of nagging
question as to use of life at all provides conceptual
framework from which modern feminism emerges.

_____ . The Second Sex, trans. H. M. Parshley. New
York: Knopf, 1953. Suggests only existentialist philo-
sophic foundation is capable of encompassing "concrete
woman" and of surpassing secondary status the male controlled environment forces on her. Part I, Destiny, and
Chapter XI, Myth and Reality, of Part III, Myths and
Reality, both in Book I, Facts and Myths, are of especial interest.

Bebel, August. Woman and Socialism. New York: Socialist
Literature, 1910. "With socialism, the issue is ... a
natural process of development. " "To women also in

general and as a female proletarian in particular, the summons goes out not to remain behind in this struggle in which her redemption and emancipation are at stake. It is for her to prove that she has comprehended her true place in the movement and in the struggles of the present for a better future; and that she is resolved to join. It is the part of the men to aid her in ridding herself of all superstition, and to step forward in their ranks. " All this because of woman's sexual nature and her propinquity to physical derangement, which places her at a distinct disadvantage to the work force. See especially ch. IV, Woman's Position as a Breadwinner, Her Intellectual Faculties, Darwinism and the Condition of Society; and ch. V, Woman's Civic and Political Status; as well as section on Population and Over-Population.

Beecher, Catharine Esther. The Evils Suffered by American Woman and American Children: The Causes and the Remedy. New York: Harper and Brothers, 1846.

_____. A Treatise on Domestic Economy for the Use of Young Ladies at Home and at School (1841). New York: Source Book Press, 1970.

_____, and Harriet Beecher Stowe. The American Woman's Home (1869). New York: Arno, 1971.

Bell, Ralcy Husted. Woman from Bondage to Freedom. New York: Critic Guide, 1921.

Benson, Mary S. Women in Eighteenth Century America: A Study of Opinion and Social Usage (1935). Port Washington, N.Y.: Kennikat, 1966.

Blackwell, Alice Stone. Lucy Stone: Pioneer of Women's Rights. Boston: Little, Brown, 1930.

Briffault, Robert. The Mothers: A Study of the Origins of Sentiments and Institutions, abr. ed. New York: Macmillan, 1927. Animal family from which humans evolved is matriarchal. Suggests this may call for reconsideration by social anthropology. Detailed analysis of matriarchy sociologically and historically. See particularly ch. VII, "The Motherhood" (including The Establishment of Masculine Domination in Some Societies in the Lowest Stages of Culture); and ch. X, The Institution of Marriage. Footnotes.

Brochett, L. P. Woman: Her Rights, Wrongs, Privileges
and Responsibilities; Her Present Legal Status in England, France and the United States, and Woman Suffrage
and Its Folly (1869). Freeport, N.Y.: Books for Libraries Press, 1970.

Catt, Carrie Chapman, and Nettie Rogers Shuler. Woman
Suffrage and Politics. Seattle: University of Washington
Press, 1969. Emphasis on "where woman movement and
American politics met in mutual menace," on those "political crises with which the suffrage cause was closely
identified and over whose motivation suffragists had to
keep sharp watch." See especially ch. X, The Invisible
Enemy, and ch. XXXII, Conclusion. Chronological table
of the suffrage victory (1878-1919) and index.

Cott, Nancy F. "In the Bonds of Womanhood: Perspective
on Female Experience and Consciousness in New England." Dissertation, Brandeis University, 1974.

Courtney, Janet. Adventurous Thirties: A Chapter in the
Women's Movement. London: Oxford University Press,
1933.

Davis, Elizabeth Gould. The First Sex. New York: G. P.
Putnam's, 1971. Plea for woman's "readmission" to
history. Traces the decline of female status from its
matriarchal origins to the present day. Part IV, The
Tragedy of Western Woman, is of especial interest, particularly chs. 19 and 20. Extensive notes and index.

De Pauw, Linda Grant. Founding Mothers: Women of America in the Revolutionary Era. Boston: Houghton, 1975.
A carefully compiled, beautifully written history of women in the colonial period which includes woman's work
in the home and commercial enterprise; woman's role,
the American Revolution and women's rights; and Black,
Indian, Loyalist and Patriot women. Topical selected
bibliography and index.

Diner, Helen. Mothers and Amazons: The First Feminist
History of Culture (1930). New York: Julian Press,
1965. Women have unique points of view. See especially III, Matriarchy (veneration of woman as goddess incompatible with making her a slave on earth); IV, The
Changing Face of Matriarchy (female-dominated vs. male-
dominated realms); X, Amazons (extremist end of matri-

archy as well as beginning and purpose in themselves); and **XXV**, Theories on Matriarchy. Index.

Edmondson, V. "Maud Younger: Feminist and Laborite." Sunset, June 1915, 1179-80. Younger was a militant labor agitator and feminist. Focused on two remedies for social wrongs: trade union and ballot. Lobbyist of temerity "fighting to the last ditch."

Ellett, Elizabeth F. The Women of the American Revolution (1873). Philadelphia: George W. Jacobs, 1900. Biographical sketches. Wide range of women, prominent and otherwise, making community appeals to home sentiment and patriotism and undergoing praise and persecution. Lady of Philadelphia: "I know this--that as free I can die but once; but as a slave I shall not be worthy of life. I have the pleasure to assure you these are the sentiments of all my sister Americans."

Farnham, Marynia, and Ferdinand Lundberg. Modern Women: The Lost Sex. New York: Harper, 1947. In ch. VII, The Feminist Complex, authors speak of instability in modern woman resulting from conflicting, irreconcilable demands placed on her by industrial society, whatever its ideology. Reaction to this dilemma was either feminism (careerists) or nonfeminism (homemakers). Authors express reservations about manner in which feminists pushed for public policy and ideology. Feminists merely exhibit female neuroticism in a way different from nonfeminists, but in so doing make obvious symptoms common to all women. Equality is the fetish of the feminist movement, as expressed in Wollstonecraft's theory. Wollstonecraft, like many feminists, was an extreme neurotic of the compulsive type. Feminist ideology based on this illness in an emotional craving for power which would result in mastery for women. "Psychologically, feminism has a single objective: the achievement of maleness by the female, or the nearest possible approach to it." See also ch. VIII, The Sex Revolution, in which it is argued that feminism failed because (1) females will never attain feelings of well-being by achieving as males do, and (2) ideology of man hunting was based on misunderstanding of source of women's problems. Appendices and extensive bibliography.

Field, Vena Bernadette. Constantia: A Study of the Life and Works of Judith Sargent Murray, 1751-1820. (University

of Maine Studies, 2d Series, no. 17.) Orono: University of Maine Press, 1931.

Flexner, Eleanor. Century of Struggle: The Woman's Rights
Movement in the United States. Cambridge, Mass.:
Harvard University Press, 1959. A careful piece of
scholarship tracing the acquisition of woman suffrage
from colonial era to its culmination, with heavy emphasis on educational attainment. Chs. XV, The Reform
Era and Woman's Rights, and XXII, Who Opposed Woman
Suffrage, help establish boundaries of feminism. "Freedom and uncertainty seem to go together. It might help
if we remembered more often ... the doubts and fears
that racked an Angelina Grimke or the seemingly intrepid
Elizabeth Cady Stanton when she stood up to make her
first public speech in the tiny Wesleyan chapel at Seneca
Falls." Illustrated and indexed with extensive notes and
bibliographic summary.

Freud, Sigmund. "Some Physical Consequences of the Anatomical Distinction Between the Sexes," in Standard Edi-
tion of the Complete Psychological Works of Sigmund
Freud, ed., trans. James Strachey with Anna Freud,
assisted by Alix Strachey and Alan Tyson. London: Hogarth Press, 1964.

_____. Three Contributions to the Theory of Sex, trans.
A. A. Brill. New York: Nervous and Mental Disease
Publishing Co., 1916.

Gage, Matilda Joslyn. "Speech at the Women's Rights Convention Held in Syracuse, 1852." Syracuse, N.Y.:
Masters' Print, 1852. Comments on inequality in marriage and the necessity for self reliance in women.

_____. Women, Church and State: An Historical Account
of the Status of Women through the Christian Ages: With
Reminiscences of the Matriarchate. Chicago: C. H.
Kerr, 1893. Begins with Mother Rule, proceeds through
Witchcraft and Wives. "The most important struggle in
history of the Church is that of women for liberation of
thought and the right to give that thought to the world."
Indexed.

Gilchrist, Beth Bradford. The Life of Mary Lyon. Boston:
Houghton, 1910. Biography of an "ill-paid teacher of
girls" who founded Mt. Holyoke College at a time when

education for women "served the purpose of the Golden
Fleece." Lyon is characterized as "a compelling figure,
standing at the beginning of today," possessed of a creative imagination, who "in company with discoverers of
all ages ... embarked on chartless seas." Illustrated,
with appendices, bibliography and index.

Gilman, Charlotte Perkins. His Religion and Hers: A Study
of the Faith of Our Fathers and the Work of Our Mothers. New York: Century Company, 1923.

_____. The Home: Its Work and Influence (1903). Ur-
bana: University of Illinois Press, 1972. Cites lack of
human progress in the material advances of the age and
attributes these to the overspecialization and individuali-
zation of each sex. Emphasis on collective socialism
within which the "true home" will be a place of rest and
order.

_____. The Man-Made World; or, Our Androcentric Cul-
ture. New York: Charlton, 1911.

_____. Women and Economics: The Economic Factor Be-
tween Men and Women as a Factor in Social Evolution.
Boston: Maynard, 1898. Unequal economic relations between women and men have resulted in woman's dependence on man and her subsequent unfitness as wife, mother and human being. Relations are beginning to change
as the social tendencies of human beings develop.

Glasgow, Ellen. The Woman Within (1944). New York: Harcourt, Brace, 1954.

Goldmark, Josephine. Impatient Crusader: Florence Kelley's Life Story. Urbana: University of Illinois Press,
1953. Kelley is characterized as cool, calculating reformer whose life was dedicated to the well being of
others. See especially ch. 15, Mrs. Kelley Opposes the
Woman's Party (polemic approach), and ch. 17, Florence
Kelley in Retrospect (New Deal labor legislation roots lie
here).

Goodsell, Willystine. Pioneers of Women's Education in the
United States: Emma Willard, Catharine Beecher, Mary
Lyon. New York: McGraw-Hill, 1931. Includes Wil-
lard's "Address to the Public ... Proposing a Plan for
Improving Female Education."

Graham, Abbie. Ladies in Revolt. New York: Woman's
    Press, 1934. Almost literary treatment, bordering on
    emotionalism, of history of the nineteenth-century wo-
    man's movement (from Mary Wollstonecraft to Carrie
    Chapman Catt) which is seen as part of a great and in-
    evitable evolutionary process.

Grimes, Alan P. The Puritan Ethic and Woman Suffrage.
    New York: Oxford University Press, 1967. Puritan
    ethic--personified in Western constituency which supported
    prohibition and immigration restriction and which believed
    woman suffrage would help guarantee these reforms--made
    important contribution to enactment of woman suffrage.

Hale, Sarah Josepha Buell. Woman's Record; or, Sketches
    of All Distinguished Women from the Creation to A.D.
    1868 Arranged in Four Eras with Selections from Author-
    esses of Each Era. New York: Harper, 1870. Ency-
    clopedic in scope, includes synopsis of woman's progress
    since 1855. Suggests change in popular attitude and femi-
    nine education. Illustrated.

Harding, M. Esther. The Way of All Women: A Psychologi-
    cal Interpretation. New York: Longmans, Green, 1943.

Hays, Elinor Rice. Morning Star: A Biography of Lucy
    Stone, 1818-1893. New York: Harcourt, Brace and
    World, 1961. Suggests Stone's fame ironically rests on
    refusing to take her husband's name. Stone was im-
    pressed by Mary Lyon. "I used to think that we girls
    (in my time) were like the cows we saw which were in
    barren pastures, but which could look over where grass
    and waving, growing grain grew beyond their reach, and
    now the bars are down and open." Illustrations, biblio-
    graphy and index.

_____. Those Extraordinary Blackwells: The Story of a
    Journey to a Better World. New York: Harcourt, Brace
    and World, 1967. Written from primary sources, excel-
    lent bibliography.

Henry, Alice. Women and the Labor Movement. New York:
    George H. Doran, 1923.

James, Edward T., ed. Notable American Women: A Bio-
    graphical Dictionary, 1607-1950. Cambridge, Mass.:
    Harvard University Press, 1971. Anne F. Scott suggests

this publication provides the social historian interested in women's history with a much-needed source for meticulously collected data. It makes possible a more in-depth understanding of feminism in America which may lead ultimately to adjustments in American social history as it is recorded now. Indexed with individual bibliographies.

Johnson, Helen Kendrick. Woman and the Republic. New York: National League for the Civic Education of Women, 1909. Survey of the woman suffrage movement and its advocates, plus arguments and radical critique which are part of an anti-suffrage statement. Indexed.

Klein, Viola. The Feminine Character: History of an Ideology. London: Kegan Paul, Trench, Trubner, 1946. Concept of feminism embodied with certain distinctive psychological traits. "The residue of typically feminist traits, connected with woman's special constitution, which is likely to remain after all is said and done about social conditioning, will have more substance and a greater scientific validity." Bibliography and index.

Lemons, J. Stanley. The Woman Citizen: Social Feminism in the 1920s. Urbana: University of Illinois Press, 1973. Suggests a linkage between women's Progressive reform activities and New Deal social legislation, but author may confuse the issue by dividing feminists into "social" and "hard-core." Ch. 7, Feminists Against Feminists, begins to document a most interesting controversy in approaches to women's rights. Extensive footnotes, index and source essay.

Lerner, Gerda, ed. Black Women in White America: A Documentary History. New York: Random, 1972. See especially A Woman's Fate in (1) Slavery; (3) A Woman's Lot; and (10) Black Women Speak of Womanhood. Extensive bibliographic notes.

_____. The Grimke Sisters from South Carolina: Pioneers for Women's Rights and Abolition. New York: Houghton, 1967. Scholarly biography, of the highest quality, of two early American women who had audacity to speak out in public, first as part of anti-slavery movement and later to assert women's rights. Notes, bibliography and index.

_____. "The Lady and the Mill Girl: Changes in the Status

of Women in the Age of Jackson." American Studies
Journal, 11 (Spring 1969), 5-15.

_____. "Women's Rights and American Feminism." The
American Scholar, 40 (Spring 1971), 235-48. Suggests
a distinction be made between feminism--that is, the
emancipation of American women--and the women's rights
movement--a phase of the feminist movement. Women's
rights movement devoted to legal changes, whereas feminist movement encompasses self-determination, autonomy
and freedom from oppressive sexual restrictions.

Lipset, Seymour Martin, ed. Harriet Martineau: Society in
America. New York: Doubleday, 1962.

Lundberg, E. O. "Pathfinders of the Middle Years." Social Service Review, 28 (March 1947), 9-11.

Martin, Anne. "Feminists and Future Political Action."
Nation, February 18, 1925, 185-86. Either American
feminists do not perceive strength of male resistance to
their program of sex equality, or there are no organized
feminists in this country. Carrie Chapman Catt sounded
death knell for feminism by urging women to work with
male parties. Woman's Party puts its own cause ahead
of that of women as a whole. Women can achieve equality only through channels of existing women's organizations
in the form of an united platform based on some common
denominator. Feminists should adopt policy of non-coop-
eration with political parties.

_____. "Political Methods of American and British Femi-
nists." Current History Magazine of the New York
Times, 20 (June 1924), 396-401.

Mitchell, Juliet. Psychoanalysis and Feminism. New York:
Pantheon Books, 1974.

Myrdal, Alva, and Viola Klein. Woman's Two Roles: Home
and Work. London: Routledge and Kegan Paul, 1956.

Nation, Carry Amelia Moore. The Use and Need of the Life
of Carry A. Nation. Topeka, Kan.: F. M. Steves,
1908. Autobiography in which Nation represents herself
as the "distracted, suffering, loving motherhood of the
world. Who, becoming aroused with a righteous fury
rebelled at this torture." See chs. IX, How I Came to

Use Hatchets as Souvenirs; XII, Woman's Mission from
Bible Standpoint; and XIII, The Rights of Mothers to Protect Their Children.

Noun, Louise R. Strong-Minded Women: The Emergence of
the Woman Suffrage Movement in Iowa. Ames: Iowa
University Press, 1969. "Now I know how Moses felt
when he viewed the Promised Land." Chronological arrangement, very good illustrations. Biographical notes,
topical bibliography, appendices and index.

O'Neill, William L. Everyone Was Brave: The Rise and
Fall of Feminism in America. Chicago: Quadrangle,
1969. Failure of feminism in the United States is attributable to its reluctance to overthrow the traditional
institutions of marriage and family and to appreciate the
environment in which it took place. Roots of feminism
lie in generalized development of nuclear family in nineteenth century and increasing gap between ideology and
actuality here. Social feminists were part of Progressive
reform era, proceeding within organizational bounds.
Hard-core feminists were interested more in equality
than reform. Failure to achieve equality nevertheless
was accompanied by considerable social good, even though
this was sometimes at expense of woman's best interest.
Index.

_____. The Woman Movement: Feminism in the United
States and England. New York: Barnes and Noble,
1969.

Potter, David M. "American Women and the American Character." Stetson University Bulletin, 62 (January 1962).
Many social generalizations made about American people
are based on masculine prototype and need to be modified
if they are to reflect women as well. American woman
maintains an equilibrium between "her general opportunities as a person and her distinctive needs as a woman."
Index.

Riegel, Robert E. American Feminists. Lawrence: University of Kansas Press, 1963.

Rossi, Alice S., ed. Essays on Sex Equality by John Stuart
Mill and Harriet Taylor Mill. Chicago: University of
Chicago Press, 1970. Includes essential writings of the
Mills regarding sex equality as well as history of their
life together and analysis of their relationship.

_____, ed. The Feminist Papers: From Adams to de Beauvoir. New York: Columbia University Press, 1973. Rossi argues in preface that feminism involves more than politics and legal changes. Each entry is preceded by a short essay commenting on the author's life and the relationship between pieces in a given section and overall. Figures and references.

Sanger, Margaret. Margaret Sanger: An Autobiography. New York: Brentano's, 1928.

_____. Motherhood in Bondage (1928). Elmsford, N.Y.: Maxwell Reprint, 1956. See ch. XVII, Life, Liberty and the Pursuit of Happiness (voluntary motherhood in fulfillment of desire, natural and desired fruition of every normal woman's life), and ch. XVIII, Conclusion.

Sarton, May. Mrs. Stevens Hears the Mermaids Singing; A Novel. New York: Norton, 1974.

Schneiderman, Rose, with Lucy Goldwaithe. All for One. New York: P. S. Erikson, 1967. "To me, the labor movement was not just a way of getting higher wages. What appealed to me was the spiritual side of a great cause that created fellowship." Illustrated.

Schneir, Miriam, ed. Feminism: The Essential Historical Writings. New York: Random, 1972. Covers 1776-1929, "old feminism" phase and themes of marriage, economic dependence and selfhood. Suggests old feminism never moved beyond advocating reform of unjust laws relating to women, within a political context, in male-defined terms. Includes Abigail Adams, Frances Wright, Sarah Grimke, Margaret Fuller, Lucy Stone and many others.

Scott, Anne Firor, ed. The American Woman, Who Was She? Englewood Cliffs, N.J.: Prentice-Hall, 1971.

_____. The Southern Lady: From Pedestal to Politics, 1830-1936. Chicago: University of Chicago Press, 1970. Suggests education and opportunities for paid employment as well as participation in the woman's club movement plus suffrage freed Southern women "for better or worse, to struggle to be themselves." See especially Part Two, The 'New Woman.' Bibliographic essay and index.

Sinclair, Andrew. The Better Half: The Emancipation of the

American Woman. New York: Harper, 1965. See Part 2, The Pioneer Feminists (where the early feminists idealistically protested worship of mother in the home, modern feminists tend to renew that worship in sociological fashion lacking idealism); Part 4, The American Lady (feminists wanted men to imitate restraint of Victorian wives); and Part 9, Nothing but the Vote (modern reformers gained support of Americans whereas "militant feminists failed to make women hate men."). Notes and index.

Smith, Florence Mary. Mary Astell. Studies in English and Comparative Literature. New York: Columbia University Press, 1916.

Smith, Page. Daughters of the Promised Land: Women in American History. Boston: Little, Brown, 1970. See especially: ch. 4, The Great Repression; ch. 5, Some Attributes of American Women: Foreign Perspectives; ch. 11, From Women's Rights to Feminism (feminism was general enough to include any reform designed to improve the status of women and did not necessarily include suffrage); ch. 19, Women and Capitalism (fluidity of American society the consequence of fluidity of American women who are essentially classless); ch. 20, The Great Withdrawal (changing ideals and aspirations); ch. 21, The Nature of Woman (women do have a nature; "it is to women that we must look for the opening up of those areas of our life which touch the spontaneous, the joyful and the responsive"); and ch. 22, The Future of Women ("It is this restless passion for 'personal fulfillment' that disfigures our life"). Footnotes and index.

Smith, Thelma M. "Feminism in Philadelphia, 1790-1850." Pennsylvania Magazine of History and Biography, 68 (July 1944), 243-68.

Sochen, June. Mover and Shakers: American Women Thinkers and Activists, 1900-1970. New York: Quadrangle, 1973.

_____. The New Woman: Feminism in Greenwich Village, 1910-1920. New York: Quadrangle, 1972.

Spencer, Anna Garlin. The Family and Its Members. Philadelphia: Lippincott, 1923.

_____. Woman's Share in Social Culture. Philadelphia: Lippincott, 1912.

Stanton, Elizabeth Cady, et al. History of Woman Suffrage (1881-1922). New York: Source Book Press, 1970. Vast and detailed treatment of the movement to pass and ratify the nineteenth amendment to the U.S. Constitution. In five volumes.

Stearns, Bertha. "Reform Periodicals and Female Reformers." American Historical Review, 37 (July 1932), 678-99.

Swisshelm, Jane Grey. Half a Century (1880). New York: Source Book Press, 1970.

Tarbell, Ida M. The Life of Madame Roland. New York: Charles Scribner's, 1896.

Taylor, Gordon Rattray. Sex in History. New York: Vanguard Press, 1954. Suggests spirit of the present times inclines toward "matrism," dominated by the masculine ideal. Battle for woman's rights began in 1840, "when an innocent wife was first granted custody of her children." Law and public opinion do not reflect matrist phase, however, because of inherent conservatism. Honoring rather than deprecating sex is source of deep anxiety to patrist. "The supposedly greater morality of patrist periods is an illusion created by turning a blind eye to the wealth of perversion and neuroses which distinguished them." "Since matrists turn their aggression inward, they harm only themselves." Appendices (see especially B, Theories of Matriarchy and Patriarchy), sources and index.

de Tocqueville, Alexis. Democracy in America (1830's). 2 vols. in 1. New York: Harper, 1966. Of especial interest is Vol. II, Part III, Influence of Democracy on Mores Properly So Called: chs. 8, Influence of Democracy on the Family; 9, Education of Girls in the United States; 10, The Young Woman as a Wife; 11, How Equality Helps to Maintain Good Morals in America; and 12, How Americans View the Equality of the Sexes. Suggests the nature of democratic equality between sexes in America consists of giving these dissimilar creatures a chance to do their jobs as well as possible. "The Americans have applied to the sexes the great principle of political

economy which now dominates industry. They have carefully separated the functions of man and of woman so that
the great work of society may be better performed." He
sees American women as dependent on the domestic
sphere but nevertheless enjoying high status.

Thorp, Margaret F. Female Persuasion: Six Strong-Minded
    Women. New Haven, Conn.: Yale University Press,
    1949. "The woman who wanted to help the world found
    that she must fight it first." Catharine Beecher, Jane
    Swisshelm, Amelia Bloomer, Sarah Lippincott, Louisa
    McCord and Maria Child were nonconformists, forgetful
    of self, from the geographic Northeast with husbands who
    functioned as fellow workers. They were individuals and
    idiosyncratic, yet they "valiantly and effectively held up
    one another's hands."

Van Kleeck, Mary. "Women and Machines." Atlantic Month-
    ly, February 1921, 250-60.

Veblen, Thorstein. "The Barbarian Status of Women."
    American Journal of Sociology, 4 (January 1899), 503-14.

_____. The Theory of the Leisure Class: An Economic
    Study of Institutions (1899). New York: Macmillan,
    1912.

Wade, Mason. Margaret Fuller: Whetstone of Genius. New
    York: Viking, 1940. See especially Part III, Feminism
    and Frustration; Part II, First Flowering, ch. VIII, The
    West and Feminism. Appendix, bibliographic notes and
    index.

Welter, Barbara. Dimity Convictions: The American Wo-
    man in the Nineteenth Century. Athens: Ohio University
    Press, 1976.

_____, ed. The Woman Question in American History.
    Hinsdale, Ill.: Dryden Press, 1973. Part I, Life (In-
    dian, eighteenth century, frontier, black, Southern wo-
    men and ladies); Part II, Liberty (ideological patterns of
    nineteenth-century feminism, opponents); and Part III,
    Pursuit of Happiness (change, character, alienation, edu-
    cation and sexual politics).

Wieth-Knudsen, K. A. Feminism: A Sociological Study of
    the Woman Question from Ancient Times to the Present

Day, trans. Arthur G. Chater. London: Constable, 1928. Ch. VII, Present-Day Feminism, includes its origin, economic and juridical feminism, propaganda of sterility and positive contributions. Bespeaks superiority of white woman whom white man idealizes as a helpmate rather than an equal and the "farrago of Feminism, pernicious alike to Man, Woman and Child, fatal to culture as no other 'movement,' a curse and a poison to all that has been built up in the sweat and blood of our race for the security of mankind's frail life upon earth."

Willard, Frances Elizabeth. Women and Temperance; or, The Work and Workers of the Woman's Christian Temperance Union. Hartford, Conn.: Park Publishing, 1883. See especially ch. III, WCTU, re-value of trained intellect and coming of Christ into five circles: heart, home, denominationalism, society, government.

Winter, Alice Ames. The Heritage of Women. New York: Minton, Balch, 1927.

NORMATIVE

Adams, Charles Francis. Familiar Letters of John Adams and His Wife Abigail Adams during the Revolution. Boston: Houghton, 1875.

Adams, Henry. The Education of Henry Adams (1907). New York: Modern Library, 1931. See ch. XXV, The Dynamo and the Virgin: "in America neither Venus nor Virgin ever had value as force--at most as sentiment.... The Woman had once been supreme.... [E]vidently America was ashamed of her.... [T]he monthly-magazine-made American female had not a feature that would have been recognized by Adam. The trait was notorious, and often humorous, but anyone brought up among Puritans knew that sex was sin." "An American Virgin would never dare command; an American Venus would never dare exist.")

Albee, Edward. Who's Afraid of Virginia Woolf? A Play. New York: Atheneum, 1962. In three acts: I, Fun and Games; II, Walpurgisnacht; III, Exorcism. "The Saddest thing about men is the way they age." "Martha's going to run things ... the little lady's going to lead the band." "GEORGE: Who's afraid of Virginia Woolf... MARTHA: I...am...George...I...am...."

Arnold, F. X. Woman and Man: Their Nature and Mission.
Montreal: Palm Publishers, 1963. Ch. VIII, Equal
Rights for Women? No, giving traditional Biblical ar-
gument against them.

Astell, Mary. A Serious Proposal to the Ladies for the Advancement of Their True and Greatest Interest (1694).
New York: Source Book Press, 1970.

_____. Some Reflections on Marriage (1730). New York:
Source Book Press, 1970.

Atherton, Gertrude. Can Women Be Gentlemen? Boston:
Houghton, 1938.

_____. The Immortal Marriage. New York: Liveright,
1927.

Bachofen, J. J. Myth, Religion and Mother Right. See entry under Complementary (Empirical).

Barth, R. "Feminist Crusade." Nation, July 17, 1948, 71-
73. The 1848 Seneca Falls Convention took place in
same year Marx issued Communist Manifesto. Feminist
movement which followed was bellicose and narrow in its
aims. Susan B. Anthony and Elizabeth Cady Stanton fos-
tered militant movement based on dogma of woman's historic subjection to man. Centennial is time for examination of founding mothers' inner motives in keeping with
modern psychiatric knowledge.

Bates, Lizzie. Woman: Her Dignity and Sphere, by a Lady.
New York: American Tract Society, 1870. Advocates
motherhood, obedience, religious fervor mixed with work
in social and domestic circle and church.

de Beauvoir, Simone. The Second Sex. See entry under
Complementary (Empirical).

Bebel, August. Woman and Socialism. See entry under
Complementary (Empirical).

Blake, Lillie Devereaux. Fettered for Life: or Lord and
Master. 1874.

Blatch, Harriot Stanton. Mobilizing Woman-Power. New
York: Woman's Press, 1918. See chs. X, As Mother

Used To Do (discussion of "Adamistic" theory), and XII, Woman's Part in Saving Civilization (women mobilize to bind up wounds and conserve civilization, things that lend themselves to the husbanding of the race by those who have borne the race). Women can save civilization only by the broadest cooperative action.

_____. A Woman's Point of View: Some Roads to Peace. New York: Woman's Press, 1920. See Part II, The Will to Heal, ch. IV, Freeing the Protective Instinct. "It is the father, not the mother, who offers up the child as a sacrifice to appease the gods" and "an endowment of motherhood is not only an assurance of care of the child, but a necessary honoring of maternity itself."

Boyd, Mary Sumner. The Woman Citizen. New York: Frederick A. Stokes, 1918. Chiefly of interest because of introduction by Carrie Chapman Catt, Passing the Federal Suffrage Amendment, in which suffrage is characterized as last task before disbanding suffragist organizations after victory or turning them into good government leagues and civic associations. Votes for women movement is concerned with "inner meanings," "informing the whole field of public life with the woman spirit." "It is these considerations and not the granting of rewards to ammunition-making women, which has made statesmen declare the ballot for women is a measure needed by a world at war as a safeguard of civilization and an assurance that the world is safe for democracy." Appendices.

Branagan, Thomas. The Excellency of the Female Character Vindicated (1808). New York: Arno, 1972.

Breuer, Elizabeth. "Feminism Is Awkward Age." Harper's Magazine, April 1925, 545-52. American feminist is a woman who attempts complete fulfillment in her job and her love life. Self-consciousness or awkwardness is only a sympton of inner aliveness. Feminism has taken on new life and direction in choosing and dividing of self. Problems of today's feminists are nearer those of the artist than of the average man in the material realm. Feminism is "an attitude of going forward."

Bromley, Dorothy Dunbar. "Feminism--New Style." Harper's Magazine, October 1927, 552-60. Pioneer feminists were hard-hitting individualists. Second generation of feminists dislike men and crave publicity, to detriment of their sex. New Style feminists are successful at marriage and art of child-rearing but have inescapable inner compulsion to be individuals in their own right. Women have a status in the arts which exceeds that in the professions. Women are progressing faster in their mental evolution than men. New Style feminist strives for economic independence and outside interest while liking men and purely feminine manners. She concludes marriage and motherhood are necessary to average woman's fullest development but insists on more freedom and honesty in marriage relationship. "She is intensely self conscious whereas the feminists were intensely sex conscious."

Buitenhuis, P. "From Daisy Miller to Julia Bride, a Whole Passage of Intellectual History." American Quarterly, 11 (Summer 1959), 136-46. A comparative essay based on two short stories by Henry James: Daisy Miller and Julia Bride. Both women are imbued with the independence displayed by American women at the turn of the century. Miller is innocent and ignorant, dies wronged, never knowing why. Bride is more jaded with depths of self-knowledge Miller never displays.

Bullough, Vern L., with the assistance of Bonnie Bullough. The Subordinate Sex: A History of Attitudes Toward Women. Urbana: University of Illinois Press, 1973.

Bushnell, Horace. Women's Suffrage: The Reform against Nature. New York: Charles Scribner's, 1869.

Butler, Josephine E., ed. Woman's Work and Woman's Culture: A Series of Essays. London: Macmillan, 1869.

Butler, Melissa A. "Early Liberal Roots of Feminism: John Locke and the Attack on Patriarchy." American Political Science Review, 72 (March 1978).

Child, Lydia Maria. Philothea: A Grecian Romance (1836). Freeport, N.Y.: Books for Libraries Press, 1969.

Christenson, R. "Political Theory of Male Chauvinism: J. J. Rousseau's Paradigm." Midwest Quarterly, 13 (April 1972), 291-99. Rousseau's political ideas assume woman's inequality to man and justify male domination in the name of freedom.

"Christian Feminism." Messenger of the Sacred Heart (Sep-

tember 1955), 10-12. Pope asked for prayers on behalf
of the problems facing women in modern world, particularly subtle undermining of feminine characteristics in
competition with men. To say women should stay at
home as God intended will not solve problem. Virgin
Mother of God has given Christian women dignity and
ideal, and Church has defined her new status. Women
must preserve natural qualities of womanliness for their
husbands. Women are free to stay single but not to sur-
render their virginity. Women can solve today's
problems by keeping sense of mission and acting as
force against secularism in business and professional
world.

Clark, David L. Brockden Brown and the Rights of Women.
Folcroft, Pa.: Folcroft Press, 1912.

Clarke, H. A. "Charlotte Perkins Stetson as Social Philosopher and Poet." Poetlore, January 1899, 124-28. Mrs.
Stetson has overemphasized certain facts and evidences
sex bias by placing responsibility of future development
entirely in woman's hands. Public opinion has agreed
to woman's dependence on her husband's support. This
is overlaid with love and devotion for most, excepting
very rich, poor and medium poor. Mrs. Stetson is not
thoroughly scientific because she ignores such classifica-
tions. Her utopia, however, is valuable contribution to
ideal of social life.

Claviere, Marie Maude la. The Women of the Renaissance:
A Study of Feminism. New York: G. P. Putnam's,
1901.

Colquhoun, Ethel Maud. "Modern Feminism and Sex Antagonism." Living Age (September 6, 1913), 579-94.

_____. The Vocation of Woman. London: Macmillan,
1913.

Cooper, James L., and Sheila M. Cooper. The Roots of
American Feminist Thought. Boston: Allyn and Bacon,
1973. Feminists need to face the problem of developing
radical ideology which will generate insight into woman's
subjection, as well as problem of propounding original
theory to account for sexism, in an essentially conservative society. Includes selections from Mary Wollstonecraft, an "enlightened rebel"; Sarah Grimke, a "radical

sectarian"; Margaret Fuller, a "romantic idealist"; John
Stuart Mill, a "utilitarian liberal"; Charlotte Perkins
Gilman, an "evolutionary socialist"; Margaret Sanger, a
"romantic irrationalist"; and Suzanne LaFollette, a "radical libertarian. "

Cross, Barbara M., ed. The Educated Woman in America:
Selected Writings of Catharine Beecher, Margaret Fuller
and ·M. Carey Thomas. New York: Teachers College
Press, Columbia University, 1965. Dealing with one aspect of the revolution in the relationship between sexes,
design of new "archetype of ideal femininity. " Beecher:
most conservative, idyll of domestic life included diligent
children and coping wives and mothers in holy home.
Fuller: set "before herself and her small self-conscious
circle the instructive mystery of feminist genius" while
rejecting Beecher's Christian terminology. Thomas: ex-
uberantly placed her faith in institutions rather than singular ecstasies or the home. These women conjointly
made "the 'feminine' seem legitimately various. "

Degler, Carl N. "Charlotte Perkins Gilman on the Theory
and Practice of Feminism, 1898-1923. " American Quarterly, 8 (Spring 1956), 21-39. Gilman's ideal was the
working girl, working wife and mother. She saw work
outside the home as a liberating force for women. Her
feminist arguments suggest women were not fulfilling
their duty to the world, and the world cannot manage unless they do so through the altruism of motherhood.
Gilman is rationalist radical. Her major contribution:
the requirement that women be in the world as well as
of it.

Ditzion, Sidney. Marriage, Morals and Sex in America: An
History of Ideas. New York: Octagon Books, 1969.
Man's economic, political, intellectual and social activities are enmeshed inextricably in his sexual activities.
Manifold social reform movements interact with sexual
reform movements. Confluence of ideas such as education of women, women's rights in the family and society,
birth control and sex education indivisibly are demonstrated aspects of sexual-social problem. Suggests feminist
movement contributed little to development of thought on
marriage relationship because of advocacy of reason
and human equality. Chapter footnotes, source note
and index.

Dorr, Rheta Childe. What Eight Million Women Want. Boston: Small, Maynard, 1910. Reformism at its most romantic (i. e. , ch. VIII, Woman's Helping Hand to the Prodigal Daughter). "Woman's place is in the home and she must not be forbidden to dwell there. " There is natural division of labor according to sex. Women have resources men lack. Illustrations including "Women's Rights Map of the U. S. " Index.

Doyle, William T. "Charlotte Perkins Gilman and the Cycle of Feminist Reform. " Dissertation, University of California, 1960.

Eliot, George. Complete Works (1867). New York: Merrill and Baker, n. d.

Elshtain, Jean Bethke. "Moral Woman and Immoral Man. " Politics and Society, 4:4 (1974), 453-73.

"Feminine vs. Feminist. " Living Age, March 9, 1912, 587-92.

Foster, G. B. "Philosophy of Feminism. " Forum, July 1914, 10-22. Primitive woman was responsible for agriculture and horticulture, forming world historical movement through which weak inherited earth. Matriarchy preceded patriarchy. This is beginning of woman's movement. At turning point of ancient civilization maternal deity Maria won primacy over all powerful church God as solution to woman question of her day. Cloister was solution to woman question in ecclesiastical Middle Ages. Woman as woman came to revolt against her inferiority to woman as nun. Woman movement in modern Protestant world is marked by revolt against ideal of virginity and angelhood. Domestic ideal of Hausfrau emphasizes woman as housekeeper, a specific social and civic character. What woman really is seeking is her self and opportunity to exist for herself.

Fuller, Margaret. "The Great Lawsuit. Man vs. Men. Woman vs. Women. " The Dial, 4 (July 1843), 1-47.

Gilman, Charlotte Perkins. His Religion and Hers. See entry under Complementary (Empirical).

_____. The Yellow Wallpaper (1899). Old Westbury, N. Y. : Feminist Press, 1973. Apparently autobiographical account of woman's retreat into madness in isolation of ideal marriage. Terrifying. Includes some footnotes in Elaine R. Hedges' afterword.

Glasgow, Ellen. Virginia (1913). Garden City, N.Y.: Doubleday, Page, 1923.

Goldwater, Ethel. "Women's Place: The New Alliance of Science and Anti-Feminism." Complementary, December 1947, 578-85.

Grand, Sarah. The Beth Book. New York: Appleton, 1897.

Grant, Jane. "Confession of a Feminist." American Mercury, December 1943, 684-91.

Griffith, Mary. Three Hundred Years Hence (1836). Philadelphia: Prime Press, 1950.

Grimke, Sarah. The Equality of the Sexes and the Condition of Woman. Boston: Isaac Knapp, 1839. Sees woman's use of reason limited by lack of education. For women to adequately perform "their sacred duties as mothers and sisters," they must do so "understandingly." Sees women as the weaker sex, but "Ah! How many of my sex feel in the dominion, thus unrighteously exercised over them, under the gentle appelation of protection, that what they have leaned upon has proved a broken reed at best, and oft a spear."

Guitton, Jean. Feminine Fulfillment, trans. Paul J. Oligny. Chicago: Franciscan Herald Press, 1965. Reveals true "Feminine Mystique," in writing "against insolence of Mme. de Beauvoir." Presents the theological and philosophical approach beginning with difference between sexes. See especially ch. 15, The Second Sex ("Woman's freedom lies in her ability to procreate").

Hale, Beatrice Forbes-Robertson. What Women Want: An Interpretation of the Feminist Movement. New York: Frederick A. Stokes, 1914.

Hale, Sarah Josepha Buell. Woman's Record. See entry under Complementary (Empirical).

Hall, Florence Howe. Julia Ward Howe and the Woman Suffrage Movement. New York: Arno, 1969.

Hamilton, Gail [pseud. for Mary A. Dodge]. Woman's Wrongs (1868). New York: Arno, 1972. Bound with John Todd, Woman's Rights (1867).

Harding, M. Esther. Woman's Mysteries, Ancient and Modern: A Psychological Interpretation of the Feminine Principle as Portrayed in Myth, Story and Dreams, rev. ed. New York: Pantheon, 1955.

Hawthorne, Nathanial. The Blithedale Romance, in The Works of Nathanial Hawthorne, vol. 3. New York: Bigelow, Brown, 1923.

Heywood, Ezra H. "Uncivil Liberty: An Essay to Show the Injustice and Impolicy of Ruling Woman without Her Consent," in Sex and Equality (1877). New York: Arno, 1974.

Howe, Julia Ward, ed. Sex and Education: A Reply to Dr. E. H. Clarke's 'Sex in Education.' Boston: Roberts Brothers, 1874. Appeals to laws of harmony to counteract dogma re female intellectual weakness. Need to educate future wives with husbands. Contains articles by Howe and Thomas W. Higginson and others as well as testimony from colleges.

James, Henry. The Bostonians. London: John Lehman, 1886.

Jepson, Weir. Feminism v. True Capitalism. Sioux City, Iowa: Hoyt-Purcell, 1932. Advocates laissez-faire economy in which women play role of creator with men as their helpmates. Suffrage did not give women the right to compete with men in industry. It was intended to correct social defects. Home is unit of consumption.

Johnston, Mary. Hagar. Boston: Houghton, 1913.

Key, Ellen. The Century of the Child. New York: G. P. Putnam's, 1909.

_____. The Renaissance of Motherhood. New York: G. P. Putnam's, 1914. Calling for social means to make renaissance of motherhood possible, and especially for education of the feelings. Concern for use women will make of their new rights, re duties of motherhood, which are of most value to race, nation and humanity. 'It was

just in order that motherliness should be able to pene-
trate all spheres of life that women's liberation emerged."

_____. War, Peace and the Future: A Consideration of
Nationalism and Internationalism, and of the Relation of
Women to War. Trans. Hildegard Norberg. New York:
G. P. Putnam's, 1916.

Kraditor, Aileen S. The Ideas of the Woman Suffrage Movement. New York: Columbia University Press, 1965.
Woman suffrage movement has no ideology but did have
standard repertoire of arguments to respond to "anti's."
Flexible revolution in woman's status equated with social
revolution. See chs. III, Two Major Types of Suffragist
Arguments (justice, expediency), and IX, Women Suffrage
in Perspective (reformist and humanitarian motives co-
existing with undemocratic attitude). Biographical data,
extensive bibliography, and index.

_____. Up from the Pedestal: Selected Writings in the His-
tory of American Feminism. Chicago: Quadrangle, 1968.

Langdon-Davis, John. A Short History of Women. New
York: Literary Guild of America, 1927.

Lasch, Christopher, ed. The Social Thought of Jane Addams.
Indianapolis: Bobbs-Merrill, 1965.

Lee, Amber. The Woman I Am. New York: Thomas Seltzer, 1925. Appears autobiographical but could be fiction.
Traces history of mental instability. Beginning is reminiscent of Gilman's Yellow Wallpaper. Considerable insight in ch. XVI: "A woman's life is so short. The best
of it is pressed into the shallow measure of twenty years.
From twenty to forty ... we women whom men buy cannot
look forward to fifty or even forty-five with any optimism."

de Leevee, Hendrick. Woman: The Dominant Sex. New
York: Thomas Yoseloff, 1957. "American women are
not only the most privileged, but, paradoxically, the most
dissatisfied persons in the world, since they want to have
their cake and eat it too. Having had liberty and un-
counted privileges dished up on a gold platter, many have
gone berserk with their newly acquired power." See chs.
3, Birth and Growth of the Feminist Movement; 4, Emancipated Women in America; 8, The American Woman vs.
the World; 10, The Domineering Matriarch; and 13, Restless Woman, the Bed of Neurosis.

Lewis, Dio. Our Girls (1871). New York: Arno, 1974.

Lewis, Sinclair. Cass Timberlane: A Novel of Husbands and Wives. New York: Random, 1945.

Lichtenberger, James. Women in Public Life. Philadelphia: Academy, 1914. Includes chapter on economic basis of feminism.

Lindbergh, Anne Morrow. Gift from the Sea. New York: Pantheon, 1955.

Lowell, Amy. The Poems of Amy Lowell. Boston: Houghton, n. d.

Lundy, Benjamin. The Poetical Works of Elizabeth Margaret Chandler with a Memoir of Her Life and Character. Philadelphia: Lemuel Howell, 1836. "Such woman is and shall proud man forbear/ The converse of the mind with her to share?/ No! She with him shall knowledge' papers scan,/ And be the partner, not the toy, of man." See especially Female Education, Fashion Spectacle, Female Character, Influence of Slavery on the Female Character.

Mailer, Norman. Barbary Shore. New York: Rinehart, 1951. "'Oh, lover, I'd do anything for you,' she said. 'You would?' His voice purred. 'I'd work for you, I'd slave for you,' she continued to declaim, 'I'd get down on my hands and knees and scrub.' 'That's not necessary....'"

Martin, Anne. "Feminists and Future Political Action." See entry under Complementary (Empiricism).

Martin, George Madden. "American Women and Paternalism." Atlantic Monthly, June 1924, 744-53. Uncle Sam is paternalistic figure in minds of American women; it is through him they must move to obtain desired ends. Women are less isolated intellectually than men, especially given activities in woman club movement; however, they have herd instinct as do men which inclines toward favoring more federal legislation rather than less.

Martin, Mr. and Mrs. John. Feminism: Its Fallacies and Follies. New York: Dodd, Mead, 1916. In Book I, From the Man's Point of View, feminism is described as dynamic movement which is powerful source of social ferment. Exists in contradistinction to humanism because it is individualistic, anarchistic, centripetal, seeing women as inferior. Book II, From the Woman's Point of View, suggests, "A taste for politics is in general a wholly artificial one for women." Fatal weakness of women voting is that men, rather than measures, are subject matter of election.

Mason, Julian, ed. The Poems of Phillis Wheatley. Chapel Hill: University of North Carolina Press, 1966.

Meikle, Wilma. Towards a Sane Feminism. New York: McBride, 1917.

Mencken, Henry Louis. In Defense of Women. Garden City, N.Y.: Garden City Publishing, 1922. Intends to expose civilized people's ideas about the woman question which have been masked and hence obscured in sentimentality. Sees major problem as that of conflict between civilization-enforced celibacy and God-implanted appetite. Maternal instinct is really compassionate irony based on perception of male puerile ego. Woman's intelligence is accompanied by special feminine character. But, "The essential feminine machine is no better than the essential masculine machine; both are monuments to the maladroitness of a much over-praised Creator." Women, however, do possess superior acumen and self-possession founded in their physical disadvantage. See especially section on Marriage ("The economic and social advantage that women thus seek in marriage ... is, by a curious twist of fate, one of the underlying causes of their precarious economic condition before marriage rescues them").

Mill, John Stuart. On Liberty (1859), ed. Curren V. Shields, Indianapolis: Bobbs-Merrill, 1956.

Miller, Alice Duer. "Who Is Sylvia?: An Aspect of Feminism." Scribner's Magazine, July 1914, 53-60.

Montague, Lady Mary Wortley. The Nonsense of Common-sense, 1737-1738. Expression of political interest in ironic tone. Feminism is "most lively topic." Concern with women as rational beings. Annotations to text and index.

More, Hannah. Hints Toward Forming the Character of a Young Princess. London: T. Cadell and W. Davies, 1805. Concern for education of Princess Charlotte of Wales. Often cited among writers at this time as having influence tantamount to that of Mary Wollstonecraft.

Murray, Judith Sargent. "On the Equality of the Sexes." The Massachusetts Magazine, March/April 1770, 132-35, 223-26. Woman's soul is equal to man's. "We can only reason from what we know, and if opportunity of acquiring knowledge hath been denied us, the inferiority of our sex cannot fairly be deduced from thence."

Nin, Anaïs The Diary of Anaïs Nin, 1931-34, ... 1934-39, ... 1939-44, ... 1944-47, ... 1947-55, and ... 1955-66. 6 vols. New York: Harcourt, Brace and World, 1966.

Owen, Harold. Woman Adrift: A Statement of the Case Against Suffragism. New York: E. P. Dutton, 1912.

Papashvely, George. All the Happy Endings: A Study of the Domestic Novel in America, the Women Who Wrote It, the Women Who Read It. New York: Harper, 1956. Description of inequalities of nineteenth-century marriage as portrayed in widely read "domestic novels," most of which were written by women.

Parker, Gail, ed. The Oven Birds: American Women on Womanhood, 1820-1920. Garden City, N.Y.: Doubleday, 1972.

Parsons, Alice Beal. Woman's Dilemma: From Colonial Times to the Twentieth Century. New York: Crowell, 1926.

Parsons, E. C. "Feminism and the Family." International Journal of Ethics, 28 (October 1917), 52-58.

Porter, John William. Feminism. Louisville, Ky.: Baptist Book Concern, 1923. In part labeled Menace of Feminism, author suggests suffrage was achieved in spite of anti-suffragists and political parties as well as Woodrow Wilson, who was overcome only by pressure. Misleading catch phrase of equal rights is abrogation of male/female biological, moral and mental differences. Feminism is rebellion against limitations and duties of sex.

Reed, Evelyn. Woman's Evolution: From Matriarchal Clan to Patriarchal Family. New York: Pathfinder Press, 1975. "Insofar as the sexes were unequally endowed by nature, the biological advantages for humanizing the species were on the side of the females, not the males." It was woman who shepherded culture and its resulting superstructure, and she did so as the biologically advantaged sex, leaving men to overcome their handicaps through totemism and taboo. Glossary, bibliography and index.

Rossi, Alice S., ed. Essays on Sex Equality. See entry under Complementary (Empirical).

_____. The Feminist Papers. See entry under Complementary (Empirical).

Rousseau, Jean Jacques. Emile (1762), trans. Barbara Foxley. New York: E. P. Dutton, 1911. Whereas Emile, prototypical young man, is taught to be self-reliant, Sophy, prototypical young woman, is viewed essentially as a child. "When women are what they ought to be, they will keep to what they understand and their judgment will be right, but since they have set themselves up as judges of literature, since they have begun to criticise books and make them with might and main, they are altogether astray."

Russell, Bertrand. "Recrudescence of Puritanism." Outlook (London), 52 (October 20, 1923), 300-02.

Saleeby, C. W. Woman and Womanhood: A Search for Principle. New York: Mitchell Kennerly, 1911. Dealing with biological problems. Woman is nature's supreme organ of the future. See especially I, First Principles; III, The Purpose of Womanhood; XII, The Maternal Instinct; XIX, The Rights of Mothers; and XX, Women and Economics. Index.

Sand, George. Indiana, in The Masterpieces of George Sand, (1831) trans. G. Burnham Ives. Philadelphia: George Barrie, 1900.

Sanger, Margaret. Motherhood in Bondage. See entry under Complementary (Empirical).

_____ . The New Motherhood. London: J. Cape, 1922.

_____ . Women and the New Race. New York: Brentano's, 1920. Women as mothers regulate birthrate and
hence human production. Woman's natural motive power
is found in feminine spirit as manifested in motherhood.
Society has alternatives of enslaving this elemental urge
or of giving women freedom to choose. "Slaves of
slaves" are not fit mothers of race. Law of woman's
being will prevail over mere man-made law. See especially I, Woman's Error and Her Debt; II, Woman's
Struggle for Freedom; IV, Two Classes of Women; and
XV, Legislating Woman's Morals.

Schneir, Miriam. Feminism: The Essential Historical Writings. See entry under Complementary (Empirical).

Schreiner, Olive [under pseud. Ralph Iron]. The Story of an
African Farm. London: Collins, 1953.

_____ . Woman and Labor. New York: Frederick A.
Stokes, 1911.

Simons, May Wood. Woman and the Social Problem. Chicago: C. H. Kerr, 1890.

Smith, Elizabeth Oakes. Woman and Her Needs. New York:
Fowler and Wells, 1851. Woman pictured as intelligent,
distinct individual whose standard should come from nob-
lest types of her sex. Treated legally as child and idiot.
Seeks her position in life through marriage, whereupon
"she becomes a reflex of the glory of another, or the recipient of all his meanness, debasement and disgrace."
Marriage is contract which presupposed equality. Suggests "it is weak and foolish to suppose that man ... wil-
fully desired to enslave us. If done at all, it was done
in blindness and ignorance."

Smith, Harrison. "Feminism in Reverse." Saturday Review,
December 25, 1954, 20.

Smith, Paul Jordan. The Soul of Woman: An Interpretation
of the Philosophy of Feminism. San Francisco: P. Ei-
der, 1916. Seeking to evoke new sympathy for motives
and ideals of feminism. Stresses Ellen Key's contribution
as "a radical, a breaker of images, a creator of new values...." Sees freedom as freedom to grow worthy of

freedom--to become free. Older phase of woman movement is dying out that feminism might prosper. Feminism
shuns conventional morality which exists for property's
sake, deferring to sociology and wisdom instead.

Spargo, John. Socialism and Motherhood. New York: B. W.
Huebsch, 1914.

Spencer, Sara Jane. Problems on the Woman Question.
Washington, D. C.: Langran, Ogilvie, 1871.

Strutt, Elizabeth. The Feminine Soul. Boston: Henry H.
and T. W. Carter, 1870.

Symes, Lilian. "Still a Man's Game: Reflections of a Slightly Tired Feminist." Harper's Magazine, May 1929, 678-
87.

Tarbell, Ida M. The Business of Being a Woman. New
York: Macmillan, 1912.

_____. The Ways of Women. New York: Macmillan,
1915.

Taylor, Gordon R. Sex in History. See entry under Complementary (Empirical).

Thayer, William M. The Poor Girl and the True Woman;
or, Elements of Woman's Success (Drawn from the Life
of Mary Lyon and Others); A Book for Girls. Boston:
Gould and Lincoln, 1859. Designed to "assist girls in
cultivating the highest virtues, and in prosecuting the
work of life with credit to themselves, and acceptance
to God."

Thompson, William. Appeal of One Half of the Human Race,
Women, against the Pretensions of the Other Half, Men,
to Retain Them in Political, and Thence in Civil and Do-
mestic Slavery, in Reply to a Paragraph of Mr. (James)
Mill's Celebrated "Article on Government" (1825). New
York: Source Book Press, 1970.

Tiger, Lionel. Men in Groups. New York: Random, 1969.
Argues that women are excluded from certain groups
typically viewed as for men only (i. e., centers of political power) in an expression of formalized hostility for
them and because there is a positive attraction between

males in an evolutionary sense. Suggests "the division of labor along sex-lines is one of the most important recurrent cross-cultural regularities which social scientists have identified" and "women are a minority in analytic terms...." Emphasizes relationship between maleness, the male bond, and aggression and violence, with resultant linkage to unhappy social consequences. "Historical evidence weighs strongly against the optimistic feminists" in terms of female access to politics. "...[W]e all share this one huge garden, our only Eden, a strangely tangled, strangely fruitful, strangely mapless garden. We also share a common responsibility to learn what our common responses to the garden are, and to its inhabitants. Only then dare we disturb the universe."

Todd, John. See Hamilton (above).

Tuttle, Florence Guertin. The Awakening of Woman: Suggestions from the Psychic Side of Feminism. New York: Abingdon, 1915. Feminism is a matter of spiritual initiative and impulse, the real cause of which is psychic awakening. Woman question is race problem, social and spiritual, existing on three planes: body, mind and spirit. It is scientific and natural, part of spiritual advancement of mankind.

Vaerting, Mathilde, and Mathias Vaerting. The Dominant Sex. New York: George H. Doran, 1923.

Violette, Augusta Genevieve. Economic Feminism in American Literature Prior to 1848. (University of Maine Studies, 2d Series, no. 17.) Orono: University of Maine Press, 1925. Analysis of early writings sympathetic to woman suffrage, from Revolution to 1848. Includes Thomas Paine, Charles Brockden Brown and John Neal as well as Sarah Grimke and Margaret Fuller. Source of title emphasis (economic feminism) not readily apparent. Bibliography and index.

Wade, Mason, ed. The Writings of Margaret Fuller. Clifton, N.J.: Augustus M. Kelley, 1973.

Wadia, A. R. The Ethics of Feminism: A Study of the Revolt of Woman. London: Allen and Unwin, 1923.

Walsh, Correa Moylan. Feminism. New York: Sturgis and Walton Co., 1917. Refers to masculinization of women

and feminization of men. "Full feminist demands that
practically all differences between the male and the female of the human species shall be obliterated except
the one big difference: begetting and bearing children
(of being mothers and fathers)." Suggests only the "se-
mi-feminist" demands from men political rights for women and then proposes waiting to see how women will
use them. Index and footnotes.

Warren, Mercy Otis. The Ladies of Castile: A Tragedy in
Five Acts, 1790.

Willard, Emma Hart. An Address to the Public Particularly
to the Members of the Legislature of New York Proposing a Plan for Improving Female Education. 1819.

Wollstonecraft, Mary. Thoughts on the Education of Daughters with Reflections on Female Conduct in the More Important Duties of Life (1787). New York: Garland, 1974.

_____. A Vindication of the Rights of Women (1790). New
York: Norton, 1967. Rationalist argument for education
of women to betterment of society, based on Rousseauian
natural rights theory.

_____. Wrongs of Women, in Posthumous Works of Mary
Wollstonecraft Godwin, ed. William Godwin (1798). New
York: Garland, 1974.

The Woman Patriot: A National Newspaper for Home and
National Defense against Woman Suffrage. Washington,
D.C.: Woman Patriot Publishing Co.; issued from April
27, 1918, to December 27, 1919.

Woollen, C. J. "Failure of Feminism." Homiletic and Pas-
toral Review, October 1949, 30-39.

Woolson, Abba Goold, ed. Dress Reform (1874). New York:
Arno, 1974.

CONGRUENT FEMINISM

EMPIRICAL

An Account of the Proceedings of the Trial of Susan B. Anthony, on the Charge of Illegal Voting at the Presidential
Election in November, 1872 (1874). New York: Arno,
1974.

Blackwell, Elizabeth. Essays on Medical Sociology (1902).
New York: Arno, 1972.

_____. Pioneer Work in Opening the Medical Profession
to Women (1895). New York: Source Book Press, 1970.

Bloomer, D. C. Life and Writings of Amelia Bloomer (1895).
New York: Schocken, 1972.

Branch, Douglas. "The Lily and the Bloomer." The Colo-
phon, 12 (1932), n. p.

Breckinridge, Sophonisba P. The Family and the State. Chicago: University of Chicago Press, 1934.

_____. Marriage and the Civil Rights of Women: Separate
Domicile and Independent Citizenship. Chicago: University of Chicago Press, 1931.

_____. Women in the Twentieth Century: A Study of
Their Political, Social and Economic Activities. New
York: McGraw-Hill, 1933. Women's organizational, occupational and political relationships and activities have
intensified in relation to their involvement in the immediate family, with their move toward emancipation. A
veritable bonanza of nicely compiled and tabulated data on
the woman's movement during the early portion of the
century.

Chafe, William H. The American Woman: Her Changing Social, Economic and Political Roles, 1920-1970. New
York: Oxford University Press, 1972. Public perceptions of woman's place, especially woman's economic
roles, and the impact of events such as war and depres-

sion on the nature of woman's sphere dictate the distribution of sexual roles and hence the distribution of power
between the sexes. A foundation for sexual equality may
have been established with the enlargement of woman's
economic sphere since 1940 and World War II. Extensive notes, selected bibliography and index.

Coleman, Elizabeth Dabney. "Penwoman of Virginia's Feminists. " Virginia Cavalcade, 6 (September 6, 1913),
579-94. Mary Johnston, novelist, assisting in organizing
Equal Suffrage League in Virginia, writes a frankly feminist proposition about girl enmeshed in class prejudices
and social intolerance who escapes by becoming a writer.
Makes plea for universal brotherhood of men and women
and champions reforms including divorce. Theory of human progress in history.

Conrad, Earl. Harriet Tubman: Negro Soldier and Abolitionist. New York: International Publishers, 1942. Short
but instructive biography. Notes Tubman's contribution to
womankind as well as to her race. Symbolizes her own
life; "in her childhood, as a slave, she was forbidden to
eat the fruit of the trees she had been made to plant....
'I liked apples when I was young and I said to myself:
"Someday I'll plant apples myself for other young folks to
eat" and I guess I did. '" Selected bibliography.

De Pauw, Linda Grant. Founding Mothers: Women of America in the Revolutionary Era. See entry under Complementary (Empirical).

Dew, Thomas. "Characteristic Differences Between the Sexes. " Southern Literary Messenger, 1 (1835), 493-512,
621-23, 672-91.

Dienes, C. Thomas. Law, Politics and Birth Control. Urbana: University of Illinois Press, 1972. Law serves
as a device by which to respond to social wants and needs
relative to change, when the interaction between the legislature and the judiciary is characterized by cooperation.
Detailed analysis of substantive area--birth control--with-
in decision-making theory. Appendices, index, extensive
bibliography and footnotes.

Dorr, Rheta Childe. A Woman of Fifty, 2d ed. New York:
Funk and Wagnalls, 1924.

Engels, Frederick. The Origin of the Family, Private Property and the State: In Light of the Researches of Lewis
H. Morgan (1891). New York: International Publishers,
1972.

Flexner, Eleanor. Century of Struggle. See entry under
Complementary (Empirical).

_____. Mary Wollstonecraft: A Biography. New York:
Coward, McCann and Geoghegan, 1972.

George, Margaret. One Woman's "Situation": A Study of
Mary Wollstonecraft. Urbana: University of Illinois
Press, 1970. Eclectic biography looking at Wollstonecraft's refusal of the feminine role and struggle with her
own sense of inferiority. See especially chs. 6 and 7,
The Independent Woman--Parts I and II. "Mary ... had
world-important things to do ... her own revolutionary
area to define, which she did, again at top speed, by
producing in six weeks of writing The Vindication of the
Rights of Women. " Index.

Gilbert, Olive. Narrative of Sojourner Truth, a Bondswoman
of Olden Time ... Drawn from Her Book of Life. Battle
Creek, Mich.: Rev. and Harold Office, 1884. Truth
emerges as profound social analyst. Includes Frances D.
Gage's report of speech at Woman's Rights Convention at
Akron, Ohio, and crowd's reaction. "Amid roars of applause, she turned to her corner, leaving more than one
of us with streaming eyes and hearts beating with gratitude. She had taken us up in her strong arms and carried us safely over the slough of difficulty, turning the
whole tide in our favor. "

Goldman, Emma. Living My Life. New York: Knopf, 1931.
Autobiography written in exile, chiefly of interest for her
sexual relationships and anarchism.

Hays, Elinor Rice. Morning Star: A Biography of Lucy
Stone, 1818-1893; Those Extraordinary Blackwells. See
entries under Complementary (Empirical).

Herschberger, Ruth. Adam's Rib. New York: Pellegrini
and Cudahy, 1948. An examination of sex roles and
their confrontation with the facts. Hard, even ironic
treatment of short shrift society gives women. Notes.

Hunt, Harriot, K. Glances and Glimpses; or, 50 Years Social, Including 20 Years Professional Life (1856). New
York: Source Book Press, 1970.

Irwin, Inez Haynes. Angels and Amazons: A Hundred Years
of American Women. Garden City, N.Y.: Doubleday,
Doran, 1933. Generalized treatment (despite details).
"This book has concerned itself with plow-women rather
than reapers; with important beginnings, no matter how
humble they seemed in their time, rather than with fulfillment." Appendices and index.

_____. Up Hill with Banners Flying (1921). Penobscott,
Me.: Traversity Press, 1964. Story of the Woman's
Party. Their strength was spirit of youth, and it pre-
vailed.

James, Edward, ed. Notable American Women. See entry
under Complementary (Empirical).

Johnson, G. G. "Feminism and the Economic Independence
of Women." Journal of Social Forces, 3 (May 1925),
612-16.

Keller, Helen. Midstream; My Later Life. New York:
Doubleday, 1929.

Lerner, Gerda. Black Women in White America; The Grimke Sisters from South Carolina; "The Lady and the Mill
Girl"; "Women's Rights and American Feminism." All
four entries see under Complementary (Empirical).

Lowi, Robert H., and Leta S. Hollingsworth. "Science and
Feminism." Scientific Monthly (September 1916), 277-84.
Feminists seeking removal of constraints on female activity are opposed because of undesirable social and ethical consequences and woman's unfitness for some activities. Authors want to look at this scientifically. Almost
everywhere woman's contribution to culture is important.
No grounds for inferring woman is inferior or superior
to man intellectually. 'It is amusing to note how every
sex difference that has been discovered or alleged has
been interpreted to show superiority of males." Restriction of woman's sphere is not natural, and there are no
scientific grounds on which to base any artificial limitation of woman's activities.

Lutz, Alma.   Created Equal: A Biography of Elizabeth Cady Stanton, 1815-1902.   New York: John Day, 1940.

_____.   Susan B. Anthony: Rebel, Crusader, Humanitarian.   Boston: Beacon Press, 1959.

McLuhan, Marshall.   The Mechanical Bride: Folklore of Industrial Man.   Boston: Beacon Press, 1974.   People have no part in making folklore.   "The display of current feminine sex power seems to many males to demand an impossible virility of assertion."   See for example How Not to Offend, From Top to Toe, Women in a Mirror, The Drowned Man, Love-Goddess Assembly Line.

Martin, Anne.   "Feminists and Future Political Action"; "Political Methods of American and British Feminists."   See entries under Complementary (Empirical).

Martineau, Harriet.   The Martyr Age in the United States.   Boston: Weeks, Jordan, 1839.

_____.   Society in America.   3 vols.   London: Saunders and Otley, 1837.

Maslow, Abraham.   "Dominance, Personality and Social Behavior in Women."   Journal of Social Psychology, 10 (1939), 3-39.

Mead, Margaret.   Male and Female.   New York: Mentor, 1955.

_____.   Sex and Temperament in Three Primitive Societies.   New York: Peter Smith, 1935.   An account of how three primitive societies in New Guinea have grouped their social attitudes toward temperament about the very obvious facts of sex differences.   "I hope this exploration of the way in which simple primitive cultures have been able to rely upon temperamental clues may be useful in shifting the present extreme emphasis upon sex roles to a new emphasis on human beings as distinct personalities who, men and women, share many of the same contrasting and differing temperamental approaches to life."   See especially Part Four, The Implications of These Results.

Newcomer, M.   A Century of Higher Education for Women.   Boston: Atheneum, 1959.

O'Neill, William L. Everyone Was Brave: The Rise and Fall of Feminism in America; The Woman Movement: Feminism in the United States and England. See entries under Complementary (Empirical).

Parkhurst, Genevieve. "Is Feminism Dead?" Harper's Magazine, May 1935, 735-45. Problems in organization of women, apathy, lack of great leaders and their ability to stand together (1920-35) discussed.

Parmalee, M. "Economic Basis of Feminism." Annals of the American Academy of Political and Social Science, 56 (November 1914), 18-26.

Riegel, Robert E. American Feminists. See entry under Complementary (Empirical).

Schneir, Miriam. Feminism: The Essential Historical Writings. See entry under Complementary (Empirical).

Scott, Anne Firor, ed. The American Woman, Who Was She? See entry under Complementary (Empirical).

Smedley, Agnes. Daughter of Earth (1943). Old Westbury, N.Y.: Feminist Press, 1973.

Sochen, June. Movers and Shakers. See entry under Complementary (Empirical).

Stanton, Elizabeth Cady. Eighty Years and More: Reminiscences of Elizabeth Cady Stanton. New York: European Publishing Co., 1898. Of especial interest is ch. XIV, Views on Marriage and Divorce. Includes index of names.

_____, et al. History of Woman Suffrage. See entry under Complementary (Empirical).

Stanton, Theodore, and Harriot Stanton Blatch, eds. Elizabeth Cady Stanton. 2 vols. New York: Arno, 1969.

Stevens, Doris. Jailed for Freedom. New York: Boni and Liveright, 1920. Militant suffragist campaign had elements of both ruthlessness and martyrdom (for a practical purpose rather than for its own sake). See especially Part III, Militancy, chs. 1-27. Experiences parallel those of more modern protesters: i.e., "Judge Mallowry addressed the prisoners with many high-sounding words about the seriousness of obstructing traffic in the national capital, and inadvertently slipped into a discourse on Russia and the dangers of revolution." Also, "The judge said that he could not possibly understand the motive for this outburst, and added 'If it is repeated, I shall consider it contempt of court.'" Of interest is characterization of a politician who failed--Woodrow Wilson. Illustrated and appendices.

Suhl, Yuri. Ernestine L. Rose and the Battle for Human Rights. New York: Reynal, 1959. Vivid account of battle for married woman's rights to her own property and earnings.

Swisshelm, Jane Grey. Crusader and Feminist: Letters of Jane Grey Swisshelm, 1858-1865, ed. Arthur J. Larsen. St. Paul: Minnesota Historical Society, 1934. Letters of one of the best-known women in America during the Civil War era. After unhappy experience as wife, Swisshelm worked to improve status of women in law. Her motto: "If the path of duty lies through the deep water, go forward and the irresistable right arm shall divide the waves." Indexed.

Talbot, Marion, and Sophonisba P. Breckinridge. The Modern Household. Boston: Whitcomb and Barrows, 1912.

Tremain, Rose. The Fight for Freedom for Women. New York: Ballantine Books, 1973. Beginning in 1867, Tremain traces struggle for woman's enfranchisement in Great Britain and the United States with unusual emphasis on violence. Wonderfully illustrated, book conveys a very real sense of struggle as well as giving attention to roots of radical feminism. Short bibliography.

Welter, Barbara, ed. The Woman Question in American History. See entry under Complementary (Empirical).

"Where Are They (National Woman's Party) Now?" Newsweek, March 23, 1970, 18. Alice Paul welcomes women's liberation to the historical woman's movement: "When you put your hand to the plow, you cannot put it down until you get to the end of the row."

Winick, Charles. The New People: Desexualization in American Life. New York: Pegasus, 1968. World War II popular cultural and social history. Author is no friend

of feminism. "... [T]housands of years have brought us
full circle to where we were.... Our awareness of the
differences between men and women has been sapped of
its vitality." See especially chs. 5, Inner and Outer
Space; 6, Childhood, a Journey with New Maps; 7, Costume and Custom: The Vanishing Difference; 8, Men,
Women, and Other Minority Groups; and 10, The Way of
the Neuter.

Winter, Alice Ames. The Heritage of Women. See entry under Complementary (Emporical).

NORMATIVE

Bazin, Nancy Topping. Virginia Woolf and the Androgynous
Vision. New Brunswick, N.J.: Rutgers University
Press, 1973. Notes Woolf sees every mind as potentially
bisexual; that is, characterized by a sense of wholeness
and unconsciousness, an equilibrium of feminine and masculine aspects of human nature. "I believe that Virginia
Woolf's experience during mania is related to what she
would have considered an essentially feminine vision of
life, and that her experience during depression is relevant to what she would have considered an essentially
masculine vision of life." See especially ch. I, A Quest
for Equilibrium. Notes, selected bibliography and index.

Billington-Grieg, Theresa. "Feminism and Politics." Contemporary Review, 100 (November 1911), 691-703.

Bjorkman, F. M. "New Prophetess of Feminism: Dora
Marsden." Forum, October 1912, 455-64. As editor of
The Free Woman, Marsden is "'spiking the suffragists'
game'" as power broker by proclaiming for extensive
changes in social structure and relations of sexes: economic independence for women; repudiation of marriage
contract by women; vast development in domestic labor
and administration which would fragment the home; increase in access points of politics and industry to accommodate more productive thinkers and workers. Feminism
defined as temporary theory of expedients and readjust-
ment to be superseded by common doctrine of humanism.
It is through self-realization rather than passive self-sacrifice that woman will become useful in highest sense.

Blackwell, Antoinette Brown. "Sex Injustice." New York:
American Purity Alliance, 1902.

_____. The Sexes Throughout Nature. New York: G. P. Putnam's, 1875.

Brackett, Anne C. "Liberal Education for Women." Harper's New Monthly Magazine, April 1877, 695-96. Number of colleges admitting women to their advantages is very small. Idea of coeducation is "to put human beings into as full possession of their faculties as they can attain minus the training for real life." Just as young men graduates will go on in life, so will young women, to rightly use opportunities offered them. The majority will hold their lives in their own control and not be swept away by the force of undisciplined impulses. "They will go on to their own place."

Buck, Pearl S. Of Men and Women. New York: John Day, 1941.

Claflin, Tennie C. Constitutional Equality: A Right of Women. New York: Woodhull, Claflin, 1871.

Cooper, James L., and Sheila M. Cooper. The Roots of American Feminist Thought. See entry under Complementary (Normative).

DeFord, Miriam A. "The Feminist Future." New Republic, September 19, 1928, 121-23.

DuBois, Ellen. "Struggling into Existence: The Feminism of Sarah and Angelina Grimke." Women; A Journal of Liberation, Spring 1970, 4-11.

"Feminine vs. Feminist." See entry under Complementary (Normative).

"Feminism in the Federal Constitution." World's Work, November 1922, 20-21. Equal rights amendment advocated by National Woman's Party proposes to make a man a woman and a woman a man. Hence same laws will exist for both, including matters of marriage and sex legislation. "If this Amendment passes, there will no longer be any such thing as sex in the United States...." Since woman is different from man, laws of application to her alone are legitimate, i.e., laws in interest of maternity. Separate Woman's Party is not in keeping with spirit of the amendment, despite being made up of extreme feminists who see any kind of sex discrimination as intolerable.

Foner, Philip S. Helen Keller: Her Socialist Years. New York: International Publishers, 1967.

Gale, Zona. Miss Lula Bett. New York: Appleton, 1921.

Goldman, Emma. Anarchism and Other Essays. Port Washington, N.Y.: Kennikat, 1910. Suggests hypocrisy of Puritanism condemns women to celibacy, indiscriminate breeding or prostitution. Woman will be free only when she asserts herself as a person rather than sex commodity, and when she refuses right of anyone to her body. See especially The Tragedy of Woman's Emancipation. The problem is "how to be one's self and yet in oneness with others; to feel deeply with all human beings and still retain one's characteristic qualities." Emancipation has brought woman economic quality with man for which she is not prepared. Also suggests love rather than marriage is the parent of true companionship and oneness.

_____. Red Emma Speaks: Selected Writings and Speeches, ed. Alix Kates Shulman. New York: Random, 1972.

_____. The Traffic in Women and Other Essays on Feminism. New York: Times Change Press, 1970.

Grimke, Angelina Emily. Letters to Catharine Beecher. Boston: Isaac Knapp, 1838. Chiding Beecher for her willingness to leave political sphere entirely to men. "When human beings are regarded as moral beings, sex, instead of being enthroned upon the summit, administering upon rights and responsibilities, sinks into insignificance and nothingness.... This regulation of duty by the mere circumstance of sex, rather than by the fundamental principle of moral being, has led to all that multifarious train of evils flowing out of the anti-Christian doctrine of masculine and feminine virtues."

Herschberger, Ruth. A Way of Happening. New York: Pellegrini and Cudahy, 1948.

Hunt, Harriot. Glances and Glimpses. See entry under Congruent (Empirical).

Ibsen, Henrik. A Doll's House (1879), trans. Eva La Gallienne. New York: Modern Library, 1953. "In his notes for this 'modern tragedy,' as he called it, Ibsen writes: 'A woman cannot be herself in the society at

present day, which is an exclusively masculine society,
with laws framed by men and with a judicial system that
judges female conduct from a masculine point of view.'"

_____. Ghosts (1881), trans. Eva La Gallienne. New
York: Modern Library, 1953.

_____. Hedda Gabbler (1890), trans. Eva La Gallienne.
New York: Modern Library, 1953.

James, Henry. The Bostonians. See entry under Complementary (Normative).

Kisner, Arlene, ed. The Lives and Writings of Notorious
Victoria Woodhull and Her Sister Tennessee Claflin.
Washington, N.J.: Times Change Press, 1972. Short
but provocative. Offers glimpses of radical feminism in
this period. "Woman's Rights movement ... pre-emi-
nently a Radical movement; for it seeks to remodel the
framework of society, as far as the relations of the
sexes are concerned...." Includes short bibliography
and illustrations.

Kraditor, Aileen S. Up from the Pedestal; Ideas of Woman
Suffrage Movement. See entries under Complementary
(Normative).

LaFollette, Suzanne. Concerning Women (1926). New York:
Arno, 1972.

Lessing, Doris. Martha Quest; A Proper Marriage; A Ripple
from the Storm; Landlocked. New York: Simon and
Schuster, 1952-1958. Traces inner and outer life of
"modern woman" from her parents' home in central Africa through two marriages and abandonment of her child,
past conventional boundaries into freedom to self actualize.

Martin, Anne. "Woman's Inferiority Complex." New Republic, July 20, 1921, 210-12.

Parker, Dorothy. After Such Pleasures. New York: Viking,
1933.

_____. Death and Taxes. New York: Viking, 1931.

_____. The Portable Dorothy Parker. New York: Viking,
1973. Includes such gems as "By the time you swear

you're his/ Shivering and sighing/ And he swears his
passion is/ Infinite, undying--/ Lady, make a note of
this:/ One of you is lying." See especially "The Sexes."

Parsons, Alice Beal. Woman's Dilemma: From Colonial
Times to the Twentieth Century. See entry under Complementary (Normative).

Pier, Florida. "The Masculine and the Feminine Mind."
Harper's Weekly, September 24, 1910, 21.

Rossi, Alice S. The Feminist Papers. See entry under
Complementary (Empirical).

Schneir, Miriam. Feminism: The Essential Historical Writings. See entry under Complementary (Empirical).

Skinner, B. F. Walden II. New York: Macmillan, 1948.

Stanton, Elizabeth Cady, et al. The Woman's Bible (1898).
Seattle: Seattle Coalition Task Force on Women and Religion, 1974. Revision of Biblical texts and chapters
pertaining to women directly and indirectly, including
Genesis through Deuteronomy (Part I) and Joshua through
Revelation (Part II). Stanton advises: "Let us remember
that all reforms are interdependent, and that whatever is
done to establish one principle on a solid basis, strength-
ens all." Ursula Gestefeld concludes: "The Bible is the
soul's guide in the fulfillment of its destiny--that destiny
which is involved in its origin; and the soul, in sleep, is
sexless. Its faculties and powers are differentiated as
masculine and feminine."

Stein, Gertrude. Painted Lace and Other Pieces [1914-1937].
New Haven, Conn.: Yale University Press, 1955.

_____. Three Lives (1901). Norfolk, Conn.: New Direc-
tions, n.d.

Stokes, Rose Pastor. The Woman Who Wouldn't. New York:
G. P. Putnam's, 1916.

Ward, Elizabeth Stuart Phelps. Hedged In. Boston: Fields,
Osgood, 1870. "Novel of hypocrisy of society in its
treatment of women who transgress against conventional
moral standards."

Wollstonecraft, Mary. Thoughts on the Education of Daugh-
ters; A Vindication of the Rights of Women; Wrongs of
Women. All three entries see under Complementary
(Normative).

The Woman's Advocate. New York: July 1869-December
1869. Collection of articles giving news and feelings of
the time re women's issues and content of feminism.

"Woman: Can She Reason?" Famous "Cynic Correspondence"
in the New York Times Saturday Review of Books and
Art. New York Times, 1899.

The Woman Voter. Official organ of Woman Suffrage Party
(a union for political work of existing equal suffrage organizations in the City of New York). February 1910-
May 1917. Encompasses a broad range of issues in addition to suffrage.

Woodhull, Victoria. The Victoria Woodhull Reader, ed.
Madeline B. Stern. Weston, Mass.: M and S Press,
1974.

Woolf, Virginia. A Room of One's Own. London: Hogarth
Press, 1931. Woolf proposes a woman must have an
independent income and a room of her own if she is to
create. Tells the tale of Shakespeare's sister who had
neither, only talent, and who lies buried at a lonely
crossroads dead by her own hand.

_____. Orlando: A Biography. New York: Harcourt,
Brace & World, 1928.

_____. Three Guineas. New York: Harcourt, Brace &
World, 1938.

Wright [D'Arusmont], Frances. Life, Letters and Lectures
1834/1844. New York: Arno, 1972.

_____. Views of Society and Manners in America, ed.
Paul R. Baker. Cambridge, Mass.: Belknap Press,
1963.

INDEX